Portraits

HBJ Reading Program

Margaret Early

Bernice E. Cullinan
Roger C. Farr
W. Dorsey Hammond
Nancy Santeusanio
Dorothy S. Strickland

LEVEL 12
Portraits

HBJ **HARCOURT BRACE JOVANOVICH, PUBLISHERS**
Orlando   San Diego   Chicago   Dallas

Copyright © 1987 by Harcourt Brace Jovanovich, Inc.

All rights reserved. No part of this publication may be reproduced or transmitted in any form or by any means, electronic or mechanical, including photocopy, recording, or any information storage and retrieval system, without permission in writing from the publisher.

Requests for permission to make copies of any part of the work should be mailed to: Permissions, Harcourt Brace Jovanovich, Publishers, Orlando, Florida 32887

Printed in the United States of America
ISBN 0-15-330512-6

Acknowledgements

For permission to reprint copyrighted material, grateful acknowledgment is made to the following sources:

Atheneum Publishers, Inc.: Adapted from *Mrs. Frisby and the Rats of NIMH* by Robert C. O'Brien. Copyright © 1971 by Robert C. O'Brien.

Bantam Books, Inc.: From *Fantastic Voyage*, a novel by Isaac Asimov, based on the screenplay by Harry Kleiner. Original story by Otto Klement and Jay Lewis Bixby. Copyright © 1966 by Bantam Books, Inc. All rights reserved. From "The Stub-Book" by Pedro Antonio de Alarcón in *Spanish Stories*, edited by Angel Flores. Copyright © 1960 by Bantam Books, Inc. All rights reserved.

Diana Chang: "Saying Yes" by Diana Chang from *Asian-American Heritage: An Anthology of Prose and Poetry*, edited by David Hsin-Fu Wand. Published by Washington Square Press, 1974.

Donald Charles (Meighan): "The Runner" by Donald Charles.

The Christian Science Monitor: "Post Early for Space" by Peter J. Henniker-Heaton from *The Christian Science Monitor*, January 10, 1952. © 1952 by the The Christian Science Publishing Society. All rights reserved.

Arthur C. Clarke and Scott Meredith Literary Agency, Inc., 845 Third Avenue, New York, NY 10022: From *Saturn Rising* by Arthur C. Clarke. Copyright © 1961 by Mercury Press, Inc.

The Coach House Press, Inc., P. O. Box 458, Morton Grove, IL 60053: From "Tom Edison and the Wonderful 'Why'" by Faye Parker. Published by The Coach House Press, Inc., 1961.

Don Congdon Associates, Inc.: "Time in Thy Flight" by Ray Bradbury from *Fantastic Universe*, June–July 1953. Copyright © 1953 by Ray Bradbury; renewed 1981 by Ray Bradbury. Published by King Size Publications, Inc.

Dodd, Mead & Company, Inc.: Adapted from "Let's Take a Trip into Space" in *Flying the Space Shuttles* by Don Dwiggins. Adapted from *The Four-Minute Mile* by Roger Bannister. Copyright © 1955, 1981 by Roger Bannister. Adapted from *Microchip: Small Wonder* by Charlene W. Billings. Copyright © 1984 by Charlene W. Billings.

Gale Research Company: Adapted from pp. 97–99 in *Something About the Author*, Volume 4, edited by Anne Commire. © 1973 by Gale Research Company.

Greenwillow Books, a division of William Morrow & Company, Inc.: Adapted from pp. 114–207 in *Willie Bea and the Time Martians Landed* by Virginia Hamilton. Copyright © 1983 by Virginia Hamilton Adoff.

Harcourt Brace Jovanovich, Inc.: From pp. 97–98, 378–379, and 430–431 in *HBJ Social Studies, The World: Past and Present*, Level 6. Copyright © 1985 by Harcourt Brace Jovanovich, Inc. From pp. 119, 131–132, and 172 in *HBJ Health*, Level Brown, Grade 6. Copyright © 1983 by Harcourt Brace Jovanovich, Inc. From pp. 158–160 in *HBJ Science*, Level Brown, Grade 6 by Elizabeth K. Cooper et al. Copyright © 1985 by Harcourt Brace Jovanovich, Inc. "They Have Yarns" from *The People, Yes* by Carl Sandburg. Copyright 1936 by Harcourt Brace Jovanovich, Inc.; renewed 1964 by Carl Sandburg. Pronunciation key from p. 33 and the short key from p. 35 in the *HBJ School Dictionary*. Copyright © 1985 by Harcourt Brace Jovanovich, Inc.

Harper & Row, Publishers, Inc. and Jonathan Cape Ltd.: "The Gift-Giving" from *UP THE CHIMNEY DOWN and Other Stories* by Joan Aiken. Copyright © 1984 by Joan Aiken.

Hastings House, Publishers, Inc.: From *True or False? Amazing Art Forgeries* by Ann Waldron. Copyright © 1983 by Ann Waldron.

Holiday House: From *The Morning the Sun Refused to Rise*, written and illustrated by Glen Rounds. Copyright © 1984 by Glen Rounds.

Houghton Mifflin Company: From pp. 91–101 in *Island of the Blue Dolphins* by Scott O'Dell. Copyright © 1960 by Scott O'Dell. From *The Sign of the Beaver* by Elizabeth George Speare. Copyright © 1983 by Elizabeth George Speare.

Houghton Mifflin Company and George Allen & Unwin (Publishers) Ltd.: "Roads Go Ever On and On" from *The Hobbit* by J. R. R. Tolkien. Copyright © 1966 by J. R. R. Tolkein.

Michele Kort: Adapted from "Joan Benoit" by Michele Kort in *Ms.* magazine, January 1985.

Little, Brown and Company, in association with The Atlantic Monthly Press: Adapted from *The Ghost on Saturday Night* by Sid Fleischman. Text copyright © 1974 by Albert S. Fleischman.

Toni Mendez Incorporated: From "The Adventure of the Blue Carbuncle" and from pp. ix–xi of the Introduction in *Sir Arthur Conon Doyle's THE ADVENTURES OF SHERLOCK HOLMES* by Catherine Edwards Sadler. Copyright © 1981 by Catherine Edwards Sadler. Published by Avon Books.

William Morrow & Company, Inc.: Adapted from *Hercules* (Titled: "The Golden Apples") by Bernard Evslin. Text copyright © 1984 by Bernard Evslin.

Mard Naman: Adapted from "Michela Aliota: Computer Teen" by Mard Naman in *Family Computing,* February 1984.

G. P. Putnam's Sons: Adapted from *HOMESICK, My Own Story* (Titled: "Homesick") by Jean Fritz. Text copyright © 1982 by Jean Fritz. Adapted from *China Homecoming* by Jean Fritz. Text copyright © 1985 by Jean Fritz.

Random House, Inc.: Adapted from "The Mystery of the Seven Wrong Clocks" in *Alfred Hitchcock's Solve-Them-Yourself Mysteries.* Copyright © 1963 by Random House, Inc. Adapted from *Incognito Mosquito Flies Again!* (Titled: "Incognito Mosquito and the Mis-cast Dancer Mystery") by E. A. Hass, illustrated by Don Madden. Copyright © 1985 by Random House, Inc.

Marian Reiner, as agent for Eve Merriam: "Think Tank" from *Out Loud* by Eve Merriam. Copyright © 1973 by Eve Merriam.

Marie Rodell—Frances Collin Literary Agency: "The Yesterdays and the Tomorrows" from *Sundial of the Seasons* by Hal Borland. Copyright © 1952, 1964 by Hal Borland. Published by J. B. Lippincott & Company.

Marjorie F. Stover: Adapted from *Trail Boss in Pigtails* by Marjorie F. Stover. Copyright © 1972 by Majorie Filley Stover. Published by Atheneum Publishers, Inc.

Yoshiko Uchida: From "The Wise Old Woman" in *The Sea of Gold and Other Tales from Japan,* adapted by Yoshiko Uchida. Published by Charles Scribner's Sons, 1965.

Walker & Company, Inc.: Adapted from pp. 22–25, 140–142 in *Letters to a Black Boy* by Bob Teague. Copyright © 1968. Published by Walker & Company, Inc.

Franklin Watts, Inc.: From *The Electronic Revolution: Robots and Computers* (Titled: "The Electronic Revolution: Robots") by Nigel Hawkes. Copyright © by Aladdin Books Ltd.

Photographs

The following abbreviations indicate the position of the photographs on the page: *t*, top; *b*, bottom; *l*, left; *r*, right; *c*, center.

Cover: HBJ Photo

Page xvi–1, 150–151, 154–155, 298–299, 302–303, 428–429, 432–433, 596–597, Ken Karp/OPC; 66, Nebraska State Historical Society; 67, Barker Texas History Center, The University of Texas at Austin; 68(t), National Archives; 68(b), Nebraska State Historical Society; 69(t), Barker Texas History Center, The University of Texas at Austin; 69(b), Nebraska State Historical Society; 97, Lee Boltin; 98, Steve E. Sutton/Duomo; 99–101(l), Focus on Sports; 101(r), David Madison/Duomo; 120, Houghton Mifflin Company; 208, NASA; 210, Sonja Bullaty/The Image Bank; 211, Thomas Hovland/Grant Heilman; 212, Scala/Art Resource; 215(t), John Walsh/Photo Researchers; 215(b), C. Falco/Photo Researchers; 216, The Bettmann Archive; 218, Tom McHugh/Photo Researchers; 219, Claude Charlier/Photo Researchers; 220, NASA; 229, Peter Aitken/Photo Researchers; 230–232, Rogers Ressmeyer/Wheeler Pictures; 234, Dan McCoy/Rainbow; 235(t), Dan McCoy/Rainbow; 235(b), Rivelli/The Image Bank; 236(t,b), Dan McCoy/Rainbow; 237(t), Joe McNally/Wheeler Pictures; 237(b), Dan McCoy/Rainbow; 247, Scala/Art Resource; 272, The Bettmann Archive; 328, Michael Fritz; 331, Delta Willis/Bruce Coleman Inc.; 334, 336, Michael Fritz; 339, Marc Riboud/Magnum Photos; 340, Michael Fritz; 348, Murray Alcosser/The Image Bank; 366, Scribner Book Company; 368, Yoshiko Uchida; 374, Lowell Georgia/Photo Researchers; 496, 498, NASA; 499, Ducharme/Gamma Liaison; 530, Eric Carle/Bruce Coleman Inc.; 535, Yamaguchi/Gamma Liaison; 536–538, Dan McCoy/Rainbow; 540, 541, NASA; 544, Culver Pictures; 564, Cox Studios/William Morris & Company, Inc.

Illustrators

Esther Baran: pp. 344–345; Floyd Cooper: 78–89, 158–171, 569–594; David Cunningham: 344–345; Rae Ecklund: 108–114, 246–253, 306–325; Paul Gourhan: 124–148, 470–485; Jeremy Guitar: 544–547; George Hamblin: 378–399; Ron Himler: 36–44, 352–358; Rosekrans Hoffman: 18–19; Barbara Hoopes: 94; Paul Lackner: 489; Tom Leonard: 436–454; Andre Licardi: 52–65; Richard Loehle: 188–202, 458–465, 490; Don Madden: 174–183, 555–559; Yoshi Miyake: 404–427; Lyle Miller: 258–267, 276–293, 492; Ed Parker: 206–207; Jim Pearson: 506–523; Arvis Stewart: 20–33; Jas Szygiel: 104, 325, 552.

Maps: Richard Sanderson, pp. 48–51.

Design, Production: Kirchoff/Wohlberg, Inc.

Contents

Unit 1 Challenges — 1

Folklore 2
    (Literature Study)

The Morning the Sun Refused to Rise 4
    by Glen Rounds (Tall Tale)

They Have Yarns 18
    by Carl Sandburg (Poem)

The Golden Apples 20
    by Bernard Evslin (Myth)

The Wise Old Woman 36
    by Yoshiko Uchida (Folktale)

Maps and Atlases 48
    (Study Skills)

Trail Boss in Pigtails 52
    by Marjorie Filley Stover (Historical Fiction)

Westward Bound 66
    (Photo Essay)

Cause and Effect 72
    (Comprehension Study with Textbook Application in Health)

Island of the Blue Dolphins 78
    by Scott O'Dell (Realistic Fiction)

vii

Draw Conclusions 92
  (Comprehension Study with Textbook
  Application in Social Studies)

Joan Benoit..................................... 98
  adapted from an article by Michele Kort   (Biography)

The Runner 104
  by Donald Charles   (Poem)

Context Clues....................................106
  (Vocabulary Study)

The Four-Minute Mile...........................108
  by Roger Bannister   (Autobiography)

Characterization 118
  (Literature Study)

Author Profile: Elizabeth George Speare 120

Bonus: The Sign of the Beaver 122
  by Elizabeth George Speare   (Historical Fiction)

Thinking About "Challenges"......................150

Read on Your Own................................152

Unit 2 Mysteries 155

Mysteries..156
  (Literature Study)

Alfred Hitchcock's The Mystery of the Seven Wrong Clocks..................158
  (Mystery)

Incognito Mosquito and the Mis-cast Dancer Mystery..................174
  by E. A. Hass   (Mystery)

Homographs....................................186
  (Vocabulary Study)

The Gift-Giving..................................188
  by Joan Aiken   (Fantasy)

Roads Go Ever On and On.........................206
  by J. R. R. Tolkien   (Poem)

Make Judgments.................................208
  (Comprehension Study with Textbook Application in Social Studies)

Microchip: Small Wonder..........................214
  by Charlene W. Billings   (Informational Article)

Think Tank.....................................224
  by Eve Merriam   (Poem)

Newspapers....................................226
  (Study Skills)

Michela Alioto: Computer Teen....................230
  by Mard Naman   (Biography)

ix

Computer Screen Imagery 234
   (Photo Essay)

Main Idea 240
   (Comprehension Study with Textbook
   Application in Health)

True or False? Amazing Art Forgeries 246
   by Ann Waldron   (Informational Article)

The Stub-Book 258
   by Pedro Antonio de Alarcón   (Folktale)

Plot 270
   (Literature Study)

Author Profile: Sir Arthur Conan Doyle 272

Bonus: **The Adventure of the Blue Carbuncle** 274
   *by Sir Arthur Conan Doyle, adapted by
   Catherine Edwards Sadler*   (Mystery)

Thinking About "Mysteries" 298

Read on Your Own 300

Unit 3 Viewpoints 303

Personal Narrative 304
   (Literature Study)

Homesick 306
   by Jean Fritz   (Autobiography)

Saying Yes 324
   by Diana Chang   (Poem)

Prefixes 326
   (Vocabulary Study)

China Homecoming 328
   by Jean Friz   (Autobiography)

The Fallow Deer at the Lonely House............344
   by Thomas Hardy   (Poem)

Fact and Opinion 346
   (Comprehension Study with Textbook
   Application in Social Studies)

Letters to a Black Boy 352
   by Bob Teague   (Autobiography)

Propaganda Techniques 362
   (Study Skills)

Yoshiko Uchida: From Japan to America, With Love ..366
   by Bernice E. Cullinan   (Biography)

Author's Purpose and Viewpoint.................372
   (Comprehension Study with Textbook
   Application in Health)

xi

The Ghost on Saturday Night 378
    by Sid Fleischman   (Humorous Fiction)

Point of View 400
    (Literature Study)

Author Profile: Robert C. O'Brien 402

Bonus: Mrs. Frisby and the Rats of NIMH 404
    by Robert C. O'Brien   (Fantasy)

Thinking About "Viewpoints" 428

Read on Your Own 430

Unit 4 Tomorrows 433

Science Fiction..434
  (Literature Study)

Fantastic Voyage...436
  by Isaac Asimov   (Science Fiction)

Time in Thy Flight...458
  by Ray Bradbury   (Science Fiction)

Multiple Meanings...468
  (Vocabulary Study)

Saturn Rising..470
  by Arthur C. Clarke   (Science Fiction)

Post Early for Space..488
  by Peter J. Henniker-Heaton   (Poem)

Predict Outcomes..490
  (Comprehension Study with Textbook
  Application in Science)

Let's Take a Trip into Space....................................496
  by Don Dwiggins   (Informational Article)

Tables and Schedules..502
  (Study Skills)

Tom Edison and the Wonderful "Why"..............................506
  by Faye Parker   (Play)

Sequence..528
  (Comprehension Study with Textbook
  Application in Social Studies)

xiii

The Electronic Revolution: Robots 534
   by Nigel Hawkes   (Informational Article)

Predictions from 1900 544
   by John Elfreth Watkins, Jr.   (Informational Article)

The Yesterdays and the Tomorrows 552
   by Hal Borland   (Poem)

Meet Don Madden 554
   by Barbara Reeves   (Biography)

Setting 562
   (Literature Study)

Author Profile: Virginia Hamilton 564

Bonus: **Willie Bea and the Time the Martians Landed** 566
   by Virginia Hamilton   (Realistic Fiction)

Thinking About "Tomorrows" 596

Read on Your Own 598

Glossary 600

Pronunciation Guide 621

Index of Titles and Authors 623

Portraits

Unit 1

Challenges

At some time in our lives, we all have adventures that challenge us. Some people's adventures involve the challenge of staying alive. Some adventures involve less dangerous challenges: taking a plane alone for the first time, winning a race, or standing up for what we believe in. Facing challenges helps us learn about ourselves. However, in order to learn, we do not have to face every challenge ourselves; we can learn by reading about how others meet challenges.

The people in this unit's stories are all adventurers about to face challenges. As you read, think about what you would do if you were in their place. Could you find the courage needed to live alone in the wilderness? Could you find the determination needed to run a 26-mile race just two weeks after having knee surgery? To get a better idea of each challenge, read on.

Literature Study

Folklore

For thousands of years people have loved to listen to and to tell stories. Some stories came from things that really happened. Others were about imaginary people or places. In many different parts of the world, stories were passed on by word of mouth for years and years before being written down. These kinds of stories usually have no known authors. They are called **folklore. Myths, folktales,** and **tall tales** are three different kinds of folklore.

Myths are traditional stories. They explain something in nature or a past event. Early peoples everywhere wondered about the same kinds of things, so many of their myths tell similar stories. Some of the most common myths are about thunder and lightning, the seasons, fire, and the sun and the moon.

Myths from many places are about heroes and heroines and their adventures. Heroes and heroines were often given the personal qualities that people admired most, such as great strength, speed, or knowledge. In ancient Greece, many of the myths were about the gods and goddesses of Mount Olympus.

We read myths today because we enjoy the stories. However, early peoples gained a greater understanding of the world around them from their myths. What things might myths have helped early peoples to understand? What are some things today that myths might help to explain?

The **folktale** is another kind of folklore. Most folktales have simple plots with ordinary people as heroes and heroines. Many were first told to teach some lesson about life. The lesson is often taught through characters who must depend on their cleverness to escape sticky situations. Folktale characters often symbolize good or evil. Some may have magical powers. In many tales, the main characters are animals that act like people. Fairy tales are considered to be folktales, too.

There are often several versions of the same folktale or fairy tale. This is because storytellers carried their tales to other parts of the world. There they were changed to show different languages and values. One such tale is "Little Red Riding Hood." Think about a folktale that you know. What examples from the story show that it is a folktale?

A **tall tale** is a funny story that may once have been based on fact. Tall tales are set in familiar places. As tall tales were told over and over, each storyteller would exaggerate the facts just a little bit more. It wasn't long before the tales were exaggerated beyond belief.

A well-known American tall-tale hero is Paul Bunyan. There may really have been an extra large, strong lumberjack like Ol' Paul, but through the years the stories of him grew taller just as he did. It is said in the tall tales that Paul's big blue ox, Babe, measured more than seven-hundred-and-fifty-four ax handles between the eyes. Can you think of your own exaggeration to tell how large Babe was?

Paul Bunyan is a legendary giant of American tall tales. In these tales, Ol' Paul meets challenges so big that most people couldn't even think about facing them! Read to find out how Paul meets the big challenge in this story.

What exaggerated facts can you spot in this traditional American tale?

The Morning the Sun Refused to Rise

by Glen Rounds

Although it happened many, many years ago, it still seems strange that so few people now remember the terrible night of the Great Blizzard. It blew across the top of the world bringing such awful cold that the Earth froze tight to its axle. It came to a full stop. And even fewer have heard of the panic that spread across the world the next morning. For the first time in history, the sun refused to rise.

And it is only in one or two crumbling copies of the oldest newspapers that one can find the account of how Paul Bunyan, the Giant Logger, by superhuman effort accomplished the seemingly impossible task of setting the world to turning again.

It is a well-known fact that the Earth spins on a great axle running through its center from top to bottom. The top end turns in a huge bearing set in the ice, and sticks up several feet in the air. This end is called the North Pole. The other end sticks out of another bearing at the

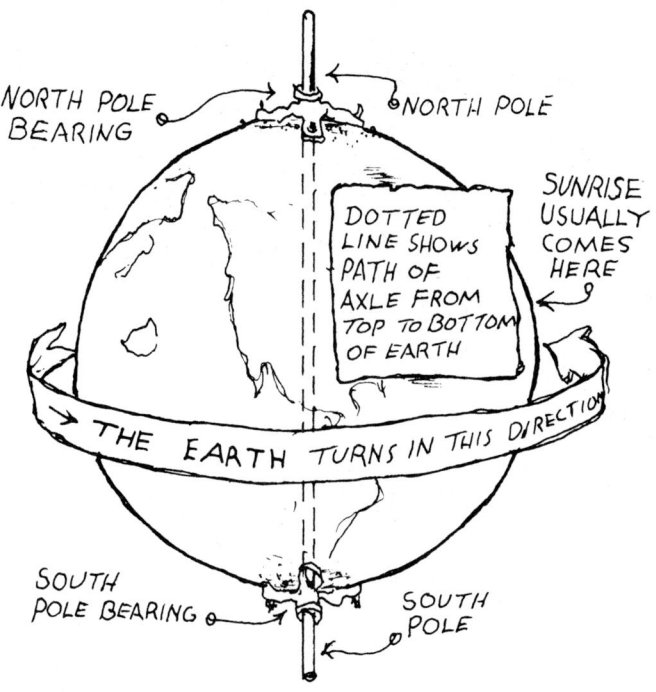

bottom of the world below South America. It is called the South Pole.

This spinning is arranged so that sunrise comes early every morning, followed by roughly twelve hours of sunshine to warm the people and give them light to do their work. Sunset comes at the end of the day, bringing night for sleeping.

This arrangement has been going on for as long as anyone can remember. Up to the time we speak of, it had worked right well. But on this particular morning, with the Earth frozen to its axle, sunrise couldn't come!

However, the spinning of the Earth is a thing that ordinary people seldom notice. The first sign that something was wrong was the fact that the roosters didn't crow.

On this terrible morning, without the light that comes before sunrise to wake them, roosters all over the world continued to sleep. And the people, hearing no crowing, slept on past their usual getting-up time.

The few people who had alarm clocks, however, were wakened at their usual time. As they built their fires, they looked out their windows and noticed that the sky was still dark, even though their clocks said it was long past time for sunrise. So they began to worry. Putting on their coats and lighting their lanterns, they hurried to wake their sleeping neighbors with the news that sunrise was long overdue. Before long, crowds began to gather in the cold darkness, wondering what had happened. Looking up at the sky, they found the stars were shining. They realized that something more than a cloudy morning was holding sunrise back.

Something was terribly wrong. The cold was becoming steadily more bitter. Panic was spreading.

The desks of Kings, Presidents, Prime Ministers, and even Senators were piled high with telegrams asking what had happened to sunrise.

But when the Government Experts looked in their books, they found instructions for dealing with such things as typhoons, hurricanes, forest fires, and hundreds of other kinds of disasters — but not a word about what to do when the sun refused to rise.

Apparently such a thing had never happened before. Then the President got a telegram from the Eskimo whose job was to grease the North Pole bearing every morning. The telegram read:

EARTH'S AXLE FROZEN IN BEARING STOP
EARTH NOT TURNING STOP

So at last the governments knew why sunrise hadn't come. The Experts hurried out with blowtorches, but the cold was so great that the flames froze and dropped off as fast as they were lighted. And of course in that country there is no wood for fires.

It is hard to know what might have happened if someone hadn't thought of Paul Bunyan, the Mighty Logger, and Babe, his Great Blue Ox and constant companion.

Ol' Paul was the legendary giant who had invented logging. He was known far and wide for his ability to do the impossible — and to often do it the hard way just for the fun of it.

It was common knowledge that with the help of the Blue Ox and a crew of the most expert loggers in the world, there was nothing Ol' Paul couldn't fix, yank straight, tear down, or rebuild.

Just how big Babe really was has long been a matter of debate. But old newspaper accounts say that on a certain Sunday a crew of lumberjacks, having nothing better to do, set out to measure the Mighty Blue Ox. By

late afternoon they had managed to measure the distance between the Great Beast's eyes—seven-hundred-and-fifty-four ax handles, two-hundred-and-four cans of tomatoes (no. 10's), and a plug of Star chewing tobacco laid edgewise.

By the time they'd done that, the cooks were calling the men to supper. They never did get around to measuring the rest of him. But it is a known fact that at every step Babe's hooves sank seven feet into the solid rock—and the many small lakes in the North Country are said to be his old tracks, now filled with water.

Ol' Paul's camp at the time was so far back in the North Woods that it was always bitterly cold there—and the trees were so thick that it was almost always as dark as night, even in the daytime. So neither Ol' Paul nor any of his men had noticed that sunrise was missing that day. But then there was a banging on the door. A

delegation of Government Men came in with a letter from the President asking Ol' Paul to try and do something to get the Earth turning so sunrise could come again.

Paul listened to them. He told them to tell the President that he'd see what he could do. Then Ol' Paul put on his heaviest fur coat (it was said to have been made from four-thousand-and-nine prime bearskins trimmed with sealskin at the collar). He walked over to the North Pole to see what had to be done.

The Great Blizzard was still blowing. The only people in sight were a few Eskimos who lived in the neighborhood. While the Eskimos watched, Ol' Paul took hold of the axle, but even his great strength couldn't move it.

Taking off a mitten to scrape frost from his beard, Ol' Paul leaned against the North Pole.

He had to figure a way to start the world to spinning again. He knew that would take some very hard thinking. Even a loaded wagon or sled is hard to get moving once it has stopped. The Earth was many, many times heavier than the heaviest wagon. Ol' Paul hurried back to camp to do some more thinking.

He went over to the mess hall. He sat there until ten o'clock, just drinking coffee and thinking. But he still couldn't think of a way to get a thing as big as the world turning on its axle again.

Ol' Paul had just refilled his fifteen-gallon coffee mug for the tenth time when he accidentally tipped over a jug of sourdough starter sitting on the back of the big range. Still stirring his coffee and thinking, he was watching the jug and listening to the odd gurgling sounds coming from inside it. Then, without warning, the cork blew out of the neck with a sound like a rifle shot.

For a moment the jug lay there, spewing a stream of sourdough as powerful as the jet from a firehose nozzle. Then it took off like a skyrocket, straight across the mess hall! Tearing a great hole in the wall, the jug whizzed over the heads of the crowd of men outside. It ploughed a deep furrow across the top of the mountain west of camp, and disappeared.

Ol' Paul stood there a minute or two, speechless with surprise. Then he let out a roar that blew out half of the mess hall windows.

"Rocket power!" he hollered. "Rocket power's the answer!"

Most rockets, even today, use gunpowder or some other explosive fuel for their power, but Ol' Paul saw no reason sourdough, which is known to be as powerful as any gunpowder ever made, shouldn't do so well. And he'd already figured out how he was going to use it.

To understand Ol' Paul's plan, one has to remember that in those days the map of the United States was much different from what it is now. Instead of the Appalachian and Rocky Mountain ranges being separated by the Middle West (as they are now), they were both in the western part of the country. The Rockies ran about where they are now, from Alaska into Mexico. Just a few miles to the east of them, across a wide valley, were the

Appalachians. And all the land from there to the East Coast was still flat prairie.

Ol' Paul's plan was to use sourdough rocket power to push eastward against the Appalachians to start the world turning on its axle again. And in less than half an

hour he had Babe hitched to his biggest sled, loaded with rock-drilling equipment and every crew he could spare.

Driving south between the two mountain ranges, he unloaded a crew every half mile from Canada to Mexico. He left them drilling tunnels into the side of the high mountain wall on the east side of the valley. By noon the men were all at work.

The entrances to these tunnels were small. They were so small that the men had to crawl on hands and knees as they worked. But further back the tunnels widened to form great cave-like chambers to hold the sourdough when it was ready.

While the tunnels were being drilled, Ol' Paul went back to camp. He put all the cooks and flunkies to work hauling flour and other such stuff away to the Sourdough Lake on top of the mountain behind the mess hall. The little steamboat that usually ran only at night mixing sourdough for each morning's breakfast flapjacks now worked night and day. As soon as one batch was mixed

and pumped into the great tank wagons, another was started. As each tank wagon was filled it was hitched onto the wagon ahead.

It was almost noon when word came that the last of the tunnels would be finished in a few minutes. So, hitching Babe to the head of the miles-long train of tank wagons, Ol' Paul drove at top speed to the valley between the two mountain ranges.

Without slowing down he had the men unhook a tank wagon by the mouth of each tunnel as he passed.

Ol' Paul's voice could be heard for almost any distance. He gave the signal. All up and down the line men started pumping the warm, bubbling sourdough into the tunnels. As each tunnel was filled, the entrance was tightly plugged with a great stopper cut from one of the biggest redwood trees in California.

As soon as the last tunnel had been filled and the redwood plug driven tightly into place, Ol' Paul sent all the men and wagons back to his camp to be out of the way of what he knew was going to happen. After that there was nothing to do but wait and see if his plan was going to work.

And just then they felt a trembling in the Earth under their feet. A little later they felt another trembling as well as small rumblings and creakings coming from deep in the ground. Suddenly the redwood plug blew out of the first tunnel mouth with a terrible bang, louder than a hundred thunderclaps.

And one by one, a dozen at a time, the plugs began blowing out of the others. Never had the world heard such a banging, rumbling, whizzing, and roaring as the great jets of steamy sourdough and sourdough gas

roared out of the line of tunnel mouths, to strike the wall of the Rocky Mountains behind them.

The sounds of the roaring sourdough jets were almost drowned by the terrible cracking of splitting rock deep beneath the mountains. It is probable that such a sound had never before been heard since the world began.

Then suddenly, as Paul sighted a dark mountaintop against a low star, he saw that the Earth was moving! It stopped, then moved again. Slowly at first, then faster and faster the Earth began to turn.

Then, the sky in the East began to lighten. People waved their hats and clapped each other on the back. Roosters everywhere took their heads from under their wings and started crowing for dawn.

The light in the East grew stronger and at 4:45 P.M., the first edge of the sun appeared over the horizon. Sunrise had come again!

People stood in the streets or on their doorsteps, cheering and clapping each other on the back. Once more Paul Bunyan had proved that he could do the impossible! And his picture was on the front page of all the papers.

But even so, not everybody was happy with the fantastic job Ol' Paul had done. For one thing, sunrise now came at 4:45 P.M. This caused some complaint since folks were not used to the idea of getting up and going to work in the afternoon instead of the morning. But someone, remembering the way the government set clocks back or ahead for daylight saving time, suggested that everybody simply turn their clocks back ten hours and forty-five minutes. That solved the problem.

But the most complaints came from the people living in the Appalachian Mountains. When daylight came that

day they found that the power of Ol' Paul's sourdough rockets had pushed the entire Appalachian range fifteen hundred miles to the East — where it stands to this day. So instead of living in Montana, Wyoming, Colorado, or some other western state, they were now citizens of West Virginia, Kentucky, and Tennessee. They began to raise a clamor because having been raised in the West, they now had trouble understanding their new neighbors, who all talked Southern.

But it all settled down after a while. Some stayed while others moved and looked for farms in the newly formed stretch of land between the Appalachians and the Rockies. That part of the country is now called the MIDWEST.

Of course all the maps of the country east of the Rockies had to be redrawn. Building roads across the new MIDWEST was something of a problem and burden to taxpayers. But all in all, in the end, Ol' Paul's sourdough rockets did more good than harm.

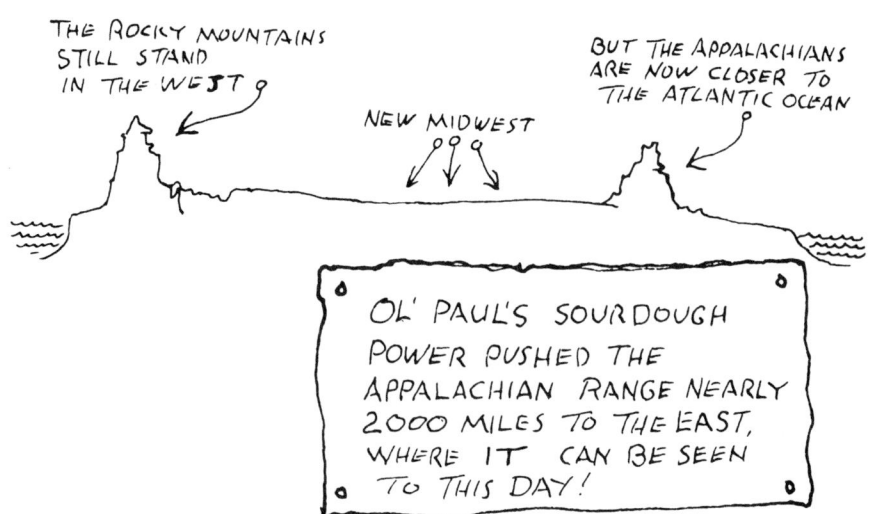

Discuss the Selection

1. How did Paul Bunyan meet the big challenge in this tall tale?
2. Where did Paul get his idea for getting the Earth to spin again?
3. If you were a tall-tale hero faced with the challenge of getting the Earth to spin again, what method might you use?
4. If Paul hadn't been successful, what might have happened to the sunless Earth?
5. At what point in the story did you realize that Paul had been successful and that the Earth had begun to turn again?

Apply the Skills

Tall tales are stories, told and retold by storytellers, that may once have been based on fact. The facts in the most entertaining tall tales have been exaggerated beyond belief.

- What are some examples of exaggeration in this tall tale about Paul Bunyan?
- What might be some of the actual facts behind the exaggerations in this story?

Think and Write

Prewrite

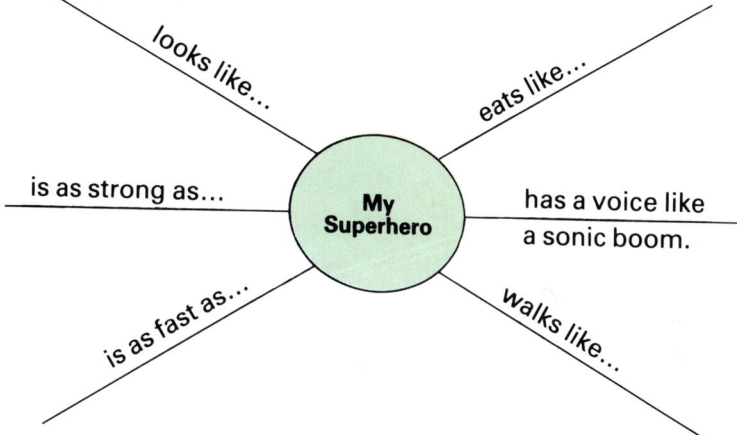

Superheroes are story characters who have unusual characteristics and can perform extraordinary deeds. Create your own tall-tale superhero.

Copy the diagram shown above. To describe your superhero, complete the unfinished similes on the diagram with your own exaggerated comparisons. If you wish, create other unusual descriptive similes for your character. Remember that similes are comparisons using *like* or *as*.

Compose

Write a paragraph describing your superhero. Use at least five similes. You might start your paragraph with this sentence: *My superhero is absolutely astounding!*

Revise

Read your paragraph, paying special attention to your similes. Are there any that you can improve to make your superhero larger than life? Revise your writing to add even more exaggeration.

They Have Yarns
by Carl Sandburg

They have yarns
Of a skyscraper so tall they had to put hinges
On the two top stories so to let the moon go by,
Of one corn crop in Missouri when the roots
Went so deep and drew off so much water
The Mississippi riverbed that year was dry,
Of pancakes so thin they had only one side,
Of "a fog so thick we shingled the barn and six feet out on the fog,"
Of Pecos Pete straddling a cyclone in Texas and riding it to the west coast where "it rained out under him,"
Of the man who drove a swarm of bees across the Rocky Mountains and the Desert "and didn't lose a bee,"
Of a mountain railroad curve where the engineer in his cab can touch the caboose and spit in the conductor's eye,
Of the boy who climbed a cornstalk growing so fast he would have starved to death if they hadn't shot biscuits up to him,
Of the old man's whiskers: "When the wind was with him his whiskers arrived the day before he did,"
Of the hen laying a square egg and cackling, "Ouch!" and of hens laying eggs with the dates printed on them.
Of the ship captain's shadow: it froze to the deck one cold winter night,
Of mutineers on the same ship put to chipping rust with rubber hammers,

Of the sheep counter who was fast and accurate: "I just count their feet and divide by four,"
Of the man so tall he must climb a ladder to shave himself,
Of the runt so teeny-weeny it takes two men and a boy to see him,
Of mosquitoes: one can kill a dog, two of them a man,
Of a cyclone that sucked cookstoves out of the kitchen, up the chimney flue, and onto the next town,
Of the same cyclone picking up wagon-tracks in Nebraska and dropping them over the Dakotas,
Of the hook-and-eye snake unlocking itself into forty pieces, each piece two inches long, then in nine seconds flat snapping itself together again,
Of the watch swallowed by a cow — when they butchered her a year later the watch was running and had the correct time,
Of horned snakes, hoop snakes that roll themselves where they want to go, and rattlesnakes carrying bells instead of rattles on their tails,
Of the herd of cattle in California getting lost in a giant redwood tree that had hollowed out,
Of the man who killed a snake by putting its tail in its mouth so it swallowed itself,
Of railroad trains whizzing along so fast they reach the station before the whistle,
Of pigs so thin the farmer had to tie knots in their tails to keep them from crawling through the cracks in their pens,
Of Paul Bunyan's big blue ox, Babe, measuring between the eyes forty-two ax-handles and a plug of Star tobacco exactly,
Of John Henry's hammer and the curve of its swing and his singing of it as "a rainbow round my shoulder."

What impossible challenge does the mighty Hercules, a hero of Greek mythology, face in this myth?

Ancient myths sometimes served to explain the mysteries of nature to early peoples. What explanations of natural phenomena does this myth contain?

The Golden Apples

by Bernard Evslin

In Greek mythology, Hercules was the strongest man in the world. From the time he was born, the jealous goddess Hera hated him. She was convinced that Hercules, who was bigger and stronger than any other human, was part god. She became obsessed with tricking Hercules into causing his own death. One day she appeared to him in a dream and showed him that he would go mad when he got older and kill his family. To prevent the horrible dream from coming true, Hercules agreed to do what Hera said. She sent him to the wicked king of Mycenae, who ordered Hercules to perform twelve superhuman tasks—any one of which, Hera hoped, would cause his death. To Hera's dismay, however, Hercules has already successfully completed six of the tasks and she must now assign him another.

Hera was furious. The Queen of the Gods could not understand how Hercules had managed to survive the perils she had flung in his path. And when she thought how he had speared the Nemean Lion, and chopped off all hundred of the Hydra's ugly heads, and managed to destroy the deadly Iron-beaks of the Marsh — as she rode in her swan-chariot thinking of how he had killed each of her pet monsters one by one, she felt herself bursting with rage.

"This time I must set him an utterly fatal task," she muttered to herself. "But what? I know! I know! I'll ask him to bring me a golden apple from the Garden of the Hesperides, that far orchard where the Titan Atlas is condemned to stand forever bearing the sky on his shoulders. Yes, Hercules shall face a double peril—for if the serpent, Ladon, who guards that tree does not devour him, then surely the foul-tempered Atlas will stomp him to bits beneath his giant feet."

She spoke her will, and Hercules once again found himself trying to get to a place he never wanted to reach. But he was fated to obey the cruel goddess through twelve labors, and knew that he would not be a free man until he had completed all twelve. So he journed to the Uttermost Island beyond the West Wind, where that part of the sky was held up by the Titan Atlas.

  It was a hilly island. Meadows ran right down to the water's edge. Deer and wild horses came down to the sea to swim. Towering above all was Atlas, snow-bearded, with huge misty eyes, holding the sky on his shoulders. If you didn't know about the Titan, you would think he was a mountain.

Fruit trees grew thickly in the orchard, and Hercules searched for a long time before he saw the golden apples flashing among dark green leaves. He came closer, stepping carefully, waiting for the serpent to show itself. Then he saw it and stood there, amazed.

He had heard that Ladon would be wrapped around the tree trunk, but the serpent had unwrapped itself and was coiled in front of the tree. It raised its head as Hercules came near—at least, he thought it must be its head because he saw two eyes. Otherwise, the serpent's body ran right into its head; its jaws were hinged at the tail. In other words, Ladon was a quarter-mile of living mouth lined with teeth.

"Well," said Hercules to himself, "how in the world am I expected to get past that monster? He's too big to strangle. No blade will pierce that leather hide. I can't use my poison arrows and spoil the fruit of the orchard and poison the rivers and streams of this beautiful island. Let me think. I fought a dragon once whose hide was like armor. The only way I could kill him was to step inside his jaws and stab upward through the roof of his mouth into the brain. But no, it won't work here. That dragon was an earthworm compared to this fellow. I daren't go anywhere near those great jaws. Whatever I do has to be done at a safe distance. Hmm. I think I feel an idea hatching."

He backed away from the serpent and angled off into the woods searching for a dead tree. He reached in and pulled out a beehive and hung it from his belt. The bees buzzed angrily. They swarmed out in a black cloud and settled on his chest and shoulders, stabbing with their stings. But his skin was too tough; the stingers broke off. The bees crept back into their hive. He searched for other hollow trees. When he came back to the orchard, his belt was hung with buzzing cones.

He walked slowly toward Hera's tree. The serpent saw him and opened its jaws. Hercules was looking right down a quarter-mile of pink and black gullet set with ivory knives. The jaws slithered toward him. He took a hive from his belt and, aiming carefully, threw it straight into the jaws, through the hedge of teeth, and saw it travel down the gullet to the jaw hinge at the serpent's tail.

One by one, he pulled the hives from his belt and hurled them into the yawning gullet. The serpent, drunk on the smell of honey, closed its jaws. But it wasn't only combs being crunched. The bees were in there too, and bees make a peppery dish. They swarmed out and thrust the wicked little hooks of their tails into the serpent's palate, the only place on its body not covered by leather hide. It was like eating fire.

In instant agony, Ladon uncoiled with the force of a thousand steel springs. High, high into the air went the serpent, tail flailing. Hercules held his oak-tree club, waiting. The serpent turned in the air and came plunging down at him. He swung his great club, smashing it into Ladon's body, splitting it open, shattering its fangs. Bits of ivory and honeycomb rained down on the meadow, and the body of the serpent, squashed like an earthworm by a gardener's spade, fell into the sea and sank out of sight.

Hercules walked toward Hera's tree. He reached for an apple. Thunder spoke out of the clear sky.

"Stop, thief!"

He dropped his hand. He knew it must be Atlas

speaking, and he remembered that he would have to meet the Titan before he could take the apples. He walked through the orchard and made his way to the other side of the island where Atlas stood. Here he saw the heavy blue bowl of the sky pressing on the shoulders of the Titan. He stood at the giant feet and looked up, up toward the snowy beard and the vast misty eyes. He heard the voice rumble again.

"Off with you, little thief, before I start an avalanche and bury you under a ton of rock."

"I'm no thief," said the young man. "I do not steal. I take. I am Hercules."

"Why didn't you say so in the first place? I've been waiting for you. I've been standing here for a thousand years, waiting."

"Waiting for what?"

"For someone strong enough to hold up my part of the sky while I take a little rest. The name they spoke was Hercules."

"They're mistaken, whoever 'they' are," said Hercules. "I haven't come here to hold up any sky, but to pick some apples."

"One little stamp of my foot and a ton of rocks will roll down on you," said Atlas. "So you won't get very far with your apples."

Indeed, just at that moment, a huge boulder came rolling down the slope of the Titan's thigh. Hercules had to leap away or he would have been crushed beneath it.

"That was just a sample," said Atlas.

"All right," called Hercules. "I'll make a bargain with

you. If you let me have an apple or two, I'll take your place for a little while."

"I agree, I agree. Take the sky."

"But only for a very short while. I'm supposed to be strong for a human being, but I'm no Titan, you know. If I take the sky from you, you must take it back quickly."

"Agreed, agreed," said Atlas. "Are you going to stand there talking about it for another thousand years? Climb to the top of that hill there, and I'll pass you the sky."

Hercules climbed to the top of a nearby hill and called out, "Before I take it, just tell me in plain words how long you'll be."

"Not long, not long. I just want to stretch my legs a bit. I'll run across to that orchard, pick your apples, and come back."

"Do you promise?"

"Upon my word as a Titan—Titans are older than the gods and much more honest."

And Atlas, moving swiftly for something so large, lifted the bowl of the sky from his shoulders and set its rim on the shoulders of Hercules. His knees sagged. He felt them sagging. He felt his spine crumbling. But he couldn't bear to show any weakness. Pride became a steel rod running from his soles to the top of his head, stiffening his backbone. His knees locked. Thighs and legs bunched like rock, welding him to the mountain top. He stood there, hunched, muscles writhing, stood there on the mountain top holding the sky on his shoulders.

Atlas skipped over the island, trampling trees and blowing eagle nests out of the cliffs with the wind of his laughter.

Hercules stood, waiting. His shoulders were on fire. He felt his ribs caving in. He could hardly turn his head. He rolled his eyes, searching for the Titan. The light faded. He felt the sinking sun warm his back, saw his own hunched shadow on the plain below. It was a sight he didn't want to see.

"Atlas," he called. "Atlas!"

A thunderous chuckle rolled across the valley.

"Atlas! Where are you? Come back!"

Thunder chuckled again. "Little fool, I'll never come back."

"You promised."

"I lied."

Hercules, with great effort, moved his head, shifting his gaze upward. The evening star had come out. It is the first star to burn in the western sky. He looked deep into its greenish blue light; it seemed to be laughing at him. He shrugged. And the star fell hissing into the sea, starting a plume of steam and leaving a scar of light in the sky.

"Hold still!" roared Atlas. "If you move, the stars will fall, and we will burn, burn...."

"I can't help moving," said Hercules. "My shoulders are sore."

"Never mind pain. It's only for eternity. Bear your burden like a man."

"I'll do my best," said Hercules. "But I'll need a pad of some kind. My lion pelt will do. If I can fold it on my shoulders under the edge of the sky, then I'll be able to stand here forever and not twitch or shake the stars."

"Very well," said Atlas. "Use your pelt."

"But you must hold the sky for a bit, while I fold the pelt on my shoulders."

"Oh, no," said Atlas. "Out of the question. Never again will I hold that sky."

Hercules shrugged. The horn of the moon snapped off

and the tide, feeling its silver reins loosen, sprang upon the beach. Atlas found himself knee-deep in water. It swirled higher and higher.

"Clumsy little idiot!" he bellowed. "Miserable weakling! You cracked the moon and unbound the tides."

"My shoulders are getting sorer and sorer," said Hercules. "And look, there are more stars out now. They'll be raining down in a minute. Better let me fix that pad."

He saw Atlas wading toward him.

"All right, all right," called the Titan. "I'll hold that accursed sky again, but just for a second. Then you must take it back and bear it forever."

"I promise," said Hercules.

Atlas groaned, hunching his back again under the awful weight of the sky. Hercules, feeling light as a feather and full of joy, raced down the slope of the mountain and splashed through the shrinking tide to where the apple tree stood. He filled his pouch with the golden fruit.

"Stop! Stop! What are you doing?" cried Atlas.

"Breaking the same promise you did. Taking a few apples."

Atlas lifted his gigantic foot, prepared to stamp and to start an avalanche that would bury Hercules under a ton of rock. But the stars were still wobbling and began to rain spears of fire. And Atlas had to steady himself quickly and quiet the sky. For in the beginning of the world, all the gods had helped adorn the heavens and were very proud of their great chandelier of stars. He did not dare let it break.

"Farewell," called Hercules. "Don't think badly of me. I, too, have burdens which I can't pass to anyone else."

Atlas didn't answer. He was weeping. His tears were snowflakes, the first of that year.

Discuss the Selection

1. What impossible challenge or heroic task did Hercules face in this myth?
2. Why did Hercules have to perform this heroic task? Why couldn't he refuse?
3. How might Atlas have felt when Hercules took the sky from him? Why might he have felt that way?
4. At what point in the story did you realize that Hercules was trying to trick Atlas?
5. Give examples from the story in which Hercules demonstrated courage in completing his task.

Apply the Skills

Many ancient myths helped early peoples understand the things they wondered about. These myths were made up to explain the mysteries of the world of nature. What explanations of natural phenomena does this myth about Hercules contain?

Think and Write

Prewrite

	Ladon	Atlas
Description		
How defeated	Bee stings and his club	
What Hercules gained from the victory	Access to the tree with the golden apples	

Copy the chart above and finish it with information about two of the creatures Hercules faced. The finished chart will compare the two creatures, showing how they were alike and different.

Compose

Use the information on the chart to write a paragraph that compares the two creatures. Include sentences that describe each creature, that tell how each was defeated, and that describe what Hercules gained from each victory. You might start with this topic sentence: *In this story, Hercules battled two very different kinds of creatures.*

Revise

Read your paragraph. Does it include all the information on the chart? If not, correct and revise your work.

In this Japanese folktale, a young man faces the challenge of saving his elderly mother from the cruel lord of a village. In the process, the cruel lord learns a valuable lesson. What is the lesson?

As you read, think about what makes this story a folktale.

The Wise Old Woman

adapted by Yoshiko Uchida

It is told that many long years ago, there lived an arrogant and cruel young lord. He ruled over a small village in the western hills of Japan.

"I have no use for old people in my village," he said haughtily. "They are neither useful nor able to work for a living. I therefore decree that anyone over seventy-one must be banished from the village and left in the mountains to die."

"What a terrible decree! What a cruel and unreasonable lord we have," the people of the village whispered. But the lord fearfully punished anyone who disobeyed him. So villagers who turned seventy-one were tearfully carried into the mountains, never to return.

Gradually there were fewer and fewer old people in the village and soon they disappeared altogether. The young lord was pleased.

"What a fine village of young, healthy, and hardworking people I have," he bragged. "Soon it will be the finest village in all Japan."

Now there lived in this village a kind young farmer and his aged mother. They were poor, but the farmer was good to his mother. The two of them lived happily together.

However, as the years went by, the mother grew older, and before long she reached the terrible age of seventy-one.

"If only I could somehow deceive the cruel lord," the farmer thought. But there were records in the village books. Everyone knew that his mother had turned seventy-one.

Each day the son put off telling his mother that he must take her into the mountains to die, but the people of the village began to talk. The farmer knew that if he did not take his mother away soon, the lord would send his soldiers and throw them both into a dark dungeon to die.

"Mother—" he would begin, as he tried to tell her what he must do, but he could not go on.

Then one day the mother herself spoke of the lord's decree. "Well, my son," she said, "the time has come for you to take me to the mountains. We must hurry before the lord sends his soldiers for you." And she did not seem worried at all that she must go to the mountains to die.

"Forgive me, dear mother, for what I must do," the farmer said sadly, and the next morning he lifted his mother to his shoulders and set off on the steep path toward the mountains. Up and up he climbed, until the trees clustered close and the path was gone. There was no longer even the sound of birds, and they heard only the soft wail of the wind in the trees. The son walked slowly, for he could not bear to think of leaving his old mother in the mountains. On and on he climbed, not wanting to stop and leave her behind. Soon, he heard his mother breaking off small twigs from the trees that they passed.

"Mother, what are you doing?" he asked.

"Do not worry, my son," she answered gently. "I am just marking the way so you will not get lost returning to the village."

The son stopped. "Even now you are thinking of me?" he asked, wonderingly.

The mother nodded. "Of course, my son," she replied. "You will always be in my thoughts. How could it be otherwise?"

At that, the young farmer could bear it no longer. "Mother, I cannot leave you in the mountains to die all alone," he said. "We are going home. No matter what the lord does to punish me, I will never desert you again."

So they waited until the sun had set and a lone star crept into the silent sky. Then in the dark shadows of night, the farmer carried his mother down the hill and they returned quietly to their little house. The farmer dug a deep hole in the floor of his kitchen and made a small room where he could hide his mother. From that day, she spent all her time in the secret room and the farmer carried meals to her there. The rest of the time, he was careful to work in the fields and act as though he lived alone. In this way, for almost two years, he kept his mother safely hidden. No one in the village knew that she was there.

Then one day there was a terrible commotion among the villagers. Lord Higa of the town beyond the hills threatened to take over their village and make it his own.

"Only one thing can spare you," Lord Higa announced. "Bring me a box containing one thousand ropes of ash and I will spare your village."

The cruel young lord quickly gathered together all the wise men of his village. "You are men of wisdom," he said. "Surely you can tell me how to meet Lord Higa's demands so our village can be spared."

But the wise men shook their heads. "It is impossible to make even one rope of ash, sire," they answered. "How can we ever make one thousand?"

"Fools!" the lord cried angrily. "What good is your wisdom if you cannot help me now?"

And he posted a notice in the village square offering a great reward of gold to any villager who could help him save their village.

But all the people in the village whispered, "Surely, it is an impossible thing, for ash crumbles at the touch of the finger. How could anyone ever make a rope of ash?" They shook their heads and sighed, "Alas, alas, we must be taken over by yet another cruel lord."

The young farmer, too, supposed that this must be. He wondered what would happen to his mother if a new lord even more terrible than their own came to rule over them.

When his mother saw the troubled look on his face, she asked, "Why are you so worried, my son?"

So the farmer told her of the impossible task ordered by Lord Higa if the village was to be spared, but his mother did not seem troubled at all. Instead she laughed softly and said, "Why, that is not such an impossible task. All one has to do is soak ordinary rope in salt water and dry it well. When it is burned, it will hold its shape and there is your rope of ash! Tell the villagers to hurry and find one thousand pieces of rope."

The farmer shook his head in amazement. "Mother, you are wonderfully wise," he said. He rushed to tell the young lord what he must do.

"You are wiser than all the wise men of the village," the lord said when he heard the farmer's solution. He rewarded him with many pieces of gold. The thousand ropes of ash were quickly made and the village was spared.

In a few days, however, there was another great commotion in the village as Lord Higa sent another threat. This time he sent a log with a small hole that curved and bent seven times through its length. He ordered that a single piece of silk thread be threaded through the hole. "If you cannot perform this task," the lord threatened, "I shall come to take over your village."

The young lord hurried once more to his wise men, but they all shook their heads in bewilderment. "A needle cannot bend its way through such curves," they moaned. "Again we are faced with an impossible task."

"And again you are stupid fools!" the lord said, stamping his foot impatiently. He then posted a second notice in the village square asking the villagers for their help.

Once more the young farmer hurried with the problem to his mother in her secret room.

"Why, that is not so difficult," his mother said with a quick smile. "Put some sugar at one end of the hole. Then, tie an ant to a piece of silk thread and put it in at the other end. He will weave his way in and out of the curves to get to the sugar and he will take the silk thread with him."

"Mother, you are remarkable!" the son cried, and he hurried off to the lord with the solution to the second problem.

Once more the lord commended the young farmer and rewarded him with many pieces of gold. "You are a brilliant man. You have saved our village again," he said gratefully.

But the lord's troubles were not over even then, for a few days later Lord Higa sent still another task. "This time you will undoubtedly fail and then I shall take over your village," he threatened. "Bring me a drum that sounds without being beaten."

"But that is not possible," sighed the people of the village. "How can anyone make a drum sound without beating it?"

This time the wise men held their heads in their hands and moaned, "It is hopeless. It is hopeless. This time Lord Higa will defeat us all."

The young farmer hurried home breathlessly. "Mother, Mother, we must solve another terrible problem or Lord Higa will take over our village!" And he quickly told his mother about the impossible drum.

His mother, however, smiled and answered, "Why, this is the easiest of them all. Make a drum with sides of paper and put a bumblebee inside. As it tries to escape, it will buzz and beat itself against the paper and you will have a drum that sounds without being beaten."

The young farmer was amazed at his mother's wisdom. "You are far wiser than any of the wise men of the village," he said. He hurried to tell the young lord how to complete Lord Higa's third task.

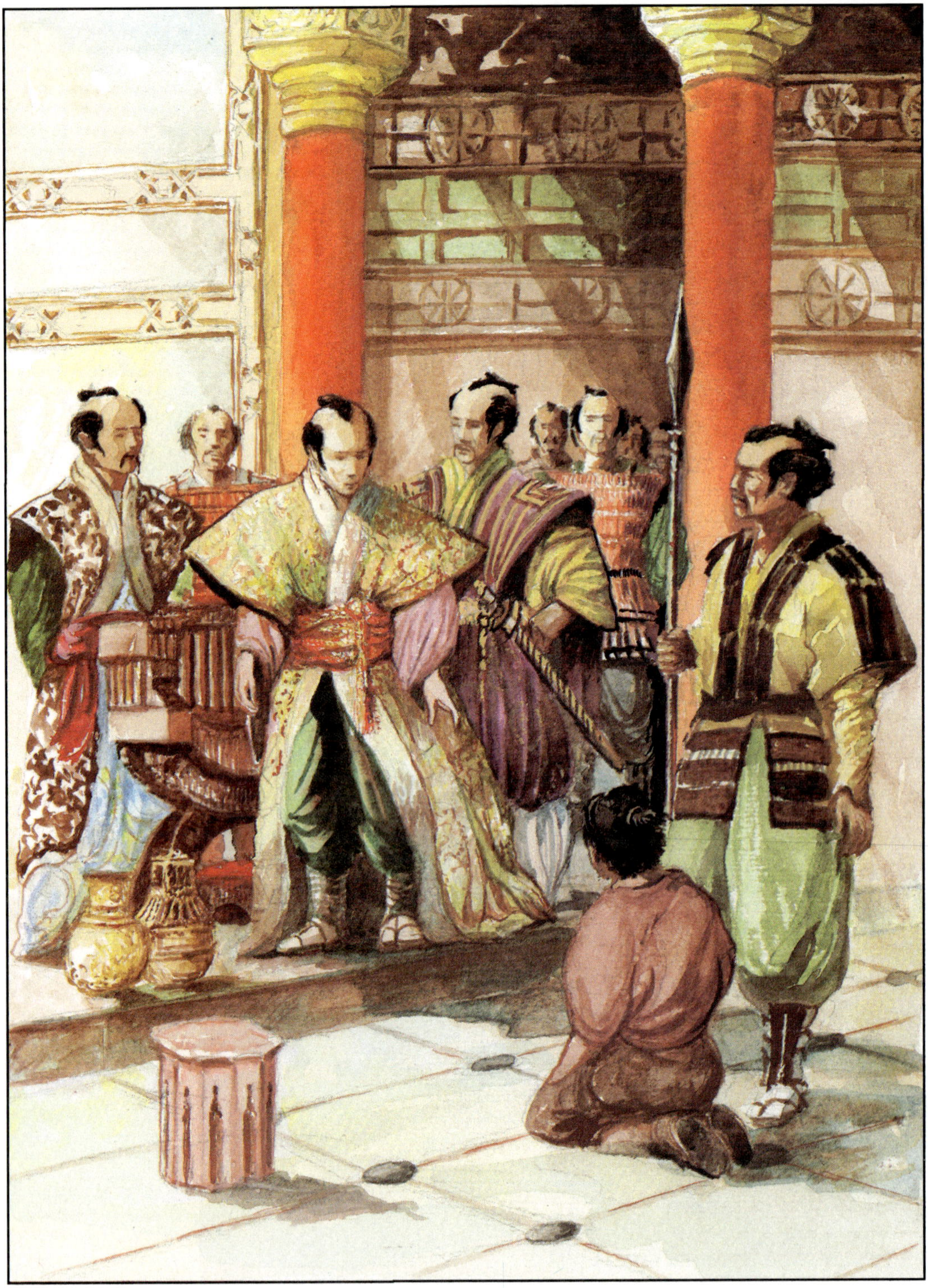

When the lord heard the answer, he was greatly impressed. "Surely a young man like you cannot be wiser than all my wise men," he said. "Tell me honestly, who has helped you solve all these difficult problems?"

The young farmer could not lie. "My lord," he began slowly, "for the past two years I have broken the law of the land. I have kept my aged mother hidden beneath the floor of my house. It is she who solved each of your problems and saved the village from Lord Higa."

He trembled as he spoke, for he feared the lord's displeasure and rage. Surely now the soldiers would be called to throw him into the dark dungeon. But when he glanced fearfully at the lord, he saw that the young ruler was not angry at all. Instead, he was silent and thoughtful. At last the lord realized how much wisdom and knowledge old people possess.

"I have been very wrong," he said finally. "And I must ask the forgiveness of your mother and of all my people. Never again will I order that the old people of our village be sent to the mountains to die. Rather, they will be treated with the respect and honor they deserve and share with us the wisdom of their years."

And so it was. From that day, the villagers were no longer forced to leave their parents in the mountains. The village became once more a happy, cheerful place in which to live. The terrible Lord Higa stopped sending his impossible tasks and no longer threatened to take over the village, for he too was impressed. "Even in such a small village there is much wisdom," he declared, "and its people should be allowed to live in peace."

And that is exactly what the farmer and his mother and all the people of the village did for all the years thereafter.

Discuss the Selection

1. Because the young man met the challenge of saving his mother, the cruel lord learned a lesson. What lesson did the cruel lord learn?
2. What did the young farmer's mother do that made it impossible for her son to leave her in the mountains?
3. Why do you think Lord Higa made such strange demands on the village?
4. Why do you think the village wise men were unable to tell the young lord how to meet Lord Higa's demands?
5. Locate the parts of the story where the young farmer's mother solved the problems presented by Lord Higa.

Apply the Skills

One type of folklore is the **folktale**. Most folktales have common characteristics: simple plots that teach readers a lesson, heroes who are ordinary people, clever characters, and story characters symbolizing good and evil. Explain how "The Wise Old Woman" exhibits each of the characteristics of a folktale.

Think and Write

Prewrite

The young farmer admitted that his wise old mother had solved the village's problems.

The cruel lord decreed that all old people must be banished from the village.

The wise old woman solved the problem of the ash rope.

The wise old woman solved the problem of the drum.

Each note card above describes a major event in the plot of "The Wise Old Woman." Think about the story. Get or make three note cards and on them describe three other events from the story. Use your notes and those above to make a list of the story events in the correct time order.

Compose

Write a summary of the major events in "The Wise Old Woman." Use your list of story events. Begin sentences with time-signaling words such as *first, next, then, following that,* and *finally* to tie your summary together. Your first sentence might be this: *A young Japanese farmer taught a cruel lord a valuable lesson.*

Revise

Read your summary. Have you included all the story events? Have you used time-signaling words? If not, revise your work.

Study Skills

Maps and Atlases

What sources would you check if you wanted to find out about a particular area? You might try a map or an atlas. The more you know about how to use a map or an atlas, the more you can learn about the areas they represent.

Maps

A **map** is a drawing of a region, such as a city, state, or country. There are even maps of the moon. A map can give us many kinds of information depending on the kind of map it is and the symbols that are used on the map.

There are many kinds of maps. Examples of two kinds appear in this lesson. A **topographical map** uses colors and shapes to show us what the land is like in an area. A topographical map of Texas appears below.

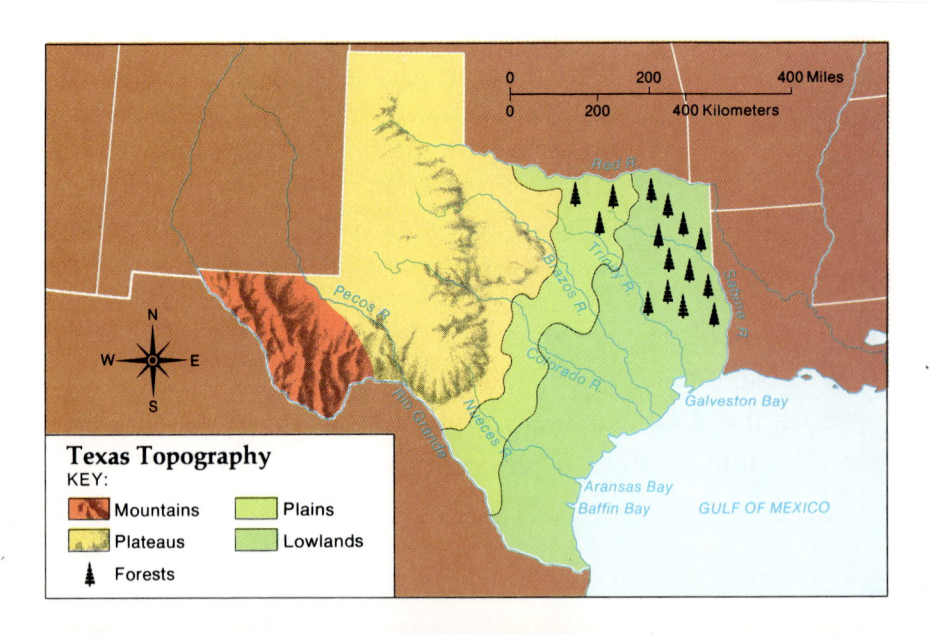

Texas Topography
KEY:
- Mountains
- Plateaus
- Plains
- Lowlands
- Forests

A **road map** shows drivers where places are located and how to get from one place to another. A road map showing part of Texas appears on the next page.

The **map key** shows what the symbols used on a map stand for. Study the symbols in the key to the topographical map of Texas. What symbol is used to show forests? A small tree symbol shows where forests are located. What kind of landforms are located in the middle of Texas?

The **compass rose** on a map shows the directions North, South, East, and West. Use the compass rose and the key on the topographical map of Texas to find in what direction the plains of Texas are from the lowlands.

The **map scale** is used to figure the distance between any two places on a map. The scale for the road map of Texas on the next page stands for distance in miles. Let's use this scale to find the distance in miles between the cities of San Antonio and Houston.

First find the dots that stand for the two cities. Then take a piece of paper and place it on the road map so that the same edge of the paper touches both dots. Make a mark on your paper at the point where each dot touches the edge.

Then move your paper so that the edge you marked is next to the map scale. Line up the left mark on your paper with the zero on the left end of the scale. Now you can see that the right-hand mark on your paper falls almost exactly on the 200-mile point on the scale. This tells us that San Antonio is about 200 miles from Houston.

Now use the road map of Texas to find the distance between the state capital and Dallas. First find the state capital, using the map key. Then repeat the steps above, using the scale to find the distance between the two cities.

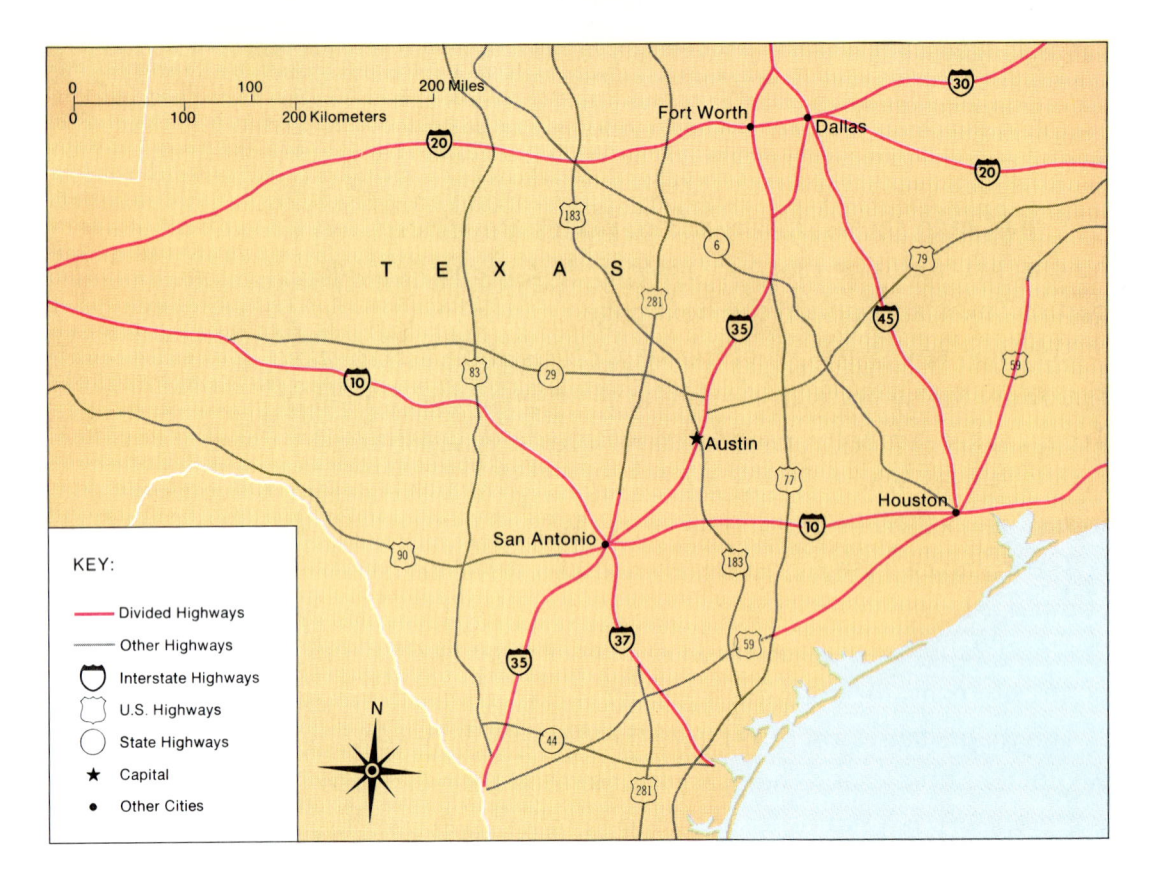

Atlases

An **atlas** is a book of maps that may also include other information about certain places. An index at the back of an atlas lists the name of each place and gives the page number of the map where it appears. The index might also list the coordinates, a letter and numeral combination that will help you to locate a specific place on a map.

How would we go about finding Clinton, Missouri, in an atlas? First we would check the index of the atlas for a listing for Clinton. It would look something like this:

Clinton, Missouri
29/C3

The first number indicates that Clinton will be on the map on page 29 in the atlas. Using the coordinates C3, which tell us the grid location, we can exactly locate Clinton on the map. The map of Missouri from page 29 of an atlas appears on this page.

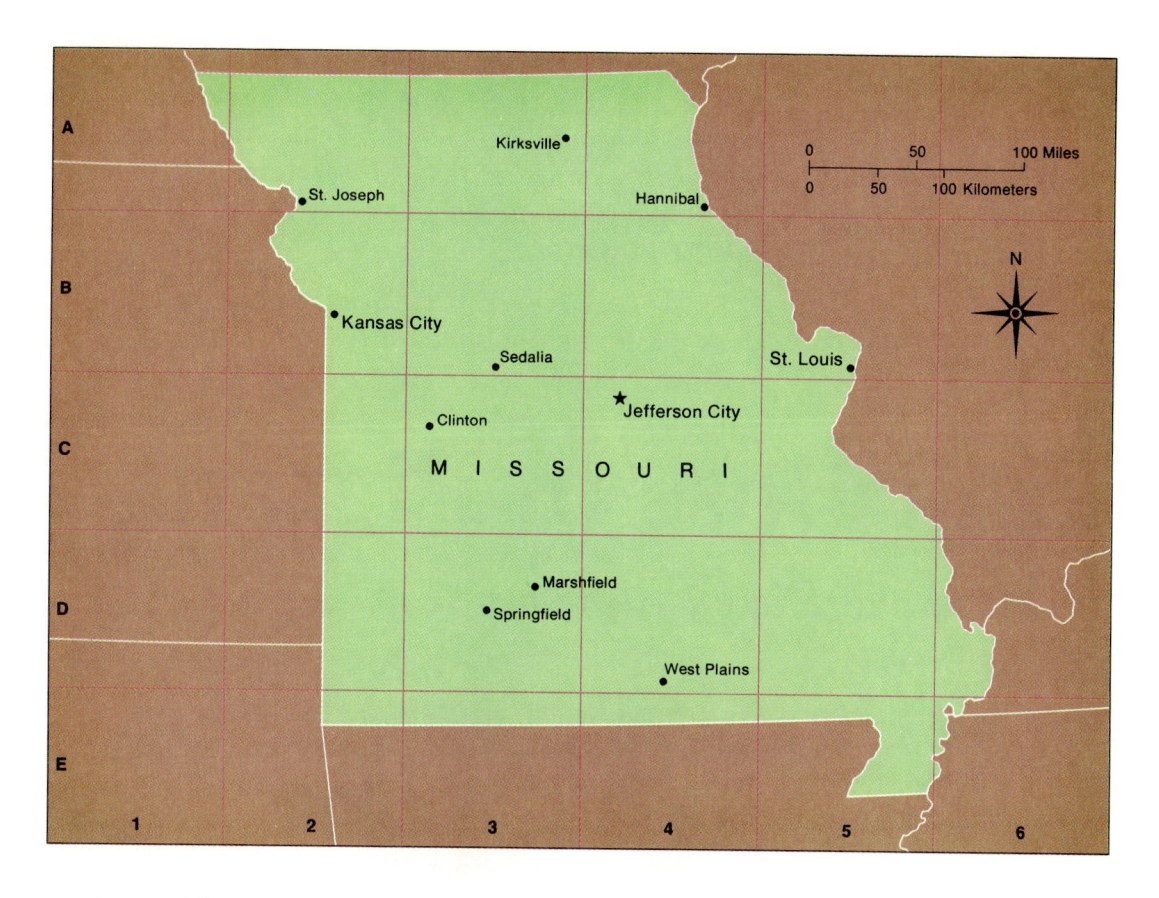

The index listing tells us that the grid location for Clinton is C3 on this map. Locate the letter C along the left-hand side of the map and place your left index finger on it. Locate the numeral 3 along the bottom of the map and place your right index finger on it. Draw an imaginary line over from C and up from 3 until your fingers meet. The point where your fingers meet is the exact C3 grid location. According to the index, this point is the approximate location of Clinton on the map. Can you find Clinton near this point?

Using steps similar to those we used to locate Clinton, find the Missouri town that appears at the grid location D4. How might the index listing for this town appear in an atlas?

51

Fourteen-year-old Emma Jane is guiding her family and their herd of longhorn cattle across Missouri, a place unfriendly to out-of-state cattle herds. How, she wonders, will she ever meet the challenge posed by the state's hostile farmers?

Maps have helped travelers for ages. How does a map help Emma Jane in this story?

Trail Boss in Pigtails

by Marjorie Filley Stover

Emma Jane Burke lived during the mid-1800's. Her family raised cattle for a living. When the Burkes set out from Texas for Illinois, Emma Jane was made trail boss because of the ill health of her father. Watching over eighty-two longhorn cattle was challenging work for the fourteen-year-old. Every day she learned more about the job, and also discovered how much more she had to learn. When Emma Jane's father died, full responsibility for the herd fell on her inexperienced shoulders. Each day presented new challenges for the spirited girl. Riding the trails was difficult work even for the most experienced herders; how much more difficult for Emma Jane and her younger brother, Martin. Emma Jane was tested again and again, but she was determined to master her grown-up job. Nothing would stop her!

Emma Jane sat thoughtfully chewing corn bread and meat while she watched the cattle browse in an open meadow. Pulling a crude map from her pocket, she turned to Martin. "If we run into trouble in Missouri, it'll be at the river crossings."

Martin nodded, and they eyed one another uneasily, remembering the warning a friendly cowboy had given them earlier. "Missouri farmers are setting up roadblocks at bridges and turning back all herds of Texas cattle," he had told them. "They claim that our longhorns infect their cattle with a disease which wipes out whole herds. 'Texas fever' they call it."

"We've got to go that way," Emma Jane insisted stubbornly. "Uncle Oscar wrote Ma he'd meet us at Alton. Our cattle aren't sick. Why blame them?"

At that time not anyone knew that Texas fever was caused by a tiny tick that clung to the longhorns which were immune to its bite.

Martin bent over the map. "Where are we now?"

Emma Jane's finger traced a line toward a black dot. "We're heading this way to the Grand River bridge near Clinton. We've got to cross that bridge."

Every day brought them closer to Clinton. If there was to be a showdown, this is where it would come, she figured.

Then one afternoon, above the medley of the cattle sounds, Emma Jane's ears caught the galloping rhythm of a horse behind her. As the sound drew closer, she flicked a glance over her shoulder and tightened her jaw. "Guess I know trouble when I see it coming," she muttered to her horse, Peanuts. Peanuts' ears twitched slightly, and he strained on the bit.

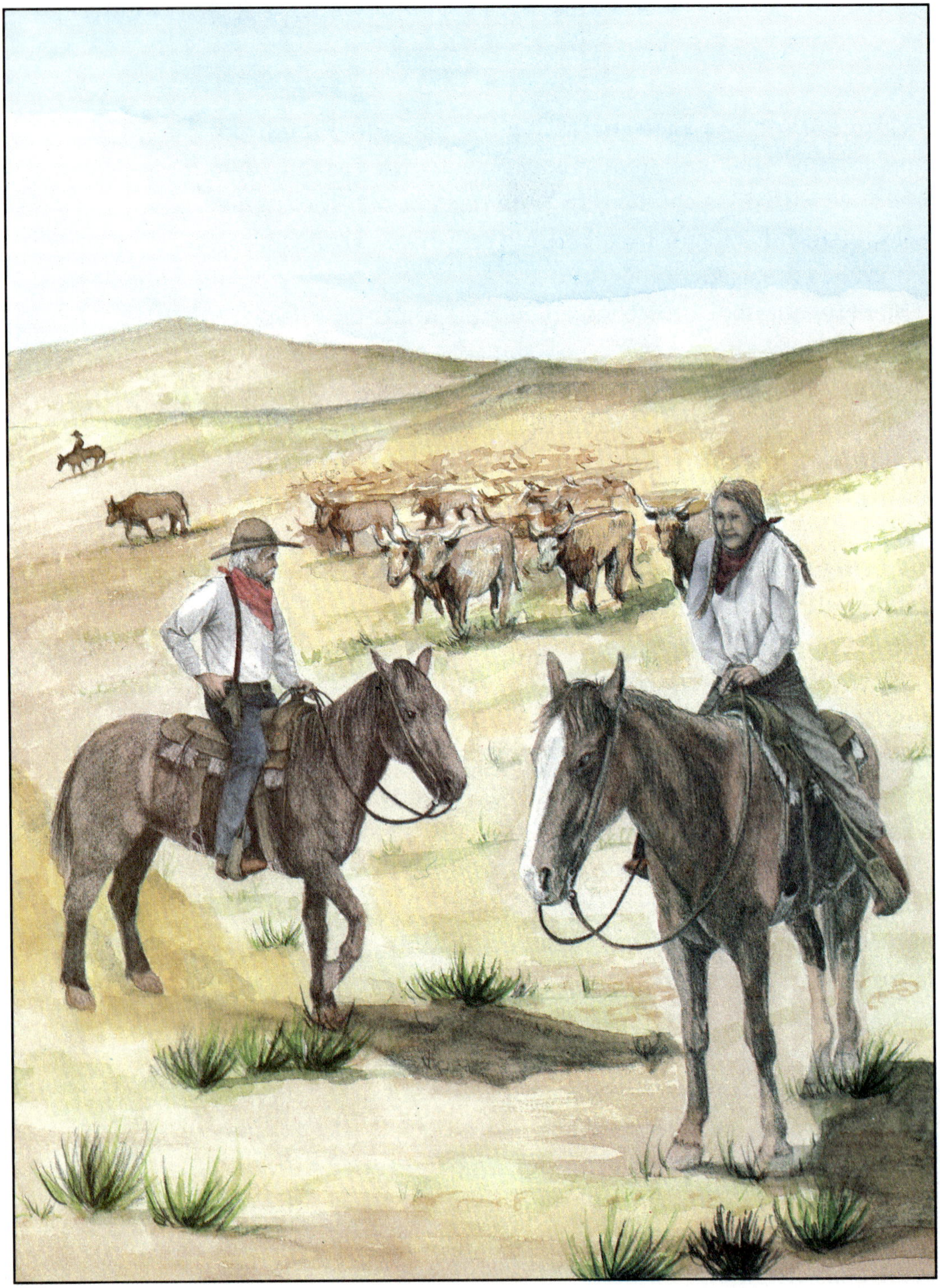

The galloping rider hauled up beside her, and a curt voice demanded, "Where do you kids think you're taking those cattle?"

Emma Jane's gray eyes swept over the man in a steady but polite gaze before she answered. A broad-brimmed hat was clamped over his iron-gray hair. His hostile blue eyes glared.

The girl kept her voice calm and mild. "We're trailin' them to market, Mister."

The blue eyes snapped. "Not across my land you're not. I don't aim to have my cattle catch the Texas fever."

Emma Jane looked at her longhorns, plodding along, and then turned back to the man. "We don't aim to go near your cattle, Mister—and anyway, these steers aren't wild. Been off the range most two years now."

The man sucked in his breath. "Now see here. Us Missouri farmers have got our rights." He tapped a holster at his hip. "I'm warning you. You better turn this herd around and head right back where you come from."

Emma Jane looked calmly at the horseman beside her. "This is just a little herd, Mister. Can't see as how they're going to do you any more harm than I could—'less you stampede 'em, of course. Then there's no tellin' where they might head or when I could stop 'em."

The man stared at her, and his voice carried a note of grudging admiration. "Well, if you aren't a cool young-un. I s'pose your pa's up ahead in the wagon." He gathered up the reins. "I'll settle this with him."

Emma Jane's voice kept the same low pitch. "Pa's dead. I'm trail boss of this outfit, Mister."

The reins dropped loose again. The man stared. "A trail boss in pigtails! How far have you come like this?"

Emma Jane pushed her feet more firmly into the stirrups and kept one eye on Peanuts' ears. "Waco, Texas."

The man exploded in a boom: "Waco, Texas!"

Peanuts bucked and reared, but Emma Jane was ready for him and held tight. "Steady, boy! Steady."

The man watched her bring the horse under control, and all the grimness disappeared from his leather face. "That horse has too much ginger for a kid—" His voice trailed into silence.

Emma Jane continued as if there had been no interruption. "Pa died in February. We left when the grass turned green. Ma drives the wagon with the little ones. Marty and I herd the cattle."

The man squinted at her from under his hat brim. "But why bring along the cattle?"

"We're goin' back to Illinois. Goin' to sell the cattle in Chicago and buy a farm."

The blue eyes blinked and the man twanged softly, "Goin' to Chicago, she says—as if it were just over the next hill."

Emma Jane flashed him a grin. "That's right. All we gotta do is keep on walking, and one day that's where Chicago will be—over the next hill."

The man's gray brows knit furiously. "Excepting there's the little matter of a few rivers and—Looky here, I'm not gonna fight kids. So, I'll let you by my place. But you'll never get past Grand River Bridge this side of Clinton. They've got a committee guarding that bridge against all out-of-state drivers. Turned back three herds numbering around two thousand in June. How do you expect to get past them?"

Emma Jane's jaw took the stubborn set her family knew so well. "I'll figure that out when we get there—just like I've been doing all the way from Texas."

"You're a spunky one, I'll say that."

The iron-gray head nodded and the man muttered, "Like you say, it's just a pint-sized herd, and they've been off the range nigh onto two years—" He pointed ahead. "That tree up yonder marks the edge of my land. Good luck—you'll need it." He touched the brim of his hat, wheeled his horse, and rode away.

Emma Jane listened to the echoing hoofbeats die in the distance, but all the while her mind was twisting, turning, probing the problems that lay ahead.

"I wonder what Pa would have done?" she asked Peanuts. She wrinkled her forehead. "I reckon he'd have outmaneuvered them somehow."

Suddenly Emma Jane's eyes lighted. "That's what I'll do. That's just what I'll do. I'll outmaneuver 'em."

A breeze cooled Emma Jane's hot cheeks late that afternoon as she sat in the worn saddle. From the top of the wooded bluff, she could see the valley spread below.

Her eye traced the river, curling and weaving its way under the fire of the sun like a scalloped pattern of molten silver. There was the brown road they must travel, threading its way to the river bank where Grand River Bridge crossed the silver stream.

As her eyes fastened on it, several toylike figures sauntered into view. Figures that when studied turned into rawboned men of muscle with glints of steel in their hands. For a moment she wavered.

Then once again she seemed to hear Pa's voice whispering, "You can do it, Emma Jane." Pa, worn with illness, from some inner depths had mustered a spark of determination and courage that he had passed on to her; and she must not fail him. "You can do it, Emma Jane, you can do it."

Her eyes went back to the bridge. She must cross the bridge. She dug her heels into Peanuts' sides and rode back to where she had left Ma and the others.

Emma Jane slid from Peanuts' back. "There's men at the bridge."

Ma nodded. "I reckon that it's pretty hard to hide even a little herd of cattle."

"That means you'll have to go ahead with the wagon."

The worry creases between Ma's eyebrows deepened. "What are you going to do, Emma Jane?"

"You get as far on the other side of Clinton today as you can. Marty and I will stay here till after dark. When the moon comes up, we'll push out and cross the bridge. They won't be expecting us then."

Without a break in his stride, Colonel was on the bridge. Emma Jane reined Star and let the proud longhorn take the lead alone.

The cattle pressed close behind Colonel. Two and three abreast they came, following their leader.

As the last of the herd gained the bridge, the noise seemed to crash and roll like thunder in Emma Jane's nervous ears.

Then the sound for which she had been tensed split the air. A voice rang out, "Hey! What's goin' on? Halt! Halt, I say!" A shot rang in the air. Then another.

Colonel had already reached the far end of the bridge when the shouts came. At the shot, he lunged forward like a greenhorn under attack for the first time. As one, the dark forms on the bridge lunged after him.

There was a thunderous noise on the wooden planks.

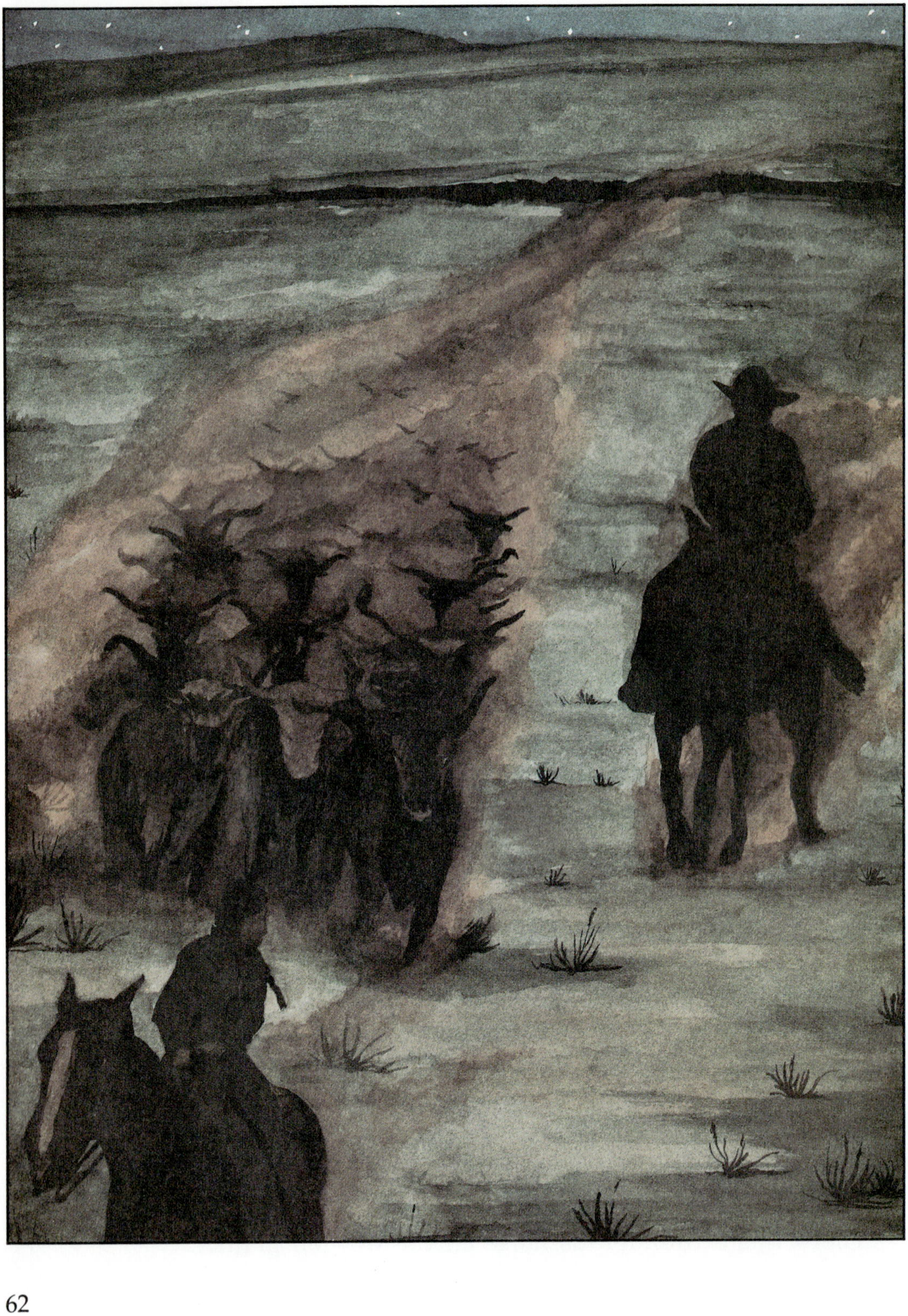

Emma Jane heard Martin yelling, "Git on there!"

Star was prancing, dancing, showing along the rear line of tails. Then the thunder of the bridge was no more than a hollow echo drowned in the thudding of more than three hundred hooves pounding the trail.

Emma Jane saw Martin on his side of the herd. Colonel had left the trail. Where were they going? She could not tell. Should she try to swing the herd to the right or the left? She did not know. There had been no time to get her bearings before the stampede began. She could only fly along with it and hope to keep her little herd intact.

Then her ears picked up a new beat of hooves. Turning around in the saddle, she saw that at least one rider was pursuing them. He was not yelling, only relentlessly riding, and gaining, gaining. Oh, what was the use? She didn't even know where they were going.

The galloping hooves beat closer. "Turn 'em left," a hoarse voice shouted. "Keep 'em out of the canebrakes along the river bottom."

She didn't know why she should obey, but she did. The stranger was making no effort to slow their swift pace. It was almost as if he were encouraging it. For a fact, he was helping them, Emma Jane realized in amazement.

Gradually the cattle slowed of their own will. They had run themselves out. They no longer remembered what had caused their mad flight.

The strange horse and rider were only a few paces behind her. "The trail's over yonder. Keep 'em moving. You still have a ways till you're out of this county."

There was something vaguely familiar about that nasal twang. "You're helping us. Why?" Emma Jane twisted around in the saddle, and for the first time, got a really good look at the stranger. The moonlight picked up the glint of silver in the iron-gray hair.

The tension drained out of her. "Oh, it's you, Mister! What about the others back at the bridge?"

"There was only one other feller. Thought I had them all talked into going home, but this feller was just too doggoned stubborn. He fired the shots."

There was a dry chuckle. "Funny thing, though. While I was getting my horse, his horse managed to break away. I reckon he hasn't caught it yet."

"But why? Why are you helping us?"

The man fumbled for a moment with his neckerchief. "I got a girl of my own with pigtails down her back. I couldn't get you out of my mind. Finally took out after you. Saw where you'd turned your stock off the trail and saw your ma and the little 'uns drive by. When you didn't come afore sundown, I figured maybe you'd try it at night. Pretty smart and pretty spunky."

The first fingers of light were streaking the sky. Emma Jane looked across the peaceably plodding longhorns and back at the man. "Thanks, Mister. Thanks a heap."

He pointed a finger down the trail. "See that old sycamore? Down right is a spot where you can rest your herd. I'll search out your ma and let her know where to find you. Beyond here you won't have too much trouble."

The man raised his wide-brimmed hat. "The farmers of this county have got their rights, but any pigtailed trail boss that's got as much spunk as you've got, has got some rights, too." He clamped the dusty hat on his head, and galloped back down the trail.

Westward Bound

"Westward, Ho!" was the call. The land west of the Mississippi was the challenge. Settlers packed a few belongings in covered wagons and traveled to the new land. All ages took part in building a home and making a living on the frontier. Children had to help out at home as well as continue their educations.

A dugout home carved out of a hillside on a North Dakota prairie in the 1890's. The sod in the wagon will be used to fix the roof.

A Texas longhorn.

A young ox driver.

Children doing their chores. Girls and boys gather the fruits of an Oklahoma farm at the turn of the century.

Moving freight in the 1860's. A wagon train, with cattle and other animals, continues its trek west through the main street of a midwestern town.

A Texan and her show horse pose for the camera.

A one-room schoolhouse in Nebraska. Children of all ages were taught by one teacher.

69

Apply the Skills

1. How did Emma Jane meet the challenge posed by the hostile Missouri farmers?
2. What were some of the things the Missouri farmer did to help Emma Jane?
3. Why do you think the Missouri farmer was surprised that Emma Jane was the trail boss?
4. Do you think Emma Jane would have been successful without the farmer's help? Why or why not?
5. Emma Jane was described by the Missouri farmer as "smart and spunky." Locate places in the story where she demonstrated these qualities.

Discuss the Selection

Maps give many kinds of information useful to travelers: directions, mileage, and locations of cities, rivers, mountains, and national parks. Emma Jane and Martin used a map to plan their journey. How did the map help them choose which way to travel?

Think and Write

Prewrite

Story	Problem	Solution
"The Morning the Sun Refused to Rise"	Paul Bunyan had to find a way to make the earth spin again.	Paul used sourdough starter as rocket power to make the earth spin.
"The Golden Apples"	Hercules needed the golden apples to complete his task.	Hercules tricked Atlas and escaped with the golden apples.
"Trail Boss in Pigtails"		

Most stories present problems that must be solved. Read the story problems and solutions in the chart above. Copy the portion of the chart for "Trail Boss in Pigtails." Fill in the story's problem and solution.

Compose

Write two paragraphs about "Trail Boss in Pigtails." In the first, state the problem. Add two or more sentences that describe the problem. In the second paragraph, state the solution. Follow with several sentences that give details about how the solution was reached.

Revise

Read your paragraphs. Check to make sure that the first paragraph clearly states the problem and that the second clearly states the solution. If they do not, revise them.

71

Comprehension Study

Cause and Effect

When something happens in a story, there is a reason why it happens. That reason can be as interesting or as important as the thing that happens. Understanding why things happen helps you understand what you read.

The reason why something happens is called the **cause.** The thing that happens is called the **effect.** There is an easy way to find the cause and the effect. As you read, ask yourself "What happened?" This will help you find the effect. Then ask yourself "Why did it happen?" This will help you find the cause. Ask yourself "What happened?" and "Why?" as you read this sentence.

Mr. Parker took his class to Bald Rock Park because he wanted the students to see the plants and animals they had studied in science.

What happened? *Mr. Parker's class went to Bald Rock Park.* That is the effect. Why did it happen? *Because Mr. Parker wanted the class to see the things they had studied.* That is the cause.

Authors sometimes use clue words that help show cause-and-effect relationships. In the example sentence, the word *because* was a clue word. There are other clue words, such as *therefore, as a result,* and *so.* Read this story part. As you read, look for a cause, an effect, and a clue word.

Nothing could possibly go wrong. Every detail of the trip had been carefully planned, so Mr. Parker sat back in his seat on the bus and relaxed.

What is the effect? *Mr. Parker sat back and relaxed.* What is the cause? *Every detail had been carefully planned.* What clue word did you find? *So.* In this selection, the cause was stated before the effect. Did you remember to ask "What happened?" and "Why?"

The cause and effect will not always be found in the same sentence. You might have to read several sentences before you can answer the questions "What happened?" and "Why?" Read the next part of the story.

> Mr. Parker gave each group of students a list of leaves and rocks to collect so they could be displayed on Parents' Night. Each group went off to collect as many of the things on the list as they could.

What is the effect? *The groups went to collect things.* What is the cause? *Their teacher gave them a list of things to find for their collections.*

One Effect from Several Causes

In each of the examples you have read, there has been one cause and one effect. Some things happen for more than one reason. The next story part gives more than one cause for one effect. Try to find all of the causes.

> Tracy's group was successful in finding everything on their list. Each member of the group had looked for one thing. When an item was found, Tracy checked it off the list. One person was in charge of the collection so nothing would be damaged.

The effect is given in the first sentence of the paragraph: *Tracy's group was successful in finding everything on their*

73

list. The causes are given in the other sentences. What are the causes? *They had each looked for one thing; they checked each item off as it was found; they protected their collection from harm.* All these things caused Tracy's group to be successful.

One Cause Leading to Several Effects

Just as one effect can have several causes, one cause can lead to several effects.

> The members of Lee's group glanced at the list and then ran off to find things. They ended up with three maple leaves and two oak leaves instead of leaves from five different trees. Everyone found a limestone rock, but no one found a seed pod. They forgot to look for other rock samples.

There is a single cause in this paragraph. What is it? *The members of Lee's group glanced at the list and then ran off to find things.* This cause had several effects: *They did not find the right kind of leaves; they did not find a seed pod; they all found the same kind of rock; and they forgot to look for other rock samples.*

Now you know that something that happens is called an effect. You know that the reason why it happens is called the cause. Sometimes one thing causes another thing to happen, and then that causes a third thing to happen. Sometimes the chain goes on and on. Then, you have many causes and many effects.

The third group of students from Mr. Parker's class had a very eventful trip. Read what happened to this group. Look for all the causes and all the effects.

> Stan's group was just about finished with their collection when Stan spotted a bird's nest on a low tree branch. The group thought it would be great to add the nest to their collection. No one had ever seen this type of bird's nest before. No one noticed the bees flying around the tree trunk, so Stan climbed up to get the nest. A bee stung Stan. Stan dropped the nest. The nest hit Andy on the back and some pieces of straw went down Andy's shirt. Andy started scratching and hopping around and he bumped into Amy. Amy stepped back and smashed a hole in their bag. Most of their collection fell out of the hole as they walked back to the bus.

Textbook Application: Cause and Effect in Health

You read a textbook to find out about things. The authors of textbooks often use cause-and-effect relationships to explain things. First, the author will tell you what happened. Then, the author will tell you why it happened. Understanding cause-and-effect relationships will help you understand the information in a textbook.

When authors use clue words such as *because*, *so*, *therefore*, and *as a result*, it is easy to find the cause and the effect. When authors do not use clue words, you need to be able to find the cause and effect in another way. Asking yourself "What happened?" will help you find the effect. Asking yourself "Why did it happen?" will help you find the cause.

Here is a selection from a health book. Read it to yourself. The sidenotes will help you find causes and effects.

At first, the effects of Roy's jogging were a shortness of breath and the pounding of his heart. What was the cause of this?

Roy decided to jog every day in order to lose weight and become more fit. At first he was short of breath after only a few minutes of exercise. He could feel his heart pounding. More oxygen and substances from food had to reach his muscles. Roy's body had to take in more air and his blood had to move faster. Jogging made Roy's lungs and circulatory system work harder than they were used to.

After a few weeks, Roy began to lose weight. He was also able to run farther without getting tired. His body had become more efficient, or able to do more with less work.

For example, Roy's lungs were able to hold more air. Lungs that can hold more air help your body work more efficiently. You do not have to breathe as hard or as often to get the oxygen you need. Improved lungs also let you get rid of more carbon dioxide when you breathe out. When wastes such as carbon dioxide are stored in your body, you feel tired. The faster you can get rid of wastes, the sooner you feel rested.

A stronger heart also helps make your body more efficient. It pumps more blood each time it beats. Your heart can move the same amount of blood with fewer beats. Jogging made Roy's heart stronger.

— *HBJ Health,*
Harcourt Brace Jovanovich

This paragraph tells some effects of Roy's continued running. What are the effects?

This paragraph tells how lungs that hold more air cause your body to be more efficient.

Here are other causes for improved efficiency. What are the causes?

Remember to look for causes and effects as you read a selection in a textbook. Asking yourself "What happened?" and "Why?" can help you understand and remember the information you read.

Karana, an Indian girl, is stranded alone on an island. How is every day of life a lonely challenge for her?

Think about causes and effects as you read this story. What effect does Karana's loneliness have on her treatment of the leader of the wild dogs?

Island of the Blue Dolphins

by Scott O'Dell

The author of *Island of the Blue Dolphins* based his book on the few facts known about an American Indian girl who was stranded on an island from 1835 to 1853. In the early 1800's, the girl's Indian tribe lived on an island off the California coast. In O'Dell's account, Aleut hunters attacked the tribe, killing most of the men. Fearful of another attack, the remaining villagers boarded a rescue ship for the mainland. When Karana, a village girl, discovered her young brother had accidentally been left behind, she dove off the ship and swam back to the island. Two days later, Karana's brother was killed by a pack of wild dogs, and she was left totally alone. This part of the story tells how Karana bravely faced the challenge of the wild dogs.

There had been wild dogs on the Island of the Blue Dolphins as long as I remember, but after the Aleuts had slain most of the men of our tribe and their dogs had left to join the others, the pack became much bolder. It spent the nights running through the village and during the day was never far off. It was then that we made plans to get rid of them, but the ship came and everyone left Ghalas-at.

I am sure that the pack grew bolder because of their leader, the big one with the thick fur around his neck and the yellow eyes.

I had never seen this dog before the Aleuts came and no one else had, so he must have come with them and been left behind when they sailed away. He was a much larger dog than any of ours, which besides have short hair and brown eyes. I was sure that he was an Aleut dog.

Already I had killed four of the pack, but there were many left, more than in the beginning, for some had been born in the meantime. The young dogs were even wilder than the old ones.

I first went to the hill near the cave when the pack was away and collected armloads of brush which I placed near the mouth of their lair. Then I waited until the pack was in the cave. It went there early in the morning to sleep after it had spent the night prowling. I took with me the big bow and five arrows and two of the spears. I went quietly, circling around the mouth of the cave and came up to it from the side. There I left all of my weapons except one spear.

I set fire to the brush and pushed it into the cave. If the wild dogs heard me, there was no sound from them. Nearby was a ledge of rock which I climbed, taking my weapons with me.

The fire burned high. Some of the smoke trailed out over the hill, but much of it stayed in the cave. Soon the pack would have to leave. I did not hope to kill more than five of them because I had only that many arrows, but if the leader was one of the five I would be satisfied. It might be wiser if I waited and saved all my arrows for him, and this I decided to do.

None of the dogs appeared before the fire died. Then three ran out and away. Seven more followed and a long time afterwards a like number. There were many more still left in the cave.

The leader came next. Unlike the others, he did not run away. He jumped over the ashes and stood at the mouth of the cave, sniffing the air. I was so close to him that I could see his nose quivering, but he did not see me until I raised my bow. Fortunately I did not frighten him.

He stood facing me, his front legs spread as if he were ready to spring, his yellow eyes narrowed to slits. The arrow struck him in the chest. He turned away from me, took one step and fell. I sent another arrow toward him which went wide.

At this time three more dogs trotted out of the cave. I used the last of my arrows and killed two of them.

Carrying both of the spears, I climbed down from the ledge and went through the brush to the place where the leader had fallen. He was not there. While I had been shooting at the other dogs, he had gone. He could not have gone far because of his wound, but though I looked everywhere, around the ledge where I had been standing and in front of the cave, I did not find him.

I waited for a long time and then went inside the cave. It was deep, but I could see clearly.

Far back in a corner was the half-eaten carcass of a fox. Beside it was a black dog with four gray pups. One of the pups came slowly toward me, a round ball of fur that I could have held in my hand. I wanted to hold it, but the mother leaped to her feet and bared her teeth. I raised my spear as I backed out of the cave, yet I did not use it. The wounded leader was not there.

Night was coming and I left the cave, going along the foot of the hill that led to the cliff. I had not gone far on this trail that the wild dogs used when I saw the broken shaft of an arrow. It had been gnawed off near the tip and I knew it was from the arrow which had wounded the leader.

Farther on I saw his tracks in the dust. They were uneven as if he were traveling slowly. I followed them toward the cliff, but finally lost them in the darkness.

The next day and the next it rained, and I did not go to look for him. I spent those days making more arrows, and on the third day, with these arrows and my spear, I went out along the trail the wild dogs had made to and from my house.

There were no tracks after the rain, but I followed the trail to the pile of rocks where I had seen them before. On the far side of the rocks I found the big gray dog. He had the broken arrow in his chest, and he was lying with one of his legs under him.

He was about ten paces from me so I could see him clearly. I was sure that he was dead, but I lifted the spear and took good aim at him. Just as I was about to throw the spear, he raised his head a little from the earth and then let it drop.

This surprised me greatly and I stood there for a while not knowing what to do, whether to use the spear or my bow. I was used to animals playing dead until they suddenly turned on you and ran away.

The spear was the better of the two weapons at this distance, but I could not use it as well as the others, so I climbed onto the rocks where I could see him if he ran. I placed my feet carefully. I had a second arrow ready should I need it. I fitted an arrow and pulled back the string, aiming at his head.

Why I did not send the arrow I cannot say. I stood on the rock with the bow pulled back and my hand would not let it go. The big dog lay there and did not move and this may be the reason. If he had gotten up I would have killed him. I stood there for a long time looking down at him, and then I climbed off the rocks.

He did not move when I went up to him, nor could I see him breathing until I was very close. The head of the arrow was in his chest, and the broken shaft was covered with blood. The thick fur around his neck was matted from the rain.

I do not think he knew I was picking him up, for his body was limp, as if he was dead. He was very heavy and the only way I could lift him was by kneeling and putting his legs around my shoulders.

In this manner, stopping to rest when I was tired, I carried him to the headland.

I could not get through the opening under the fence, so I cut the bindings and lifted out two of the whale ribs and thus took him into the house. He did not look at me or raise his head when I laid him on the floor, but his mouth was open and he was breathing.

The arrow had a small point, which was fortunate, and came out easily though it had gone deep. He did not move while I did this, nor afterwards as I cleaned the wound with a peeled stick from a coral bush. This bush had poisonous berries, yet its wood often heals wounds that nothing else will.

I had not gathered food for many days and the baskets were empty, so I left water for the dog and, after mending the fence, went down to the sea. I had no thought that he would live, and I did not care.

All day I was among the rocks gathering shellfish and only once did I think of the wounded dog, my enemy, lying there in the house, and then to wonder why I had not killed him.

He was still alive when I got back, though he had not moved from the place where I had left him. Again I cleaned the wound with a coral twig. I then lifted his head and put water in his mouth, which he swallowed. This was the first time that he had looked at me since the time I had found him on the trail. His eyes were sunken and they looked out at me from far back in his head.

Before I went to sleep I gave him more water. In the morning I left food for him when I went down to the sea, and when I came home he had eaten it. He was lying in the corner, watching me. While I made a fire and cooked my supper, he watched me. His yellow eyes followed me wherever I moved.

That night I slept on the rock, for I was afraid of him, and at dawn as I went out I left the hole under the fence open so he could go. But he was there when I got back, lying in the sun with his head on his paws. I had speared two fish, which I cooked for my supper. Since he was very thin, I gave him one of them, and after he had eaten it he came over and lay down by the fire, watching me with his yellow eyes that were very narrow and slanted up at the corners.

  Four nights I slept on the rock, and every morning I left the hole under the fence open so he could leave. Each day I speared a fish for him, and when I got home he was always at the fence waiting for it. He would not take the fish from me so I had to put it on the ground. Once I held out my hand to him, but at this he backed away and showed his teeth.

On the fourth day when I came back from the rocks early he was not there at the fence waiting. A strange feeling came over me. Always before when I returned, I had hoped that he would be gone. But now as I crawled under the fence I did not feel the same.

I called out, "Dog, Dog," for I had no other name for him. I ran toward the house, calling it. He was inside. He was just getting to his feet, stretching himself and yawning. He looked first at the fish I carried and then at me and moved his tail.

That night I stayed in the house. Before I fell asleep I thought of a name for him, for I could not call him Dog. The name I thought of was Rontu, which means in our language Fox Eyes.

The white men's ship did not return that spring or in the summer. But every day, whether I was on the headland or gathering shellfish on the rocks or working on my canoe, I watched for it. I also watched for the red ship of the Aleuts.

I was not sure what I would do if Aleuts came. I could hide in the cave which I had stored with food and water, for it was surrounded by thick brush and the mouth of the ravine could only be reached from the sea. The Aleuts had not used the spring and did not know about it because there was another closer to where they had camped. But they might come upon the cave by chance and then I must be ready to flee.

For this reason I worked on the canoe I had abandoned on the spit. I went to the place where the others were hidden, but they were dried out and cracked. Also they were too heavy for a girl to push into the water, even a girl as strong as I was.

The tides had almost buried the canoe, and I labored many days to dig it out of the sand. Since the weather was warm, I did not go back and forth to my house on the headland, but cooked my meals on the sandspit and at night slept in the canoe, which saved much time.

Even this canoe was too big for me to pull easily in and out of the water, so I set about making it smaller. I did this by loosening all the planks, by cutting the sinews and heating the pitch that bound them together. I then shaped these planks to half their length, using sharp knives made from a black stone which is to be found at one place on the island, and bound them back together with fresh pitch and sinews.

The canoe when I had finished was not so beautiful as it had been before, but I could now lift one end of it and drag it through the waves.

All the time I was working on the canoe, which was most of that summer, Rontu was with me. He was either sleeping in the shade of the canoe or running up and down the sandspit chasing the pelicans that roost there in great numbers because there were numerous fish nearby. He never caught any of the birds, yet he would keep trying until his tongue hung out of his mouth.

He had learned his name quickly and many words that meant something to him, *zalwit*, for example, which is our word for pelican, and *naip* which means fish. I talked to him often, using these words and others and many that he did not understand, just as though I were talking to one of my people.

"Rontu," I would say after he had stolen a special fish I had speared for my supper, "tell me why it is that you are such a handsome dog and yet such a thief."

He would put his head on one side and then the other, although he knew only two of the words, and look at me.

Or I would say, "It is a beautiful day. I have never seen the ocean so calm and the sky looks like a blue shell. How long do you think these days will last?"

Rontu would look up at me just the same, though he understood none of the words, acting as if he did.

Because of this I was not lonely. I did not know how lonely I had been until I had Rontu to talk to.

Discuss the Selection

1. How was every day of life on the island a challenge for Karana?
2. Which of the dogs did Karana especially want to kill? Why?
3. Why do you think Karana didn't shoot the wounded leader of the dogs when she found him?
4. On the fourth day, the dog was not waiting at the fence when Karana returned home. Why do you think Karana had a "strange feeling" when he was not there?
5. Rontu became a good companion for Karana. Find examples in the story that show how Rontu helped ease Karana's loneliness.

Apply the Skills

When something happens in a story, there is a reason for it to happen. Why things happen is the *cause*; what happens is the *effect*. Thinking about causes and effects as you read will help you to better understand what you read.

- What effect might Karana's loneliness have had on her treatment of the leader of the wild dogs?
- What things caused Rontu's behavior toward Karana to change in the story?

Think and Write

Prewrite

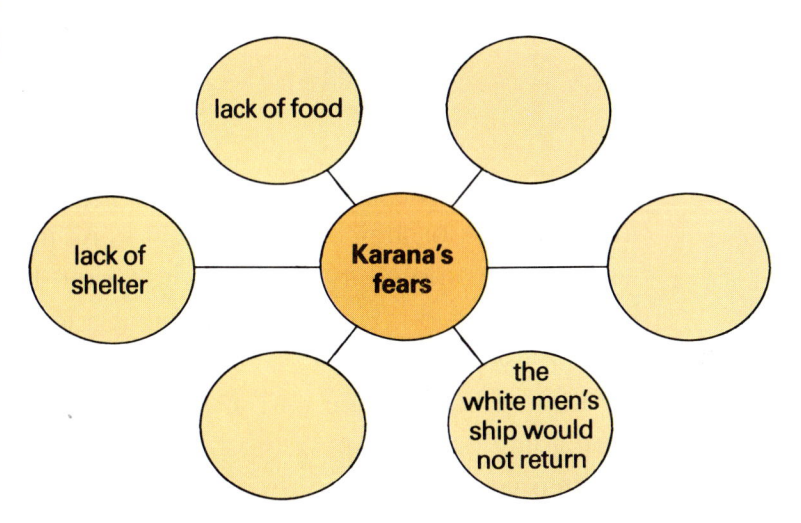

```
        lack of food       ( )
   lack of                      
   shelter    Karana's     ( )
              fears              
       ( )   the white men's
             ship would
             not return
```

This diagram might be called an *"ideaburst."* The words in the center, *Karana's fears*, are the central idea. The phrases around them all relate to the central idea; they name Karana's fears. Copy the ideaburst and fill it in with other things Karana feared.

Compose

Write a first-person account describing Karana's fears. You might begin with the topic sentence: *While I was stranded on the island, I feared many things.*

Follow this with supporting sentences explaining the fears named in your ideaburst.

Revise

Read your paragraph. Does each supporting sentence tell about the main idea? Is each sentence written in the first person? Revise your writing until you can answer "yes" to each question.

Comprehension Study

Draw Conclusions

If you saw your neighbors putting a tent and sleeping bag into the trunk of their car, you might think that they were going on a camping trip. Two things would help you come to this conclusion. First, you know that a tent and sleeping bag are used for camping. Second, you saw the neighbors put these things in their car, so you would think that they were going on a camping trip.

When you read a story or a book, you often need to **draw conclusions** about what is happening. In drawing these conclusions you use two kinds of information: You use the facts the author gives you, and you use what you already know about the subject. Read the sentences below. What conclusion can you draw?

> Karen likes to play golf, tennis, and baseball. For her birthday, her aunt sent her a package of new balls. Now Karen can hardly wait until it gets warm enough outside to go to the course and try out her birthday present.

Did you conclude that Karen got golf balls for her birthday? The author gives you three facts. First, Karen likes to play golf, tennis, and baseball. Second, Karen got a package of new balls. Third, Karen has to go to a course to use her new balls. You also had to use what you know about sports to help you draw the conclusion. You know that golf, tennis, and baseball are all played with balls. You also know that tennis is played on a court and baseball is played on a field. You used all these facts to come to a conclusion.

Drawing More Than One Conclusion

Sometimes you can use one set of facts to draw several conclusions. Read the following paragraphs:

> Scientists know that animals have teeth that are adapted to the kind of food the animal eats. Some animals eat only soft plants. These animals are called herbivores. They have flat teeth for grinding. Carnivores are animals that eat meat. They have sharp, pointed teeth for tearing. Some animals eat both plants and meat. These animals are called omnivores. They have some sharp, pointed teeth and some flat teeth.
>
> When scientists put together dinosaur skeletons, they can tell what each kind of dinosaur ate by looking at its teeth. Most dinosaurs, including the brontosaurus and the stegosaurus, ate plants. A few, such as the tyrannosaurus, ate meat.

Look at the conclusions below. Use the facts from above to decide which ones are correct.

1. Most dinosaurs were herbivores.
2. Some dinosaurs were omnivores.
3. Meat-eating animals need more food than plant-eating animals.
4. Tyrannosaurus had sharp, pointed teeth.
5. Stegosaurus had flat teeth.

Three conclusions are correct: 1, 4, 5. What facts from the reading support conclusion 1: *Most dinosaurs were herbivores?* You read that animals that eat plants are called herbivores. Then you read that most dinosaurs ate plants. What facts support conclusion 4: *Tyrannosaurus had sharp, pointed teeth?* You read that animals that eat meat have sharp, pointed teeth. You also read that tyrannosaurus ate meat. What facts support conclusion 5: *Stegosaurus had flat teeth?* You read that it ate plants. You also read that plant-eating animals have flat teeth.

You could not conclude that some dinosaurs were omnivores (conclusion 2). No facts were given about dinosaurs that had both flat and pointed teeth. You could not conclude that meat-eating animals need more food than plant-eating animals (conclusion 3). The facts did not tell how much food the animals need.

Drawing Conclusions from Graphic Aids

You can also use graphic aids to help you draw conclusions. Look at the graph below. What conclusions can you draw?

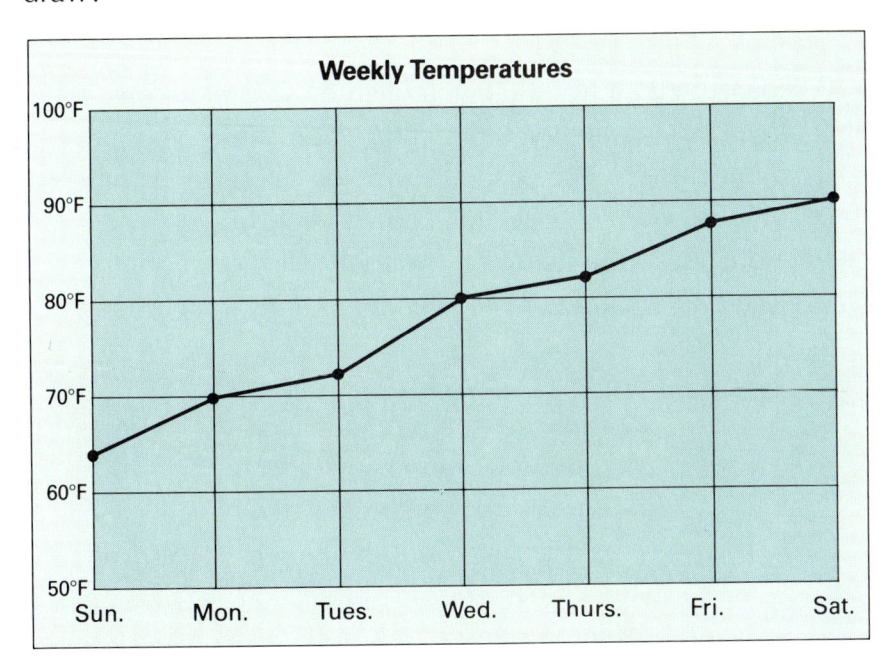

Weekly Temperatures

[Line graph showing temperatures: Sun. ~65°F, Mon. 70°F, Tues. ~72°F, Wed. 80°F, Thurs. ~82°F, Fri. ~88°F, Sat. ~90°F]

Which of these conclusions are correct?

1. It was warmer on Wednesday than it was on Monday.
2. It rained on Tuesday.
3. The temperature went up all week.

Look at the graph. It was 80° on Wednesday and only 70° on Monday. These facts support the first conclusion: *It was warmer on Wednesday than it was on Monday.* The line on the graph goes upward. This fact leads us to the third conclusion: *The temperature went up all week.* The graph does not give any facts about rain. You cannot conclude that it rained on Tuesday.

95

Textbook Application: Draw Conclusions in Social Studies

When you read a textbook, you often draw conclusions about the ideas the author is presenting. Sometimes you have to draw conclusions from only the facts on the page. At other times, you use what you already know to help you draw conclusions. Read the following textbook selection. Use the facts given and what you already know to draw conclusions.

> From this paragraph, you can conclude that a better kind of armor was needed.

> What can you conclude about chain mail? Was it better?

Armor

Soldiers, fighters, and knights during the Middle Ages wore many different kinds of armor. At first, armor consisted of specially treated leather worn on the legs, chest, and arms. It offered some protection but was no defense against blows from heavy metal swords.

Later, leather armor was combined with **chain mail**. Chain mail was a type of armor made of small loops of iron or steel. A suit of chain mail resembled a long shirt that was slit up the middle. In that way a soldier's legs could move while still being protected. Chain mail was almost as flexible as cloth or leather, but it was also heavy. It was, however, effective against swords.

As time went on, another kind of metal armor replaced leather and chain mail. This armor fit the shape of a knight's body. Movable joints were fastened to the armor at the elbows, knees, hips, and ankles. This let the limbs move as they would normally. A horse and knight fully covered in metal armor acted as the "armored tank" of the Middle Ages.

— *The World Past and Present,*
Harcourt Brace Jovanovich

What can you conclude about metal armor? What do you know about an "armored tank" that will help you?

Remember to try to draw conclusions as you read. Make sure that you can support your conclusions with facts from the selection. Be sure to use what you already know to help you draw your conclusions.

> *In 1984, over forty women from all over the world faced the 26.2-mile challenge of the first women's Olympic marathon. Joan Benoit, a U.S. runner, faced more of a challenge than most of the runners. What was that challenge?*
>
> *What information in the selection helps you draw the conclusion that Joan Benoit will continue to race in the future?*

Joan Benoit

adapted from an article by Michele Kort

Joan, far ahead of her competitors, enters the Los Angeles Memorial Coliseum to the cheers of the 77,000 fans in the stadium.

There were many women who took part in the 1984 Summer Olympics. One of these women showed all the dedication, the sportsmanship, and the talent of an Olympic athlete. That woman was Joan Benoit, who won the gold medal for the women's Olympic marathon. This was the first Olympic marathon race ever held for women runners.

At the beginning of the 26.2-mile race, Benoit set a surprising pace. She moved to the front of the runners in the third mile and ran in the lead for the rest of the race. She did not seem to be worried about the danger of burning herself out. By the end of the race, no other runner could catch her. Benoit was the first runner to enter the Los

Angeles Coliseum. She finished the race 500 meters ahead of the second-place runner.

Many people were surprised that Benoit was able to run in the Olympics. To qualify, she had to run in a trial marathon. She had to finish as one of the top three runners to be chosen for the Olympics. Only 17 days before the trial race, Benoit had surgery on her knee. Everyone thought it would be impossible for her to be well enough to compete.

While she was still in bed recovering from surgery, Benoit worked a hand-pedaled bike to make her heart pump hard. Two weeks later, she

Joan began the race running in the middle of the pack, but she didn't stay there for long.

Joan running a victory lap after winning the marathon.

ran in the trial marathon. She finished the 26.2 miles with tears of pain running down her face. She not only finished the trial race — she *won* it. This victory was as important to Joan Benoit as the Olympics themselves.

Benoit on the victor's stand: "After watching some of the guys who had won," she says, "I was determined not to cry. But I sure blinked a lot."

Knowing about her surgery, no one would have been disappointed if Benoit had not won the Olympic gold medal. But she was no ordinary patient. In 1981, she had surgery on both her Achilles tendons and had to give up running for ten weeks. With casts on both feet, Benoit climbed on a stationary bicycle. She pedaled until she was worn out in order to keep her heart and lungs working as hard as possible. Her coach has called her "the toughest athlete I've ever seen."

Benoit returned to racing and set the American women's record in the marathon in 1982. In 1983, she broke the women's world record in the Boston Marathon. She ran the race nearly three minutes faster than any other woman has ever run the race.

Joan Benoit grew up in Maine with her three sports-minded brothers. She joined in sports with the same energy as the boys. "It was survival of the fittest," she has said. "I had to hold my own from the start."

Skiing was Benoit's favorite sport, but she broke her leg when she was in high school. She began to run to get back in shape. In college she played field hockey, with running as her second sport. One day she ran a half-marathon. She was too worn out to play hockey the next day, so the hockey coach benched her. She left the team. "Who knows, maybe I would have been on the Olympic hockey team," she joked before the Olympics.

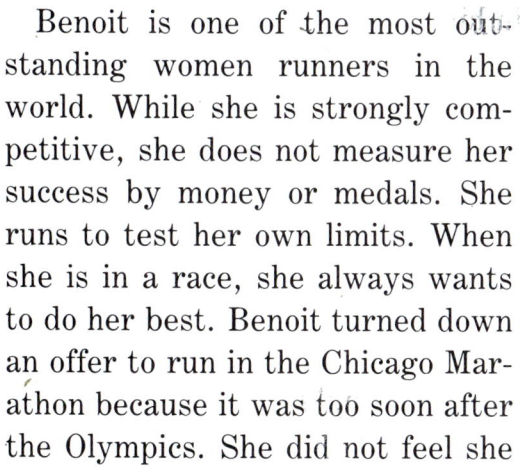

Joan on a training run with her dog, Creosote, who is doing his best to keep up.

Benoit skis the Maine woods with her father.

Benoit is one of the most outstanding women runners in the world. While she is strongly competitive, she does not measure her success by money or medals. She runs to test her own limits. When she is in a race, she always wants to do her best. Benoit turned down an offer to run in the Chicago Marathon because it was too soon after the Olympics. She did not feel she could give a world-class performance.

Joan Benoit symbolizes the rewards of hard work, determination, and commitment to a very special talent. As she says, "It's just one challenge after another." That is true for everyone. Joan Benoit's Olympic victory helps us recognize that there could be a hero or heroine in each of us.

101

Discuss the Selection

1. What challenge did Joan Benoit face in the Olympic marathon?
2. Why was the women's marathon in the 1984 Olympics an important event?
3. Why was it dangerous for Benoit to run ahead of all the other runners in the Olympic marathon?
4. Find the sentences that tell what Benoit did both times she was injured.
5. What words might a writer use to describe Joan Benoit? Use story information to support your answers.

Apply the Skills

Conclusions are decisions based on facts. You draw conclusions from the information given in a selection. What information from the selection helps you to conclude that Joan Benoit will continue to run races, even though she has won an Olympic gold medal?

Think and Write

Prewrite

Who?	What?	Where?	When?	Why?	How?
Joan Benoit			Aug. 5, 1984	because she was skilled and fiercely competitive	

News articles report events that have recently taken place; they describe events in a brief, factual, and interesting way. News articles answer six basic news-gathering questions: Who? What? Where? When? Why? How?

Copy the chart shown above and finish it with information about Joan Benoit's victory at the 1984 Olympics. The finished chart will show the important details of her victory.

Compose

Write a short news article about Joan Benoit. Use the information on the chart. Be sure to include answers to the six basic news-gathering questions.

Revise

Read your news article. Check to be sure that you have included the answers to the six basic questions. If not, correct and revise your work.

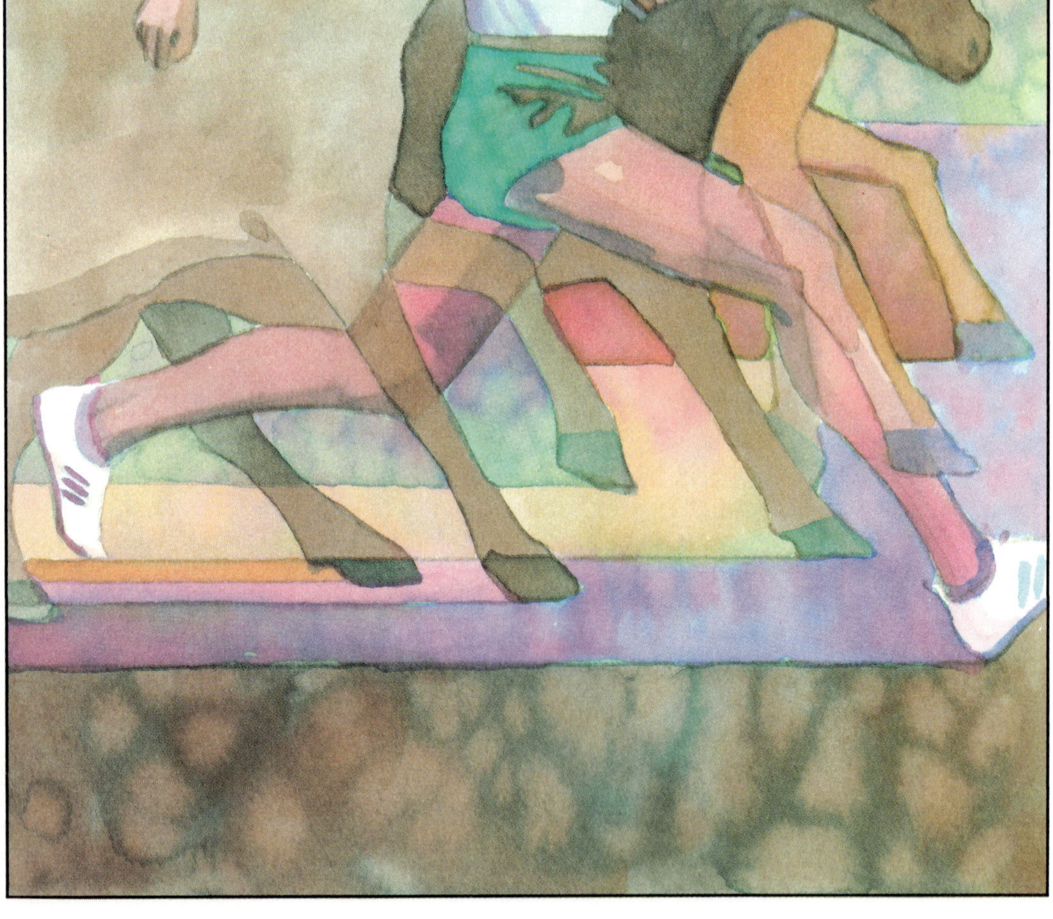

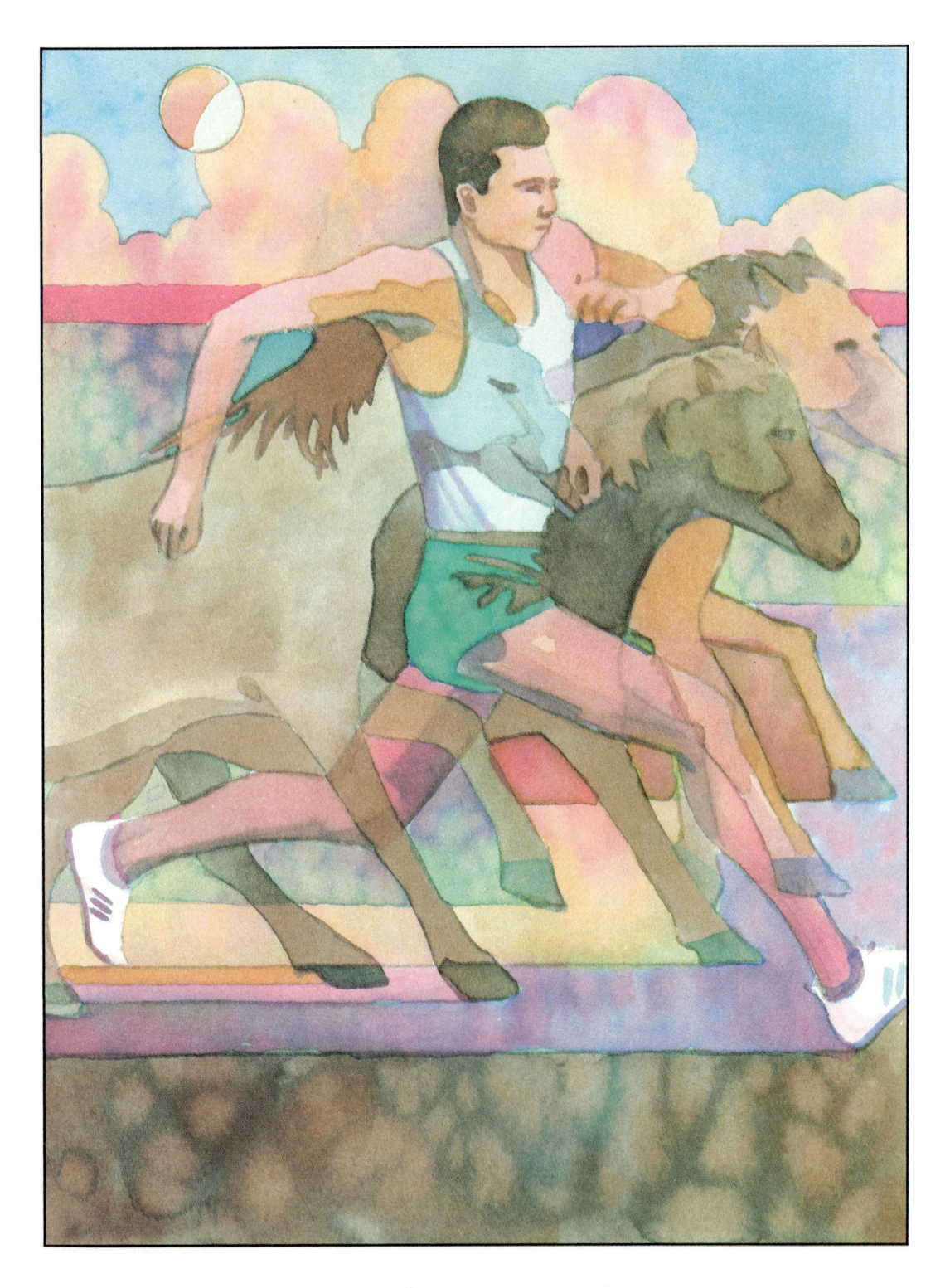

The Runner
by Donald Charles

People see me jogging by
Almost unseen, unfelt, a fleeting thought.
What drives my feet
Along this pointless path, the endless steps repeated
   like a drum?
What words set me on this timeless run:
"Improve yourself, compete and win, the joy is in the
   doing"?
No, not great thoughts
Of health or fame from victories won could keep me in
   this lonely game.
My world is private: Sometimes,
Though the legs grow heavy and the lungs are tight
   with pain,
Although the breath of life
Is squeezed, these mortal bones grow sore and skin is
   raw;
All that falls away!
And suddenly, like standing on the brink of clouds,
I feel some long lost joy,
And hear soft echoes of a day when wondrous wild
   horses ate the wind.

Vocabulary

Study

Context Clues

When you are reading a story or an article, you may find words you do not know. You can stop and look up each word in a dictionary, or you can use the hints the author gives about what a word means. We call these hints **context clues**.

Sometimes the context clue will be a definition of the word right in the same sentence. Read this sentence to find out what *mollusk* means.

> Clams and snails are mollusks; that is, they are animals with shells.

What is a mollusk? *A mollusk is an animal with a shell.* The author gave you the meaning of the word in the same sentence. The words *that is* are a clue that the author is going to explain the word. An author might also use the words *in other words* as a clue.

Practice looking for this kind of context clue. Here is another sample sentence. Look for the meaning of the word *optimist*.

> Jennifer is an optimist; in other words, she always thinks things will turn out well.

Another kind of context clue gives a word or group of words that mean the same thing as the word you don't know. Read this sentence to find out what *portal* means.

> We pushed on the huge portal, but the big door refused to open even an inch.

Did you guess that a portal is a door? The author used the words *big door* in the same sentence to mean the same thing as the words *huge portal*.

Here is another sample. Look for a context clue to explain the word *bogus*.

> The salesperson could tell the bogus bill was fake because the picture of George Washington showed him wearing glasses.

Sometimes the author will explain elsewhere in the selection what a word means. You may have to read several sentences to figure out a word's meaning. Read all of these sentences to find out what *portage* means.

> When the water was shallow, we had to make portage with the canoe. Shelley lifted one end and I lifted the other. We carefully carried the canoe over the sandbar and into deeper water.

Did you guess that *portage* means "picking up the canoe and carrying it"? You had to read all of the sentences.

Practice looking for context clues. Read these sentences to find out what the word *vacant* means.

> The old house had been vacant for years. No one had lived there since the Smith family moved away and left it empty.

When you find a word you don't understand, remember that an author often gives clues that can help you define the word. The author might tell you the meaning of the word farther on in the sentence. The author might use a different word that means about the same thing as the word you do not know. Sometimes the author explains the word in another part of the selection. Keep looking for context clues. You may be surprised at the number of words whose meanings you can figure out for yourself.

Athletic competition challenges athletes, and so do records that are meant to be broken. How does Roger Bannister prepare to break an especially challenging record?

As you read, remember to use context clues to figure out the meaning of words you do not know.

The Four-Minute Mile

by Roger Bannister

I expected that the summer of 1954 would be my last competitive season. It was certain to be a big year in athletics. There would be the Empire Games in Vancouver, Canada, and the European Games in Berne, Switzerland. Hopes were running high for a four-minute mile.

Whether as athletes we liked it or not, the four-minute mile had become rather like Mount Everest—a challenge to the human spirit. By a strange coincidence it happened that the round figure of four minutes was just below the existing world record for the mile. It was a barrier that seemed to defy all attempts to break it.

If I were to attack the four-minute mile, the problem was to decide how and where the race should be run. There were four essential requirements—a good track, absence of wind, warm weather, and even-paced running. Some people thought that a four-minute mile might result from normal competition. But it could only happen if there was an opponent capable of forcing the pace, right up to the last 50 yards. It was easier to race an opponent than the clock.

In my hardest training Chris Brasher was with me. He made the task very much lighter. On Friday evenings he took me along to where his coach, Franz Stampfl, held a training session. On weekends Chris Chataway would join us. In this friendly atmosphere the very severe training we did became most enjoyable.

We started a new intensive course of training in December, 1953. We ran several times a week a series of ten consecutive quarter-miles, each in 66 seconds. Through January and February, 1954, we gradually speeded them up. By April we could run them in 61 seconds, but however hard we tried it did not seem possible to reach our target of 60 seconds. We were stuck, or as Chris Brasher expressed it — "bogged down." The training had stopped doing us any good. We needed a change.

Chris Brasher and I drove up to Scotland overnight for a few days' climbing. The weekend was a complete mental and physical change.

After three days our minds turned to running again, and we decided to return. We had slept little and eaten poorly. But when we tried to run those quarter-miles again, the time came down to 59 seconds!

It was now less than three weeks to the Oxford University versus the Amateur Athletic Association race. This was the first chance of the year to attack the four-minute mile. Chris Chataway had decided to join Chris Brasher and myself on the A.A.A. team.

I had now abandoned the severe training of earlier months and was concentrating on gaining speed and freshness. I had to learn to release in four short minutes the energy I usually spent in half an hour's training.

There was no longer any need for my mind to push my legs to run faster. I never thought of length of stride or style, or even of my judgment of pace. All this now happened automatically. There was more enjoyment in my running than ever before. It was as if all my muscles were a part of a perfectly tuned machine. I felt fresh now at the end of each training session.

I had been training every day since the previous November. Now that the race at Oxford was approaching I barely knew what to do with myself. Each night in the week before the race there came a moment when I saw myself at the starting line. My whole body would grow nervous and tremble. I ran the race over in my mind. Then I would calm myself and sometimes get off to sleep.

Finally, it was Thursday, May 6, 1954. I decided to travel up to Oxford alone because I wanted to think quietly. I took an early train. As I opened the door of the compartment, quite by chance, there was coach Franz Stampfl inside. I was delighted to see him. He was a friend with the kind of cheerful personality I badly needed at the moment.

We talked about my decision. This was my first race in eight months and all this time I had been storing nervous energy. In my mind I had chosen this as the day when, with every ounce of strength I had, I would attempt to run the four-minute mile. I knew that I had reached my peak. There would never be another day like this one.

But it seemed that a high wind was going to make success impossible. A wind of gale force was blowing which would slow me up by a second a lap. In order to succeed I must run not merely a four-minute mile, but the equivalent of a 3-minute 56-second mile in calm weather.

Franz understood my concern. He thought I was capable of running a mile in 3 minutes 56 seconds, or 3.57, so he argued that it was worthwhile making the attempt. "With the proper motivation, that is, a good reason for wanting to do it," he said, "your mind can overcome any kind of problem. In any case the wind might drop. And what if this were your only chance?"

He had won his point. Racing has always been more of a mental than a physical problem to me. He went on talking, but I heard no more. The idea left uppermost in my mind was that this might be my only chance. "How would you ever forgive yourself if you rejected it?" I thought, as the train arrived in Oxford.

Now the wind was almost gale force. I walked around the deserted track. A flag on a nearby church stood out from the flagpole. The attempt seemed hopeless, yet for some unknown reason I tried out my two pairs of spikes. I had a new pair which were made just for me. They were built with the weight of each running shoe reduced from six to four ounces. This saving in weight might well mean the difference between success and failure.

In the afternoon I called on Chris Chataway. He smiled and said, just as I knew he would, "The day could be a lot worse, couldn't it? The forecast says the wind may drop toward evening. Let's not decide until five o'clock."

I spent the afternoon at the window, watching the swaying of the leaves. Later, on the way down to the track, there was a shower of rain. The wind blew strongly, but now and then came in gusts, as if uncertain. As Brasher, Chataway, and I warmed up, we knew the eyes of the crowd were on us. They were hoping that the wind would drop just a little—if not enough to run a four-minute mile, enough to make the attempt.

No one tried to persuade me. The decision was mine alone. And the moment was getting closer. As we lined up for the start I glanced at the flag again. It fluttered more gently now. Yes, the wind was dropping slightly. This was the moment when I made my decision. The attempt was on.

There was complete silence on the ground . . . a false start. I felt angry that precious moments during the lull in the wind might be slipping by. The gun fired a second time . . . Brasher went into the lead. I slipped in effortlessly behind him, feeling tremendously full of running. My legs seemed to meet no resistance at all, as if propelled by some unknown force.

We seemed to be going so slowly! Impatiently I shouted "Faster!" But Brasher kept his head and did not change the pace. I went on worrying until I heard the first lap time, 57.5 seconds. In the excitement the thought of pace had deserted me. Brasher could have run the first quarter in 55 seconds without my realizing it, but I should have had to pay for it later. Instead, he made success possible.

At one and a half laps I was still worrying about the pace. A voice shouting "Relax" penetrated to me above the noise of the crowd. I learned afterwards it was Stampfl's. Unconsciously I obeyed. If the speed was wrong it was too late to do anything about it, so why worry? I was relaxing so much that my mind seemed almost detached from my body. There was no strain.

I barely noticed the half-mile, passed in 1 minute 58 seconds, nor when, round the next bend, Chataway went into the lead. At three-quarters of a mile the effort was still barely noticeable. The time was 3 minutes 0.7 seconds. By now the crowd was roaring. Somehow I had to run the last lap in 59 seconds. Chataway led around the next bend and then I pounced past him at the beginning of the back straight, three hundred yards from the finish.

I had a moment of mixed joy and anguish, when my mind took over. It raced well ahead of my body and drew my body forward. I felt that the moment of a lifetime had come. There was no pain, only a great unity of movement and aim. The only reality was the next two hundred yards of track under my feet.

I felt at that moment it was my chance to do one thing supremely well. I pressed on, driven by a combination of

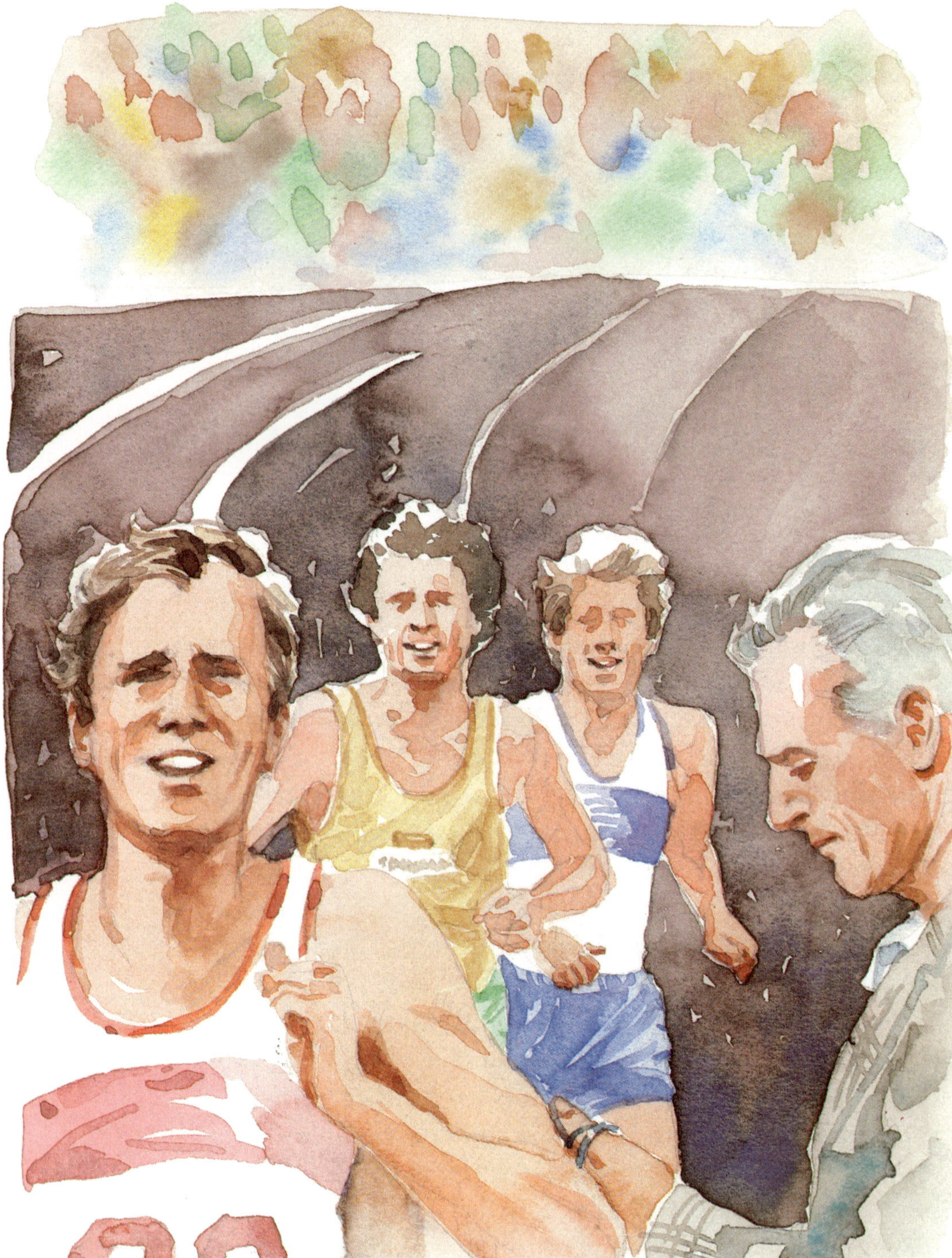

fear and pride. I turned the last bend and there were only fifty yards more.

My body had long since exhausted all its energy, but it went on running just the same. This was the crucial moment when my legs were strong enough to carry me over the last few yards as they could never have done in previous years. With five yards to go the tape seemed almost to move away from me. Would I ever reach it?

Those last few seconds seemed never-ending. The faint line of the finishing tape stood ahead as a haven of peace, after the struggle. I leapt at the tape like a man taking his last spring to save himself.

My effort was over and I collapsed.

It was only then that the real pain overtook me. It was as if all my limbs were caught in an ever-tightening vise. I knew that I had done it before I even heard the time. I was too close to have failed, unless my legs had played strange tricks at the finish by slowing me down and not telling my brain that they had done so.

The stopwatches held the answer. The announcement came — "Result of one mile . . . time, 3 minutes" — the rest was lost in the roar of excitement. I grabbed Brasher and Chataway. Together we scampered round the track in a burst of spontaneous joy. We had done it — the three of us!

We shared a place where no one had yet ventured — secure for all time, however fast athletes might run miles in the future. We had done it where we wanted, when we wanted, how we wanted, in our first attempt of the year. In the wonderful joy my pain was forgotten. I wanted to prolong these precious moments of realization.

I felt suddenly and gloriously free of the burden of athletic ambition that I had been carrying for years. After the four-minute mile, I ran almost daily for the next twenty years, but I never competed again.

Discuss the Selection

1. Why was a four-minute mile considered to be such a challenge for a runner?
2. How did Bannister prepare to break the world record?
3. What do you think Bannister meant when he said that racing had always been more a mental than a physical problem?
4. What did Brasher and Chataway do to help Bannister set the record?
5. What qualities did Bannister have that made him able to achieve his goal? Give examples from the story to support your answer.

Apply the Skills

When you read, context clues can help you to figure out the meaning of words you don't know. Use the clues in the sentence below to explain what the word *motivation* means. Explain what kind of context clues the author used to define the word *motivation*.

The coach told Bannister, "With proper motivation, that is, a good reason for wanting to do it, your mind can overcome any kind of problem."

Think and Write

Prewrite

> **Roger Bannister's Run**
> I. Before the race
>   A. _____
>   B. _____
> II. Day of the race
>   A. Worried about wind
>   B. _____
> III. _____
>   A. Ran a victory lap
>   B. Ran for 20 years
>   C. Never raced again

A good way to prepare to write is to outline your ideas. Copy the story outline above. Use "The Four-Minute Mile" to help you complete the outline.

Compose

Follow the outline to write a three-paragraph summary of the story. First develop a topic sentence for each of the three main topics (I., II., III.) in the outline. The first might be *Roger Bannister carefully prepared to attempt the first four-minute mile.*

Use the subtopics (A., B., C.) in the outline for supporting sentences that give details about each main topic.

Revise

Compare your summary with your outline. Are all the topics mentioned? If not, correct and revise your work.

Literature Study

Characterization

When you read a good book or story, you may feel that you know the characters. You care about what happens to them. You understand why they do the things they do. Knowing what a character is like helps you understand and enjoy a book or story.

Fictional characters, like real people, have qualities that you can recognize. They may be daring or shy, industrious or lazy, careful or carefree. These qualities are called **character traits.** An author often gives a character several traits. This makes the character seem more real because real people always have several traits.

Read the story below. What character traits does Ted have?

> "The park district has two great bus tours this Saturday," said Ted. "One bus is going to the space center. The other bus is going to the animal park. I just can't decide which tour to take. Can you help me, Rosa?"
>
> "It seems to me you had the same problem last spring," said Rosa. "You couldn't decide whether to join a softball team or a soccer team. You took so long to make up your mind that the softball teams were all full, so soccer won because it was all that was left."
>
> Ted felt a little embarrassed, but he smiled good-naturedly. "The trouble was, I really liked to play

both games, but I couldn't practice for two teams at once. Now I want to see the rockets at the space center, but I also want to see the new animals at the animal park. Say, maybe I should just pack a lunch and stand around until one of the buses is full; then I'll get on the other one!"

You can tell from this story that Ted has trouble making up his mind. You can also tell that he is curious—he is eager to learn about things. Ted can also laugh at himself—he has a sense of humor.

There are three ways that you can learn about a character in a book or story. One way is through the character's own words and actions. We know that Ted cannot make up his mind because he says, "I can't decide which tour to take." We know that he is curious because he wants to see both the space center and the animal park.

A second way to find out about a character is through the words of other characters. Rosa reminded Ted that he could not choose what sport to play. Rosa's words tell you that Ted cannot make decisions.

Finally, the author may tell you about the character. The author describes what happens, or how the character feels. The author of this story told you that Ted felt a little embarrassed. The author also said that Ted smiled good-naturedly.

It is important to remember that a story may not tell the reader exactly what a character's traits are. You may have to figure out the traits from the words, actions, and descriptions of the character. For example, no one in the story used the word *curious* to describe Ted. You had to discover that Ted was curious from knowing that he wanted to see both the space center and the animal park.

As you read, use the information the author gives you to look for the traits of characters in stories and books.

Author Profile

Elizabeth George Speare

Elizabeth George Speare has always loved to write. In fact, she can't remember a time when she didn't want to become a writer. During her childhood, she remembers, "Whenever our families met, a favorite cousin just my own age and I, with barely a greeting to anyone else, used to rush into a corner clutching fat brown notebooks. There we breathlessly read out loud to each other the latest stories we had written."

The story you are about to read, "The Sign of the Beaver," is part of one of Elizabeth George Speare's books. It is about a real boy who was left alone for a summer in 1769 in the Maine wilderness.

The author's interest in colonial times, the subject of all of her books, began early for her. She was born in Massachusetts and has lived and worked all her life in New England. "It is easy for me to feel right at home in colonial times," Speare says, "because in some ways the countryside and the New Englanders themselves have not changed very much in three hundred years."

But how can Elizabeth George Speare write so realistically about things that happened so long ago? She does research. She begins with a real event in history. Then she learns everything she can about the lives of people in that time and place. She says, "Gathering the material for a book takes me a year or more. To truly share the adventures of my imaginary people, I have to know many things about them — the houses they lived in, the clothes they wore, the food they ate, what they did for fun, and what things they cared about. You can call this research if you like, but that seems to be a dull word for such a fascinating pursuit."

While she is taking notes in libraries and museums, her story is growing little by little in her mind. When she finally begins to write, she fills in the real event with new people and scenes from her own imagination. She writes slowly, doing only a few pages a day, trying to make every sentence say exactly what she means.

Speare's books are so beautifully written and her characters so real that she has won the Newbery Medal, the highest award a children's book author can receive, twice! Her first award was made in 1959 for *The Witch of Blackbird Pond* and her second in 1962 for *The Bronze Bow*. *The Sign of the Beaver* was a runner-up for the Newbery Medal in 1984.

Left alone to care for the family's cabin, Matt was worried. How could he possibly meet the challenges involved in living alone in the forest?

As you read, try to decide what character traits Matt has that help him meet this challenge.

The Sign of the Beaver

by Elizabeth George Speare

The year was 1769. Large parts of North America were still undiscovered and unexplored. Twelve-year-old Matt and his father built a cabin on the family's land in the wilderness of Maine. Matt's father then journeyed hundreds of miles back to their old home in Quincy, Massachusetts, to get Matt's mother and sister. A worried Matt was left to care for the cabin. Alone in the middle of a huge forest, Matt found that he had to learn many things very quickly. However, Matt was not completely alone. He was watched over by his neighbors, the Indians of the Beaver clan. When Matt was attacked by swarming bees, the Indian chief, Saknis, rescued him and sent his grandson, Attean, to help Matt learn to live in the forest. Despite Attean's suspicion of white people, he and Matt were becoming friends.

Attean had come without his dog. So there was no warning.

Matt was in fine spirits that day, because he had managed by a magnificent stroke of luck to hit a rabbit with his bow and arrow. It was the first time this had happened, and it was more the rabbit's doing than his own. The silly creature had just sat there and let him take careful aim. All the same, he was pleased with himself, and even more pleased that Attean had been there to see it.

Matt was walking behind Attean, swinging the rabbit carelessly as Attean always did, when the Indian suddenly halted, his whole body tensed. Matt could see nothing unusual, and he had opened his mouth to speak, when Attean silenced him with a jerk of his hand. Then he heard a sound in the underbrush ahead. Not a rustle like a grouse or a snake. Not a trapped animal. This was a stirring of something moving slowly and heavily. He felt a cold prickle in his stomach. He stood beside Attean, his own muscles tight, scarcely breathing.

A low bush bent sideways. Through the leaves a brown head thrust itself. Bigger than that of a dog, and shaggier. It was a small bear cub. Matt could see the little eyes peering at them curiously, the brown nose wrinkling at the strange smell of a human boy. The little animal looked so comical that Matt almost laughed out loud.

"Hsst!" Attean warned under his breath.

There was a crashing of bush and a slow, snarling growl. An immense paw reached through the thicket and tumbled the cub over and out of sight. In its place loomed a huge brown shape. Bursting through the leaves was a head three times as big as the cub's. No curiosity in those small eyes, only an angry reddish gleam.

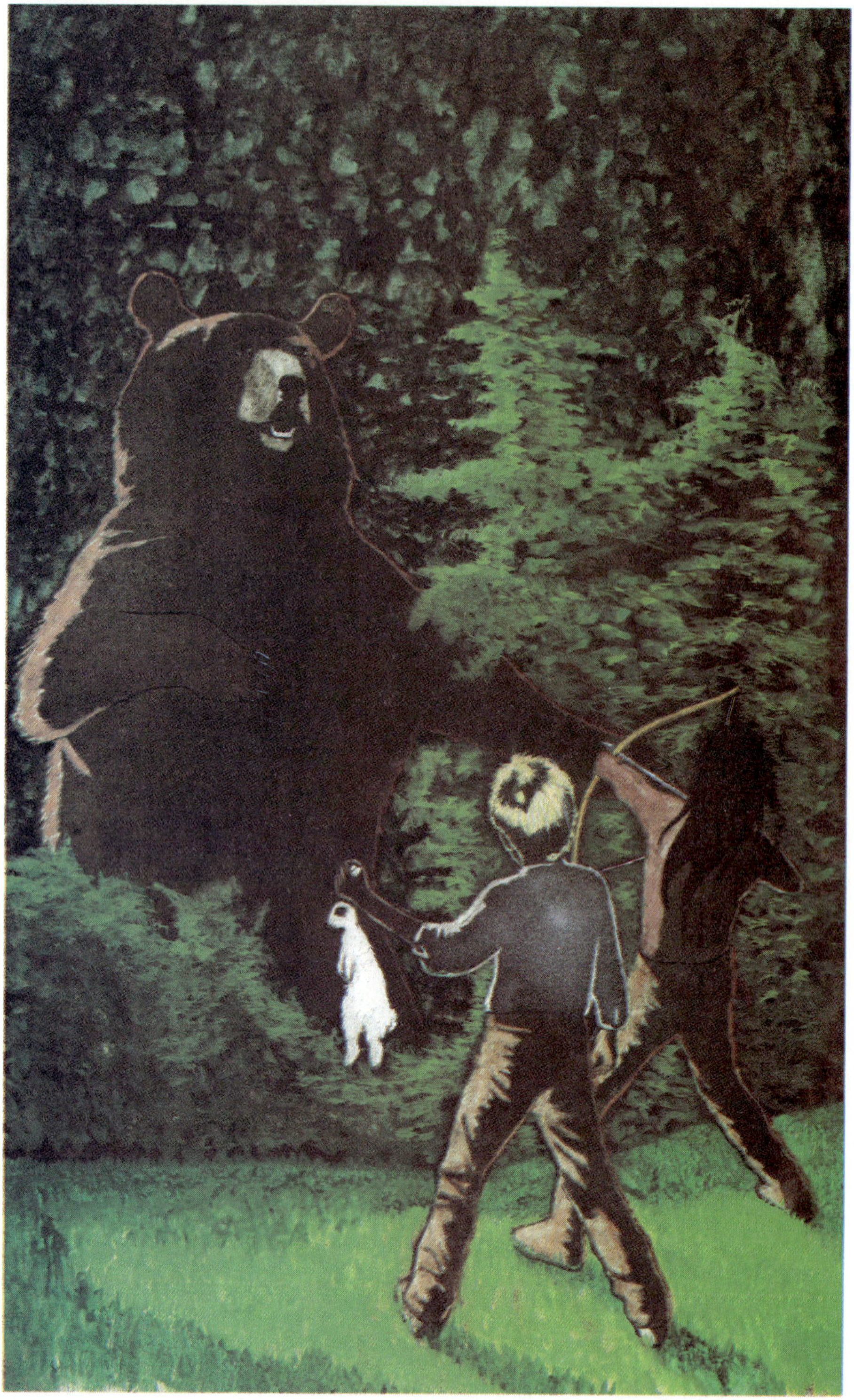

Somehow Matt had the sense not to run. He stood frozen on the path. A bear could overtake a running man in a few bounds. And this one was only two bounds away. The bear's head moved slowly from side to side. Its heavy body brushed aside the branches as though they were cobwebs. It swayed, shifting its weight from one foot to the other. Slowly it rose on its hind legs. Matt could see the wicked curving claws.

Matt would never know why he acted as he did. He could not remember thinking at all, only staring with numb horror at the creature about to charge. Somehow he did move. He swung the dead rabbit by its ears and hurled it straight at the bear's head. The tiny body struck the bear squarely on its nose. With a jerk of her head the bear shook it off as though it was a buzzing mosquito. The rabbit flopped useless to the ground. The bear did not even bother to look down at it. She had been distracted for only an instant, but in that instant something flashed through the air. There was a sharp twang and the dull thud of a blow. Just between the eyes of the bear, the shaft of Attean's arrow quivered. As the waving forepaw began to lower, a second arrow struck just below the bear's shoulder.

The great head shuddered and sank toward the ground. With a wild yell, Attean sprang forward and thrust his knife deep just behind his first arrow. Still scarcely aware that he moved at all, Matt leaped after him. Jerking his own knife from his belt, he sank it into brown fur. His blow had been misplaced, but it was not needed. The bear's side was heaving. The boys stood watching, and in a few moments it lay still.

Matt stared down at the creature in horror. The fearsome yellow teeth were still bared in a snarl. The little eyes that had glittered so savagely were filmed over. The long, sharp claws hung powerless, clotted with pawed-up earth.

Now that there was nothing to fear, Matt felt his knees shaking. He hoped that Attean would not notice, and he managed a wide grin to hide his trembling. But Attean did not grin back. He stood over the bear, and he began to speak, slowly and solemnly, in his own tongue. He spoke for some time.

"What were you saying?" Matt demanded when the speaking was over.

"I tell bear I do not want to kill," Attean answered. "Indian not kill she-bear with cub. I tell bear we did not come here to hunt."

"But it might have killed us both!"

"Maybe. I ask bear to forgive that I must kill."

"Well, I'm mighty thankful you did," Matt said stoutly. He was about to say that he had never been so scared in his life, but he thought better of it.

Attean looked at him, and his solemnness suddenly dissolved in a grin. "You move quick," he said. "Like Indian."

Matt felt his cheeks turn red. "You killed him," he said honestly. Yet he knew that he had had a part. He had given Attean just that instant in which to notch his arrow.

Attean nudged the bear with his toe. "Small," he said, "Just same fat. Good for eat."

Small! That monstrous creature! It certainly was too big for two boys to carry. It appeared that Attean had no intention of trying.

"Belong squaw now," he said. "I go tell."

"You mean a squaw is going to carry that heavy thing?"

"Cut up meat, then carry," Attean answered.

"The cub," Matt remembered now. It was nowhere in sight.

Attean shook his head. "Let cub go," he said.

"Take rabbit," Attean reminded him. Matt looked with distaste at the rabbit, almost covered by the bear's heavy paw. He would rather not have touched it, but obediently he pulled it out. It was his dinner, after all. And he knew that in Attean's world everything that was killed must be used. The Indians did not kill for sport.

When Attean had disappeared into the forest, Matt still stood looking down at the first bear he had ever seen. He felt resentful. Attean had killed the bear, of course. It was his by right. But Matt would have liked just a small share of that meat, or even one of those big claws to show his father. Then he remembered the Indian boy's tribute. He had moved fast, like an Indian. That would have to be share enough.

In the late afternoon Matt sat in his cabin doorway. He couldn't think of any work to do. He felt restless, the excitement still jumping about inside him. He needed to talk to someone. He wanted to tell his father about the bear. Thinking of his father, he felt that snake of worry crawling about behind every other thought. What could have kept his father so long?

Suppose some accident had befallen him? The meeting with the bear had shaken Matt's trust in the forest. Now it seemed to close him in on every side, dark and threatening. Suppose his father had met with a bear? Suppose he never got back to Quincy? How would his mother know where to find this place, or even where to send anyone to look for him? Matt hugged his arms around his chest. But the cold was inside. It would not go away.

Something moved at the edge of the woods. Matt leaped to his feet. A stranger came walking into the clearing. With an ugly chill against his backbone, Matt stared at the hideously painted face. Then he recognized Attean, a very different Attean from the boy who had walked with him in the forest that morning. The Indian boy had washed his body, and it shone with fresh grease. He had combed his tangled black locks. Down his cheeks on either side and on his forehead ran broad streaks of blue and white paint. On a cord around his neck dangled a row of new bear's claws.

In case Attean had noticed his first alarm, Matt greeted him boldly. "What's the war paint for?" he demanded.

"Not war paint," Attean answered. "Squaws made feast with bear. My grandfather say you come."

Matt hesitated, unable to believe his ears. It took him a moment to realize that this was actually an invitation.

"Thanks," he stammered. "I'd sure like some of that bear meat. Wait till I get my jacket."

"Shut door," Attean reminded him. "Maybe another bear come." Attean was in a good humor. He had made one of his unexpected jokes.

"Long way," Attean said, after a time. Matt was certain they must have been walking fast for more than an hour. He remembered that Attean had already walked all this way to fetch him and he kept silent. It was so dark now that he could barely see to put one foot before the other, but he realized that they were on a well-beaten trail. Just as the last light was glinting above the treetops, they reached a river bank. Drawn up at its edge was a small birch canoe. Attean motioned him to step into it. Then he gave a push and leaped nimbly into the stern. His paddle moved soundlessly. Grateful to sit still, Matt was entranced by the speed, the silence, the gliding shadows on the silver river. He was regretful when in a very few strokes they reached the other side.

Now Matt could see a glimmer of light deep in the woods. Attean led him toward it, and presently their way was barred by a solid wall of upright posts. A stockade. For the first time a quiver of uneasiness made Matt falter. But stronger than any doubt, curiosity drove him on. Not for one moment would he have turned back.

Eagerly he followed Attean through a gateway into an open space filled with smoke and moving shadows and wavering patches of light cast by birchbark torches.

All around him in a circle rose the dim shapes of cabins and cone-shaped wigwams. In the center of the circle a long, narrow fire was burning between walls of logs. Suspended on timbers hung three iron pots, sending up rosy curls of steam in the smoky air. The fragrance of boiling meat and pungent herbs made Matt's stomach crawl.

Then he was aware of the Indians. They sat silently on either side of the fire, their painted faces ghastly in the flickering light. They were clad in an odd medley of garments, some in Englishmen's coats and jackets, others with bright blankets draping their shoulders. A few had feathers standing straight up from headbands. Everywhere there was the gleam of metal on arms and chests. Women in bright cloth skirts and odd pointed caps moved about without a sound, adding wood to the fire or stirring the contents of the kettles. Light glinted on their silver armbands and necklaces. Clearly the Indians had put on their finest array for this feast. It came over Matt with a rush of shame how very shabby he must look in their eyes. Even if Attean had warned him, what could he have done? He had no other clothes to wear. Probably Attean had known that and so had said nothing.

No one seemed to notice him. Yet he was conscious of the unblinking stare of the row facing him. The others did not turn their heads. They seemed to be waiting. In the silence, Matt's heart beat so loudly they all surely must have heard it.

After a long pause, one man rose slowly and came toward him. It was Saknis, Attean's grandfather, his paint-streaked face barely recognizable. He wore a long red coat decorated by a handsome beaded collar and metal armbands. A crown of feathers rose from the beaded band around his forehead. He stood very tall, and there was pride in his stern features. Why, Matt thought, he looked like a king!

"*Kweh*," Saknis said with dignity. "White boy welcome."

In a sudden terrifying yell the rows of Indians echoed this greeting. "*Ta ho,*" they shouted. "*Ta ho. Ye hye hye.*"

"*Kweh,*" Matt stammered in return, then more boldly, "*Kweh.*"

The Indians seemed satisfied. Smiles flashed in their dark faces. There was rough laughter, and then, seeming to forget him, they began to jabber to each other. From nowhere, children suddenly crowded around him, giggling, daring each other to touch him. Matt's heart slowed its pounding. There was nothing to fear in this place, but after the weeks of stillness in his cabin the noise was confusing. He was grateful when Attean came to his rescue and led him to a seat at the end of the log. An old woman approached and held out to him a gourd cup. It contained a sweetish drink, acid and flavored with maple sugar, good on his dry tongue.

Saknis raised his arm, and instantly the clamor was silenced. There was no doubt Attean's grandfather was the leader here. The rows of Indians waited respectfully for him to speak. Instead the old man turned to his grandson.

Attean stepped into the center of the clearing. In the firelight he stood straight and slender, his bare arms and legs gleaming. Matt had never seen him like this. Proudly he began to speak.

Matt did not need to understand the words. He soon realized that Attean was recounting the morning's adventure. Watching his gestures, Matt felt himself living again the walk through the woods, the meeting with the small cub, the fearsome mother about to charge. As Attean spoke, the Indians urged the boy on with grunts and shouts of approval and pleasure. Attean tensed his body. He uttered a sharp cry, pointed at Matt, and made a flinging sweep in his arm, hurling an imaginary rabbit. The seated figures broke into loud cries, shouting "*He*," grinning and pointing at Matt, swinging their own arms in imitation. Matt's cheeks were hot. He knew they were making fun of him. But boisterous as it was, the sound was friendly.

Now they turned back to Attean and followed his story with growing excitement.

Attean certainly made a very good story of it. His telling took a lot longer than the actual event. Plainly they all enjoyed it, and in listening they were all taking part in it. Attean was a skillful storyteller.

When the narrative was over, the Indians sprang to their feet. They formed a long line. Then began a sound that sent a tingle, half dread and half pleasure, down Matt's spine. A lone Indian had leaped to the head of the line, beating a rattle against his palm in an odd, stirring rhythm. He strutted and pranced in ridiculous contortions, for all the world like a clown in a village fair. The line of figures followed after him, aping him and stamping their feet in response.

Attean was at his side again, "Dance now," he said. "Then feast."

The rhythm of the rattle quickened. The line of figures wove round the fire, faster and faster. Women joined now, at the end of the line, linking their arms, swaying. Finally the children, even small children, were dancing, stamping their small naked feet.

"Dance," Attean commanded. He seized Matt's arm and pulled him into the moving line. The men near him cheered him on, laughing at Matt's stumbling attempts. Once he caught his breath, Matt found it simple to follow the step. His confidence swelled as the rhythm throbbed through his body, loosening his tight muscles. He was suddenly filled with excitement and happiness. His own heels pounded against the hard ground. He was one of them.

He came back to earth with a stitch in his side. His legs threatened to give way under him. The dancing seemed to have no end. Determined that Attean should not see him weakening, he moved faster and stamped harder. Finally, when he felt he could not make the circle one more time, the dance ended.

The feasting began. A squaw brought him a wooden bowl filled with thick, hot stew and a curiously carved wooden spoon. The first steaming mouthful burned his tongue, but he was too hungry to wait. He thought nothing had ever tasted so good, dark and greasy and spicy. So this was bear meat!

Presently he noticed that Attean sat beside him, eating nothing.

"You're not eating," he said, with a sudden doubt. "Have you given me your share?"

"This my bear," the boy answered. "I kill. Not eat. Maybe not get any more bear." He didn't sound as if he minded in the least, as if, in fact, he was proud of not eating.

When Matt's bowl was empty, the squaw refilled it. By the time he finished, sleepiness began to drag at his eyelids. He could scarcely hold them open. Attean seemed in no hurry to leave. The Indians were enjoying themselves, refilling their bowls and shouting at each other.

At last, however, they fell silent, and Matt saw that one of them was beginning another story. It promised to be a long one. Matt's head drooped and came up with a painful jerk. He had almost fallen asleep sitting up. Attean laughed and motioned him to his feet. At the thought of tramping all the way back to the cabin, Matt groaned. It must be close to midnight.

Then he saw that Attean did not mean to go back. He led Matt toward one of the wigwams and pulled back the flap of deerskin that hung across the door. Inside, a small fire burned, and by its faint light Matt saw a low platform covered with matting and fur. Attean made a silent motion, and Matt, too sleepy to question, gratefully let his tired body sink down on the soft skins. Attean stirred up the fire and left him alone. Once, long after, Matt roused to hear the rattle and the pounding of feet. The Indians were dancing again, and he was thankful to stay right where he was.

Over and over, though he knew the number only too well, Matt counted his notched sticks. He kept hoping he had made a mistake. Always they were the same. Ten sticks. That meant that August had long since gone by. He couldn't remember exactly how many days belonged to each month, but any way he reckoned it the month of September must be almost over. He only needed to look about him.

The maple trees circling the clearing flamed scarlet. The birches and aspens glowed yellow, holding a sunlight of their own even on misty days. The woods had become quieter. Jays still screamed at him, and chickadees twittered softly in the trees, but the songbirds had disappeared. Twice he had heard a faraway trumpeting and had seen long straggles of wild geese like trailing smoke high in the air, moving south. In the morning, when he stepped out of the cabin, the frosty air nipped his nose. The noonday was warm as midsummer, but when he came inside at dusk he hurried to stir up the fire. There was a chilliness inside him as well that neither the sun nor the fire ever quite reached. It seemed to him that day by day the shadow of the forest moved closer to the cabin.

Why was his family so late in coming?

He was troubled too because the autumn weather seemed to have brought about a restlessness in Attean. There were days when the Indian boy did not come. He never offered a word of explanation. After a day or two he would simply walk into the cabin and sit down at the table. He rarely suggested that they hunt or fish together. Day after day Matt tramped the woods alone, trying to shake the doubts that walked beside him like his own shadow.

As he walked, Matt was careful to cut blazes in the bark of trees. They gave him courage to walk farther into the forest than he had ever dared before, since he was sure of finding his way back to the cabin. He also watched for Indian signs, and sometimes he was sure he had detected one. One day, looking up, he saw on a nearby tree the sign of the turtle clan, the sign marking this as their hunting land. Time to turn back, he told himself. He felt secure now in the territory of the beaver clan, but he wasn't so certain that a strange people would welcome a white trespasser.

As he started to retrace his steps, he heard, some distance away, the sharp, high-pitched yelp of a dog. It didn't sound threatening, but neither did it sound like the happy, excited bark of a hound that had scented a rabbit. It sounded almost like the scream of a child. When it came again, it died away into a low whining.

Attean had warned him to have nothing to do with a turtle trap. But he hesitated, and the sound came again. No matter what Attean had told him, he could not bring himself to walk away from that sound. Warily, he made his way through the brush.

It was a dog dirt-caked and bloody, a scrawny Indian dog. As Matt moved closer he saw through the blood, the white streak down the side of its face, then the chewed ear and the stubby porcupine quills. Only one dog in the world looked like that. It was caught by its foreleg and it was frantic with pain and fear. Its eyes were glazed, and white foam dripped from its open jaws. Matt felt his own muscles tense with anger. His mind was made up in an instant. It had been bad enough to leave a fox to suffer. Turtle tribe or no, he was not going to walk away from Attean's dog. Somehow he had to get that dog out of the trap.

But how? As he bent down, the dog snapped at him so ferociously that he jumped back. Even if it recognized him, Attean's dog had never learned to trust him. Now it was too crazed to understand that Matt meant to help. Matt set his teeth and stooped again. This time he got his hands on the steel bands of the trap and gave a tug. With a deep growl, the dog snapped at him again. Matt started, scraping his hand against the steel teeth. He leaped to his feet and stared at the red gash that ran from his knuckles to his wrist. It was no use, he realized. There was no way he could get that trap open with the dog in this maddened state. Somehow he would have to find Attean.

He began to run through the forest, back over the way he had come, back along the trails he knew, searching his memory for the signs he remembered that led to the Indian village. Luck was with him. There was the sign of the beaver cut into a tree, and here were the fallen logs. He was never absolutely sure, but he knew he walked in the right direction, and after nearly an hour, to his great relief, he came out on the shore of the river. There was no canoe waiting, as there had been when Attean had led him there. But the river was narrow, and placid. Thank goodness he had grown up near the ocean, and his father had taken him swimming from the time he could walk. He left his moccasins hidden under a bush and plunged in. In a few moments he came out, dripping, within sight of the stockade.

He was greeted by a frenzied barking of dogs. They burst through the stockade and rushed toward him, halting only a few feet away, menacing him so furiously that he dared not take another step. Behind them came a group of girls who quieted the dogs with shrill cries.

"I have come for Attean," Matt said, when he could make himself heard.

The girls stared at him. Tired, wet, and ashamed of showing his fear of the dogs, Matt could not summon up any politeness or dignity. "Attean," he repeated impatiently.

One girl, bolder than the others, answered him, flaunting her knowledge of the white man's language. "Attean no here," she told him.

"Then Saknis."

"Saknis not here. All gone hunt."

Desperately Matt seized his only remaining chance. "Attean's grandmother," he demanded. "I must see her."

The girls looked at each other uneasily. Matt pulled back his shoulders and tried to put into his voice the stern authority that belonged to Saknis. "It is important," he said. "Please show me where to find her."

Amazingly, his blustering had an effect. After some whispering, the girls moved back out of his way.

"Come," the leading girl ordered, and he followed her through the gate.

He was not surprised that she had led him straight to the most substantial cabin in the clearing. He had recognized on the night of the feast that Saknis was a chief. Now facing him in the doorway was a figure even more impressive than the old man. She was an aging woman, gaunt and wrinkled, but still handsome. Her black braids were edged with white. She stood erect, her lips set in a forbidding line, her eyes brilliant, with no hint of welcome. Could he make her understand? Matt wondered in confusion.

"I'm sorry, ma'am," he began. "I know you don't want me to come here. I need help. Attean's dog is caught in a trap, a steel trap. I tried to open it, but the dog won't let me near it."

The woman stared at him. He could not tell whether she had understood a word. He started to speak again, when the deerskin curtain was pushed aside and a second figure stood in the doorway. It was a girl, with long black braids hanging over her shoulders. She was dressed in blue, with broad bands of red and white beading. Strange, Matt thought, how much alike they looked, the old woman and the girl, standing side by side so straight and proud.

"Me Marie, sister of Attean," the girl said in a soft, low voice. "Grandmother not understand. I tell what you say."

Matt repeated what he had said and waited impatiently while she spoke to her grandmother. The woman listened. Finally her grim lips parted in a single scornful phrase.

"*Aremus piz wat*," she said. Good-for-nothing dog.

Matt's awe vanished in anger. "Tell her maybe it is good for nothing," he ordered the girl, "but Attean is fond of it. And it's hurt, hurt bad. We've got to get it out of that trap."

There was distress in the girl's eyes as she turned again to her grandmother. He could see that she was pleading, and that in spite of herself the old woman was relenting.

After a few short words, the girl went into the cabin and came back in a moment holding in her hand a large chunk of meat, a small blanket folded over her arm.

"Me go with you," she said. "Dog know me."

In his relief, Matt forgot the torn hand he had been holding behind him. Instantly the old woman moved forward and snatched at it. Her eyes questioned him.

"It's nothing," he said hastily. "I almost got the trap open."

She gave his arm a tug, commanding him to follow her.

"There isn't time," he protested.

She silenced him with a string of words of which he understood only the scornful *piz wat*.

"She say dog not go away," the girl explained. "Better you come. Trap maybe make poison."

Having no choice, Matt followed them into the cabin. He saw now that the woman's straight posture had been a matter of pride. She was really very lame, and stooped as she walked ahead of him. While she busied herself over the fire, he sat obediently on a low platform and looked about him. He was astonished that the little room, strange, and so unlike his mother's kitchen, seemed beautiful. It was very clean. The walls were lined with birchbark and hung with woven mats and baskets of intricate design. The air was sweet with fresh grasses spread on the earth floor.

Without speaking, the woman tended him, washing his hand with clean warm water. From a painted gourd she scooped a pungent-smelling paste and spread it over the wound, then bound his hand with a length of clean blue cotton.

"Thank you," Matt said when she was finished. "It feels better."

She dismissed him with a grunting imitation of Saknis's "Good." The girl, who had been watching, moved swiftly to the door. As Matt rose to follow her, the grandmother held out to him a slab of corn bread. He had not realized how hungry he was, and he accepted it gratefully.

The girl took the lead, brushing aside the curious children and the still-suspicious dogs. At the river's edge she untied a small canoe, and Matt stepped into it, thankful that his half-dried clothes would not have to be drenched again. Once on the forest trail, she set the pace, and he did not find it easy to keep up with her swift, silent stride. She was so like Attean, though lighter and more graceful.

At last they heard the yelping just ahead of them and they both began to run. Even in his terror, the dog recognized the girl, and greeted her with a frantic beating of his tail. He gulped at the meat she held out to him. But he still would not let either of them touch the trap. The girl had come prepared for this, and she unfolded the blanket she had carried, threw it over the dog's head, and gathered the folds behind him. With surprising strength, she held the struggling bundle tightly in her arms while Matt took the trap in both hands and slowly forced the jaws open. In a moment the dog was free, escaping the blanket, bounding away from them on three legs, the fourth paw dangling at an odd angle.

"I'm afraid it's broken." Matt said. He was still breathing hard from the last run and from the effort of tugging those steel jaws apart.

"Attean mend," the girl said, folding up the blanket as calmly as though she was simply tidying up a cabin.

The dog hobbled slowly after them along the trail, lying down now and then to lick at the bleeding paw. They made slow progress, and now that the worry was over Matt was aware how tired he was. It seemed as though he had been walking back and forth over that trail all day, and the way to the village seemed endless. He was thankful when, halfway to the river, he saw Attean approaching swiftly along the trail.

"My grandmother send me," he explained. "You get dog out?"

"I couldn't do it alone," Matt admitted.

Attean stood watching as the dog came limping toward him. "Dog very stupid," he said. "No good for hunt. No good for turtle smell. What for I take back such foolish dog?"

His harsh words did not fool Matt for a moment. Nor did they fool the dog. The scruffy tail thumped joyfully against the earth. The brown eyes looked up at the Indian boy with adoration. Attean reached into his pouch and brought out a strip of dried meat. Then he bent and very gently took the broken paw into his hands.

"Grandmother say you come to village today," Attean announced two days later.

"That's kind of her," Matt answered. "But my hand is just about healed. It doesn't need any more medicine."

"Not for medicine."

Matt waited uncertainly.

"My grandmother very surprise white boy go long way for Indian dog," Attean explained. "She say you welcome."

So once again Matt crossed the river into the Indian stockade. This time, though the dogs barked at him and children stared and giggled, he did not feel so much like a stranger. Saknis held out a hand of welcome. Attean's grandmother did not exactly smile, but her thin lips were less grim. Behind her, Attean's sister smiled but did not speak. The old woman dipped a clamshell ladle into a kettle and filled bowls with a stew of fish and corn.

After the meal Attean did not hurry him away. He rather grandly played host and led Matt about the village. Attean produced from nowhere a soft ball made of deerskin. Instantly the other Indian boys raced off in all directions and came back carrying thin sticks. One of these was thrust at Matt. It was a curious sort of bat, light and flexible with a wide, flat curve at the tip. Matt suddenly grinned. With a bat in his hand he could hold his own with any Indian.

The boys back in Quincy could have told them that. Eagerly he joined in the scramble of choosing sides.

But never had he played a game like this, so fast and merciless. The ball could not be touched by hands or foot. It was kept flying through the air by the sticks alone. If it fell to the ground, some player scooped it up with the tip of his bat and sent it spinning again. The Indian boys were bewilderingly quick and skillful, and they wielded their bats with no heed for each other's heads, and certainly not for Matt's. It was no accident, he knew, when an elbow jabbed suddenly into his right eye. These boys were putting him to the test. Ignoring the blows that fell on his head and shoulders, Matt swung grimly at the whirling ball, missing it over and over, but sometimes feeling the satisfying thwack of bat against leather. Finally, by pure luck, he sent the ball into the hole in the ground that marked the goal. Out of breath and dripping, he grinned as his side generously cheered him and whacked his sore shoulders.

Then, with a whoop, they raced all together through the stockade gate down to the river and went leaping like frogs into the water. Matt floated face down, grateful for the coolness against his burning cheeks. All at once a brown arm circled his neck and dragged him under. Squirming free, he seized a black head in both hands, and the two boys went down together. They came up gasping and grinning. Suddenly Matt was enjoying himself. It was almost as good as being back in Quincy again.

The sun had reached the tops of the pines when he went to Attean's cabin to bid the grandmother goodbye. She stood studying him, and he flushed under her sharp eyes. He must look a sight, he knew. There was a lump as big as an egg on his forehead, and his right eye was probably turning black.

Before they left, the old woman gave each of them a slab of cake heavy with nuts and berries. Her eyes, as she looked at her grandson, were warm and bright. Matt was reminded how his mother had often looked at him, pretending to be angry with him but not able to hide that she was mighty fond of him just the same. Suddenly he felt a sharp stab of homesickness.

Outside the cabin Attean's dog was waiting. He limped after them to the river, and when Matt stepped into the canoe the dog jumped in after him and settled down only a few inches from Matt's knees. He had never willingly come so close before.

Attean noticed and commented. "Dog remember."

Was that possible? Matt wondered. Could a dog caught in a trap, even though he snapped out in pain and fear, sense that someone was trying to help him? Could the dog remember that terrible ordeal at all? You couldn't read a dog's mind. Very slowly Matt reached down and laid his hand on the dog's back. The dog did not stir or growl. Gently, Matt scratched behind the ragged ear. Gradually, against the bottom of the canoe, the thin tail began to thump in a contented rhythm.

At the opposite bank Attean watched Matt climb out of the canoe, but he did not follow. Apparently this was as far as he intended to go. As Matt hesitated, Attean lifted his hand. It occurred to Matt that this might be a compliment. Without saying a word, Attean was acknowledging that Matt could find his own way through the forest. Returning his wave, Matt set out with a confidence he did not quite feel. It was growing dark. He would have to walk fast or he would not be able to mark the signs along the trail.

   He was very tired. The bump on his forehead was throbbing. He was sore from head to toe, and his eyes were almost swollen shut. But to his surprise, deep inside he felt content. Was it because Attean's dog had finally trusted him? No, more than that had changed. He had passed some sort of test. Not by any means with flying colors; he had plenty of bruises to remind him of that. But at least he had not disgraced Attean. He felt satisfied. And for the first time since his father had left him, he did not feel alone in the forest.

Discuss the Selection

1. What challenges did Matt meet while living alone in the forest?
2. How did Matt prove his friendship for Attean and the Indians to Attean's grandmother?
3. Why do you think Matt took the rabbit from under the bear, even though he did not want to do so?
4. Matt felt that his day in the Indian village showed that he had passed a test. How did he know that he had passed?
5. Going to the Indian village was very special for Matt. Find the parts of the story that describe his visits to the village and tell why he went there.

Apply the Skills

Story characters have traits you can recognize. These traits make the characters real to readers. What character traits did Matt have that helped him face the challenges of living in the forest?

Thinking About "Challenges"

In these stories, you've read about people from the past, from the present, from the world of make-believe, and from our real world. Each of these people met their challenges head-on.

Paul Bunyan and Hercules faced bigger-than-life tasks with confidence and cleverness. The Japanese farmer courageously risked his life for his mother and taught the cruel lord a lesson. Emma Jane Burke faced unfriendly farmers and her own inexperience with determination. Matt and Karana bravely fought wild animals and loneliness. Joan Benoit and Roger Bannister became the best as they trained their bodies to win.

All these people grew through their experiences. While they may have wondered whether they could measure up to their challenges, all were successful. In meeting their challenges, they learned things about other people and about themselves. Some learned that they could do much more than they had ever hoped.

Did you think about what you would have done in each person's place? Would you have had his or her courage and determination? These stories show that, when faced with a challenge, we can all look inside ourselves and somehow find what it takes.

1. Hercules and Paul Bunyan are both folklore heroes. Name two character traits that both heroes have in common. Explain how each character demonstrated these traits.

2. Karana and Matt both faced a similar challenge—survival. In what ways was Karana's struggle to survive like Matt's struggle? In what ways was it different?

3. Sometimes a little ingenuity, or cleverness, can help someone meet a challenge or solve a problem. Choose the two characters from this unit who you think showed the most ingenuity. Explain why you think they were ingenious.

4. Think of a myth, tall tale, or folktale in which a character faces a challenge. Briefly describe the story plot and how the character meets the challenge.

5. The characters of Emma Jane, Karana, and Matt are all based on the lives of real people. Which of these three do you think faced the greatest challenge? Explain your answer.

6. Being the first to do something is a challenge that has attracted people for years. What real-life challenges in this unit were firsts? What challenges to be first might you like to face?

7. A person who successfully meets a challenge usually feels great satisfaction in the accomplishment. Which story characters in this unit do you think felt satisfaction? Explain your answer.

Read on Your Own

My Mother Is the Smartest Woman in the World by Eleanor Clymer. Atheneum. Kathleen's mother has so many great ideas that Kathleen suggests she run for mayor. This fun-filled story details her exhausting, exciting campaign.

Hercules by Bernard Evslin. William Morrow. In this suspenseful Greek myth, Hercules bravely faces twelve terrible tasks.

Children of the Wild West by Russell Freedman. Clarion Books. This fascinating book brings to life the experiences of pioneer and Indian children in the days of the Wild West.

My Side of the Mountain by Jean George. E.P. Dutton. Every day of life is an adventure for young Sam Gribley, who runs away and lives alone for a year in the wilderness of the Catskill Mountains.

Perfect Balance: The Story of an Elite Gymnast by Lynn Haney. G.P. Putnam's Sons. Photographs help to illustrate this interesting book about the training of a young gymnast whose goal is to compete in the Olympics.

Space Challenger: The Story of Guion Bluford by Jim Haskins and Kathleen Benson. Carolrhoda Books. This biography tells how Guion Bluford overcame many challenges to become an aerospace engineer and the first black American in space.

Saint George and the Dragon adapted by Margaret Hodges. Little, Brown. Saint George, a brave knight, courageously battles a dreadful dragon in this beautifully illustrated legend.

Island of the Blue Dolphins by Scott O'Dell. Dell. A young Indian girl is stranded alone on a California island. This book tells of her long and lonely struggle to survive.

The Sign of the Beaver by Elizabeth George Speare. Houghton Mifflin. This is the exciting story of Matt, a fourteen-year-old boy left alone to care for his family's cabin in the Maine wilderness in 1769.

Trail Boss in Pigtails by Marjorie Stover. Atheneum. When Emma Jane Burke's father dies, she is left with an adult job: driving her family's herd of eighty-two longhorn steers from Texas to Illinois.

Two Pairs of Shoes retold by P.L. Travers. Viking. In these beautifully illustrated folktales, two pairs of shoes teach two different truths about the men who own them.

The Surprising Things Maui Did by Jay Williams. Four Winds Press. Long ago the people of Hawaii were poor and hungry, cold and sad. In this myth, Maui does some *very* surprising things to improve their lives.

ve hAve kiDnaPPeD YOur
end. DrOP The
Money
at The

Unit 2
Mysteries

A mystery is something that is not understood or explained. People have long sought to understand the mysteries of the world around them. Detectives of long ago—scientists and explorers—tried to discover the "hows" and "whys" of our world. The answers they found have helped broaden the horizons of our knowledge. Although many of the world's mysteries have been solved, there are still many questions that remain unanswered.

In the stories in this unit, you will read about old and new mysteries. You will meet many different kinds of detectives. The detectives are all careful observers. They rely on their powers of observation and on their ingenuity to gather clues. Then they put together the clues to solve each mystery. Some even use computers in their investigations.

As you read the stories in this unit, have fun matching wits with the detectives. Use your powers of observation to become a reading detective. Perhaps you will discover new ways to look at the mysteries and problems you meet. You may even find new ways to broaden your own horizons.

Literature Study

Mysteries

A **mystery** story is one in which a puzzling or unusual event occurs that is not explained. Sometimes this puzzling event happens as the story opens. Sometimes the event has already occurred before the story begins. In either case, the characters in the story are often as baffled by the event as the reader.

In a mystery story, usually at least one of the main characters in the story becomes intrigued with the mystery. The story then tells how that character works to gather clues to solve the puzzle. At the end of the story, the mystery is unraveled and the meaning of the clues is explained.

There are many different kinds of mystery stories. One of the most popular is the detective story. In this type of mystery, a crime is committed, and a detective tries to figure out who committed it. Some mystery stories are scary and filled with suspense. Others tell tales of people involved in strange situations or investigating odd phenomena.

The reader of a mystery story pays special attention to the author's use of foreshadowing. **Foreshadowing** is mentioning something early in a story that gives the reader a clue to what might happen next. In a mystery, foreshadowing keeps the reader involved in trying to solve the mystery. Look for an example of foreshadowing in this paragraph:

> The Millers got out of their car and looked at their new home. "What a big house!" Mrs. Miller exclaimed. "Just like you see in the movies," said Tommy as he put down the family dog, Rags. As

soon as Rags got to the ground, she yelped and hid under the car. "What's the matter, Rags?" asked Tommy. "Why are you afraid?"

After much coaxing, Tommy was able to pick up the dog and walk to the house. "What's there to be afraid of?" he wondered.

The author of this paragraph uses Rags's fearful reaction to the house as foreshadowing. The author is giving the reader clues that the house is somehow dangerous.

A **flashback** is an interruption of a story to tell about an event that happened at an earlier point in time. Mystery writers sometimes use flashback to explain an unusual event to the reader. Read the following paragraph. Look for an example of flashback.

Elena sat by her grandmother's desk, trying to figure out what kind of signal the spies could be using. She heard the tolling of her grandmother's clock in the background and suddenly recalled her experience the week before. Elena had been in the courthouse at midnight when she heard the huge courthouse clock strike. At the time, she had thought she was imagining things. But now she realized what had happened: The clock really had struck thirteen. That was the spies' signal!

The writer of this paragraph uses flashback to take Elena back in time and place to the courthouse the week before. Elena's memories help her to solve her mystery.

As you read the stories that follow, think about what makes them mysteries. Do they have intriguing puzzles, mysterious clues, and searching detectives? Don't forget to be a detective yourself as you read. How fast can you solve each mystery?

How could seven clocks mysteriously communicate a message? Read the story to find out how clocks help Peter Perkins solve a crime.

Clues are present in all mystery stories. How did Peter identify the clues in this story?

Alfred Hitchcock's
The Mystery of the Seven Wrong Clocks

Alfred Hitchcock Speaking: In everyday life, time is flexible. It can crawl by like a snail going to the dentist, or it can race past like an orbiting satellite. It can even turn backward—which is exactly what happens in this story. The clues are present. You are invited to turn detective and help solve the mystery.

Peter Perkins, puzzle and cryptogram editor of the *Sunday Morning Star*, was strolling along the boardwalk at Atlantic Beach.

It was dusk, and the boardwalk was deserted except for him. The amusement park, which took up six blocks of the shoreline of the small city of Atlantic Beach, was silent and empty, filled only with the whispering ghosts of merrymakers long since gone. Actually, the whispering ghosts were only leaves, but Perkins had a lively imagination.

In an effort to shake himself out of his strange mood, the puzzle editor increased his pace. He was heading toward Atlantic Street, a block from the beach, to call on his old friend Fritz Sandoz, who had a watch and clock repair shop and was also a great puzzle enthusiast. They worked puzzles together one night a week.

Fritz was a wizard at repairing any kind of clock. He and Peter had been good friends for many years. Peter went around to the back of the shop and opened the special lock on the door, as he had done on so many other evenings. He walked into the dark room and called out, "Fritz? Fritz?"

A voice roared in his ear, "I've got you!" Huge hands grabbed him. Helpless as a baby, Peter Perkins was dragged into the back room of the Clock Hospital, where lights blazed brightly.

"I caught the killer," a deep voice said in his ear, "returning to the scene of the crime."

In front of him he saw Detective Sergeant Magrue of the local police force. Two other men were bending over something on the floor a few feet away, at the foot of a fine old grandfather's clock.

With a shock of horror, Peter Perkins saw what the men were bending over. It was his old friend, Fritz, and he knew — there could be no doubt of it — that Fritz was dead.

His gaze came back to the bulldog features of Detective Magrue, whom he knew from the past. Magrue looked at him.

"Let him go, Snider," he said. "That's Peter Perkins, the puzzle pest. He's a nuisance, but not a killer."

Magrue fixed the puzzle editor with a steely eye. "What are you doing here, sneaking in the back way?"

"I wasn't sneaking in," Perkins said. "Fritz and I were going to work puzzles together."

"Work puzzles together?" Magrue asked.

"Fritz was a very good puzzle solver," Peter said. "He and I both belong to the National Puzzle League."

"Well, this is no puzzle game," Magrue said. "This is murder. And I don't want any interference from you."

"Who killed him?" Peter asked. "Who killed Fritz?" He tried to keep his voice steady but was not successful.

"That's what *I'm* here to find out," Magrue said. "It happened last night. He was in here, winding his clocks, so that means it had to be midnight. He wound his clocks at midnight every night on the dot."

Peter nodded. That was true.

"Someone slipped in, using a duplicate key—anyway, the door wasn't forced. The murderer came up behind Fritz and hit him over the head. We know that much."

"It had to be someone who knew him," Peter said. "Someone who knew that Fritz distrusted banks and kept all his money in a secret drawer in his desk. He didn't have any enemies so it had to be someone who did it to get the money."

"That much we figured," Magrue said, "seeing as how the drawers of his desk were pried open. Now you go sit in his office, just in case I need to ask you any questions. And don't touch anything!"

Peter Perkins wanted to ask many questions, but he knew Magrue's temper. Silently he walked to the little office and workshop which opened off the big back room. He put his derby on the desk and sat down in an easy chair. One obvious place to look for possible clues was right there, in the office-workshop. Sitting quite still, Peter began to study the room. He studied the shelves which held clocks that had been repaired. He studied the big board full of little hooks from which hung watches of all kinds. He studied the desk, which also served as Fritz's workbench. Fritz's tools were still laid out on top of it. A clock he had been working on—an electric clock, Peter noted with surprise—also stood on top of the desk. Fritz was very neat. He

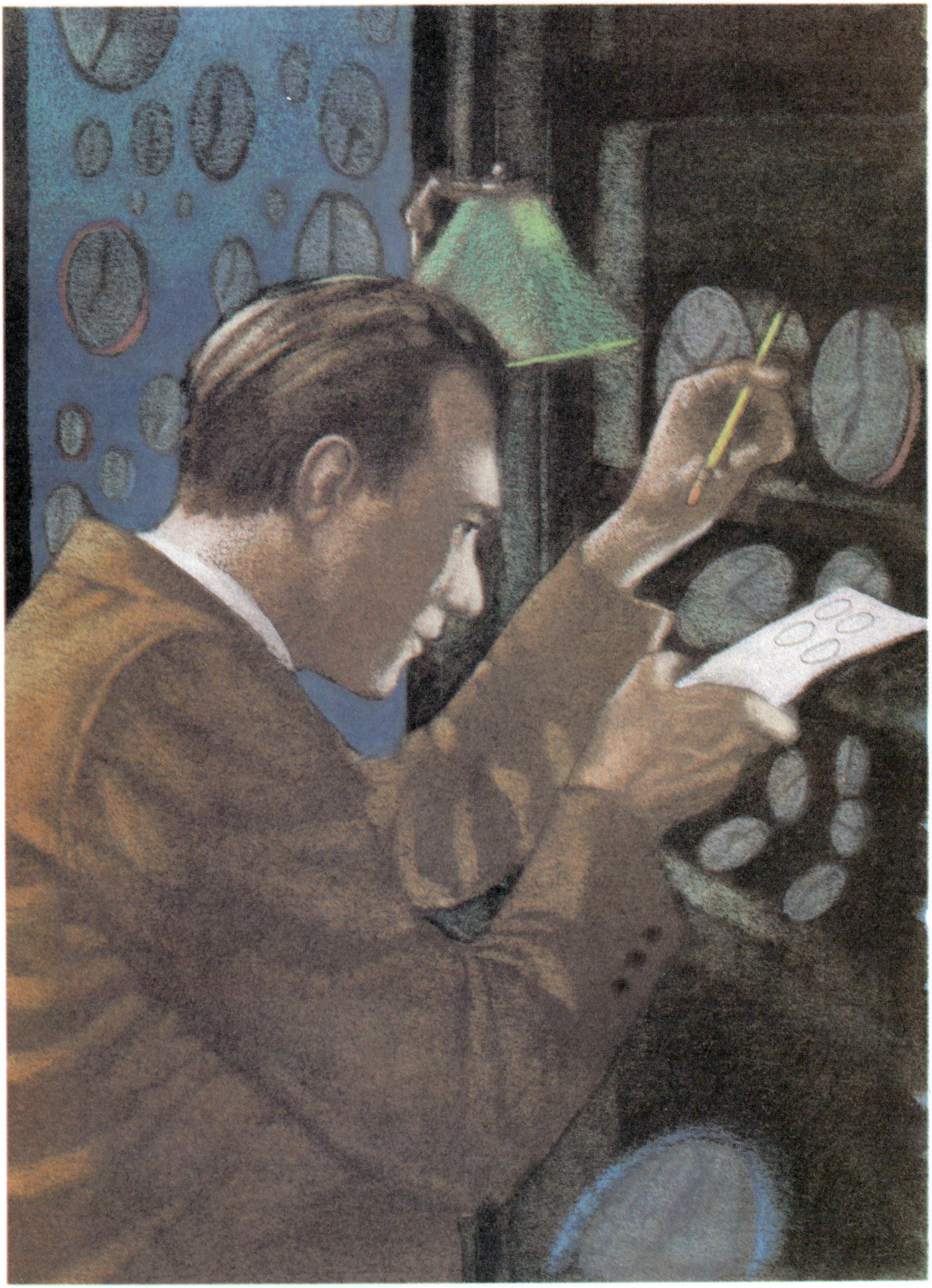

always put away his tools when he stopped work. It was quite obvious, Peter realized, that Fritz had been interrupted in his work.

His gaze started to move onward. Then a realization of something queer brought it back again. The clock—there was something peculiar about the clock. It was running backward!

Staring at it, watching the second hand spin in the wrong direction, Peter Perkins felt a peculiar chill. Clocks always ran forward. Yet here was one running backward in the shop of Fritz Sandoz, whose great pride had been his ability to make clocks keep perfect time.

It was so strange that Peter Perkins felt that it must mean something. It *had* to mean something. But what?

Peter Perkins took a pad of paper from his pocket and a pencil. He made two small drawings and labeled them:

THE CORRECT TIME   THE TIME OF THE
                          BACKWARD CLOCK

He bent over and looked at the clock carefully. It was a very old electric clock—apparently one of the first ever made. A screwdriver lay beside the clock as if Fritz had just put it down. Peter had the feeling that Fritz had actually been setting the clock when he had been interrupted. Suppose he had just set the clock to the correct time? Then he had looked up—perhaps to see the intruder. He had started the clock running backward. But why?

Peter Perkins was lost in thought when one of the many clocks began to strike. He waited for the others; Fritz had kept them in such perfect order that they all struck almost at once. To his amazement, none of the other clocks struck. He looked for the clock that had struck, and then he gasped out loud. A whole row of Fritz Sandoz's precious clocks was telling the wrong time, and each one was telling a *different* wrong time! It was simply incredible — as incredible as the clock that was running backward. Sudden excitement gripped Peter. Did the clocks have a message to convey by their very wrongness?

The first three clocks in the row told the correct time. Then came the wrong clocks. Then came two more clocks telling the right time.

Peter took out his paper and pencil and sketched rapidly:

CORRECT CLOCKS   **WRONG CLOCKS**

WRONG CLOCKS (Continued)   **CORRECT CLOCKS**

As he sketched, he realized that all the clocks in the room had stopped except for the twelve grandfather's clocks. Fritz Sandoz probably hadn't had time to wind them the previous night, so they had run down. Peter tried to reconstruct what might have happened.

Fritz had locked up at six o'clock as he always did. Then he had fixed himself some supper in his living quarters and probably at about seven he had gone into his workshop, where he usually stayed until midnight. At midnight exactly, he went in to wind his clocks.

It looked as if he had started to wind the clocks and then had been struck down by someone who had slipped into the shop. So it looked as if he had been killed at midnight.

Peter Perkins did not believe it. He was sure Fritz had been busy in his workshop when the intruder had slipped in, startling him. Probably the thief had had a gun. He or she had threatened Fritz—and Fritz had started the electric clock running backward. Then the intruder had made Fritz wind twelve of the clocks to make it look to the police as if the murder had happened at midnight. Fritz, knowing his life was in danger, had deliberately changed the clock hands while winding them. He had done it because he was trying desperately to leave some kind of message.

Sometime later Detective Magrue came out and dropped down onto a chair beside Peter Perkins.

He said grimly, "Now this is how I figure it. The killer has to be someone who knew Fritz, who knew his habits and who knew about the money. It had to be someone who came here often enough to make an impression of the front door key and have a duplicate made. I hate to say it, but that means it must be someone who lives and works right in this neighborhood."

Peter nodded in agreement.

"Now Fritz was killed last night, at midnight, as we can tell because he was winding his clocks . . ."

"Detective Magrue," Peter began, "that's what I want to talk . . ."

"Don't interrupt, Perkins!" Magrue bellowed.

"Now, my staff has been busy. I've got a list of names of five people who live on this very block who knew Fritz well—and they are all having money troubles. I'm pretty certain one of them did the job."

He showed Peter Perkins a penciled list on which were the following names: Ann Harrison, painter; Thomas Fentriss, jeweler; Bill Lawden, grocer; Joseph Finchly, barber; Laura Rogers, key maker.

"All of them were often in and out of Fritz's shop, and could have made an impression of the key," Magrue told Peter. "I'm going to question them and see who doesn't have an alibi for midnight last night."

"But, Magrue," Peter tried again, "don't you see, the killer . . ."

"Perkins, stick to your puzzles and leave homicide to the experts," Magrue advised. "Now go on home."

Peter Perkins picked up his hat and his cane, his mind troubled, and went home to his apartment. Before he went to bed, he spent an hour staring at the sketches he had made of the clocks, but no inspiration came to him.

> *Alfred Hitchcock Speaking*: I wonder if you spotted an important clue in the last few pages, or if it slipped right by you. It did? Don't feel bad. Peter Perkins missed it, too.

Next day, in his tiny office at the newspaper, Peter was unusually absent-minded. He opened letters from readers who sent him puzzles, scarcely reading them.

If he could only talk to someone—another puzzle fan, perhaps—who could give him a fresh viewpoint. Absently he opened a letter and looked at it. It was a cryptogram— quite a good one. It was signed, *Submitted by Donna Magrue*.

Peter did a double take. Donna Magrue! Why, that was Detective Magrue's daughter, and she was a puzzle fan!

165

The puzzle editor noted the street address, grabbed his derby and cane, and almost ran from his office. A taxi took him to the address in ten minutes. A tall, perky girl was raking leaves in the front yard. Peter hurried up the walk.

"Donna Magrue?" he asked.

"Why, hello, Mr. Perkins," the girl said. "I recognize you from your picture in the paper. Did you get the cryptogram I sent you?"

"Yes, and I'm going to use it," Peter said. "But I'm here on something much more important."

He swiftly told Donna Magrue all about Fritz Sandoz and the wrong clocks.

"So you see," he finished, "I'm positive he was trying to leave a message when he changed the hands of those clocks. Look, here's a sketch I made." He showed Donna the sketch of the wrong clocks.

Peter said, "Fritz was an expert in codes and he probably expected me to be able to read this one because he knew I'd understand he was trying to leave us a message. I can't see any way to crack a code with so few letters. Maybe you can see something I missed."

"I bet it is a code." Donna sat down on the porch steps and Peter sat down beside her. They both studied the drawing. At last Donna Magrue looked up.

"You know," she said, "these clock hands make me think of semaphore flags spelling out a message. I suppose that's really wild, but . . ."

"Semaphore code!" shouted Peter. "Fritz was in the Swiss Army Signal Corps when he was young. He must have

167

known semaphore. But I don't. I've only studied secret codes."

"I may be wrong, Mr. Perkins," Donna said. "At summer camp I studied semaphore, but the position of these clock hands doesn't spell anything. They're just a few odd letters, and some aren't even letters."

"That's it, Donna!" Peter Perkins' eyes were bright with excitement now. "The clocks aren't telling the time Fritz set them for. They have all moved ahead since he set them. In order to read the message, we'd have to know when the hands were set, and figure out how they looked originally."

"Gosh, then I guess Mr. Sandoz's message is impossible to decode," Donna sighed. "Mr. Sandoz had a good idea, but he didn't realize how tough a message he was leaving us."

"But he did, Donna, he did." Peter Perkins almost shouted the words. "That's why he started the clock backward. What can you tell from a stopped clock?"

"That's easy. The correct time—twice a day." Donna stared at him. "What kind of clock can run backward?"

"A very old electric clock, one of the first models. They had such simple motors that the hands could move in either direction," Peter said. "Now look at this." He showed Donna the sketch he had made of the electric clock.

"So the correct time was six-forty," Donna mused. "But the backward clock said ten after twelve."

"If we move the hands of the backward clock backward some more, and of the forward clock forward some more, the point where they both tell the same time is the time the backward clock was started. Or, in other words, the approximate time Fritz was killed!" Peter exclaimed. "Oh, but wait a minute!"

"Something wrong, Mr. Perkins?" Donna asked.

"We've made a mistake," Peter Perkins groaned. "Since one clock is going forward and one backward, the hands will indicate the same time every six hours, or four times every twenty-four hours. Two of those times will be the moment at which they started, and two will be wrong by six hours."

"Gosh," Donna said. "How can we ever figure out which is which?"

Peter Perkins thought for a long minute, his face a scowl of concentration. Then gradually the scowl cleared.

"I think I've got it," he said. "Your father told me that the suspects all have alibis for after 10:00 p.m. and we're sure the crime was committed after 6:00 p.m. That means the actual time of the crime was between six and ten. Correct?"

Donna nodded. "That's absolutely right, Mr. Perkins."

"Then let's figure out the next time the hands will indicate the same time, if both clocks were still running. If it is between six and ten, we'll know it's the time we're looking for. If it is between ten and four, we figure the alternate time, which will be just six hours later."

Donna nodded. "Let's use our watches and turn the hands," she said.

After a few moments she exclaimed, "We've done it! The two clocks will tell the same time at 9:25, which is in the correct time period between six and ten. So Mr. Sandoz set the electric clock running backward at nine-twenty-five the night he was killed!"

"Precisely," Peter agreed.

"Now we know what time Fritz must have changed the hands of the clocks telling the wrong time," Peter said.

"Allow five minutes or so and it would have been about half-past nine when he started winding them and setting the hands to spell out a message."

"It was six-forty-five when you saw them and sketched them," Donna Magrue said eagerly. "The difference between nine-thirty and six-forty-five is two hours and forty-five minutes. If we add two hours and forty-five minutes to the time of each wrong clock, we'll have the position at which Mr. Sandoz put the hands just before he was killed."

"Which will only take a moment, my girl!"

It took several moments, but presently Peter had another sketch:

THE POSITIONS AT WHICH SANDOZ SET THE WRONG CLOCKS

Then he made a few more swift sketches, drawing under each a little figure holding semaphore flags in the position of the clock hands.

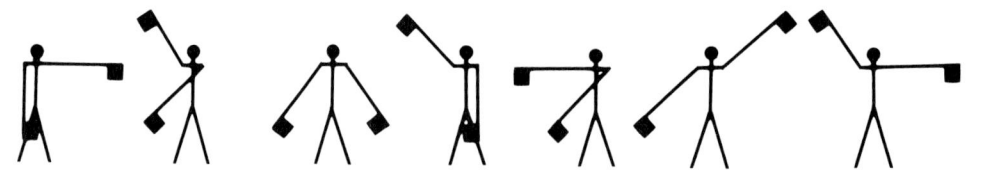

"There. Does that spell anything?"

"It sure does, Mr. Perkins!" Donna said. "In semaphore code that's . . ."

She wrote a letter underneath each figure.

Peter stared at it and swallowed hard.

"Donna," he said, "that's the name of one of the suspects on your father's list. You've solved the mystery!"

If you have any doubts as to how Fritz Sandoz's ingenious message worked, get some clocks, preferably not your family's favorites. Follow the deductions made by Peter Perkins and Donna Magrue, actually turning the clock hands as suggested. I believe you will find it all works out neatly, simply and correctly. What about that clue I mentioned that Peter missed? Really, it's so simple, but if you insist. Go back and observe that exactly seven clocks were changed to give the code message. There was only one suspect with seven letters in his name. So you could easily have picked out Finchly, couldn't you? And if you didn't think to count the wrong clocks — well, what's the title of our story? Exactly! The principal clue you needed was staring you in the face all along, but it's so easy to overlook the obvious, isn't it? Well, on to the next case! Oh, by the way, when Finchly was questioned by Detective Magrue, he confessed. His motive: Business was poor and he was deeply in debt. He wanted the money so that he could live out his life on a tropical island. Instead he spent the rest of his days in jail.

Discuss the Selection

1. How did the seven clocks help Peter Perkins solve the mystery?
2. How were Peter Perkins and Donna Magrue able to figure out the meaning of the wrong clocks?
3. How did you feel about Peter Perkins's ability as a detective? Explain your answer.
4. How was Peter Perkins's ability to work puzzles helpful in solving the mystery of the wrong clocks?
5. Were you able to predict who the murderer was? What clues helped you discover that it was Finchly? Locate those clues in the story.

Apply the Skills

In a mystery story, clues are present for the detective, and the reader, to find. In this story, all the clues were in the office-workshop. What were the clues? What did Peter know about Fritz that led Peter to identify the clues?

Think and Write

Prewrite

1. Peter Perkins became a detective because he found out that his friend Fritz Sandoz had been killed.

2. Because the clocks had stopped and one was running backward, _____
_____
_____

3. Peter Perkins and Donna Magrue figured out the code by _____
_____
_____

A good detective knows there is a reason for everything that happens. Part of solving a mystery depends on knowing what happened and why it happened. The chart above contains sentences that state causes and effects. The first sentence has been completed for you. Use the story to complete the rest of the sentences with either a cause or an effect.

Compose

Using the sentences from the chart as a guide, write a summary of "The Mystery of the Seven Wrong Clocks." Include at least two additional sentences that contain causes and effects.

Revise

Read your summary to make sure that you have included two more examples of cause and effect. Check to see that all of your sentences help to summarize the story.

173

Criminals are no match for the brilliant detective, Incognito Mosquito. How does he use his keen powers of observation to get to the bottom of this mystery?

As you read, hunt for clues along with Incognito Mosquito. What clue helps him solve the case?

Incognito Mosquito and the Mis-cast Dancer Mystery

by E. A. Hass

CONFIDENTIAL

The following information can be released only to individuals with the highest security clearance. But, as long as you've gotten this far . . .

The case you are about to read comes from the files of one Incognito Mosquito, Private Insective. No criminal is immune from the biting wit and stinging intelligence of Mosquito. He is capable of nipping bugs so mean and sinister that they think the evil Mr. Hive is Dr. Jekyll's better half; thugs so greedy that the only thing they'd share with you is a communicable disease; insect fiends so cruel that they make their prisoners eat spaghetti—through a straw.

Only in the files of Incognito Mosquito will you find such tales of slime and pun-ishment. Fortunately. Now it's all up to you. So give it a buzz—before you bug out!

I had just taken my seat at the ballet and was looking forward to a terrific evening. This was the gala premiere of the St. Vitus Dance Troupe's newest production, *The Grasshopper Suite.*

Suddenly, I felt a slap on my shoulder. There in the seat next to mine was the Chief, Inspector Insector, who practically dragged me out of my seat and into the lobby. "I'd really like to make this an open-and-shut case, Mosquito," the Chief said under his breath. "As soon as you open your mouth, I'd like to shut this door in your face. But it seems that the ballet master, one Mr. R. Abesque, thinks you have culture and taste. Little does he know that your taste is all in your mouth."

"Well, actually, Chief, he's not too far off. I have always considered myself a peon of the arts."

The Chief wasted no time, either in listening to me or in explaining what was going on. It seemed that the St. Vitus Dance Troupe wanted to present a very valuable gold medal to the world-famous dancer Mikhail Baryshnimoth at a special ceremony following tonight's performance. Mr. Baryshnimoth had indeed arrived on schedule, but somehow something was wrong.

There was some question as to the identity of the guest. A telegram had arrived earlier explaining that the dancer had to cancel his appearance due to a terrible accident, and yet here was someone claiming to be the great Baryshnimoth himself. There was no way of telling whether this was the real dancer or not! You see, Mr. B. *had* been in this terrible accident recently, so his face was totally bandaged. Also, his left leg was broken, making any dancing out of the question.

So the troupe was faced with the embarrassing predicament of risking the presentation of the medal to an impostor, or canceling the entire ceremony and possibly offending what could be the real Baryshnimoth. The Chief was faced with an even more embarrassing predicament—calling me.

But as usual, he handled the situation with great tact. That's one thing you have to say for the Inspector. He's very tacky. The Chief explained that in order not to arouse suspicion, I was to be introduced as the ballet critic for that snobbish dance magazine *Too-Too*. Then we went backstage to meet either one of the world's greatest dancers or a very clever impostor.

And clever he was. The supposed Mr. Baryshnimoth was charming but sneaky. The Chief was right. The dancer's face was totally bandaged, and his left leg was in a cast to his hip. He leaned heavily on the crutch under his right wing. Every traditional means of identification was a dead end. We chatted casually about the dance, but this bug pulled off his ballet ruse well. He went through all of the positions, really kept me on my toes.

To be honest, I myself have never really understood the principles of ballet. I've never gotten the "pointe" of it, so to speak. I mean, if they want bigger ballerinas, why don't they just get girls a foot taller instead of making them walk around on their toes all the time? And if the girls weren't wearing themselves out by walking around on tiptoe, the boys wouldn't always have to pick them up and carry them all over the place. This would leave a lot more time for dancing, don't you think? When I asked the alleged Baryshnimoth to explain this, for my readers of course, he looked confused.

The Chief didn't look confused. He turned bright red and muttered, "Mosquito, I don't understand why you call yourself a private insective. Public defective is more like it!"

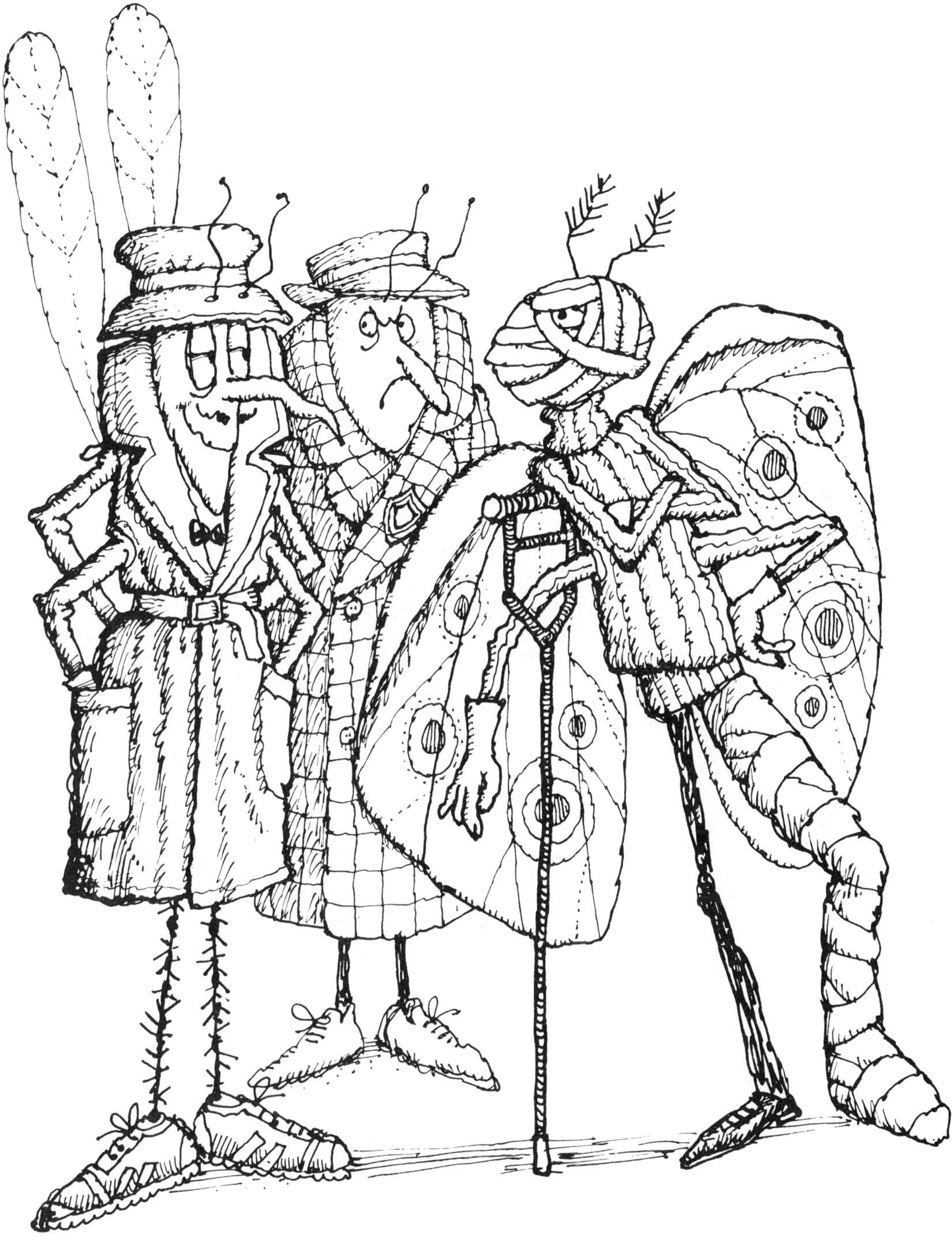

All this time, the ballet had been proceeding on schedule. Dancers whisked by us in tu-tus, three-threes, and four-fours, clad in multicolored tights (and looses), doing arabesques and araworsques, pliés and pliebies. It was growing dangerously close to presentation time, time for the case's finale, and for me to bow out gracefully. There was just one problem — I still had not solved the mystery. Was the bug standing before me an invalid impostor or an innocent invalid? I just wasn't sure. I began to wonder if this was to be my farewell appearance, my swan song, whether I had pirou-ed my last ette.

Then astonishingly an idea hit me like a ton of bricks. Or like a sandbag. Actually, it *was* a sandbag. I'd accidentally bumped into the rope that held the bag high above the stage, thereby triggering its (and my) downfall. Excusing myself, I headed dizzily for the little bugs' room and whipped out my Newly Perfected, Highly Effective Insective Detective Kit the moment I was out of sight.

Without wasting a minute (or any more than I'd already wasted), I grabbed the bottle I was looking for and began to rub the clear liquid on my palms. A special solution of my own invention, this stuff would harden into a gel that would faithfully record the fingerprints of anyone who shook my hand. Then I could instantly match those fingerprints with the fingerprints of the real Baryshnimoth. There was just one bug in the system ... but I'll get to that later. Now it was time to catch a fly in my ointment. (A moth actually, but I'm not picky.) I ran backstage, prepared to leave my mark on the Baryshnimoth case. Or to have Baryshnimoth leave his mark on me.

   The Chief was where I'd left him, making small talk with the dancer. The Inspector is known for his tremendous presence of mind at times like this. He has often also commented on my absence of brain.

"I just wanted to applaud Mr. Baryshnimoth," I explained, while clapping my hands. "And also to shake the wing of a great dancer." At that point I tried to extend my right hand, but that was where the trouble started. I had forgotten the stickiness effect of my potion if not used immediately. In the few minutes since I'd applied it, the stuff had stuck my hands together. The more I pulled, the stickier it got. I tried frantically to wipe the stuff off, but you know what they say—"If the glue fits, wear it." In this case I didn't have much of a choice.

The Chief stepped forward looking ready to explode. "Mosquito, don't ever let anyone tell you that you're a stupid, incompetent fool. I want to be the one to tell you!"

Fortunately, at that moment the supposed Mr. Baryshnimoth smiled apologetically, saving me from what could have been a very sticky situation. "Don't worry about it," he said sweetly. "I couldn't shake your hand even in a pinch. You see, if I let go of this crutch I'll fall flat on my face."

At that moment I realized that the impostor had accidentally upstaged himself. It was curtains for him. "I'm afraid you've already fallen flat on your face." I smiled graciously. "And you don't even have a leg to stand on."

HOW DID INCOGNITO MOSQUITO KNOW THAT THE SUPPOSED MIKHAIL BARYSHNIMOTH WAS ACTUALLY AN IMPOSTOR?

HERE'S HOW:

If he were the *real* Baryshnimoth with a *real* broken left leg, he would have carried a crutch under his left wing to support himself. So ... he would have had no trouble extending his right wing for Incognito to shake.

The only way that the bug would have fallen over while shaking Incognito's hand is if he carried the crutch under his right wing—the wrong wing.

While the impostor had danced the performance of a lifetime—without ever lifting a toe—the time had come for him to bow out. Say for about twenty years.

Discuss the Selection

1. How did Incognito Mosquito use his keen powers of observation throughout the story to help him get to the bottom of the case?
2. How did Incognito Mosquito become involved in the Mis-cast Dancer Mystery?
3. What part of the story did you think was the funniest? Why?
4. Even though Incognito Mosquito's fingerprint solution didn't work as planned, how did it help him identify the alleged Baryshnimoth as an impostor?
5. When did you first begin to think that the moth behind the bandages might be an impostor? Find that part of the story.

Apply the Skills

A good detective is always on the lookout for clues. Those clues sometimes come in the form of unlikely things. What unlikely clue helped Incognito Mosquito unravel this mystery? How did it help?

Think and Write

Prewrite

Story	Problem	Solution
"The Mystery of the Seven Wrong Clocks"	Who killed Fritz Sandoz?	The seven clocks spelled the killer's name.
"Incognito Mosquito and the Mis-cast Dancer Mystery"	Is the alleged Mikhail Baryshnimoth an impostor?	

All good mystery stories present puzzling problems and their solutions. Read the first mystery story problem and solution above. Copy the portion of the chart for "Incognito Mosquito and the Mis-cast Dancer Mystery." Fill in the story's solution.

Compose

Write two paragraphs about "Incognito Mosquito and the Mis-cast Dancer Mystery." In the first paragraph, state the problem as the topic sentence. Then write at least two sentences that provide details about the problem.

In the second paragraph, state the solution as the topic sentence. Follow with several sentences that give details about the solution.

Revise

Read your paragraphs. Make sure that each paragraph has a topic sentence followed by two or more sentences that provide details. Revise any sentences that do not relate to the topic sentence of the paragraph.

Vocabulary Study

Homographs

The sole way to win this race is to keep on running.

I'll never reach the finish line because there's something stuck to the sole of my sneaker!

Look at the word *sole* in both of the sentences above. *Sole* is one of many words that are called homographs. **Homographs** are words that are spelled the same way but have different meanings.

In the first sentence, *sole* means "one and only." In the second sentence, *sole* means "bottom of a shoe." Read the following conversation to find another meaning for the word *sole*.

"Dad, what are we having for dinner?"
"We're having sole. Your mom thinks we should cut down on meat and eat more fish."

You can figure out the meaning of a homograph by looking at the way the word is used in a sentence.

Look at the word *pitch* in the following sentences. In each sentence, *pitch* has a different meaning.

1. The pitch on the new roof was sticky when the roofers applied it.
2. Ted wound up and sent the pitch right over home plate.
3. The forest clearing was the best place to pitch the tent.

Here are three meanings for the word *pitch*. Match each meaning with one of the sentences you just read.

   a. throw
   b. set up
   c. black tar

All of the homographs you have read about so far are pronounced in the same way. Sometimes homographs can have different pronunciations. Read these sentences, paying close attention to the words in italics.

   1. I wonder what kind of birthday *present* I should get for Jenny?
   2. I'd like to *present* my gift to her tomorrow.
   3. She might *object* because tomorrow is not her birthday.
   4. But she probably wouldn't if I surprised her with a beautifully wrapped *object*.

Match the homograph in each sentence above with its meaning below.

   a. give   **c.** thing
   b. gift   **d.** complain

Can you think of another meaning for the word *present*? Pronounce it the same way you would the word meaning "gift."

All the words below are homographs. Write two sentences for each word. Use a different meaning for the homograph in each sentence.

   a. crane   **d.** bow
   b. rock   **e.** steer
   c. swallow

187

Blind Grandmother had a special, mysterious gift. How did Sammle and Mark save her life when the mysterious gift disappeared?

As you read, look for homographs. To figure out their meanings, look at the way they are used in the sentences.

The Gift-Giving

by Joan Aiken

The weeks leading up to Christmas were always full of excitement, and tremendous anxiety too, as the family waited in suspense for the Uncles, who had set off in the spring of the year, to return from their summer's traveling and trading. Uncle Emer, Uncle Acraud, Uncle Gonfil, and Uncle Mark always started off together, down the steep mountainside, but then, at the bottom, they took different routes along the deep narrow valley. Uncle Mark and Uncle Acraud rode eastward, toward the great plains, while Uncle Emer and Uncle Gonfil turned west, toward the towns and rivers and the western sea.

Then, before they were clear of the mountains, they would separate once more, Uncle Acraud turning south, Uncle Emer taking his course northward, so that, the children occasionally thought, their family was scattered over the whole world, netted out like a spider's web.

Spring and summer would go by in the usual occupations: digging and sowing the steep hillside garden beds, fishing, hunting for hares, picking wild strawberries, making hay. Then, toward St. Drimma's Day, when the winds began to blow and the snow crept down, lower and lower, from the high peaks, Grandmother would begin to grow restless.

Silent and calm, all summer long she sat in her rocking chair on the wide wooden porch, wrapped in a patchwork comforter, with her blind eyes turned eastward toward the lands where Mark, her dearest and firstborn, had gone. But when the winds of Michaelmas began to blow, and the wolves grew bolder, and the children dragged in sacks of logs day after day, then Grandmother grew agitated indeed.

When Sammle, the eldest granddaughter, brought her hot milk, she would grip the girl's slender brown wrist and demand: "Tell me, child, how many days now to St. Froida's Day?" (which was the first of December).

"Eighteen, Grandmother," Sammle would answer, stooping to kiss the wrinkled cheek.

"So many, still? So many till we may hope to see them?"

"Don't worry, Granny, the Uncles are certain to return safely. Perhaps they will be early this year. Perhaps we may see them before the feast of St. Melin" (which was December the fourteenth).

And then, sure enough, sometime during the middle weeks of December, their great carts would come jingling and trampling along the winding valleys. Young Mark (son of Uncle Emer), from his watchpoint up a tall pine over a high cliff, would catch the flash of a baggage-mule's brass brow-medal, and would come dashing back to report.

"Granny! Granny! The Uncles are almost here!"

Then the whole household, the whole village, would be filled with turmoil. Wives would build the fires higher, fetch out the best linen and dried meat, set dough to rising, and bring up stone jars of preserved strawberries from the cellars. And the children, with the servants and half the village, would go racing down the perilous zigzag track to meet the cavalcade at the bottom.

The track was far too steep for the heavy carts, which would be dismissed and the carters paid off to go about their business. Then with laughter and shouting, amid a million questions from the children, the loads would be divided and carried up the mountainside on muleback, or on human shoulders. Sometimes the Uncles came home at night, through falling snow, by the smoky light of torches. But the children and the household always knew of their arrival beforehand, and were always there to meet them.

"Did you bring Granny's Chinese shawl, Uncle Mark? Uncle Emer, have you the enameled box that Aunt Grippa begged you to get? Uncle Acraud, did you find the glass candlesticks? Uncle Gonfil, did you bring the books?"

"Yes, yes, keep calm, don't deafen us! Poor tired travelers that we are, leave us in peace to climb this hill! Everything is there, set your minds at rest—the shawl, the box, the books—besides a few other odds and ends, pins and needles and fruit, and a few trifles for the village. Now, just give us a few minutes to get our breath, will you, kindly—" as the children danced round them, helping each other with the smaller bundles, never ceasing to pour out questions: "Did you see the Grand Cham? Did you go to Cathay? Did you travel by ship, by camel, by llama, by elephant?"

And, at the top of the hill, Grandmother would be waiting for them, out on her roofed porch. No matter how wild the weather or how late the time, she sat in majesty with her furs and patchwork quilt around her, while the Aunts ran to and fro with hot stones to place under her feet. And the Uncles always embraced her first, very fondly and respectfully, before turning to hug their wives and sisters-in-law.

Then the goods they had brought would be distributed through the village—the scissors, tools, medicines, plants, bales of cloth, ingots of metal, and musical instruments. After that there would be a great feast.

Not until Christmas morning did Grandmother and the children receive the special gifts that had been brought for them by the Uncles. And this giving always took the same ceremonial form.

Uncle Mark stood behind Grandmother's chair, playing on a small pipe that he had acquired somewhere during his travels. It was made from hard black polished wood, with silver stops, and it had a mouthpiece made of amber. Uncle Mark invariably played the same tune on it at these times, very softly. It was a tune that he had heard for the first time, he said, when he was much younger, once when he had narrowly escaped falling into a crevasse on the hillside, and a voice had spoken to him, as it seemed, out of the mountain itself, bidding him watch where he set his feet and take care, for the family depended on him. It was a gentle, thoughtful tune, which reminded Sandri, the middle granddaughter, of springtime sounds.

While Uncle Mark played on his pipe, Uncle Emer would hand each gift to Grandmother. And she—here was the strange thing—she, who was stone-blind all the year long, could not see her own hand in front of her face, she would take the object in her fingers and instantly identify it. "A mother-of-pearl comb, with silver studs, for Tassy . . . it comes from Babylon. A silk shawl, blue and rose, from Hind, for Argilla. A wooden game, with ivory pegs, for young Emer, from Damascus. A gold brooch, from Hangku, for Grippa. A book of rhymes, from Paris, for Sammle, bound in a scarlet leather cover."

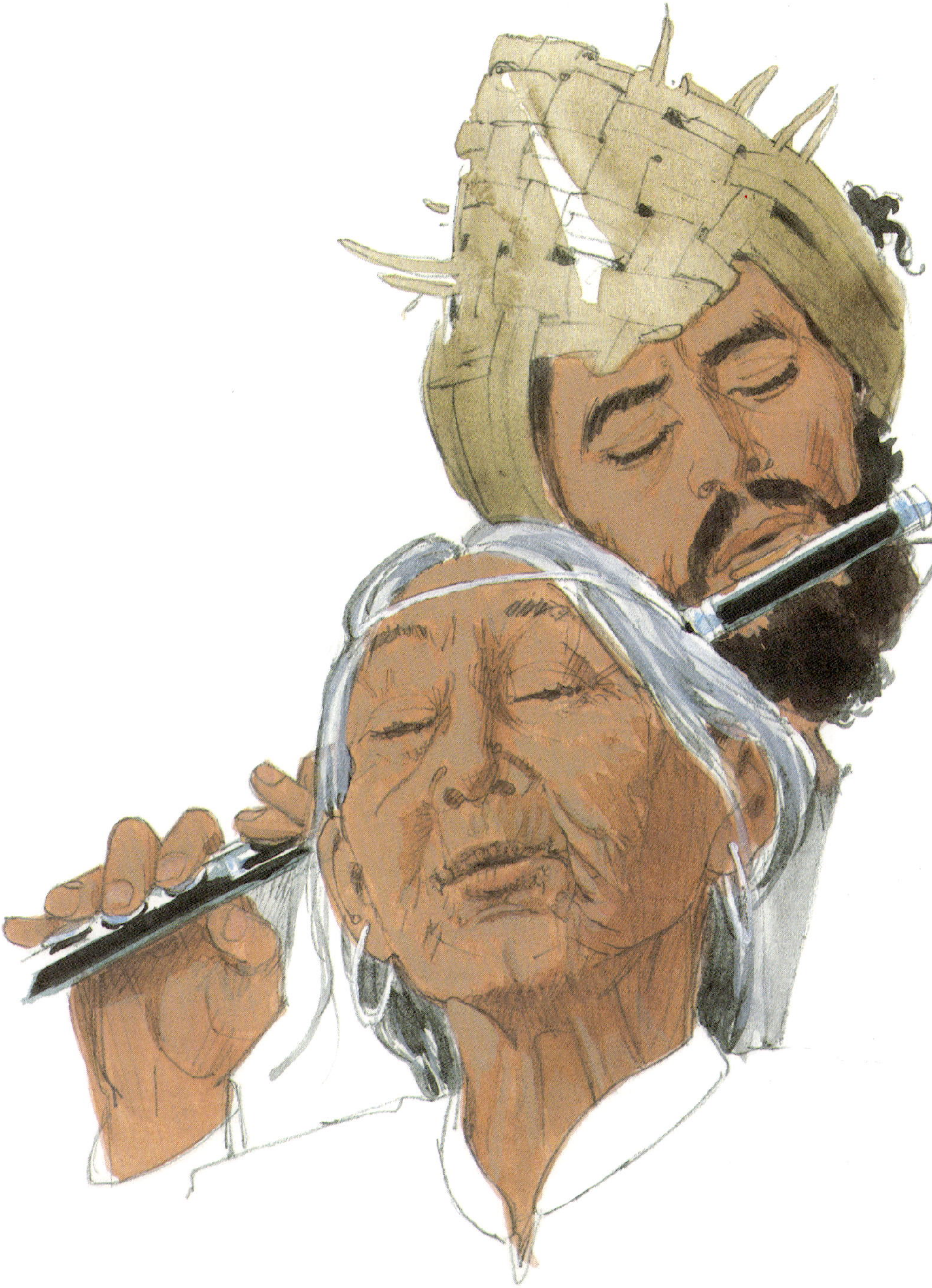

By stroking each gift with her old, blotched, clawlike fingers, frail as quills, Grandmother, who lived all the year round in darkness, could discover not only what the thing was and where it came from, but also the color of it, and that in the most precise and particular manner, correct to a shade. "It is a jacket of stitched and pleated cotton, printed over with leaves and flowers. It comes from the island of Haranati, in the eastern ocean. The colors are leaf-brown and gold and a dark, dark blue, darker than mountain gentian flowers—" for Grandmother had not always been blind. When she was a young girl she had been able to see as well as anybody else.

"And this is for you, Mother, from your son Mark," Uncle Emer would say, handing her a tissue-wrapped bundle, and she would exclaim, "Ah, how beautiful! It's a coat of tribute silk, of the very palest green, so that the color shows only in the folds, like shadows on snow. The buttons and the button-toggles are of worked silk, lavender-gray, like pearl, and the stiff collar is embroidered with white roses."

"Put it on, Mother!" her sons and daughters-in-law would urge her, and the children, dancing 'round her chair, clutching their own treasures, would chorus, "Yes, put it on, put it on! Ah, you look like a queen, Granny, in that beautiful coat! The highest queen in the world! The queen of the mountain!"

Those months after Christmas were Grandmother's happiest time. Secure, thankful, with her sons safe at home, she would sit in the warm fireside corner of the big wooden family room. The wind might shriek, the snow gather higher and higher out of doors, but that did not concern her, for her family, and all the village, were well supplied with flour, oil, firewood, meat, herbs, and roots. The children had their books and toys, they learned lessons with the old priest, or made looms and spinning wheels, carved stools and chairs and chests with the tools their uncles had brought them. The Uncles rested and told tales of their travels as Uncle Mark played his pipe for hours. Uncle Acraud drew pictures in charcoal of the places he had seen, and Granny, laying her hand on the paper covered with lines, would expound while Uncle Mark played: "A huge range of mountains, like wrinkled brown lines across the horizon; a wide plain of sand with patches of pale blue. I think it is not water but air the color of water. Here are strange lines across the sand where men once plowed it, long, long ago; and a great patch of crystal green, with what seems like a road crossing it. Now here is a smaller region of plum-pink, bordered by an area of rusty red. I think these are the colors of the earth in these territories. It is very high up, dry from height, and the soil glittering with little particles of metal."

"You have described it better than I could myself!" Uncle Acraud would exclaim, while the children, breathless with wonder and curiosity, sat cross-legged round her chair. And she would answer, "Yes, but I cannot see it at all, Acraud, unless your eyes have seen it first, and I cannot see it without Mark's music to help me."

"How does Grandmother *do* it?" the children would demand of their mothers, and Argilla, or Grippa, or Tassy would answer, "Nobody knows. It is Grandmother's gift. She alone can do it."

On many evenings thirty or forty people of the village would be there, silently listening. When Grandmother retired to bed, which she did early for the seeing made her weary, the audience would turn to one another with deep sighs, and murmur, "The world is indeed a wide place."

But with the first signs of spring the Uncles would become restless again. They began looking over their equipment, discussing maps and routes, mending saddlebags and boots, and gazing up at the high peaks for signs that the snow was in retreat.

Then Granny would grow very silent. She never asked them to stay longer, she never disputed their going, but her face seemed to shrivel. She grew smaller, wizened and huddled inside her quilted patchwork.

And so, St. Petrag's Day, when the Uncles set off, when the farewells were said and they clattered off down the mountain through the melting snow and the trees with pink luminous buds, Grandmother would fall into a silence that lasted, sometimes, for as much as five or six weeks. All day she would sit with her face turned to the east, wordless, motionless, and would drink her milk and go to her bed-place at night still silent and dejected. It took the warm sun and sweet wild hyacinths of May to raise her spirits.

Then, by degrees, she would grow animated, and begin to say, "Only six months, now, till they come back."

But young Mark observed to his cousin Sammle, "It takes longer, every year, for Grandmother to grow accustomed."

And Sammle said, shivering though it was warm May weather, "Perhaps one year, when they come back, she will not be here. She is becoming so tiny and thin. You can see right through her hands, as if they were leaves." And Sammle held up her own thin brown young hand against the sunlight to see the blood glow under the translucent skin.

"I don't know how they would bear it," said Mark thoughtfully, "if when they came back we had to tell them that she had died."

But that was not what happened.

One December the Uncles arrived much later than usual. They did not climb the mountain until St. Misham's Day, and when they reached the house it was in silence. There was none of the usual joyful commotion.

Grandmother knew instantly that there was something wrong. "Where is my son Mark?" she demanded. "Why do I not hear him among you?" And Uncle Acraud had to tell her: "Mother, he is dead. Your son Mark will not come home, ever again."

"How do you *know*? How can you be *sure*? You were not there when he died?"

"I waited and waited at our meeting place, and a messenger came to tell me. His caravan had been attacked by wild tribesmen, riding north from the Lark Mountains. Mark was killed, and all his people. Only this one man escaped and came to bring me the story."

"But how do you know he told the *truth*?"

"He brought Mark's ring."

Emer put it into her hand. As she turned it about in her thin fingers, a long moan went through her.

"Yes, he is dead. My son Mark is dead."

"The man gave me this little box," Acraud said, "which Mark was bringing for you."

Emer put it into her hand, opening the box for her. Inside lay an ivory fan. On it, when it was spread out, you could see a bird, with eyes made of sapphires, flying across a valley, but Grandmother held it listlessly, as if her hands were numb.

"What is it?" she said. "I do not know what it is. Help me to bed, Agrilla. I do not know what it is. I do not wish to know. My son Mark is dead."

Her grief infected the whole village. It was as if the keystone of an arch had been knocked out. There was nothing to hold the people together.

That year spring came early, and the three remaining Uncles, melancholy and restless, were glad to leave on their travels. Grandmother hardly noticed their going.

Sammle said to Mark: "You are clever with your hands. Could you not make a pipe—like the one my father had?"

"I?" he said. "Make a pipe? Like Uncle Mark's pipe? Why? What would be the point of doing so?"

"Perhaps you might learn to play on it. As he did."

"I? Play on a pipe?"

"I think you could," she said. "I have heard you whistle tunes of your own."

"But where would I find the right kind of wood?"

"There is a chest, in which Uncle Gonfil once brought books and music from Leiden. I think it is the same kind of wood. I think you could make a pipe from it."

"But how can I remember the shape?"

"I will make a drawing," Sammle said. She drew with charcoal on the whitewashed wall of the cowshed. As soon as Mark looked at her drawing he began to contradict.

"No! I remember now. It was not like that. The stops came here—and the mouthpiece was like this."

Now the other children flocked 'round to help and advise.

"The stops were farther apart," said Creusie. "And there were more of them and they were bigger."

"The pipehole was longer than that," said Sandri. "I have held it. It was as long as my arm."

"How will you ever make the stops?" said young Emer.

"You can have my silver bracelets that Father gave me," said Sammle.

"I'll ask Finn the smith to help me," said Mark.

Once Mark had got the notion of making a pipe into his head, he was eager to begin. But it took him several weeks of difficult carving; the black wood of the chest proved hard as iron. And when the pipe was made, and the stops fitted, it would not play. Try as he would, not a note could he fetch out of it.

Mark was dogged, though, once he had set himself to a task. He took another piece of the black chest and began again. Only Sammle stayed to help him now. The other children had lost hope, or interest, and gone back to their summer occupations.

The second pipe was much better. By September, Mark was able to play a few notes on it. By October he was playing simple tunes made up out of his head.

"But," he said, "if I am to play so that Grandmother can see with her fingers—if I am to do *that*—I must remember your father's special tune. Can *you* remember it, Sammle?"

She thought and thought. "Sometimes," she said, "it seems as if it is just beyond the edge of my hearing—as if somebody were playing it, far, far away, in the woods. Oh, if only I could stretch my hearing a little farther!"

"Oh, Sammle! Try!"

For days and days she sat silent or wandered in the woods, frowning, knotting her forehead, willing her ears to hear the tune again. And the women of the household said, "That girl is not doing her fair share of the tasks."

They scolded her and set her to spin, weave, milk the goats, and throw grain to the hens. But all the while she continued silent, listening, listening to a sound she could not hear. At night, in her dreams, she sometimes thought she could hear the tune, and she would wake with tears on her cheeks, wordlessly calling her father to come back and play his music to her, so that she could remember it.

In September the autumn winds blew cold and fierce. By October snow was piled around the walls and up to the windowsills. On St. Felin's Day the three Uncles returned, but sadly and silently, without the former festivities; although, as usual, they brought many bales and boxes of gifts and merchandise. The children went down, as usual, to help carry the bundles up the mountain. The joy had gone out of this tradition, though, and they toiled silently up the track with their loads.

It was a wild, windy evening. The sun set in fire, the wind moaned among the fir trees, and gusts of sleet every now and then dashed in their faces.

"Take care, children!" called Uncle Emer as they skirted along the side of a deep gully. His words were caught by an echo and flung back and forth between the rocky walls: "Take care—care—care—care—care . . ."

"*Oh!*" cried Sammle, stopping precipitately. "I have it! I can remember it! *Now* I know how it went!"

And, as they stumbled on up the snowy hillside, she hummed the melody to her cousin Mark, who was just ahead of her.

"Yes, that is it, yes!" he said. "Or, no, wait a minute, that is not quite right—but it is close, it is very nearly the way it went. Only the notes were a little faster, and there were more of them—they went up, not down—before the ending tied them in a knot—"

"No, no, they went down at the end, I am almost sure—"

Arguing, interrupting each other, disputing, agreeing, they dropped their bundles in the family room and ran away to the cowhouse where Mark kept his pipe hidden.

For three days they discussed and argued and tried a hundred different versions. They were so occupied that they hardly took the trouble to eat. But at last, by Christmas morning, they had reached agreement.

"I *think* it is right," said Sammle. "And if it is not, I do not believe there is anything more that we can do about it."

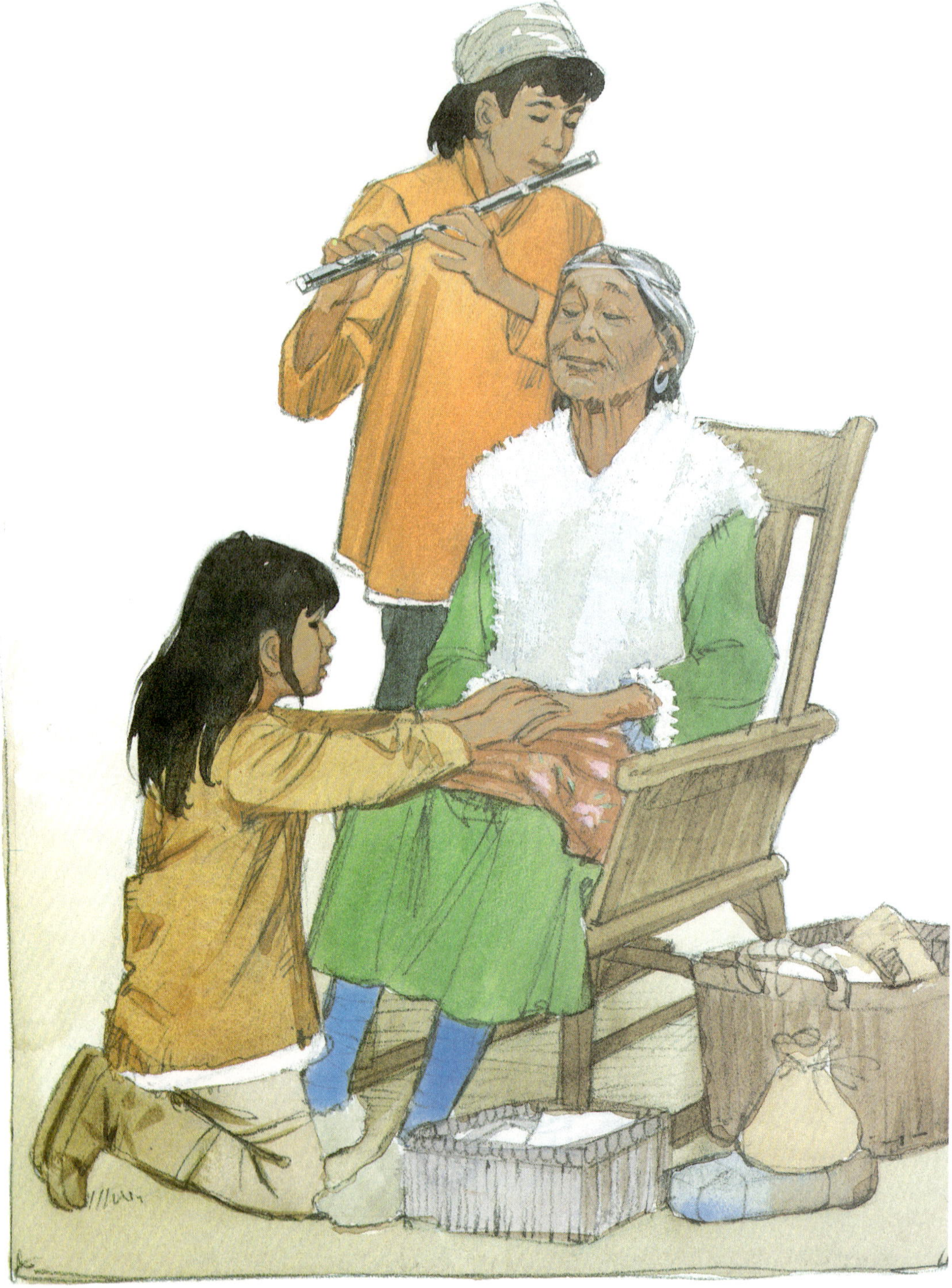

"Perhaps it will not work in any case," said Mark sadly. He was tired out with arguing and practicing.

Sammle was equally tired, but she said, "Oh, it *must* work. Oh, let it work! Please let it work! For otherwise I don't think I can bear the sadness. Go now, Mark, quietly and quickly, go and stand behind Granny's chair."

The family had gathered, according to Christmas habit, around Grandmother's rocking chair. The faces of the Uncles were glum and reluctant, their wives dejected and hopeless. Only the children showed eagerness, as the cloth-wrapped bundles were brought and laid at Grandmother's feet.

She herself looked wholly dispirited and cast down. When Uncle Emer handed her a slender, soft package, she received it apathetically, almost with dislike, as if she would prefer not to be bothered by this tiresome gift ceremony.

Then Mark, who had slipped through the crowd without being noticed, began to play on his pipe just behind Grandmother's chair.

The Uncles looked angry and scandalized. Aunt Tassy cried out in horror: "Oh, Mark, wicked boy, how *dare* you?" But Grandmother lifted her head, more alertly than she had done for months past, and began to listen.

Mark played on. His mouth was quivering so badly that it was hard to grip the amber mouthpiece, but he played with all the breath that was in him. Meanwhile, Sammle, kneeling by her grandmother, held, with her own young hands, the old, brittle ones against the fabric of the gift. And, as she did so, she began to feel what Grandmother felt.

Grandmother said softly and distinctly: "It is a muslin shawl, embroidered in gold thread, from Lebanon. It is colored a soft brick red, with pale roses of sunset pink, and thorns of silver-green. It is for Sammle . . ."

Discuss the Selection

1. How did Sammle and Mark save Grandmother's life when the mysterious gift disappeared?
2. Why did Grandmother lose her gift?
3. What did you think of Sammle's idea?
4. What two types of gifts might the title refer to?
5. Locate the parts of the story that describe the gift-giving. How are the ceremonies different? How are the ceremonies the same?

Apply the Skills

Homographs are words that are spelled the same but have different meanings. Some, like *sole*, are pronounced the same. Others, like *present*, are pronounced differently. You can figure out the meaning of a homograph by looking at the way it is used in a sentence.

Read each of the following sentences. Define the italicized homograph as it is used in each sentence. Then explain another meaning that the homograph can have.

1. When Uncle Mark played his tune, Grandmother saw a huge *range* of mountains across the horizon.
2. Sammle offered her silver bracelets to Mark for making the pipe *stops*.

Think and Write

Prewrite

Object	Sound	Sight	Taste or Smell	Touch
toast	crunchy	square, brown		
cotton		puffy		soft
new tire		black	rubbery	

In "The Gift-Giving," Grandmother is blind. Yet she has a special ability to describe vividly the things she cannot see. The chart above categorizes the sensory details of four familiar objects. How would you describe them to someone who cannot see them? Think of other words that describe each object. Copy and complete the chart.

Compose

Pick any object. You may use an object listed on the chart if you wish. Write a paragraph describing the object to someone who cannot see it. Appeal to as many of the senses as you can in your description.

Revise

Read your description carefully. Make sure that you have included sensory details. If necessary, revise to add descriptive details.

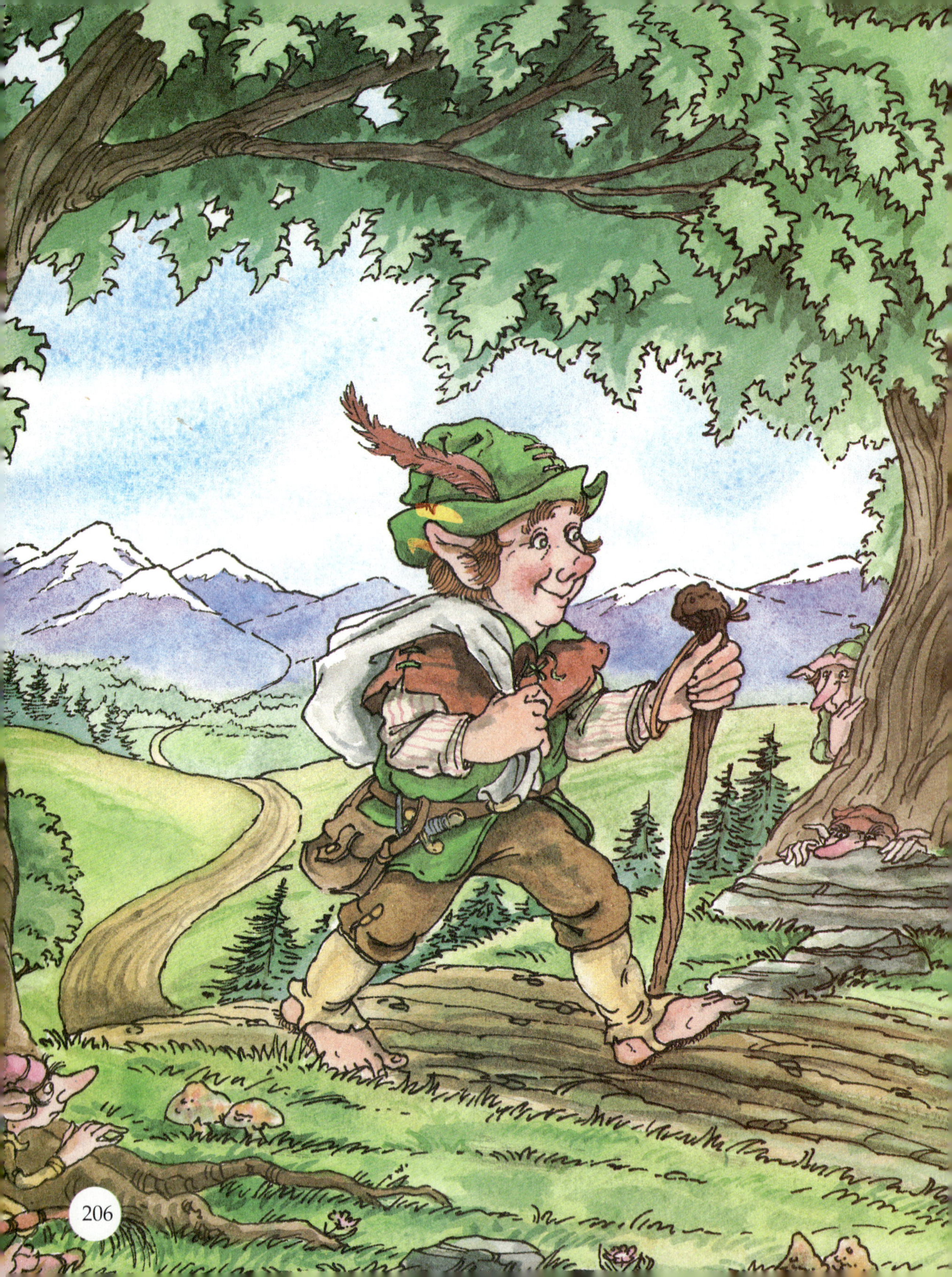

Roads Go Ever On and On

by J. R. R. Tolkien

Roads go ever on and on,
   Over rock and under tree,
By caves where sun has never shown,
   By streams that never find the sea;
Over snow by winter sown,
   And through the merry flowers of June,
Over grass and over stone,
   And under mountains in the moon.

Comprehension Study

Make Judgments

One way to understand more fully what you read is to **make judgments.** When you make a judgment, you form an opinion about what you read. How do you know whether the judgment you make is correct? You can study the details in the passage to see if they support your judgment.

Read the following passage. Think about a judgment you can make based on what you read.

> A computer can store great amounts of information about illnesses. It can store descriptions of the symptoms and methods of treatment for thousands of different illnesses. A doctor can call up a specific bit of information about an illness just by pressing a button.

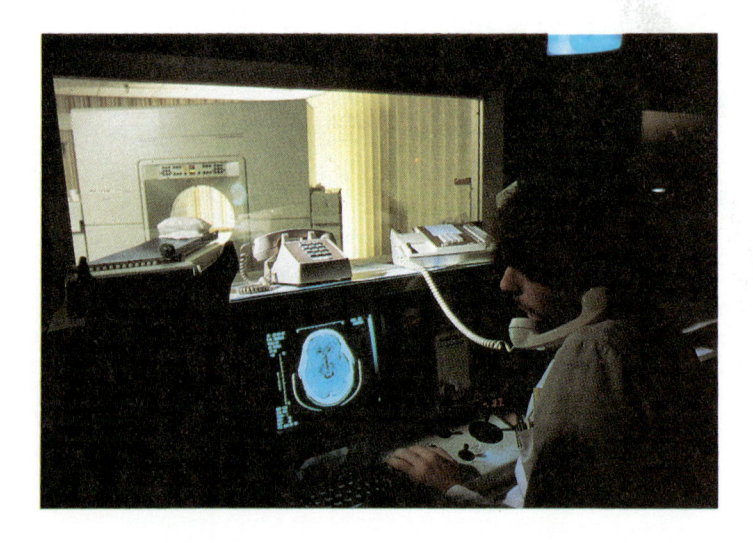

Based on details in the passage, you can make the following judgment: The computer is becoming very useful to doctors. You can use the information in the passage to support that judgment.

Validity and Accuracy of Judgments

A good question to ask yourself when you are making a judgment is *Is my judgment valid?* The word *valid* means "based on evidence." Is there enough evidence to support the judgment that computers can be useful to doctors? The answer is yes, so the judgment is a valid one.

Another question you need to ask yourself is whether the information in the passage is accurate. In other words, is the information correct? If the information is not correct, you can't expect to make a valid judgment.

There are several questions to ask yourself to determine whether the information you read is accurate:

1. Does it agree with other information I have heard or read about the subject?
2. Are specific examples given?
3. Is the information made up of facts or opinions that can be supported?

If you can answer yes to each question, the information in the passage is probably accurate. You will be able to make a valid judgment.

Author's Judgment

Another task you will need to perform when you read is to determine whether an author's judgment is valid. Read the following passage:

> The population of the mountain states will continue to grow over the next twenty years. The populations of the mountain states of Montana, Idaho, Wyoming, Colorado, New Mexico, Arizona, Utah, and Nevada are growing. In the 1990's, the number of people in the mountain states is expected to increase by more than 30 percent. A computer made this prediction from information collected in the 1980 population census.

In the first sentence of the passage, the author makes the judgment that the population of the mountain states will continue to grow. Are there facts that support the judgment? Are the facts accurate? Is the author's judgment valid? Because the answers to these questions are yes, the judgment is valid.

How can you recognize an author's judgment that is not valid? Often you will not need any special knowledge to do this. Read the following passage:

> Most people in the United States are learning to live off the land. Many grow their own fruits and vegetables. They raise animals to get meat and eggs. Instead of burning gas or oil, they heat their homes with wood from trees they chop down themselves.

Based on your own experience, you know that most people shop in supermarkets and heat their homes with gas or oil. Therefore, the author's judgment in the first sentence of the passage is incorrect.

How would you turn an incorrect judgment into a valid judgment? You might say that some people are learning to live off the land. You would probably want to check the accuracy of the facts before making a judgment.

Why should you think about accuracy and validity as you read? Making valid judgments, and knowing how authors make them, can help you understand and evaluate what you read.

Textbook Application: Making Judgments in Social Studies

How do you recognize an author's judgment in a textbook, and how do you know if the judgment is valid? You look for facts and opinions in a passage and then look for details that support them.

As you read the following selection from a social studies book, look for sentences in which the author makes judgments.

These details will help the author make judgments in the next paragraph.

Artifacts as Clues

We do not know the oral history of the world's earliest peoples. They and their languages died out long ago. We do have other records of their lives. Some of these records are in the form of things that the people made. Tools, clothing, and other objects that people make and use are called **artifacts** (AHR-tuh-faktz). Ancient peoples left some artifacts behind when they moved. They buried other artifacts with their dead.

Artifacts give clues about early peoples' feeling and beliefs. Painted pots, decorated clothes, and jewelry show that their makers cared about beauty, just like people of all other times. Artifacts that were buried with the dead suggest that some ancient peoples believed in a life to come.

In most cases, artifacts were not intended to be records. Early peoples left more purposeful records in the form of pictures. Paintings in certain caves in France and Spain may be 20,000 years old. They show that even so long ago, people looked carefully at their world and took the time and trouble to record what they saw.

—*The World Past and Present,*
Harcourt Brace Jovanovich

Here the author makes judgments about what ancient peoples believed. Look for details that support the judgments.

In the last sentence, the author makes a judgment. Is the judgment valid?

Remember to think about authors' judgments when you read textbooks. Ask yourself whether the judgments are supported by details and whether the details are accurate. Asking these questions will help you to better understand what you read.

Microchips are tiny, amazing little tools. What kinds of mysteries have they helped people to solve?

As you read, look for the facts in the article that help you to make judgments about the usefulness of microchips.

Microchip: Small Wonder

by *Charlene W. Billings*

Think about an object that can fit on the tip of your finger. It is so light you could blow it away with a puff of your breath. It is so small an ant could carry it.

Yet this object is making your life far different from your mother's or father's life. This object is one of the most important inventions of recent years. It is called the chip.

Chip is a nickname for *microchip. Micro* means "very small." At first glance, a chip could be mistaken for a spot of gray paint. If you look more carefully, you will see that it is a perfect square and about as thick as a thumbnail. Each side of the square is only one-quarter of an inch long.

There is a pattern on the surface of the chip. The pattern is too small to see with the naked eye. You need a very strong magnifying glass or microscope to see the pattern clearly. The pattern looks like the map of a city. Row upon row of "streets" overlap and cross. These "streets" are really circuit lines. They serve as wires to carry electricity through the chip.

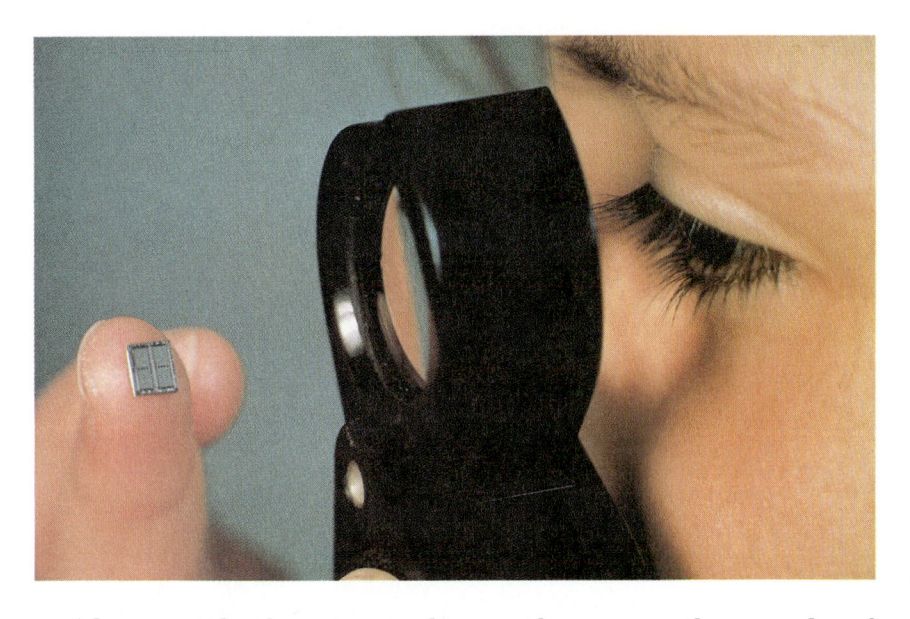

A microchip so small it can fit on the tip of a finger.

    Along with the circuit lines, there are thousands of very, very tiny electronic parts built into the chip. The circuit lines and electronic parts control electricity as it passes through the chip.

    The microchip is amazing because it can take the place of thousands of much larger wires and parts. It can work better and faster than anything was able to do before.

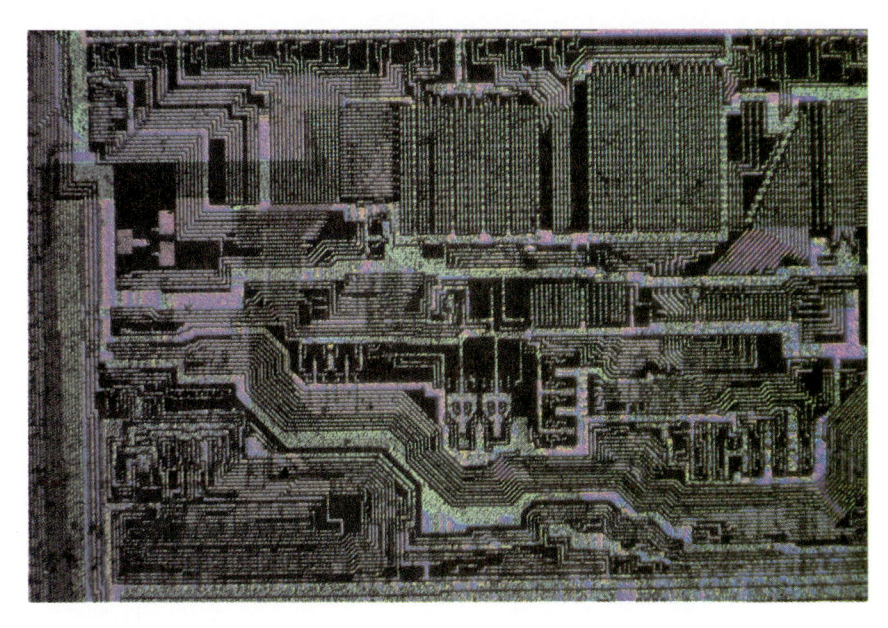

A microchip enlarged to fourteen times its actual size.

215

ENIAC, one of the first electronic computers.

The first computers were built in the early 1940's. One of these computers was called ENIAC (which stands for Electronic Numerical Integrator and Calculator). It was a thirty-foot-by-fifty-foot giant that filled a room as big as a school gym. ENIAC weighed over thirty tons! It had more than 18,000 glass electronic tubes and miles of wires. It took over two and one-half years to put ENIAC together. ENIAC cost millions of dollars. Not even big businesses wanted to spend that much for a computer. By the early 1960's, scientists had found ways to put smaller transistors and circuit lines on a single sliver of material. The microchip was a reality!

The microchip uses very small amounts of electricity. It costs little to run. Because no wires can come loose within the chip, a computer built with microchips is far less likely to fail. Thus, the chip has reduced the size and cost of computers.

The tiny chip is awe-inspiring. But it cannot do anything on its own. Someone must give directions to the microchips in a computer that tell them exactly what to do. These directions are called a *program*. The program can be entered into the chips of a computer by typing it on the computer keyboard. Later, the instructions in a program can be changed if needed.

Chips are the "brains" in today's computers. But there are many other things around us that are made with microchips. Tiny calculators owe their size to the chip. In 1970, a palm-sized calculator cost over four hundred dollars. It used so much power that its batteries would last only about ten hours. Today, a calculator costs under ten dollars. It may be no bigger than a few playing cards stacked together. It will run on one battery the size of a shirt button for a year or more.

You may be wearing microchips on your wrist. In a digital watch, microchips take the place of the many little gears of the wind-up watch. The chips not only measure time, they also control the display of the numbers on the face of the watch. Digital watches will run for a year or more, using small batteries. They are known for their accuracy. At the end of a full year of keeping time, digital watches will still be within a second or two of the exact time.

When you think of robots, do you think of microchips as well? Through computers, chips control the actions of robots that are at work in factories all over the world. Many of these robots spray paint or carry heavy items for people. They also weld, assemble, polish, shape, mix, or cut materials. Robots are useful to do hazardous tasks too. In the future, robots may fight fires. They may even mine minerals from deep under the sea.

A robot is being developed to explore other planets. It will be able to collect rocks and other samples as it moves along the surface. On its own, it will avoid craters, cliffs, and other dangers.

When you play a video game you are using microchips. Hidden inside the game are chips that keep track of the time and the score. If you have played these games, you know that a lot can happen in a blink of time. Some of these games even have sounds such as a victory tune when you win — or a *"BLAT"* when you lose.

A robot arm used for welding automobiles.

A "seeing-eye" robot guiding a blind person.

Microchips also help doctors. The chips inside computers can store descriptions of thousands of illnesses and their treatments. They can remember more than doctors could possibly remember by themselves. A doctor can enter a patient's symptoms into a computer and get back a possible diagnosis and treatment. A bank of information like this is especially valuable to care for rare diseases that are not often seen by doctors.

Handicapped people are being aided by the chip as well. Devices small enough to be placed permanently under the skin or scalp can bring back some sight or hearing for blind or deaf people. Better artificial limbs with more lifelike control are available for those who have lost arms or legs.

During Discovery's fourth day in orbit, a Mission Specialist on the ground controls the unfolding of a solar experiment.

The exploration of space would be impossible without the microchip. The United States sent the *Viking* spacecrafts to Mars, and *Voyager 1* and *2* flew by Jupiter and Saturn. The crafts sent back information and photographs of these planets. The pictures were not like any ever seen before. Space shuttles have flown into space and returned to Earth to fly again. Lightweight computers made with microchips control every phase of these missions.

Chips are in things as different as cash registers and heart pacemakers. They control traffic lights, heat in buildings, and the newest household appliances. Chips are inside radios, television sets, and cameras, as well. There are many more uses for microchips. Most were hardly imagined only a few years ago.

People can use microchips to solve an almost endless number of problems or to do many jobs. Therefore, they are one of the most important inventions of our time.

What is in the future?

People who make microchips are still trying to put more and more circuit lines and transistors onto each sliver. By creating chips that can do more, engineers will make new computers that will be easier for people to use. These "user-friendly" computers will be able to respond to spoken commands. They will even be able to tell one person's voice from another.

Scientists will be able to store much more information inside the microchips of the future. Tomorrow's computers will be able to translate back and forth between languages such as Japanese (which uses thousands of difficult characters) and English (which uses the alphabet).

Some scientists are working on new kinds of electronic switches. One kind works at very high speed when kept very cold. Chips made with these switches could bring about supercomputers that carry out 60 million instructions each second. This is ten times faster than today's best computers.

Microchips have already brought about astonishing changes. In the years to come, chips will be more powerful than ever. They will help us in ways we can hardly imagine today.

Discuss the Selection

1. What kinds of mysteries have microchips helped people to solve?
2. How were computers different before the microchip?
3. How has the microchip affected your life, either directly or indirectly?
4. How might microchips help humankind in the future?
5. Locate the part of the article in which you learned about the sharp contrast between computers of years ago and computers today.

Apply the Skills

As you read, you make many judgments. You evaluate these judgments using the facts and details provided. Facts and details tell you whether your judgments are valid and accurate.

Which facts and details in the article would you use to support the judgment that the microchip is one of the most important inventions of recent years?

Think and Write

Prewrite

	Older Calculators	Modern Calculators
Size	palm-sized	
Price	over $400	
Uses	add, subtract, multiply, divide	
Battery-life		

Copy and complete the chart above to contrast important facts about old and modern calculators. Use the facts provided in "Microchip: Small Wonder."

Compose

Use the information on the chart to write a paragraph that contrasts today's calculators with older calculators. Include sentences that tell about the size, price, uses, and battery life of each. Begin with a topic sentence. Then write four supporting sentences about older calculators and four sentences about today's calculators.

Revise

Read your paragraph. Make sure it includes all of the information on the chart. If it does not, revise your work.

Think Tank

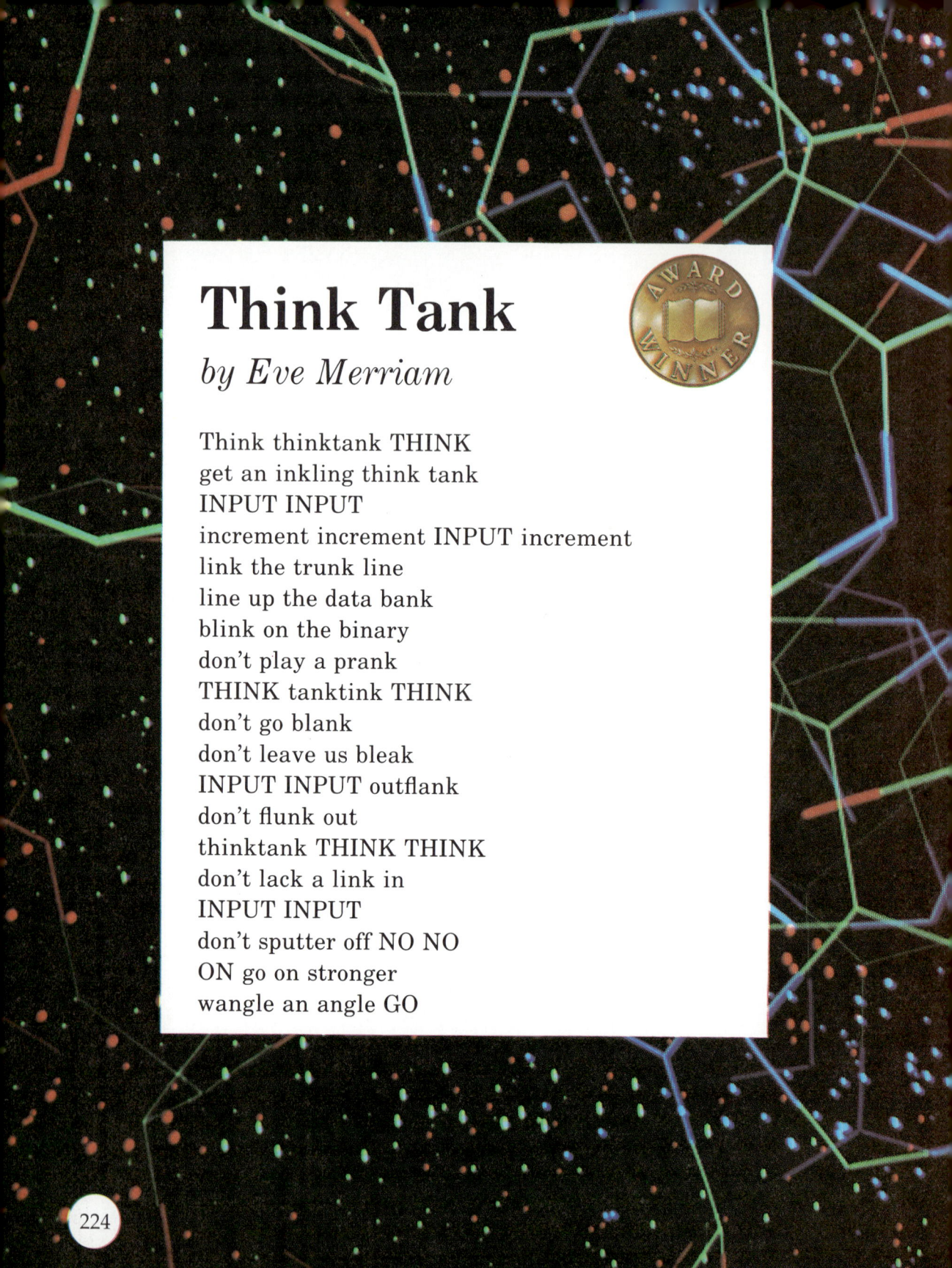

by Eve Merriam

Think thinktank THINK
get an inkling think tank
INPUT INPUT
increment increment INPUT increment
link the trunk line
line up the data bank
blink on the binary
don't play a prank
THINK tanktink THINK
don't go blank
don't leave us bleak
INPUT INPUT outflank
don't flunk out
thinktank THINK THINK
don't lack a link in
INPUT INPUT
don't sputter off NO NO
ON go on stronger
wangle an angle GO

thinktank THINK
don't put us out of luck stuck
on the brink
don't conk out
INPUT INPUT
something bungled
mangled rattled
RETHINK thinktank RETHINK
disentangle
unwrinkle
undo the junk CLUNK
plug up the CHINK the leak
don't peter out be fleet
be NEAT
we hunger for hanker for answer
print out print out print out
THANK you THINKTANK THANKTANK THINK
you TANKYOU out THINK
REPEAT REPEAT
REPEAT
THANK YOU THINKTANK
THINK
TANK
DONE
THUNK

Study Skills

Newspapers

The best way to learn what's new in the world is to read a newspaper. A newspaper is filled with news stories. News stories are reports about events that have recently happened in the world, in the nation, or in your town. News stories always answer six questions: Who? What? Where? When? Why? How?

What will you find in a newspaper besides news stories? There are letters to the editor and editorials. There are sports pages and puzzles. There are also many advertisements, a weather map, movie and TV listings, and book, movie, and theater reviews. All of these are regular features in a newspaper. Regular features appear in a paper every day.

The Newspaper Index

Many newspapers have an index on the first page of the paper. The index below is a list of the kinds of features you'll find in many newspapers.

Advice Columns Answers to letters from readers

Classified A section of ads bought by people who offer jobs, have things for sale or rent, and so on

Obituaries A list of people who have recently died

Index

Advice Columns	D2	Health/Science	D1-3
Arts	B8-9	Letters to the Editor	B11
Business	B7	Movie Times	B9
Classified	D4-12	Obituaries	B6
Comics	C6-7	Sports	C1-5
Crossword	C7	Television	C8
Editorials	B10	Weather	A8

Each section of a newspaper contains articles about the subject featured in that section. You might find articles about exercising or about discoveries in medicine on the *Health/Science* pages. What kind of article would you be likely to find under the heading *Arts*? You probably would find movie, theater, and book reviews. You might find an article about a young cartoonist from your town, or an article about a new play at the local theater.

Most daily newspapers are printed in sections. This newspaper index shows that the sections are labeled A, B, C, and D. The letters tell you the section of the newspaper where the feature is found. Notice that only the weather feature is listed in Section A. That's because Section A is the news section. A newspaper's index does not list news stories.

Many papers give summaries of the day's news stories on the front page. The summary helps you decide which stories you want to read. It also helps you quickly find a story. The index headings list the news by categories. Use the index shown to tell the section in which you would find an article about a new vaccine for measles discovered in France. In which section would you find an article about a lost dog in your town?

STORY SUMMARIES

World

A new supertrain runs in Japan.	A2
Elections are held in Spain.	A3

Nation

A cold wave freezes the Southeast.	A1
The cost of food climbs sharply.	A6

Local

A sixth-grader wins a medal.	B1
Road work slows traffic flow.	B2

Facts and Opinions in Newspapers

The main purpose of a newspaper is to report news. Reporters and editors try to make sure that a news story tells facts only. Here is a news article:

Warehouse Collapses in Fire

A fire that blazed for seven hours last night destroyed an old warehouse on Weston Road. Three firefighters escaped from the blaze just before the roof of the warehouse caved in. Two others were overcome by smoke and treated at the scene of the fire.

The fire chief, Paul Lee, said he did not know the cause of the fire. The fire department will begin its investigation today.

Although news stories tell only facts, newspapers also give opinions. You can find opinions in the movie, book, or theater reviews; advice columns; editorials; letters to the editor; and some feature articles.

The following article is an editorial. **Editorials** are written by newspaper editors. They tell the newspaper management's opinion.

Protect Our Firefighters

The recent fires in several empty warehouses on Weston Road are a danger to our firefighters. Let's not wait until one of them is killed or injured under a falling roof. The Town Council must take some action to prevent these fires. Tearing down the warehouses would be a good way to begin. Only direct action can protect those who must risk their lives every day.

Notice that an editorial states opinions based on facts. What is the editor's opinion of the empty warehouses? What does the editor think the Town Council should do about the warehouses?

The following article is a **book review**. A book review expresses an opinion.

The ABCs of Carpentry by Jane Anderson is a wonderful how-to guide for the beginning woodworker. In a clear, concise way, the author guides the reader through the step-by-step process of creating a finished piece of furniture. More than ten projects are discussed in great detail. This is certainly a book no amateur carpenter should be without.

How did the reviewer feel about the book? What words give clues to the writer's opinion?

The newspaper is a valuable tool. It can keep you up-to-date on what is going on in the world, in our country, and in your town. Learning how to use a newspaper will help you find exactly what you are looking for quickly and efficiently.

Computers are used today to solve many medical mysteries. How have computers changed Michela Alioto's life?

As you read, look for answers to the six basic news-gathering questions: Who? What? When? Where? Why? How?

Michela Alioto: Computer Teen

by Mard Naman

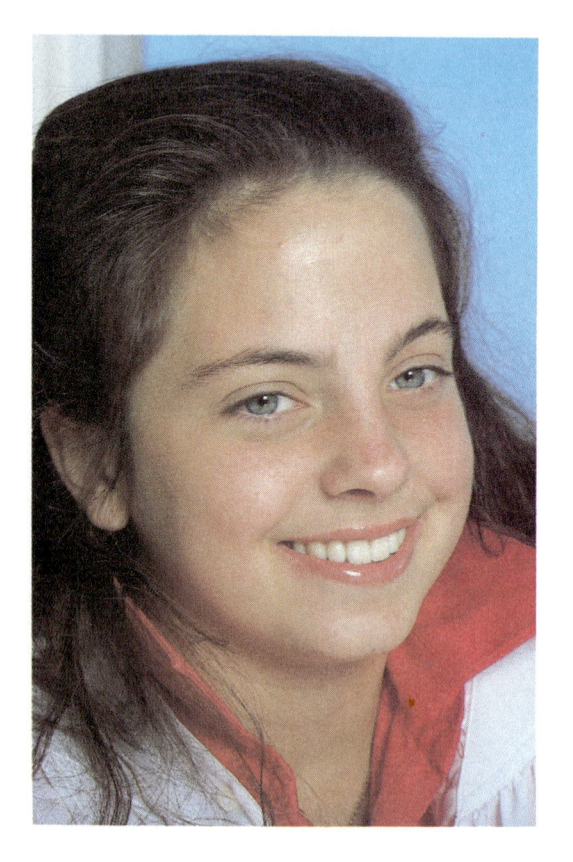

It took a tragedy for the Alioto family of San Francisco to find out how important home computers could be. In April 1981, Michela Alioto fell 30 feet from a ski lift. The accident left Michela—the granddaughter of former San Francisco Mayor Joseph L. Alioto — paralyzed from the waist down. She now lives mostly out of her wheelchair.

Before her accident, Michela had never really thought about computers. Now she thinks about them all the time. They not only help keep her healthy, they also hold the key to her future ability to walk. Michela's computer helps keep her leg muscles as toned as the leg muscles of any of her friends. Michela has been paralyzed for several years and one would expect her legs to look weak from lack of use. But her legs look perfectly normal. It soon becomes clear why she is in such good shape.

Twice a week, Michela rolls into a San Francisco orthopedic center for some computer-age exercising. She's assisted by a physical therapist, Stephanie Earle. Ms. Earle attaches three electrodes to each of Michela's legs. She then goes to the computer keyboard to type in directions. The computer asks which muscles are to be exercised and how much weight is to be lifted. Earle types in the answers. She also types in the range of movement for each leg and how fast the legs should move. The computer asks if it should begin the exercises. The therapist pushes one more button and Michela's legs begin to move.

First, there are stretch exercises. Then there are leg kicks. First the right leg moves, then the left . . . right leg, left leg . . . again and again and again. The computer counts off seventy-five repetitions. When the required number of kicks has been done, the computer plays a little victory march.

Michela's doctor, Robert Gordon,

The same computer Michela and her friends use to play video games also helps to exercise her legs.

lives on the same block as the Aliotos. They all began to learn about computers as a result of Michela's accident. Dr. Gordon and Michela's parents took a computer class together. They needed to know if computers could help with Michela's therapy.

Dr. Gordon gets very excited when he talks about computers. "We use the computer as a substitute for the small part of the brain that controls the muscles we want to exercise. Michela, like others we work with, has a normal brain and normal muscles. But no messages can be sent from brain to muscles across Michela's severed spinal cord, so we're bypassing it. We're substituting a mini-brain — the computer — which connects directly to the muscles."

When we move, the brain sends electrical messages in a specific order to specific muscles in the body. A computer can be programmed to do the same thing. It can send out bursts of electricity to make the right muscle move at the right time, just as the brain would.

The computer exercises are important for keeping Michela's body

Michela, helped by Stephanie Earle, exercises with the help of the computer.

healthy. They prevent the muscles from shrinking. If this happened, the bones would become so brittle they would break with almost no pressure. The computer exercises also build up the muscles and bones. It's as though Michela has actually been lifting weights or jogging.

Dr. Gordon says, "We're not only exercising the muscles, we're also exercising the heart and lungs. For people who have no use of their arms or legs, this would be impossible without the computer. The computer can make the muscles work together. The motion is surprisingly natural."

Dr. Gordon thinks that someday a computer can be programmed to help people walk. Of course, the number of muscles used to walk is much greater than the number of muscles used to do simple exercises. Michela now uses three electrodes on each leg for a leg kick. To walk, she would need about eighteen electrodes on each leg. Many scientists and doctors believe that computer-assisted walking may be possible within five to ten years.

At present, the best use of computers is to keep the muscles and bones strong. Says one worker in the field, "Computers help maintain healthy bodies between now and the time when we find a cure for spinal paralysis."

Michela waits for the day when she can walk again, but her life is far from dull. She goes to school and spends time with her friends. If you ask Michela what she can't do now that she did before her accident she'll say, "Nothing — except walk." Anyone who knows her says that she is a positive, independent person. Michele and Joseph Alioto, Michela's parents, bought her a car with hand controls so that she could get around on her own.

Michela has taken trips to Europe and even to the Far East. She was asked to represent American disabled youth at a conference held in Japan in the summer of 1985. She is active in other organizations, as well. She was the youngest person ever to speak before the National Council for the Disabled. She later became a member of its advisory board.

Michela and her family have high hopes for the future. Michela plans to go to college and get a law degree. Then she would like to go into politics. At the same time, Michela will continue to work with computers. Computers give Michela and her family their greatest hope. In their search, the computer has become like another member of the family.

Computer Screen Imagery

People communicate with computers through screens. The computer screen is a valuable tool. Scientists, engineers, artists, and even athletes use the images, or pictures, on computer screens in their work. These photographs show just some of the hundreds of uses of computer screens.

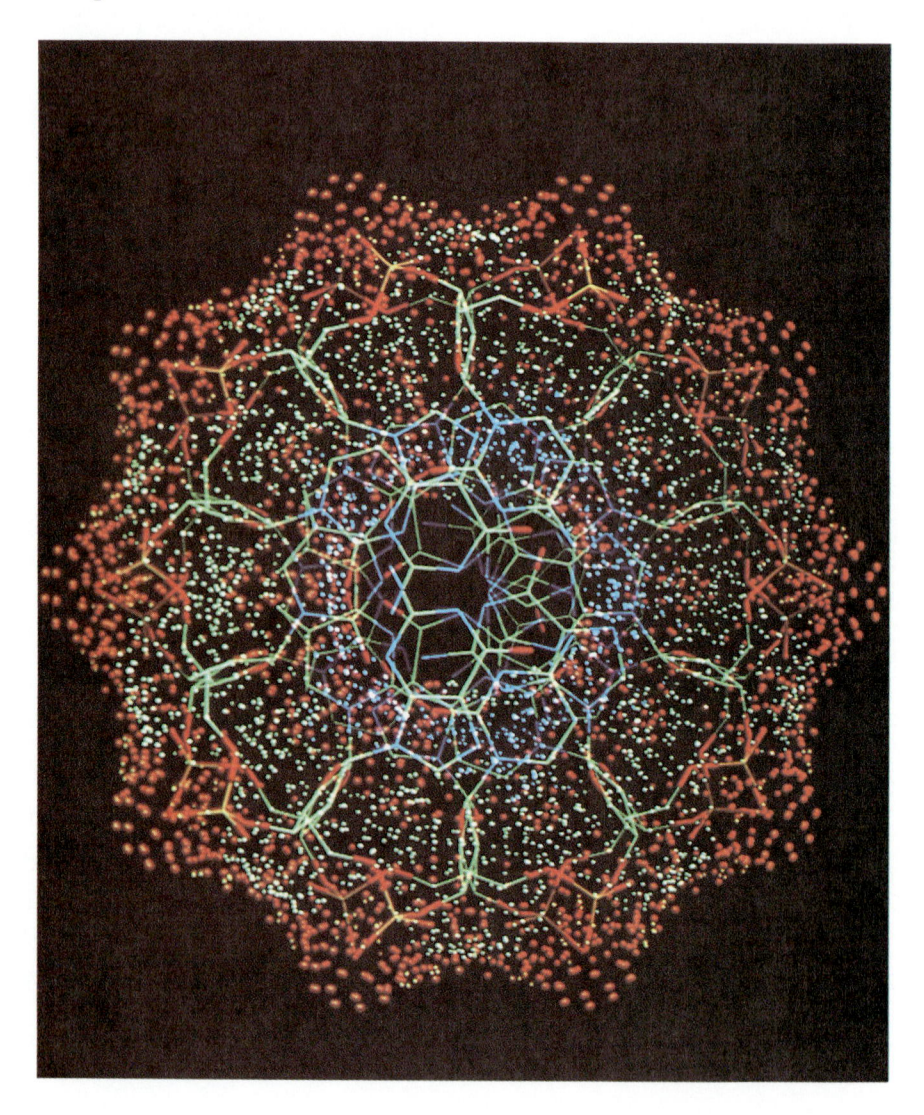

Computer image of a DNA molecule. We are looking up from within the molecule.

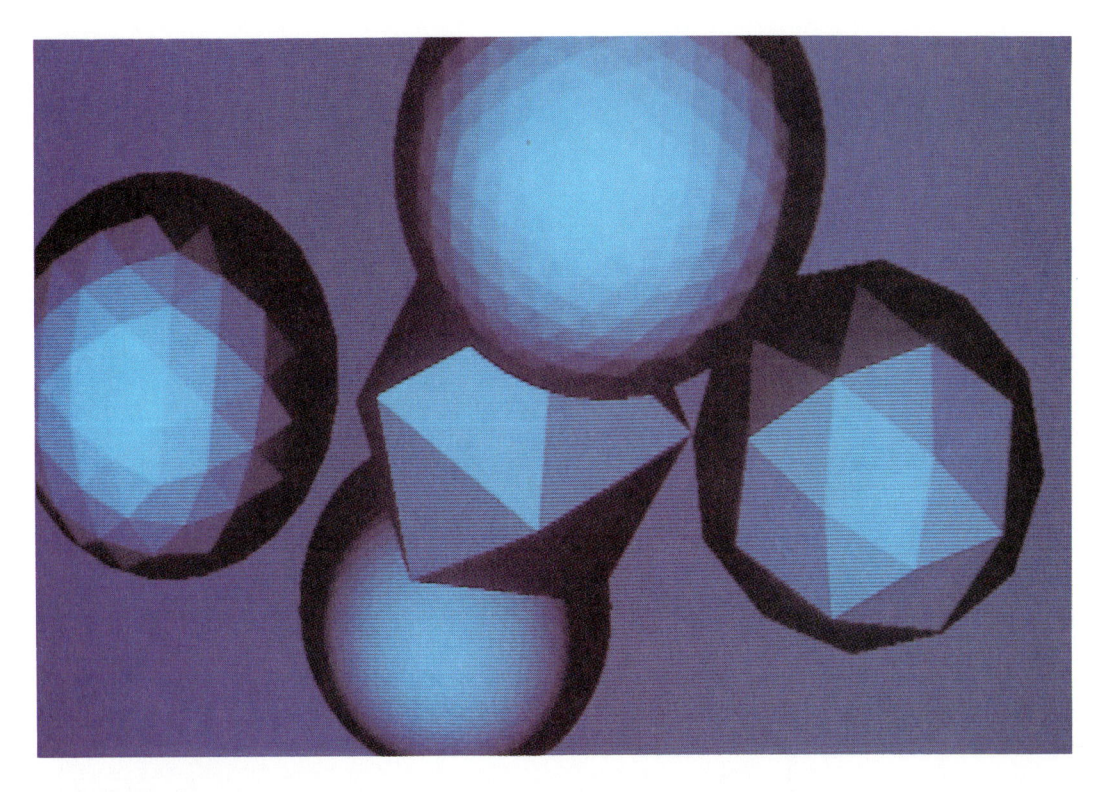

Geometric shapes created on the computer.

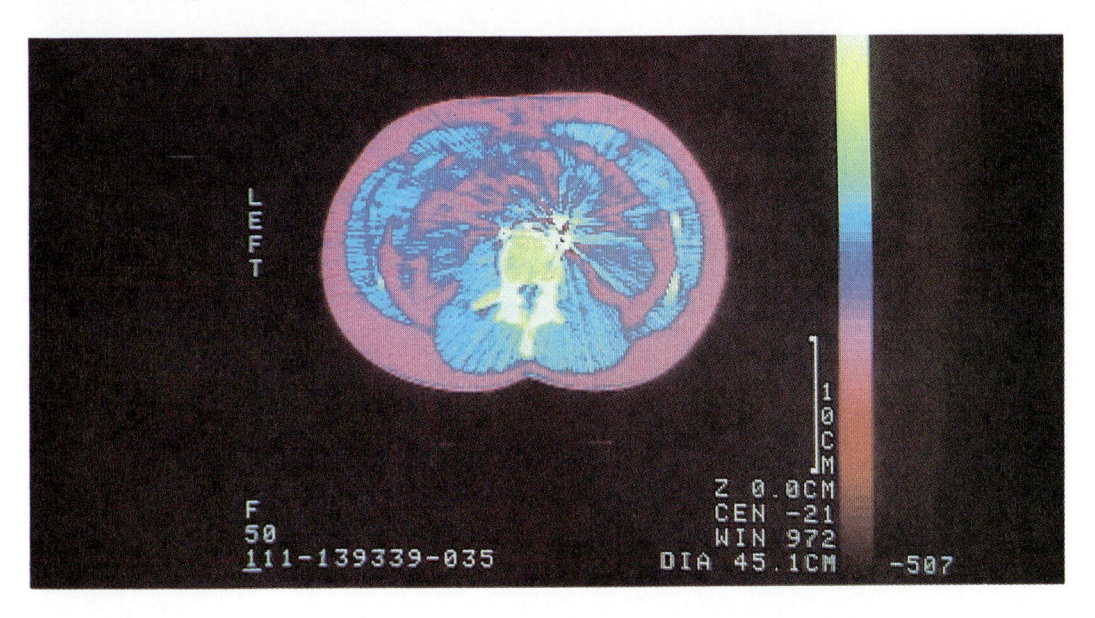

Medical doctors use computer technology to perform brain scans.

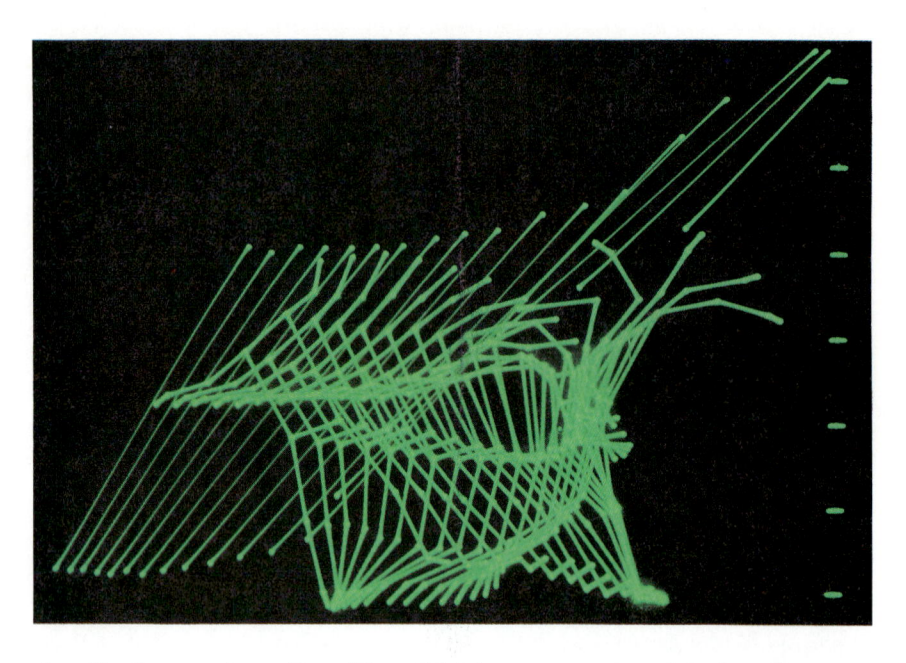

Javelin thrower in action. The athlete's movements, picked up by sensors attached to the body, are displayed on the computer screen. This allows the athlete to study and improve performance.

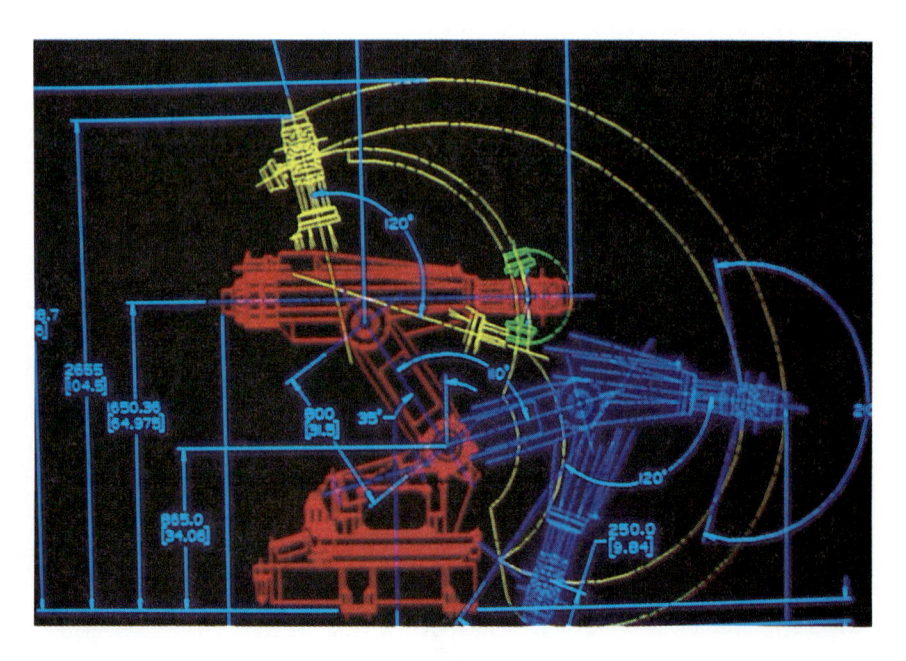

Designing a new robot arm for a factory. Computer graphics show engineers the kinds of movements that can be made by the robot arm.

Computer graphics. Computer graphics systems allow artists to create illustrations and even cartoons.

Discuss the Selection

1. How have computers changed Michela Alioto's life?
2. How did a computer serve as a substitute for the brain to control Michela's muscles?
3. What kind of person do you think Michela Alioto is? Explain your answer.
4. How might computers help Michela Alioto in the future?
5. Might computers someday be used to help paralyzed people walk? Find the part of the selection that answers this question.

Apply the Skills

A news story reports the important facts about a subject or event. A news story always contains answers to the six basic news-gathering questions: Who? What? Where? When? Why? How?

Some facts from "Michela Alioto: Computer Teen" are listed below. Each fact answers one of the six news-gathering questions. Identify which fact answers each question.

1. twice a week
2. Michela Alioto
3. leg muscles exercised by computer
4. a San Francisco orthopedic center
5. to give Michela better use of her legs
6. computer sends bursts of electricity to the muscles

Think and Write

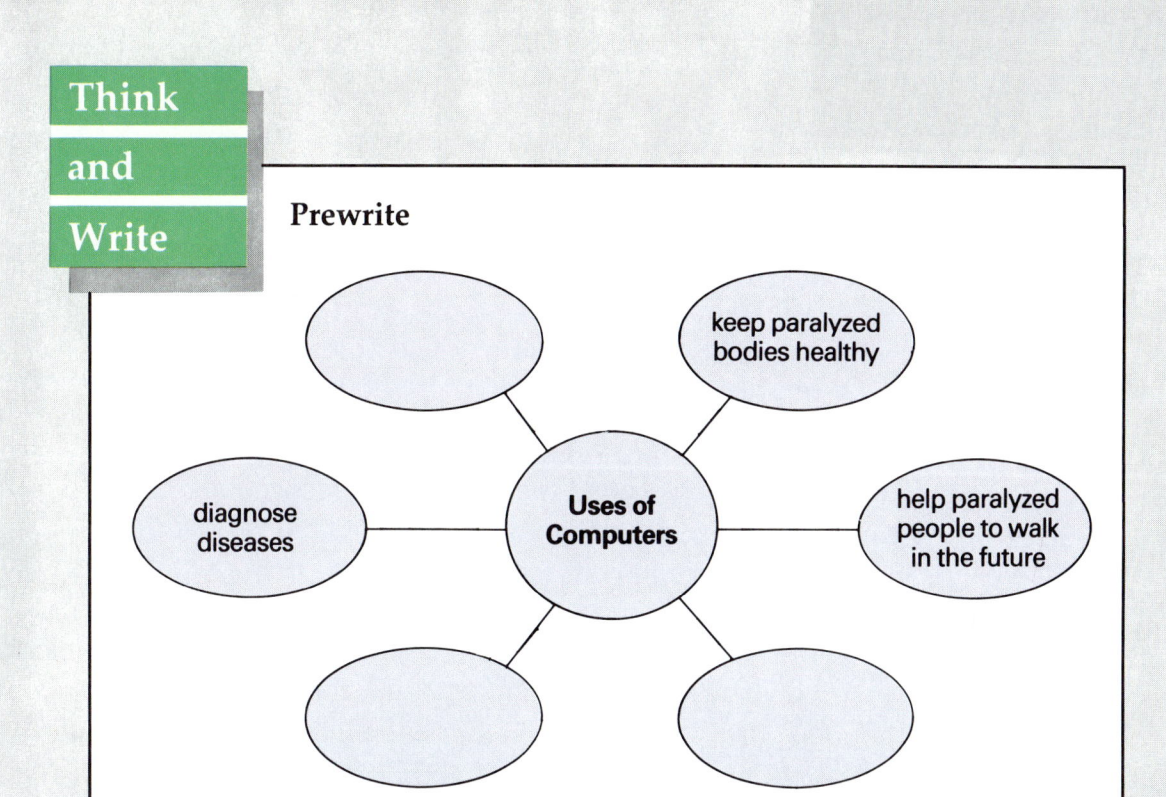

Prewrite

Ideaburst diagram with "Uses of Computers" in the center, surrounded by: "keep paralyzed bodies healthy", "help paralyzed people to walk in the future", "diagnose diseases", and three empty ovals.

The words in the center of this ideaburst, *Uses of Computers*, are a central idea. The phrases around them all relate to the central idea; they give some of the uses of computers. Copy the ideaburst. Use the selections "Michela Alioto: Computer Teen" and "Microchip: Small Wonder" to fill in the ideaburst with other uses of computers.

Compose

Write a paragraph describing the many uses of computers. You might begin with this topic sentence: *Computers are used for many things in today's world.* Follow this with supporting sentences explaining the uses named in your ideaburst.

Revise

Read your paragraph. Does each supporting sentence tell about the main idea? If not, revise your work.

Comprehension Study

Main Idea

The **topic** of a paragraph is what the paragraph is all about. A statement giving important general information about the topic is called the **main idea.** Recognizing the topic and the main idea of a paragraph will help you to understand and remember what you read.

Finding the Topic and the Main Idea

As you read the following paragraph, find the topic by asking yourself, "What is the one thing that all or most of the sentences in this paragraph tell about?" Find the main idea by asking yourself, "Which sentence in the paragraph makes an important general statement about the topic?"

Scientists are studying the ability of apes to use language as humans do. They train gorillas and chimpanzees to recognize geometric symbols and to understand spoken words. Because apes are physically incapable of producing the sounds of human speech, scientists teach them how to communicate with symbols or sign language.

Which of the following is the topic of the paragraph?

1. how apes communicate

2. apes and human language

3. apes and geometric symbols

All of the sentences in the paragraph are about apes and human language; therefore, choice 2 is the topic of the paragraph. Choice 1 is not the topic because it is too broad. The paragraph deals only with how apes communicate using human language. Choice 3 is not the topic because it is too narrow. The paragraph deals with more than apes and geometric symbols.

Once you have found the topic, look for a sentence that gives a general statement about the topic. In the paragraph about the apes, the main idea is stated in the first sentence: *Scientists are studying the ability of apes to use language as humans do.*

Notice that the main idea sums up important information in the paragraph in a general statement. The other sentences give examples of and details about the main idea.

The main idea of a paragraph is not always stated in the first sentence. It may be given in the last sentence or in one of the middle sentences. Which sentence in the following paragraph states the main idea?

> One ape signaled a request for a kitten. Another frequently communicated a wish to watch television. Still another asked for forgiveness after he had been punished for misbehaving. The range of the apes' communications often surprised scientists.

Did you find the main idea? It is given in the last sentence: *The range of the apes' communications often surprised scientists.* The other three sentences are examples of the apes' communications.

Main Ideas Stated in Two Sentences

Sometimes two sentences are equally important parts of the main idea of a paragraph. When this happens, you have to combine the information from both sentences to come up with the main idea.

As you read the following paragraph, look for the main idea in more than one sentence.

> You probably think of gold as having a yellowish color and being stacked in piles of bullion. Yellow is only one of a variety of colors in which gold is found. Some gold appears white because it is mixed with silver and platinum impurities. Some gold appears red because it contains copper. Iron in gold causes it to look green. Gold also appears in different forms. You might be familiar with gold bars and coins of the finished product. But some gold is found in rocks that are called nuggets, and some is found as flecks in streams.

The topic of this paragraph is gold, because all of the sentences tell about this precious metal. Which of the following sentences best states the main idea of the paragraph?

1. Yellow is only one of a variety of colors in which gold is found.
2. Gold appears in different forms.
3. Gold is found in different colors and forms.

The first sentence states part of the main idea, but it doesn't mention any information given in the second part of the paragraph. Sentence 2 mentions part of the main idea too, but it doesn't mention anything about the colors of gold. Sentence 3, then, states the complete main idea.

Unstated Main Ideas

In some paragraphs, the main idea is not directly stated, so you have to figure it out for yourself. First, decide what the topic is, and then decide what all the sentences tell you about the topic. When you add up all these clues, you will be able to state the main idea in a sentence.

The main idea of the following paragraph is not stated. Use the sentences to figure out the topic, and then see if you can state the main idea in your own words. Remember, the main idea should state important general information about the topic of the paragraph.

> Before the time of refrigeration, people preserved food by drying it in the sun or smoking it over fires. This protected it from spoiling. The heat removed moisture from the food, which in turn prevented the growth of harmful bacteria. Salting and pickling were two other methods used to prevent bacteria from growing and so preserve food.

Before stating a paragraph's main idea, determine the topic by asking yourself, "What is the paragraph about?" Preserving food is the topic because all the sentences say something about it. How would you state the main idea of the paragraph in a sentence? Here is an example: *Long ago, people found several ways to preserve food.* Notice that the main idea sums up the details in the paragraph.

243

Textbook Application: Main Idea in Health

Finding topics and main ideas in your textbooks is a good way to study. The main idea may be a sentence at the beginning, in the middle, or at the end of a paragraph. Sometimes it is divided between two sentences. At other times the main idea is not stated at all. You have to figure it out.

As you read this selection from a health textbook, use the sidenotes to help you find topics and main ideas.

The main idea is the first sentence in this paragraph.

Which sentence contains the main idea in this paragraph?

What is the topic of this paragraph? The main idea is not stated in one sentence. Think of a sentence that states the main idea.

What Happens When You Sleep?

When you fall asleep, many parts of your body change. Your muscles relax. Your heartbeat and your breathing slow down. Your senses are dulled.

This slowdown in the way your body works saves energy. Your body uses the extra energy to repair itself. It builds new cells to replace worn-out ones. Sleep gets your body ready for the next day's activities.

What Happens When You Dream?

When you first fall asleep, you go into a dreamless sleep. After about 90 minutes, your eyes begin to move around very quickly under your closed eyelids. You are in a period of **REM, or rapid eye movement, sleep**. REM sleep is sleep with dreams. You usually have four or five periods of REM sleep a night. Periods of REM sleep last from 5 to 15 minutes. Between these periods you go back into dreamless sleep.

During REM sleep most of your muscles stay relaxed. But your **brain waves** show that your mind is very active. Brain waves are tiny waves of energy that your brain produces as it works.

Scientists do not know why people dream, but they have several ideas. One idea is that dreams are made up of bits of memory in no special order. When you dream, your brain may be sorting through these bits of memory and deciding which ones to store.

Another idea is that dreams contain thoughts and feelings that you do not want to think about when you are awake. They may include problems you do not want to face, secret fears, or wishes for things you cannot have. In your dreams, you go through these thoughts and feelings. You may dream that your problems have been solved or that some wishes have come true. For example, you may be worried about a test the next day. You may dream about taking the test and doing well on it.

Scientists have learned that everyone needs to dream. If people do not dream enough one night, they make up for it by dreaming more the next night.

—*HBJ Health,*
Harcourt Brace Jovanovich

> What two sentences contain the main idea in this paragraph?

> Notice that the main idea is the first sentence. The rest of the paragraph tells about one of the ideas scientists have about dreams.

> What is the topic of this paragraph?

Looking for topics and main ideas can help you understand what you read. It will also help you to remember what you study.

Some mysteries will probably never be solved. Is this mysterious story behind one of the greatest art thefts in history true? Judge for yourself.

As you read, remember to think about the selection's main idea.

True or False? Amazing Art Forgeries

by Ann Waldron

The Mona Lisa is, without a doubt, the most famous painting in the world. Everyone knows what it looks like, and everyone agrees it's the masterpiece of Leonardo da Vinci, who painted it around 1503 in Florence. The Mona Lisa found its way into the art collection of the French kings and from there it went to the Louvre, the French national museum of art.

Who would dare try to forge the Mona Lisa? Many people have copied it. At least eighty fairly good copies of the painting exist around the world, all of them known to museum officials. How many more there are is anybody's guess. It is known that several forgeries of the Mona Lisa were sold to Americans during the early part of this century. It is known that the Mona Lisa was stolen in August 1911, recovered in Italy, and returned to its place in the Louvre two years later.

There is a story that ties the theft and the forgeries together, creating one of the cleverest art capers of all time.

Leonardo da Vinci's "Mona Lisa"

    It begins with Eduardo Valfierno, who called himself the Marques de Valfierno, and a Frenchman named Yves Chaudron. Chaudron had worked as a restorer, repairing old and damaged paintings. He was not a creative painter, but he was an excellent copyist. He moved into forging.
    The story goes that the Marques and Chaudron sold forged paintings to rich Americans and gave them forged

247

documents proving their authenticity. This began to seem like small potatoes after a while, and the Marques began to dream of the crime of a lifetime — no, the crime of a century.

"Could you sell somebody a forged Mona Lisa?" he wondered. "Would anybody buy a forged Mona Lisa and believe he had the real thing?"

The Marques claimed he did sell somebody a copy of the Mona Lisa, telling his American client that the picture hanging in the Louvre was a copy that had been substituted. (French newspapers inadvertently helped him along by running stories about a rumor that a copy had been substituted for the real Mona Lisa.)

The Marques decided that collectors were so greedy that it didn't matter what you told them, as long as they thought they were getting a bargain. In fact, he decided that he and Chaudron would sell not one but several Mona Lisas. He had Chaudron make six copies. Artists were free to go to the Louvre and copy any painting, as long as they didn't make the copy the same size as the original. Chaudron made one small copy of the Mona Lisa in the Louvre and went home to his studio and turned out six copies the same size as the real Mona Lisa. He sawed up an antique Italian bed to get old walnut to paint on. As Chaudron finished the copies, the Marques shipped each one to a partner in America. He had no trouble getting through customs — there is no law against selling copies, as long as you don't claim they are the originals.

Now came the hard part. The Marques had six Mona Lisas safely in America. If buyers thought they were getting the real thing, they would pay a fortune for it. But to make buyers think they were getting the original, it was necessary for the real Mona Lisa to be stolen from the Louvre. The theft of the Mona Lisa would cause a worldwide sensation, and would help persuade gullible buyers that they had a chance of a lifetime — a chance to own the world's most famous masterpiece. Each buyer, of course, would be sworn to secrecy. No one would be likely to disclose the purchase in any case.

But how on earth could you steal the Mona Lisa? It was France's most valuable painting, France's celebrated treasure. It was kept under glass in the guarded room at the Louvre. You *couldn't* steal the Mona Lisa.

Oh, yes, you could, the Marques said. He located a man named Vincenzo Peruggia, who had once worked in the Louvre. Peruggia knew all the nooks and crannies of the museum, the back stairways and cleaning closets and courtyards and side entrances.

Peruggia, who had been present not long before when the painting had been taken down to get a new frame, said the picture was too heavy for one man. Leonardo painted the Mona Lisa on a heavy wooden panel an inch and a half thick, 20 by 30 inches, which weighed 18 pounds. Furthermore, it was braced against warping by a heavy cradle of ebony, which weighed 110 pounds. The Renaissance frame weighed 25 pounds and the shadow box within which the picture was placed weighed 15 pounds. The heavy plate glass in the shadow box weighed 25 pounds. All together, the Mona Lisa weighed 220 pounds. The Marques and Chaudron would have to be there to help.

The Marques knew that workers at the Louvre wore white workshirts. He figured that three men in white workshirts could wander about the museum without arousing suspicion.

The Louvre closed at 4:00 P.M. on Sunday afternoons and remained closed all day Monday in those days. The Marques, Peruggia, and Chaudron went into the museum on Sunday afternoon, August 20, 1911, dressed like ordinary visitors. When closing time came, Peruggia showed them a tiny room where cleaning materials were stored, and here they spent the night. The next morning, before the staff came to work, they put on their white workshirts and headed for the Salon Carrée, where the Mona Lisa hung. They had to wait for some workers in the next gallery to leave but, as soon as they had gone, Peruggia and the others lifted the Mona Lisa down from the wall.

The three men carried it through the corridors, prepared to say, if anybody stopped them to ask what they were doing, that they were taking the Mona Lisa to the room where the museum photographers worked on Monday mornings.

In fact, at 8:35 on Monday morning, one of the head workers at the Louvre passed through the Salon Carrée and noticed that the Mona Lisa was gone. He assumed it was in the photographers' room.

The three men took the painting through several galleries and turned sharply into a door that led to a cramped, winding stairway. They went down, stopped on the stairs, and struggled to get the painting out of the heavy cradle, shadow box, and frame. At last, they had the panel out. They left the frame and cradle at the bottom of the stairway, and raced for the door that led to the courtyard and escape.

Here the men had their first real scare. They couldn't get the door open. It was locked and they had no key. In desperation, Peruggia whipped out a screwdriver and took off the doorknob so he could get at the latch mechanism. Just then someone started down the stairway.

The men jumped back from the door. Perruggia hid the Mona Lisa under his shirt and waited as footsteps descended. The man coming down the stairs was the chief plumber for the Louvre.

"I can't get the door open because the knob is missing," complained Peruggia, who knew the plumber.

The plumber obligingly opened the door for them with his own key and ushered them outside. He did not notice the frame, cradle, and shadow box lying by the stairs.

The three men walked across the courtyard, through a gate to the street, and disappeared. The porter at the gate was dozing under his red umbrella and did not see them.

Nobody noticed that the Mona Lisa was missing until Tuesday morning when an artist came in to copy it and couldn't find it. At first, the guards thought the painting was still at the photographers', but soon they realized it was really missing.

They found the frame and cradle at the foot of the stairs and noticed the doorknob was missing. The police were called. All of France went into shock.

"Unimaginable!" trumpeted the headline in *Le Matin*, a newspaper.

The country became hysterical over the theft. Every visitor to Paris had wanted to see the towers of Notre Dame and the smile of Mona Lisa, and now Mona Lisa was gone. The picture "belongs to humanity," wrote one reporter, "and France, the faithless guardian, cannot hold up her head."

"To steal the crown jewels is a crime," said another, "but to steal a masterpiece is a sacrilege."

The police could find no leads, and as their helplessness became more apparent, the public became more upset.

Meanwhile, Peruggia, Chaudron, and the Marques separated. The Marques is supposed to have headed for America to pick up the six fake Mona Lisas, which he then sold for fancy prices to millionaires who believed they were getting the real Mona Lisa, stolen from the Louvre just for them.

How much of all this is fact, and how much is fiction? It's a known fact that the Mona Lisa was stolen on August 21, 1911, by men who apparently had spent the night in the museum. The cradle, frame, and shadow box were indeed found at the foot of a stairway, and it's true that the porter at the gate was sleeping.

But did the Marques plan the daring robbery so that he could sell six forged Mona Lisas and make a fortune? The answer is veiled in mystery. We do know that the real Mona Lisa turned up in Italy in 1913. In the autumn of that year an art dealer from Florence named Alfredo Geri put an advertisement in several Italian newspapers saying that he was in the market for all kinds of art objects. He got a letter from a man who signed his name "Leonardo Vincenzo." He said he had the real Mona Lisa and would like to sell it to Geri because it really belonged "to Italy."

Geri thought the man probably had one of the many existing copies of the Mona Lisa. He wrote to him and said that he did not buy copies, but that he would pay any price for the true Mona Lisa.

On December 10, a man came to Geri's gallery who said that he was "Leonardo Vincenzo." He announced he had brought the Mona Lisa from Paris. The original was in his hotel room and Geri could examine it. He wanted half a million lire, and a guarantee that it would always hang in the Uffizi Gallery in Florence.

Geri told Vincenzo he'd come to the hotel the next day, but that he had to bring the director of the Uffizi Gallery, Giovanni Poggi, with him.

Geri notified Poggi and the police, who surrounded Vincenzo's hotel the next day. When Geri and Poggi got to the room, Vincenzo was waiting for them, smiling and confident. He opened a small, unpainted wooden trunk, and pulled out a pair of shoes, a shirt, and some woolen underwear. He then lifted out a false bottom, and there was the Mona Lisa herself, back home in Florence.

Poggi examined the painting and recognized the Louvre's seal and number on its back. He told Vincenzo that he wanted to take the Mona Lisa to the Uffizi to compare it with other works of da Vinci's and he calmly picked up the masterpiece and left the room.

Inch-by-inch inspection with photographs proved that this was indeed the real Mona Lisa. Vincenzo was happy. He talked freely to the police. He was, of course, Vincenzo Peruggia. And he had indeed worked at the Louvre. He said he had decided to steal the Mona Lisa and take it back to Italy. He believed that Napoleon had stolen it from Italy, and he wanted to return the painting to its supposed rightful home.

The Italian and the French people were both ecstatic that the Mona Lisa had been found. The painting stayed in Florence on display at the Uffizi for a few months, and then went to Rome and Milan and finally back to Paris and the Louvre.

Peruggia was tried in Florence in June, convicted, and sentenced to a year and fifteen days in prison. Geri received a small reward.

Discuss the Selection

1. Is this mysterious story of the theft of the Mona Lisa true? Explain your opinion.
2. Why was the theft of the Mona Lisa a great shock to many people?
3. As you read, did you expect that the three art thieves would be caught? Why or why not?
4. How did Giovanni Poggi identify the painting he saw in 1913 as the real Mona Lisa?
5. When did you first learn that the story of the theft and forgeries would be part fact and part fiction? Find that part of the story.

Apply the Skills

The main ideas in a selection are always supported by details. The details supply examples of and information about the main idea.

Each of the following sentences is either a main idea or a supporting detail. After reading each sentence, identify it as either a main idea or a supporting detail.

1. Peruggia remembered a tiny room in the Louvre where three men could hide overnight.
2. While the Mona Lisa itself weighed only 18 pounds, its Renaissance frame weighed 25 pounds.
3. The Mona Lisa was too heavy for one person to carry.
4. Vincenzo Peruggia knew enough about the Louvre to make the theft successful.

Think and Write

Prewrite

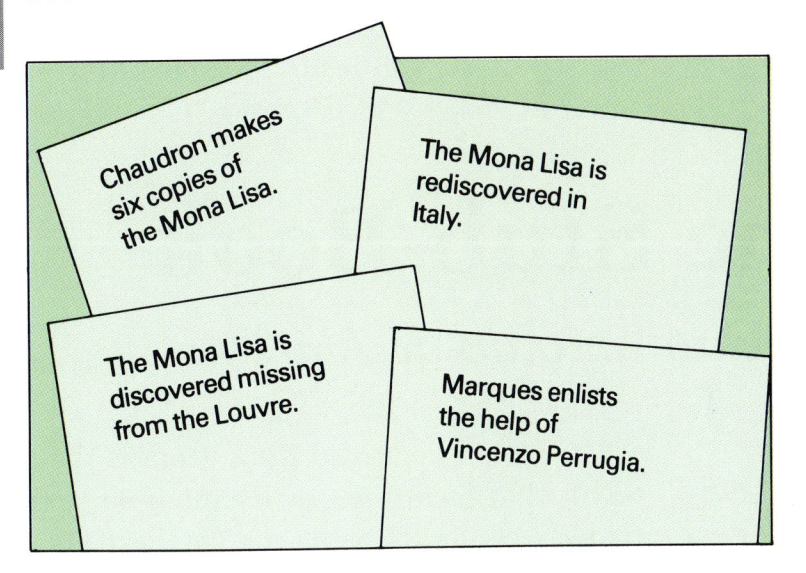

- Chaudron makes six copies of the Mona Lisa.
- The Mona Lisa is rediscovered in Italy.
- The Mona Lisa is discovered missing from the Louvre.
- Marques enlists the help of Vincenzo Perrugia.

Each note card above describes a major event in "True or False? Amazing Art Forgeries." Make three note cards and on them describe three other events from the story. Use your notes and those above to make a list of the story events in the correct time order.

Compose

Write a summary of the major events in "True or False? Amazing Art Forgeries." Use your list of story events. Begin sentences with time-signaling words, such as *first, next, then, following that*, and *finally* to tie your summary together. Begin with a topic sentence that expresses the main idea.

Revise

Read your summary. Have you included all of the story events? Have you used time-signaling words? If not, revise your work.

> *Not all mysteries are solved by professional detectives. When tío ("uncle") Buscabeatas's pumpkins are stolen, he not only has to find them, he has to undeniably prove that they are his. How can he do this?*
>
> *As you read, think about the main idea of this storyteller's tale.*

The Stub-Book

by Pedro Antonio de Alarcón

The action begins in Rota. Rota is the smallest of the towns that form the great semicircle of the bay of Cádiz. Despite its being the smallest, the grand duke of Osuna preferred it. There he built his famous castle, which I could describe stone by stone. But now we are dealing with neither castles nor dukes. We are dealing with the fields around Rota, and with a most humble gardener, whom we shall call tío Buscabeatas, though this was not his true name.

From the fertile fields of Rota, particularly its gardens, come the fruits and vegetables that fill the markets of Huelva and Seville. The quality of its tomatoes and pumpkins is such that in Andalusia the Roteños are always referred to as pumpkin- and tomato-growers, titles which they accept with pride.

And, indeed, they have reason to be proud. The soil of Rota produces so much. That is to say, the soil of the gardens, which produces three or four crops a year, is not soil, but sand, pure and clean, cast up by the ocean, blown by the furious west winds and scattered over the entire region of Rota.

But the ingratitude of nature is more than made up for by the constant diligence of humans. I have never seen, nor do I believe there is in all the world, any farmer who works as hard as the Roteño. Not even a tiny stream runs through those fields. No matter! The pumpkin-grower has made many wells from which he draws the water that is the lifeblood of his vegetables. The tomato-grower spends half his life seeking substances which may be used as fertilizer. And when he has both elements, water and fertilizer, the gardener of Rota begins to fertilize his tiny plots of ground. In each of them he sows a tomato seed, or a pumpkin pip, which he then waters by hand, like a person who gives a child a drink.

From then until harvest time, he attends each day, one by one, to the plants which grow there. He treats them with a love only comparable to that of parents of children. One day he applies to such a plant a bit of fertilizer. On another day he pours a pitcherful of water. Today he kills the insects which are eating up the leaves. Tomorrow he covers with reeds and dry leaves those which cannot bear the rays of the sun, or those which are too exposed to the sea winds. One day he counts the stalks, the flowers, and even the fruits of the earliest ripeners. Another day, he talks to them, pets them, kisses them, blesses them, and even gives them names in order to tell them apart and individualize them in his mind.

Without exaggerating, it is now a proverb (and I have often heard it repeated in Rota) that the gardener of the region touches with his own hands at least forty times a day every tomato plant growing in his garden. This explains why the gardeners of that region get to be so bent over that their knees almost touch their chins.

Well, now, tío Buscabeatas was one of those gardeners. He had begun to stoop at the time of the event which I am about to relate. He was already sixty years old . . . and had spent forty of them tilling a garden near the shore.

That year he had grown some pumpkins that were already beginning to turn yellow, which meant it was the month of June. Tío Buscabeatas knew them perfectly by color, shape, and even by name, especially the forty fattest and yellowest, which were already saying "cook me."

"Soon we shall have to part," he said tenderly.

Finally, one afternoon he made up his mind and pronounced the dreadful sentence.

"Tomorrow," he said, "I shall cut these forty and take them to the market at Cádiz. Happy the people who eat them!" Then he returned home and spent the night as anxiously as a parent whose child is to be married the following day.

"My poor pumpkins!" he would sigh, unable to sleep. But then he thought about it and concluded by saying, "What can I do but sell them? For that I raised them! They will be worth at least fifteen duros!"

Imagine, then, how great was his astonishment, his fury and despair when he went to the garden the next morning. He found that, during the night, he had been robbed of his forty pumpkins. He began calculating coldly. He knew that his pumpkins could not be in Rota, where it would be impossible to sell them without the risk of his recognizing them.

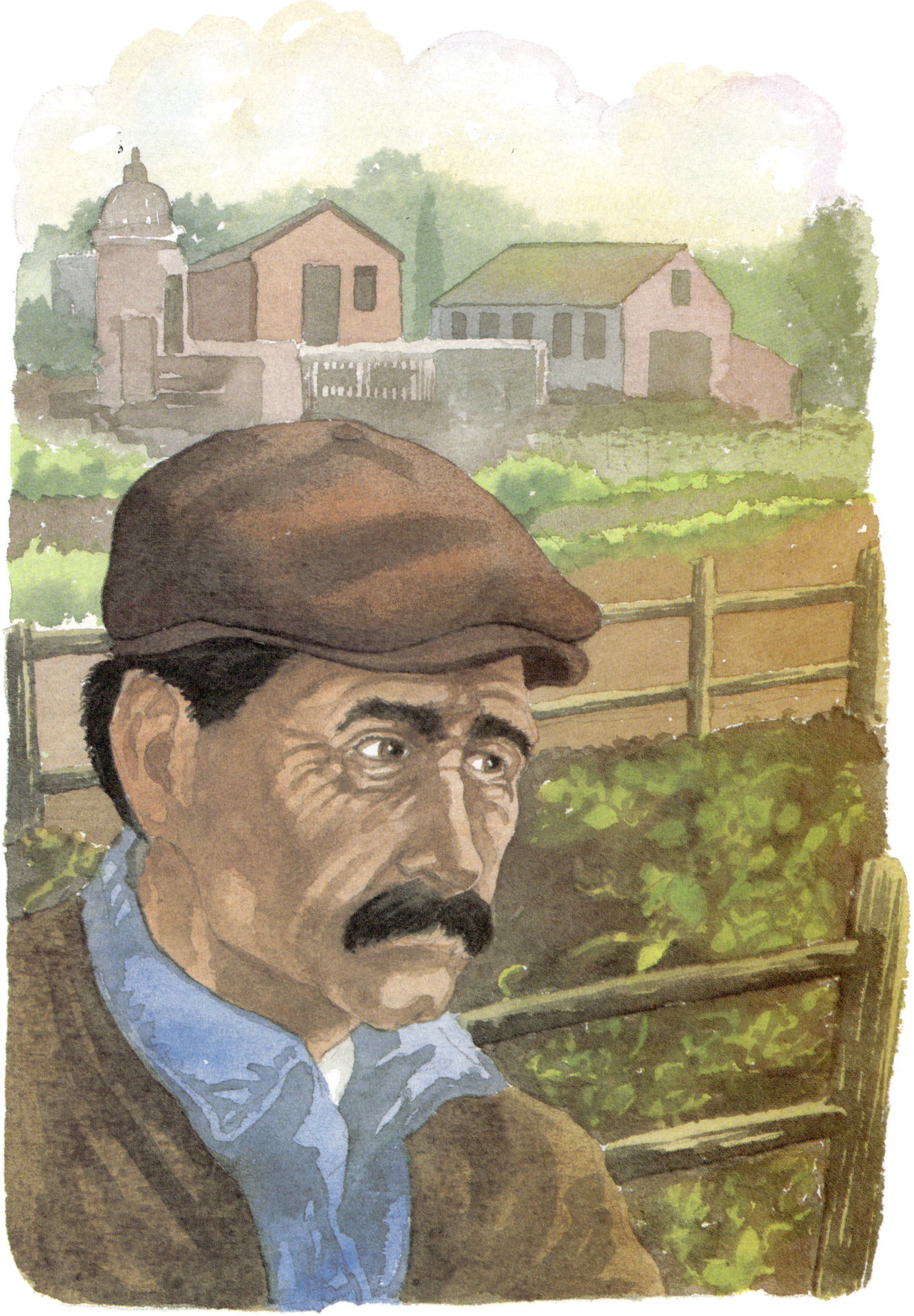

"They must be in Cádiz. I can almost see them!" he suddenly said to himself. "The thief who stole them from me last night, at nine or ten o'clock, escaped on the freight boat. . . . I'll leave for Cádiz this morning on the hour boat. In Cádiz, I'll catch the thief and recover my pumpkins!"

So saying, he stayed for some twenty minutes more at the scene of the catastrophe. He counted the pumpkins that were missing, and at about eight o'clock, he left for the wharf.

Now the hour boat was ready to leave. It was a small boat which carries passengers to Cádiz every morning at nine o'clock, just as the freight boat leaves every night at twelve, laden with fruit and vegetables.

The former is called the hour boat because in an hour, and sometimes less, it cruises the three leagues separating Rota from Cádiz.

It was, then, ten-thirty in the morning when tío Buscabeatas stopped before a vegetable stand in the Cádiz market. It was then he said to a police officer who was nearby: "These are my pumpkins! Arrest that man!" and pointed to the vendor.

"Arrest *me*?" cried the vendor, astonished and angered. "These pumpkins are mine. I bought them."

"Tell that to the judge," answered tío Buscabeatas.

"No, I won't"

"Yes, you will!"

"You old thief!"

"You old scoundrel!"

"Keep a civil tongue. People shouldn't insult each other like that," said the officer very calmly, giving them each a push.

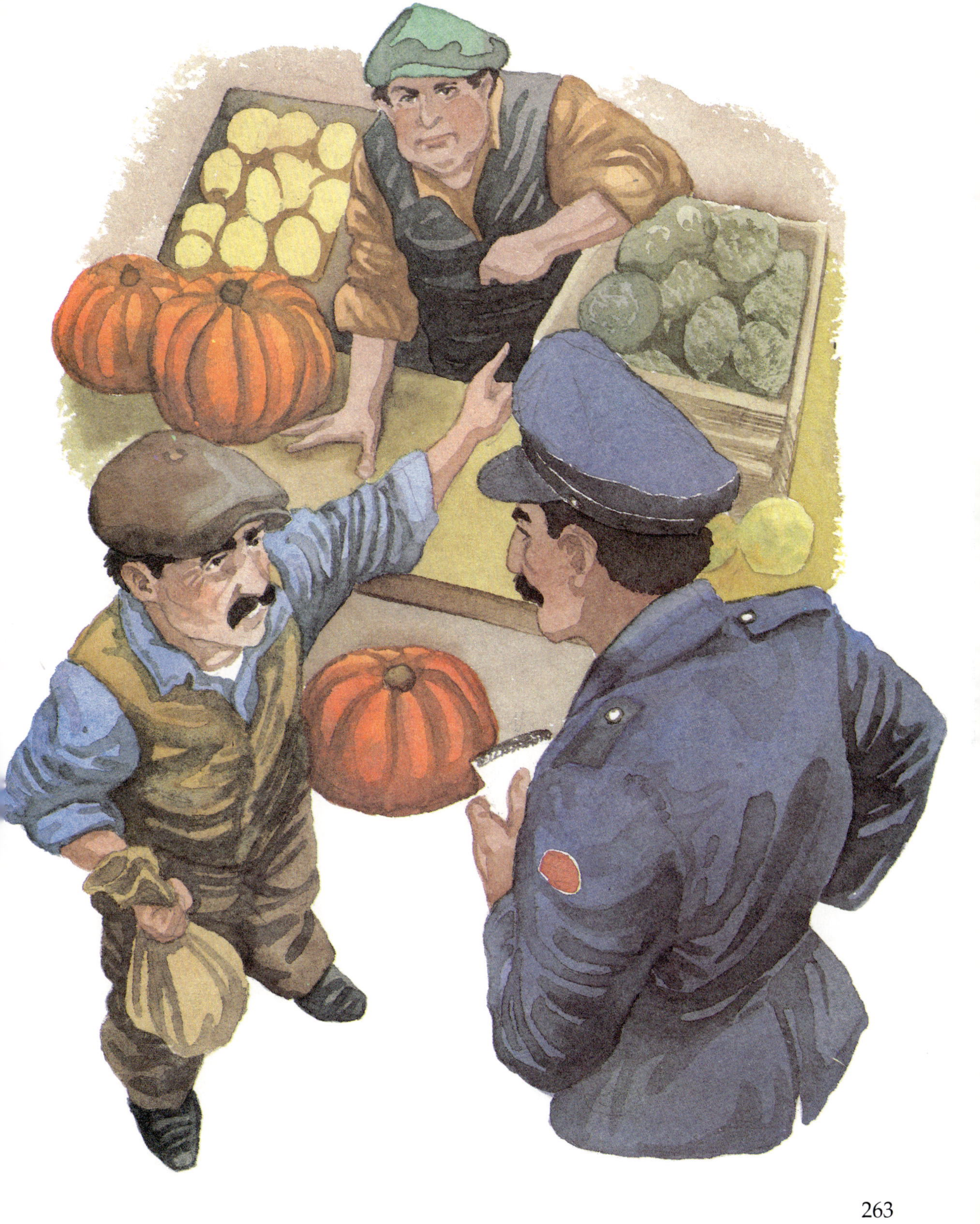

By this time several people had gathered, among them the inspector of public markets. When the officer had informed the inspector of all that was going on, the inspector asked the vendor: "From whom did you buy these pumpkins?"

"From tío Fulano, near Rota," answered the vendor.

"He would be the one," cried tío Buscabeatas. "When his own garden, which is very poor, yields next to nothing, he robs from his neighbors'."

"But, supposing your forty pumpkins were stolen last night," said the inspector, addressing the gardener, "how do you know that these, and not some others, are yours?"

"Well," replied tío Buscabeatas, "because I know them as well as you know your children, if you have any. Don't you see that I raised them? Look here, this one's name is Fatty, this one, Plumpy Cheeks, this one, Pot Belly, and this one, Manuela, because it reminds me so much of my youngest daughter."

And the poor old man started weeping like a child.

"That is all very well," said the inspector. "But it is not enough for the law that you recognize your pumpkins. You must identify them with undeniable proof. Gentlemen, this is no laughing matter. I am a lawyer!"

"Then you'll soon see me prove to everyone's satisfaction, without stirring from this spot, that these pumpkins were raised in my garden," said tío Buscabeatas.

Throwing on the ground a sack he was holding in his hand, he kneeled, and quietly began to untie it. The curiosity of those around him was overwhelming.

"What's he going to pull out of there?" they wondered.

At the same time another person came to see what was going on in that group. When the vendor saw the newcomer, he exclaimed:

"I'm glad you have come, tío Fulano. This man says that the pumpkins you sold me last night were stolen. Answer . . ."

The newcomer turned yellower than wax, and tried to escape, but the others prevented him. The inspector himself ordered him to stay.

As for tío Buscabeatas, he had already faced the supposed thief, saying:

"Now you will see something good!"

Tío Fulano recovered his presence of mind. He replied: "You are the one who should be careful about what you say, because if you don't prove your accusation, and I know you can't, you will go to jail. Those pumpkins were mine. I raised them in my garden, like all the others I brought to Cádiz this year. And no one could prove I didn't."

"Now you shall see!" repeated tío Buscabeatas, as he finished untying the sack.

A multitude of green stems rolled on the ground. The old gardener, seated on his heels, addressed the gathering as follows:

"Friends, have you never paid taxes? And haven't you seen that green book the tax-collector has, from which he cuts receipts? He always leaves a stub in the book so he can prove afterwards whether the receipt is counterfeit or not."

"What you are talking about is called the stub-book," said the inspector gravely.

"Well, that's what I have here: the stub-book of my garden; that is, the stems to which these pumpkins were attached before this thief stole them from me. Look here. This stem belongs to this pumpkin. No one can deny it. This other one . . . now you're getting the idea . . . belongs to this one . . . exactly! And this one to that one . . . that one, to that one over there . . ."

And as he spoke, he fitted the stems to the pumpkins, one by one. The spectators were amazed that the stems really fitted the pumpkins exactly. Delighted by such strange proof, they all began to help tío Buscabeatas.

"He's right! He's right! No doubt about it. Look. This one belongs here . . . That one goes there . . . That one there belongs to this one . . . This one goes there . . ."

The laughter of the men and women mingled with the catcalls of the children, the joyous and triumphant tears of the old gardener, and the shoves the police officers were giving the convicted thief.

Needless to say, besides going to jail, the thief was compelled to return to the vendor the fifteen duros he had received. The thief handed the money to tío Buscabeatas, who left for Rota very pleased with himself, saying, on his way home:

"How beautiful they looked in the market! I should have brought back one to eat tonight and kept the seeds."

Discuss the Selection

1. How did tío Buscabeatas undeniably prove that the stolen pumpkins were his?
2. How did tío Buscabeatas first show that he knew his pumpkins as well as he knew his children?
3. Do you think the inspector was justified in demanding undeniable proof that the pumpkins belonged to tío Buscabeatas? Give reasons for your answer.
4. Why did tío Buscabeatas compare his proof to a tax collector's stub-book?
5. The storyteller claimed that the gardeners of Rota get so bent over that their knees almost touch their chins. Find the part of the story that explains why this is so.

Apply the Skills

The main ideas in a selection are always supported by details. In "The Stub-Book," the storyteller presents this main idea: *The gardeners of Rota treat their crops with a love only comparable to that of parents of children.*

Find details in the selection that support this main idea.

Think and Write

Prewrite

Object	Descriptive Words	Rhyming Words
pumpkin	round	ground sound mound
bird	fly	sky high
	wings	sings
tree	green	scene
	tall	

A thing of beauty often inspires a person to write a poem. Tío Buscabeatas thought his pumpkins were beautiful. The chart above might be called a "Poet's Idea Chart." Copy the chart. Then write words in the last column that rhyme with the descriptive words. Add other objects and descriptive words of your own.

Compose

Write a short poem using rhyming words from your chart. Tío Buscabeatas might have written a poem like this:

> See the pumpkins
> On the ground,
> Growing so beautifully
> Orange and round.

Revise

Read your poem again. Do some of the words rhyme? Is there rhythm to the poem? Can you add other words to make it more descriptive? If so, revise it.

Literature Study

Plot

If you ask someone "What happens in that story?" you are asking for the story plot. A **plot** is made up of individual events that, when added to one another, form a story. The events are like the links of a chain. Each link is connected to the next until the chain is complete. In the same way, each story event is connected to the next until the plot is complete.

A good plot usually presents a story problem and a solution to the problem. The plot unfolds by following these steps:

1. The problem is presented.
2. Events occur in which attempts to solve the problem are made.
3. A climax takes place.
4. A solution is presented.

Problem

A story plot usually begins by describing the **problem**. It quickly tells what is going on to gain the reader's interest. In describing the problem, the plot introduces the main characters and makes the setting obvious. In "The Mystery of the Seven Wrong Clocks," the problem—who murdered Fritz Sandoz—was presented immediately. The main character, Peter Perkins, quickly set out to gather clues. Think about "Incognito Mosquito. . . ." What problem was presented as the story opened?

Events

After the problem has been stated, the plot describes the **events** as the main characters attempt to solve the problem. These attempts build the dramatic conflict of the story. They create tension and suspense that hold the reader's interest. In Incognito Mosquito's encounter with The Mis-cast Dancer, the accident with the glue was one of the events that led to the eventual solution of the problem. What events took place as Peter Perkins attempted to solve the mystery of Fritz Sandoz's murder?

Climax

Events in a story build until they reach a climax. A **climax** is the most exciting part of a story's plot. Many readers consider the climax to be the most enjoyable part of a story. When Incognito Mosquito finally found the clue he needed, the climax of the story was reached.

Solution

Most plots end with a solution. A plot's **solution** is an explanation of the way the problems or complications in the plot are resolved. The solution always follows the climax. The solution in "The Mystery of the Seven Wrong Clocks" explained how Perkins used the clock clues to solve the mystery, gave the clue that Perkins missed, and told what happened to the murderer. As you read the story that follows, "The Adventure of the Blue Carbuncle," decide what makes its solution unusual.

Think about all the parts of a plot—the problem, events, climax, and solution—as you read the next story. An awareness of each of these will help you to better understand and enjoy what you read.

Author Profile

Sir Arthur Conan Doyle

Sir Arthur Conan Doyle was born in Edinburgh, Scotland, in 1859. When he was seventeen years old, he entered Edinburgh Medical College to study medicine. There he met a professor named Joseph Bell. On hospital rounds, Bell amused his students in a most unusual way. He told a patient's history before the patient said a single word! What first seemed like a mysterious trick was nothing of the kind. Bell carefully noted the exact appearance of the patient, down to the smallest details. He looked at marks on the hands, stains on the clothing, and the jewelry worn. From these observations, he made deductions—intelligent guesses—about the life and work of the patient.

For example, Bell observed a tattoo on a man's wrist and a certain way of walking and made the deduction that the man had been a sailor. Time and again, Professor Bell's deductions were correct.

To Doyle, who loved mysteries, Bell's methods were fascinating. He had always enjoyed detective stories and decided to write one. His main character would be a new kind of detective who would solve mysteries as Bell did. Not surprisingly, Doyle's detective looked like Bell—thin, with sharp features. He acted like Bell, too. Doyle's detective observed the smallest details and, with extraordinary cleverness, solved his cases and captured his criminals. The detective is Mr. Sherlock Holmes. In Doyle's first Sherlock Holmes story, he introduced Dr. Watson, Holmes's sidekick. Watson is much like Arthur Conan Doyle himself — easygoing, a writer and a doctor. He admires Holmes, just as Doyle admired his professor.

In 1886, Doyle began to write stories at his office while waiting for the few patients who came to see him. He finished the first of many stories, "A Study in Scarlet," in just two months. So began a new career for Dr. Arthur Conan Doyle who, in years to come, would be knighted.

Sir Arthur Conan Doyle died in 1930. In all, he wrote sixty Sherlock Holmes stories. The earliest was set in the time of gaslight and horse-drawn carriages; the later ones in the time of airplanes and telephones. Holmes has been kept alive for a hundred years by readers around the globe. It seems a safe deduction that Sherlock Holmes, the world's most famous detective, will go on living for many years to come.

Sherlock Holmes's keen powers of observation note even the smallest of details. What details does the famous detective notice that solve this mystery?

As you read, think about each part of the plot in this mystery story.

The Adventure of the Blue Carbuncle

by Sir Arthur Conan Doyle
adapted by Catherine Edwards Sadler

I called upon my good friend, Mr. Sherlock Holmes, on the second morning after Christmas. I wanted to wish him the compliments of the season. I found Holmes lounging on the sofa. A huge pile of newspapers lay beside him. Next to the couch was a wooden chair. On its back hung a rather worn black felt hat and on its seat was a large magnifying glass . . . a tool which suggested Holmes had been closely examining the hat.

"You are engaged," I said. "Perhaps I interrupt you . . ."

"Not at all! I am glad to have a friend with whom I can discuss my results. The matter is a small one," Holmes said, pointing to the hat. "But it is interesting in its own way."

I seated myself in his armchair and warmed my hands before his crackling fire. Outside a sharp frost had set in and the windows were thick with icicles.

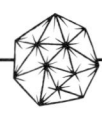

"I suppose," I remarked, "this hat has some deadly story linked to it. Is it the one clue that will guide you to solve some mystery and punish some criminal?"

"No, no! No crime," answered Sherlock Holmes, laughing. "Do you know Peterson, the commissionaire?"

"Yes," I replied.

"He found this hat. Its owner is unknown. It arrived on Christmas morning in the company of a good fat goose—which is now roasting in front of Peterson's fire. The facts are these: About four o'clock on Christmas morning, Peterson was walking home. The street was well-lit by a nearby gaslight. A tallish man was walking in front of him. He carried a white goose over his shoulder. At the corner stood a small gang of young ruffians. As the stranger approached, they began to bother him. One knocked off his hat. In defense, the stranger swung his walking stick over his head. The stick accidentally broke a shop window behind him. Peterson rushed forward to protect the stranger, but the man was shocked at having broken the window. On seeing an official-looking person rush toward him, he dropped his goose and took to his heels. The gang also fled. Peterson was left with this battered hat and a beautiful Christmas goose."

"Why didn't he return them to their rightful owner?" I asked.

"My dear fellow, there lies the problem. A small card was attached to the bird's left leg. On it was printed: FOR MRS. HENRY BAKER. The initials H. B. are written on the lining of the hat. But there are thousands of Bakers and hundreds of Henry Bakers in London. It is not easy to return property to any one of them."

"What did Peterson do?"

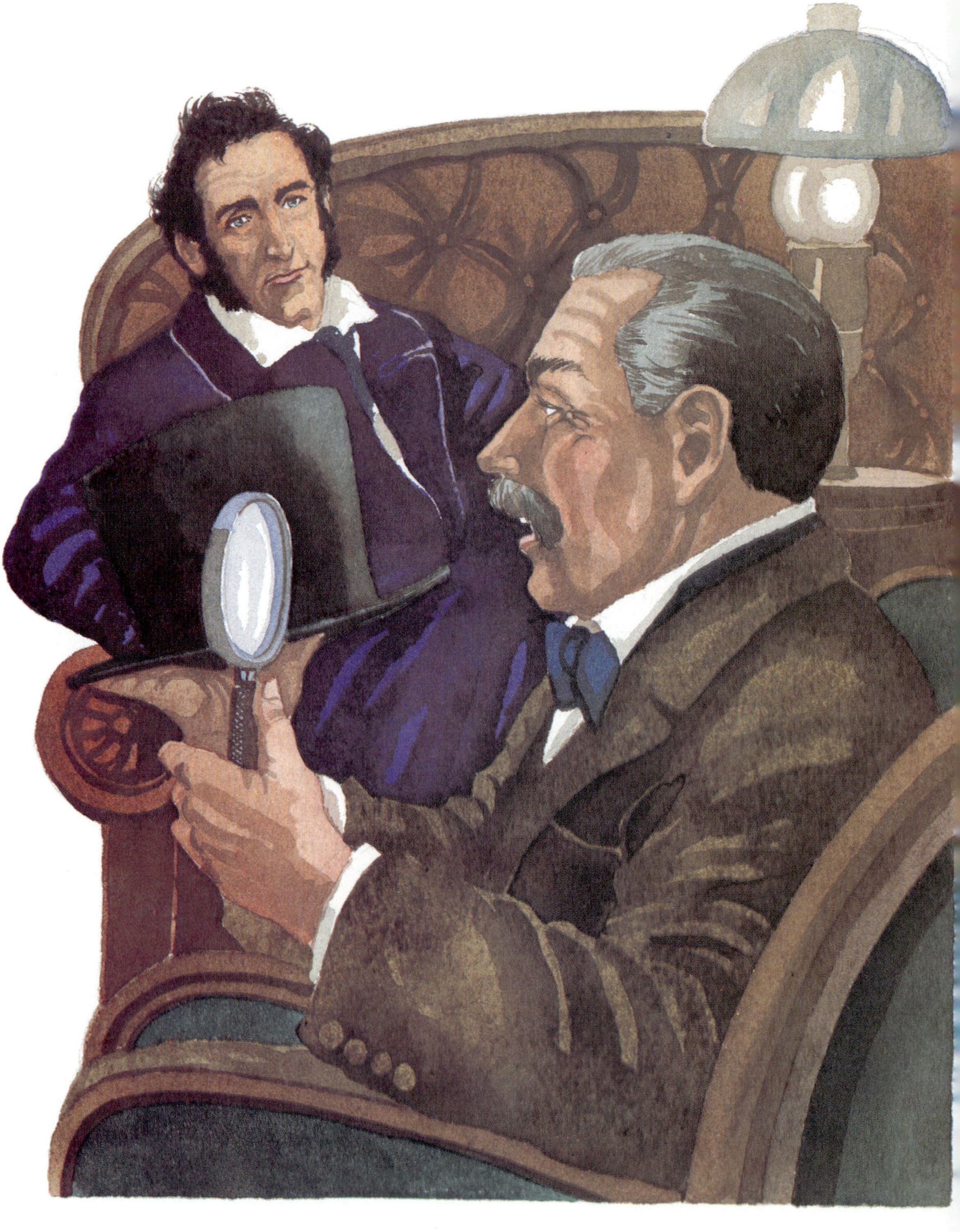

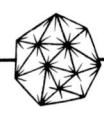

"He brought the hat and the goose to me. He knew such problems are of interest to me. We kept the goose till this morning when we realized, despite the slight frost, it should be eaten without unnecessary delay. Its finder took it home while I have the hat of the unknown gentleman who lost his Christmas dinner."

"Did he not advertise?"

"No."

"Then what clues could you have to his identity?"

"Only as much as we can deduce," answered Holmes.

"From his hat?" I asked.

"Precisely."

"But you are surely joking. What can you gather from this old battered felt hat?"

"Here is my lens," Holmes said as he handed me his magnifying glass. "You know my methods. What can you learn from this hat about its owner?"

I took the tattered hat in my hands and turned it over. It was a very ordinary round felt hat—very much the worse for wear. There was no maker's name. However, the ititials H. B. were written on one side. It was cracked, exceedingly dusty, and spotted in several places. Ink had been smeared on some of the spots to hide them.

"I can see nothing out of the ordinary," I said and handed Holmes back the hat.

"On the contrary, Watson. You can see everything. However, you fail to reason from what you see."

"Then tell me what you can find out from this hat," I responded.

Sherlock Holmes picked up the hat and gazed at it intensely. "The owner was highly intelligent. He was fairly well-to-do within the last three years and has fallen on bad times. However, he has not lost his self-respect. These are the most obvious facts that can be deduced from his hat."

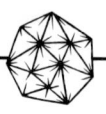

"You are certainly joking, Holmes!" I exclaimed.

"Not in the least. Can it be that even after I have given you these facts you cannot see how I deduced them?"

"I must confess I cannot follow you. For example, how did you deduce that this man was intelligent?"

Holmes placed the hat on his head. It came right down over his forehead and settled on the bridge of his nose.

"It is a question of cubic capacity," he said. "A man with so large a brain must have something in it."

"The decline of his fortune then?" I asked.

"This hat is three years old. These flat brims were popular then. It is a hat of the very best quality. Look at the band of ribbed silk and the excellent lining. This man could afford to buy an expensive hat three years ago. However, he has had no new hat since. His fortunes have assuredly gone down. But, he has tried to conceal some of the stains with ink. He has certainly not lost his pride."

"Your deductions are remarkable," I said. "But you said no crime has been committed and no harm done. It seems a waste of your energy."

Holmes had just opened his mouth to answer, when the door was flung open. Peterson, the commissionaire, rushed into the room. His cheeks were flushed and he seemed dazed.

"The goose, Mr. Holmes! The goose, sir!" he gasped.

"What of it?" Holmes asked. "Has it returned to life and flapped off through the kitchen window?"

"See here, sir! See what my wife found in its belly." He held out an open hand. A small but brilliant blue stone dazzled in its palm.

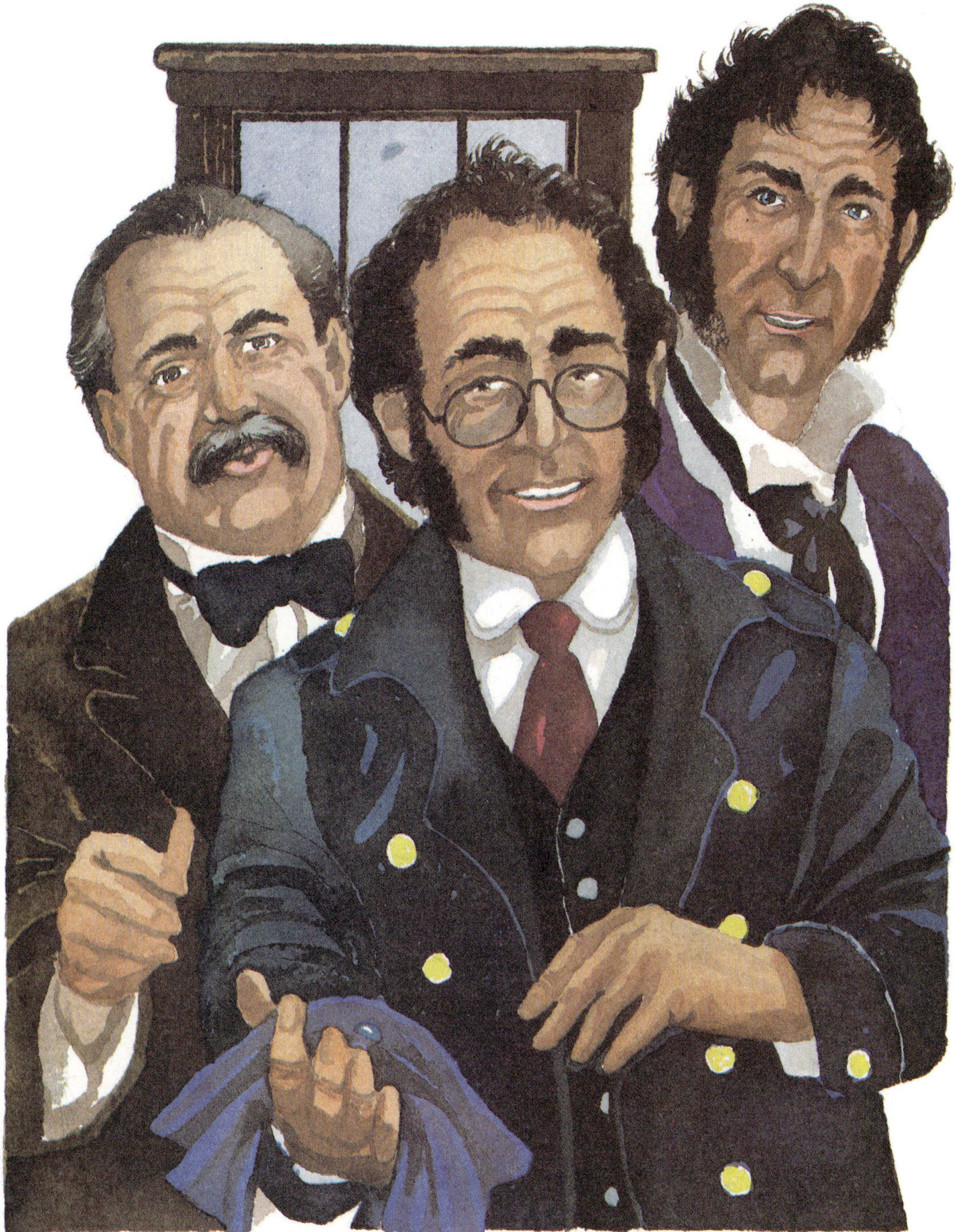

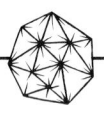

Sherlock Holmes sat up with a whistle. "By Jove, Peterson!" he exclaimed. "This is a treasure! Do you know what you have there?"

"A diamond, sir! A precious stone! It cuts into glass as though through putty."

"It's more than a precious stone. It is *the* precious stone!"

"Not the Countess of Morcar's blue carbuncle?" I exclaimed.

"Precisely so. I ought to know its size and shape," said Holmes. "I have read about it every day in the *Times*. The stone is absolutely unique. Its value can only be guessed at. The reward of one thousand pounds is certainly not a twentieth its market price."

"A thousand pounds!" gasped the commissionaire. He plumped himself down into a chair and stared at us in disbelief.

"It was lost, if I remember correctly, at the Hotel Cosmopolitan," I said.

"On the twenty-second of December, just five days ago," said Holmes. "John Horner, a plumber, was charged with stealing it from the Countess's jewel case." Holmes began to rummage through his pile of newspapers. At last he found the page he was looking for. He smoothed it out, doubled it over, and read the following paragraph:

Hotel Cosmopolitan Jewel Robbery

John Horner, 26, plumber, was charged with the robbery of the Countess of Morcar's valuable gem known as the Blue Carbuncle. The hotel manager, Mr. James Ryder, stated that he had taken Horner up to the Countess's room to mend the bathroom grate. He remained with Horner for some time, but was finally called away. On returning, he found that Horner had disappeared. The bureau had been forced open and the jewel case lay empty on the dressing table. Ryder instantly gave the alarm. The Countess's maid, Miss Catherine Cusack, heard Ryder's cry. She rushed into the room and found matters exactly as described by the hotel manager. Horner was found that same evening. The stone was neither on his person nor in his rooms. Since he had been convicted of a similar crime once before, he was arrested. Proceedings were started against him immediately. The accused man protested his innocence.

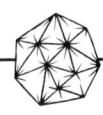

"Hum!" said Holmes. "We must now figure out the sequence of events that lead a precious stone from a countess's jewel case to the belly of a Christmas goose! You see, Watson, our little deductions suddenly take on meaning. Here is the stone. The stone came from the goose . . . and the goose came from Mr. Henry Baker. We must now find him and learn what part he played in this mystery. To do this, we must try the simplest means first . . . an advertisement in the evening newspapers. If this fails, I shall have to resort to other methods."

"What will you say?" I asked.

"Give me a pencil and that slip of paper. Now then:

Found: A goose and a black felt hat. Mr. Henry Baker can have the same by applying at 6:30 this evening at 221B Baker Street.

"I believe that will do. Peterson, please run down to the advertising agency and have this printed in the evening papers. I shall keep the stone here and shall drop the

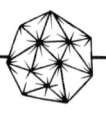

Countess a note telling her that we have found it. On your way back buy a goose. We must have one to give to Mr. Baker in place of the one your family is devouring right now!"

That evening at half-past six I returned to Baker Street. Holmes and I had agreed to have dinner together after our visitor left. As I approached the house I saw a tall man waiting outside. Just as I arrived the door was opened. We were both shown up to Sherlock Holmes's rooms.

"Ah, Watson, you have come at the right time," said Holmes. He turned to the tall man, "Mr. Henry Baker, I believe. Pray take this chair by the fire." He handed the man the hat and added, "Is this your hat, Mr. Baker?"

"Yes, sir," replied Baker. He was a large man with rounded shoulders, a massive head, and a broad, intelligent face. His black frock coat was buttoned high in front with the collar turned up and no sign of either cuff or shirt.

"Why didn't you advertise your loss?" Holmes asked.

Our visitor gave a rather shamefaced laugh.

"Shillings have not been as plentiful with me as they once were," he remarked. "I assumed the gang of ruffians carried off both my hat and the bird. I did not care to spend money in a hopeless attempt to recover them."

"Naturally. By the way, about the bird—we were compelled to eat it."

"To eat it!" exclaimed our visitor. He half rose from his chair in agitation.

"Yes, it would have been no use to anyone had we not done so. But I presume this other goose on the sideboard will do. It is about the same weight and perfectly fresh."

"Oh, certainly, certainly!" answered Mr. Baker with a sigh of relief.

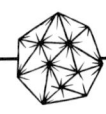

"Of course, we still have the feathers, legs, belly and so on of your own bird. So if you wish . . ."

"They might be useful to me as relics of my adventure," said Baker, "but beyond that I can hardly see what use they would be."

Holmes glanced sharply across at me. He shrugged.

"There is your hat and there is your bird. By the way," Holmes said, "would it bore you to tell me where you got the other one from? I am somewhat of a fowl fancier and I have seldom seen a better-grown goose."

"Certainly, sir. A number of my friends and I often visit the Alpha Inn near the museum. This year our good host, Mr. Windigate, started a goose club. We were to pay a few pennies each week and in exchange receive a goose at Christmas. I paid my weekly pennies and was taking home the bird the other night. You know what followed." Mr. Henry Baker took up his bird and hat, thanked us, and departed.

"So much for Mr. Henry Baker," said Holmes. "It is quite certain that he knows nothing about the matter. Shall we turn our dinner into a late supper and follow up our clue while it is hot?"

"By all means!" I agreed enthusiastically.

We bundled up and went outdoors. It was a bitter night and the breath of passersby hung in the air like smoke. Our footsteps rang out crisply as we walked. In a quarter of an hour we were at the Alpha Inn. Holmes immediately ordered two glasses of cider from the ruddy-faced landlord.

"Your cider should be excellent if it is as good as your geese!" Holmes told the landlord.

"My geese!" exclaimed the landlord, Windigate.

"Yes. I was speaking only half an hour ago to Mr. Henry

Baker. He is a member of your goose club."

"Ah yes, I see. But they weren't my geese."

"Indeed!" said Holmes. "Whose then?"

"Well, I got the two dozen from a salesman in Covent Garden Market."

"I know some of them!" exclaimed Holmes. "Which salesman was it?"

"Breckinridge is his name."

"Ah! I don't know him. Well, here's to your good health and to the prosperity of your inn." Holmes drank his cider, rose from his seat, and motioned for me to follow. In a moment we were standing outside once again.

"Now for Mr. Breckinridge," Holmes said. "Remember,

Watson, a man may get seven years imprisonment if we cannot prove his innocence. Our only clue is a Christmas goose that somehow had a gem in its belly. Our inquiry may lead to Horner's guilt, but we must follow it through to the bitter end."

By the time we reached Covent Garden Market it was near closing time. There were still many people milling about. One of the largest stalls bore the name of Breckinridge. Beneath the sign stood the man himself. He had a rather sharp face and trim side-whiskers and was helping a boy shut up the shutters.

"Sold out of geese, I see," Holmes commented, pointing at the bare slabs of marble.

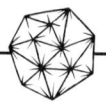

"Let you have five hundred tomorrow morning," muttered Breckinridge.

"That's no good," Holmes answered.

"Well, there are still some at the next stall," replied the salesman.

"Ah, but I was recommended to you."

"Who by?" he asked.

"The landlord of the Alpha."

"Ah yes, I sent him a couple of dozen," Breckinridge answered.

"Fine birds they were too," Holmes replied. "Where did you get them from?"

To my surprise the question provoked a burst of anger from the salesman.

"What are you driving at?" he asked. "Let's have it straight now."

"It is straight enough," said Holmes. "I'd like to know who sold you the geese which you sold to Alpha."

"Well, I shan't tell you!" responded Breckinridge.

"Oh! It is a matter of no importance. But I don't know why you should be so hot over such a small thing."

"Hot! You'd be hot, if you were as pestered as I am. When I pay good money for a good article that should be an end to the business. But it's 'Where are the geese?' and 'What will you take for the geese?' and 'Who did you sell the geese to?' One would think they were the only geese in the world to hear the fuss that is made over them."

"Well, I have no connection with any other people," Holmes said carelessly. "But I bet five pounds that the bird I ate was country bred."

"Well then, you've lost your money. It was town bred," snapped the salesman.

"It was nothing of the kind!" insisted Holmes.

"I say it was!"

"I don't believe it."

"Do you think you know more about birds than I do?" asked Breckinridge. "I've been handling them since I was a child. I tell you all the birds that went to the Alpha were town bred."

"Will you bet then?" prodded Holmes.

"It's merely taking your money, for I know I am right. But I'll bet just to teach you not to be so stubborn."

The salesman chuckled grimly. "Bring me my books, Bill," he ordered.

The boy brought back a small ledger and a large greasy one. He placed them both on a slab of marble beneath a hanging lamp.

"You see this little book," said Breckinridge. "It contains a list of the people from whom I buy. Here on this page are the country folk and the numbers after their names are where their accounts are in the big ledger. You see this other page in red ink? Well, this is a list of my town suppliers. Now, look at the third name. Just read it out to me."

"Mrs. Oakshott, 117 Brixton Road—page 249," read Holmes.

"Quite so. Now turn to page 249 in the large ledger." Holmes turned to that page. On it was written: "Mrs. Oakshott, 117 Brixton Road, egg and poultry supplier."

"Now what is the last entry?" asked the salesman.

"December 22, twenty-four geese."

"Quite so. There you are . . . and underneath?"

"Sold to Mr. Windigate of the Alpha."

"What have you to say now?" asked Breckinridge triumphantly.

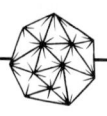

Holmes looked deeply upset. He drew a coin out of his pocket and threw it down onto the slab. Then he turned away in disgust. A few yards off he stopped under a lamppost and laughed in a hearty, noiseless fashion. "Well, Watson," he said to me. "I fancy we are nearing the end of our quest. The only question that remains is whether we should go on to this Mrs. Oakshott's tonight or tomorrow. It is clear there are others who are anxious about the matter, and I should . . ."

Just then a commotion broke out at the stall we had just left.

"I've had enough of you and your geese!" Mr. Breckinridge was shouting at a cringing man. "If you come pestering me anymore with your silly talk I'll set the dog on you. You bring Mrs. Oakshott here and I'll answer her, but what have you to do with it? Did I buy the geese off you?"

"No, but one of them was mine just the same," whined the little man.

"Well, then ask Mrs. Oakshott for it!"

"She told me to ask you."

"You can ask the King of Prussia for all I care! I've had enough. Get out!!!" He rushed fiercely forward. The little man ran quickly into the darkness.

"Ha, this may save us a visit to Brixton Road," whispered Holmes. My companion speedily overtook the man and touched him on the shoulder. The man sprang around nervously. I could see by the gaslight that his face was deathly pale.

"Who are you? What do you want?" he asked in a shaken voice.

"My name is Sherlock Holmes. It is my business to know what other people don't know."

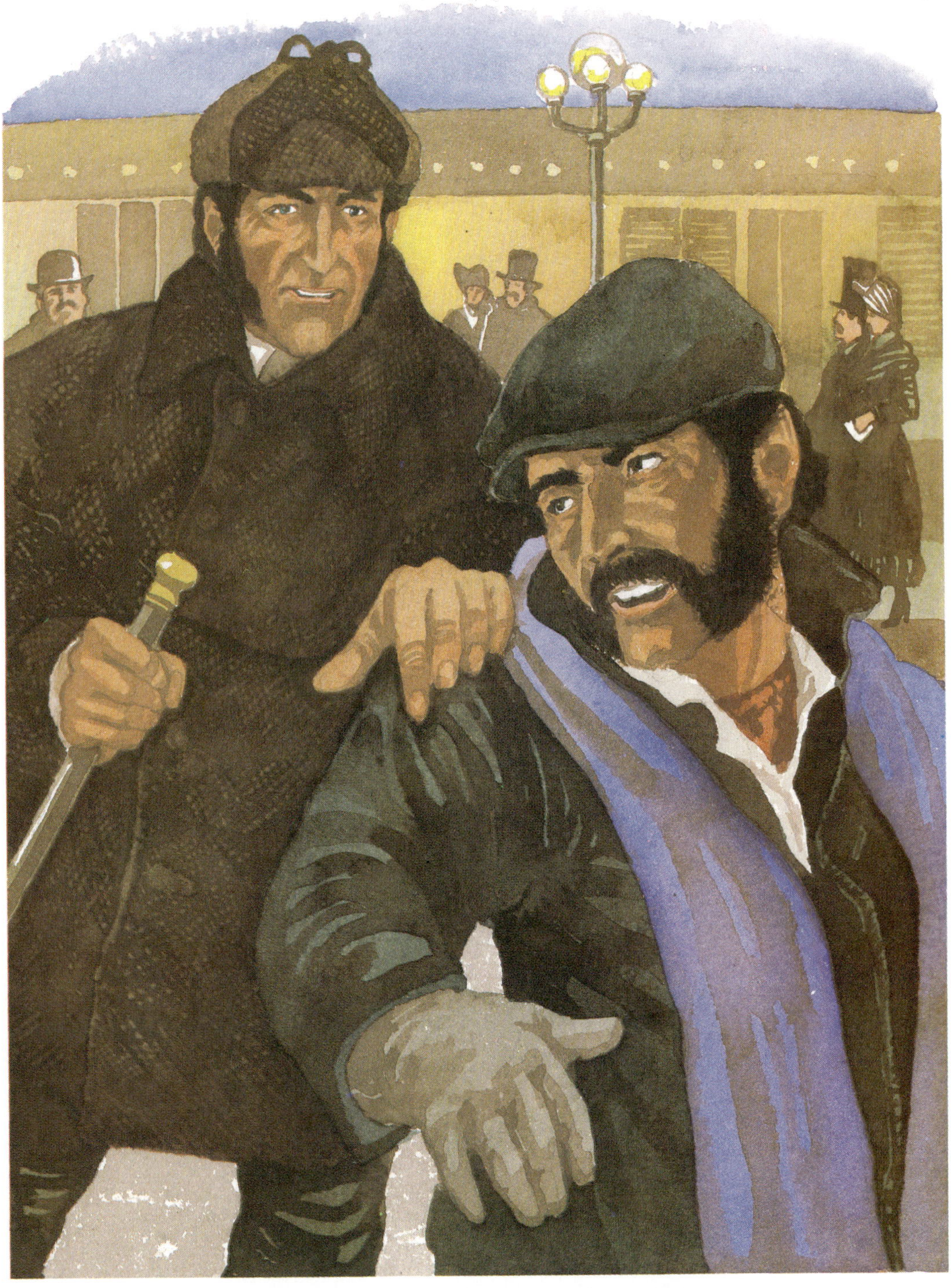

"But you know nothing of this," the man insisted.

"Excuse me, I know everything of it," Holmes replied. "You are trying to trace some geese. They were sold by Mrs. Oakshott of Brixton Road to a salesman named Breckinridge. They were in turn sold to Mr. Windigate of the Alpha and by him to Mr. Henry Baker."

"Oh sir, you are the very man whom I have longed to meet," cried the little fellow.

Sherlock Holmes hailed a cab. "In that case we had better discuss the matter in the privacy of my rooms. Who do I have the pleasure of assisting?"

"My name is John Robinson," he answered.

"No, no. The real name," said Holmes, sweetly. "It is always awkward doing business with an alias."

The stranger's cheeks turned red. "Well, then," he said, "my real name is James Ryder."

"Precisely so! Manager of the Hotel Cosmopolitan! Step into the cab and I shall be able to tell you everything you wish to know presently." Holmes motioned toward the waiting cab.

The little man stood glancing from one of us to the other. His eyes were half frightened and half hopeful. Then he stepped into the cab. In half an hour we were back at Baker Street. Nothing had been said during the drive. But our companion's heavy breathing told us how nervous he was.

"Here we are!" said Holmes cheerfully as we filed into the room. "The fire looks very seasonable in this weather. You look cold, Mr. Ryder. Take this basket-chair. I will just put on my slippers before we settle this little matter of yours. Now then! You want to know what became of those geese? Or rather, of that goose. It was one bird, I imagine, which interests you — white with a black bar across its tail."

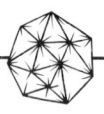

Ryder quivered with emotion. "Oh, sir," he cried, "can you tell me where it went?"

"It came here."

"Here?"

"Yes and a most remarkable bird it proved to be. I don't wonder that you should take an interest in it. It laid an egg after it was dead—the brightest little blue egg that ever was seen. I have it right here."

Our visitor staggered to his feet and steadied himself against the mantelpiece. Holmes unlocked his strong box and held up the blue carbuncle. It shone out like a star. Ryder glanced at it, uncertain whether to claim it or disown it.

"The game's up, Ryder," Holmes said quietly. Ryder staggered, nearly falling into the fire. I helped him into his chair. He sat staring at his accuser.

"I have deduced most of the facts of this case. There is little for you to tell me," said Holmes. "Still, that little may as well be cleared up. How did you first learn of the Countess's stone?"

"It was Catherine Cusack who told me of it," he said.

"I see. Her ladyship's maid. And the temptation of easy wealth was too much for you. You knew the plumber Horner had once been involved in a similar matter. He would immediately be suspected. So what did you do? You created a job for him in the Countess's room. When he was done, you stole the gem, raised the alarm and had him arrested. You then . . ."

Ryder threw himself on the rug. "Have mercy," he shrieked. "Think of my father! Of my mother! It would break their hearts. I never went wrong before! I never will again. I swear it. Oh, don't bring it into court!"

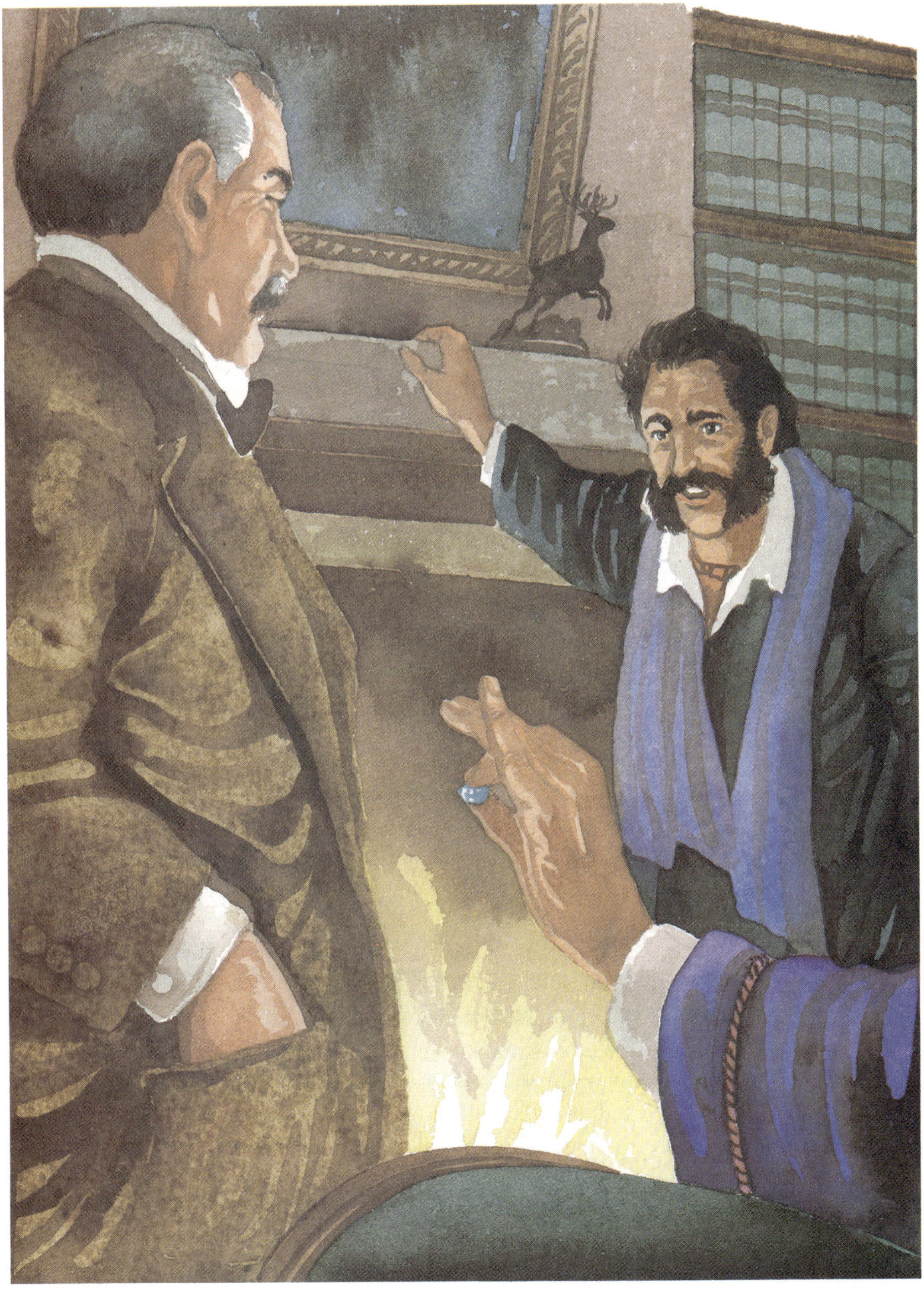

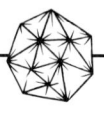

"Get back into your chair!" said Holmes sternly. "It is all very well for you to cringe and crawl now. You thought little of poor Horner in prison for your crime."

"I will flee, Mr. Holmes. I will leave the country. Then the charge against him will be dropped."

"Hum! We will talk about that later. And now let us hear the true account of the next act. How did the stone come to be in the goose and the goose come to be in the market? Your safety depends on your telling us the truth."

Ryder passed his tongue over his parched lips. "I will tell you just as it happened, sir," he said. "I had to hide the stone. There was no safe hiding place in the hotel. After Horner was arrested, I went to my sister's house. She is married to a man named Oakshott. She lives on Brixton Road and breeds birds in her backyard. Along the way I suspected each man I saw of being a police officer or detective. By the time I got to Brixton Road sweat was pouring down my face. My sister asked me what was the matter. I told her the robbery at the hotel had upset me. Then I went into the backyard and wondered what to do.

"I remembered a friend called Maudsley. He knew the ways of thieves and how they got rid of what they stole. I made up my mind to go to Kilburn where he lived. He would show me how to turn the stone into money. But how to get it to him? . . . At any moment I could be seized and searched. And there was the stone in my pocket. I looked down at the geese waddling about my feet. Suddenly an idea came into my head — one which would stump the best detective that ever lived!

"My sister had promised me a goose for Christmas. I would take my goose now and in it I would carry my stone to Kilburn. I spotted a fine white bird with a distinctive barred tail. I caught the bird and pried open its bill. Then I thrust the stone down its throat. The bird gave a gulp. I felt the stone pass along its gullet and into its belly. The bird flapped and struggled. Out came my sister. As I turned to speak to her, the bird broke loose and joined the others.

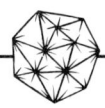

" 'Whatever were you doing with that bird, Jim?' she asked.

" 'Well, you said you'd give me one for Christmas. I was feeling to see which one was the fattest.'

" 'Oh! We've set yours aside for you. Jim's bird, we call it. It's the big, white one over yonder. There's twenty-six of them, which makes one for you and one for us and two dozen for the market.'

" 'Thank you, Maggie,' says I. 'But if it is all the same to you, I'd rather have the one I was handling just now.'

" 'The other is a good three pounds heavier,' she said. 'We fattened it expressly for you.'

" 'Never mind, I'll have the other and I'll take it now.'

" 'Very well,' she answered. 'Kill it and take it with you.'

"Well, I did what she said, Mr. Holmes, and I carried the bird all the way to Kilburn. I told my pal what I had done and he laughed until he nearly choked. We got a knife and opened the goose. But there was no stone. I immediately knew there had been some terrible mistake. I left the bird and rushed back to my sister's. But there was not one bird to be seen.

" 'Where are they all, Maggie?' I cried.

" 'Gone to the dealer's, Jim.'

" 'Which dealer's?'

" 'Breckinridge of Covent Garden.'

" 'But was there another with a barred tail?' I asked. 'The same as the one I chose?'

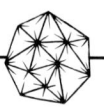

" 'Yes, Jim,' she answered. 'There were two barred-tailed ones. I could never tell them apart.'

"Well, then I realized what had happened. I ran off as fast as my feet would carry me to Breckinridge. He had sold them and wouldn't tell me where they had gone. You heard him yourselves. My sister thinks I am going mad. Sometimes I think I am, too! And now — and now I am myself a branded thief. Without ever having touched the wealth for which I sold my character!" He burst into sobs and buried his face in his hands.

There was a long silence broken only by Ryder's sobs and Holmes's fingers tapping on the table beside him. Finally my friend rose and threw open the door.

"Get out!" he told the man.

"What, sir?" Ryder exclaimed. "Oh, bless you!"

"No more words. Get out!"

And no more words were needed. There was a sudden rush to the door, a clatter on the stairs, the bang of the front door, and the rattle of running footsteps from the street.

"After all, Watson," said Holmes, "I am not employed by the police. If Horner were in danger it would be another thing. But this fellow will not testify against him. The case will collapse. I suppose I should turn him in. But perhaps by setting him free I am saving his soul. This fellow will not go wrong again. He is too frightened. Send him to jail now and you make him a jailbird for life. Besides, it is the season of forgiveness. Chance put a curious mystery in our hands. Our solution is our reward.

"And now, Dr. Watson. Please ring Mrs. Hudson, the housekeeper . . . It is time to investigate yet another bird — one which she kindly prepared for our supper."

Discuss the Selection

1. What details did Sherlock Holmes notice that solved this mystery?
2. How did Sherlock Holmes deduce that Henry Baker knew nothing of the gem's theft?
3. Which of Holmes's deductions did you think was the cleverest? Why?
4. How was Holmes able to deduce that James Ryder was involved in the jewel theft?
5. Were you able to guess that Ryder was involved in the theft? Find the part of the story that led you to suspect Ryder's guilt.

Apply the Skills

Most story plots have four basic parts: a problem, events in which attempts are made to solve the problem, a climax, and a solution.

Think about the plot of "The Adventure of the Blue Carbuncle." Look at the outline below. Decide what is needed to complete the outline. Then tell the plot of the story.

"The Adventure of the Blue Carbuncle"

I. Problem
   A. Finding the goose and hat's owner
   B. Finding out who stole the blue carbuncle

II. Events
   A. Newspaper ad brings Henry Baker in
   B.
   C.

III. Climax
   A.
   B.

IV.
   A. Ryder describes his crime
   B. Holmes lets Ryder go free

Thinking About "Mysteries"

In this unit you've read about all kinds of mysteries. You've met many kinds of detectives, from real-life medical researchers to joke-cracking insects.

The detectives in this unit solved mysteries in many ways. Peter Perkins and Donna Magrue used careful deductions. Incognito Mosquito used sharp observation. Sammle used her keen memory. Sherlock Holmes, the master detective, drew conclusions based on his careful observations.

You have read about some mysteries in the real world. Police detectives have carefully pieced together clues to try to explain one of the biggest art thefts in history. Medical detectives have used computers to help them find a way to keep paralyzed Michela Alioto healthy. Scientists are using computers on rockets to learn about the mysteries of the universe.

Reading these stories should have improved your detective skills. You may have discovered new ways to look at the mysteries and problems you meet. You may have found new ways to broaden your own horizons.

1. Think about the personalities of Peter Perkins, puzzle enthusiast, and Sherlock Holmes, master detective. Explain how the two men are alike.

2. What did the fictional detectives you read about have in common with the doctors who developed Michela Alioto's exercise program?

3. Think about the detectives you met in this unit. How does a detective go about solving a mystery? Summarize the steps of the method.

4. Which of the characters you read about in this chapter would you most like to spend time with? Why?

5. How might detectives and police officers use computers in their work?

6. Do you know someone who might make a good detective? Tell about that person. Explain why he or she might be a good mystery solver.

7. Think about the mysteries of our world that are still unsolved. Describe one that you might like to solve.

Read on Your Own

The Microchip: Small Wonder by Charlene W. Billings. Dodd, Mead. A history of the computer, from the thirty-ton giants of the 1940's to today's desktop models.

The Mystery of Stonehenge by Franklyn M. Branley. Harper & Row. The story of Stonehenge, a group of huge stones raised 4,000 years ago in England. Why and how the stones were raised is something people have wondered about for centuries.

Of Quarks, Quasars and Other Quirks: Quizzical Poems for the Supersonic Age edited by Sara and John E. Brewton and John Brewton Blackburn. Harper & Row. Zany poems about the world of computers, quarks, atoms, and sonic booms.

Great Mysteries of the Sea by Edward F. Dolan, Jr. Dodd, Mead. Deep-sea mysteries explored in this book include a triangle of water where ships vanish, ships that sail for years without a crew, and ghost ships.

The House of Dies Drear by Virginia Hamilton. Macmillan. Thirteen-year-old Thomas and his family move to a house that was once a station for the underground railroad. A frightening mystery unfolds, and Thomas decides to solve it.

Incognito Mosquito, Private Insective by E. A. Hass. Lothrop. Solving mysteries as he goes, this unusual hero makes his way through the hum of the insect underworld, wearing an assortment of flea-brained disguises. He always gets his bug.

Alfred Hitchcock's Solve-Them-Yourself Mysteries. Random House. This is a book for those who like to test their detective skills. As each of the five mysteries unfolds, Hitchcock points out important clues and challenges the reader to solve the case.

Computers That Think? The Search for Artificial Intelligence by Margaret O. Hyde. Enslow. This book tells the story of computers that make decisions, diagnose illnesses, translate from foreign languages, help the blind, and learn from experience.

Loads of Codes and Secret Ciphers by Paul B. Janeczko. Macmillan. A history of ways in which people have communicated in secret. You may enjoy using the special languages discussed in this book.

The Master Puppeteer by Katherine Patterson. Avon. Jiro, an apprentice puppeteer, tries to find the link between the puppet theater and a mysterious bandit who robs the rich and gives to the poor.

Sir Arthur Conan Doyle's *The Adventures of Sherlock Holmes* adapted for young readers by Catherine Edwards Sadler. Avon. Stories detailing the adventures of Holmes and Watson. Includes puzzling mysteries, brilliant solutions, and captured criminals.

Computer Kids by George Sullivan. Dodd, Mead. Eight computer wizards tell how they first got interested in computers, and the games and programs some of them created.

True or False? Amazing Art Forgeries by Ann Waldron. Hastings. The story of the forgery of great works of art—how it is done and why, and the ways in which the forgers are caught.

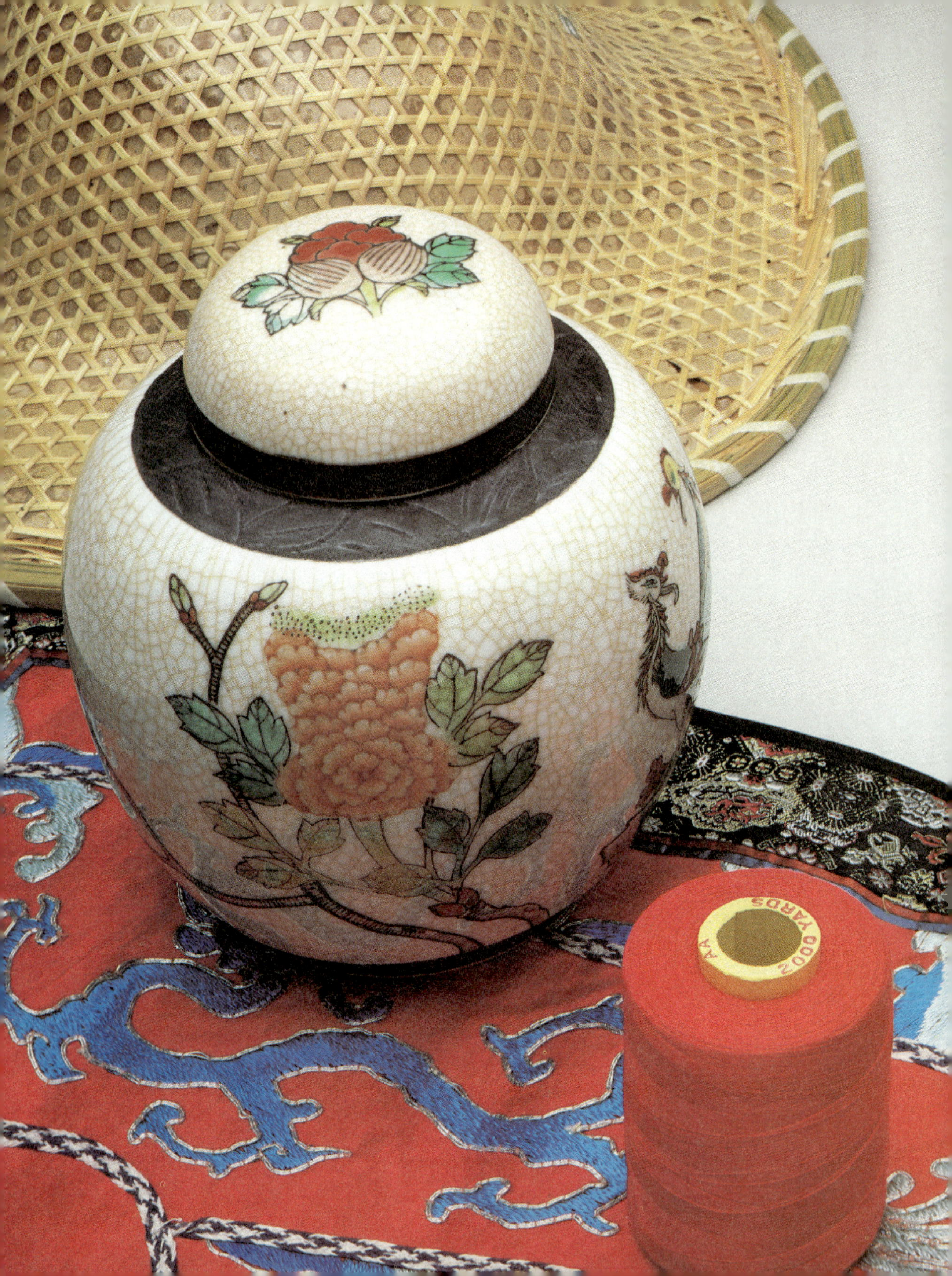
AA 2000 YARDS

Unit 3
Viewpoints

Wouldn't the world be a dull place if everyone had the same thoughts, the same opinions, and the same feelings? Fortunately, there's little chance of that ever happening! Each person is unique. Each of us has his or her own point of view.

We have many ways of expressing our personal points of view. Words are the most common means. But art, music, and dance also communicate ideas and feelings. Even the way we dress can say something about our views.

Writers, of course, rely on words. The stories that follow are expressions of the ideas and feelings of their authors. You may share a writer's viewpoint, or you may find one different from your own. You may even find a viewpoint that reveals something about the world or about people that you have never thought of before.

Literature Study

Personal Narrative

Sometimes you have experiences that you can't wait to tell your friends about. You might tell your friends how you felt or what you thought as things were happening. You would probably use phrases such as "First, I . . ." and "Then we . . ." You would be telling a story about something that really happened. Your story would be a personal narrative. A **personal narrative** is a true story about an event or an experience told by the person who had the experience.

You can tell when a story is a personal narrative. The author uses personal pronouns such as *I*, *we*, *me*, and *my* to tell the story. You use the same words to tell about your experiences.

Authors often write about their own experiences. When a person writes in a diary, he or she is writing down experiences to remember. Later, the writer might publish the diary so that others can read it. This is one kind of a personal narrative.

In another kind of personal narrative, an author tells a story about something he or she did. The author is a character in the story. The author tells how he or she felt as the event was happening. The author also tells you the things he or she thought about. Reading a personal narrative can make you feel you know the author very well and that you are sharing the experience.

An **interview** is another form of personal narrative. In an interview, a writer asks questions. The person being interviewed answers the questions from his or her point of view. The writer keeps a record of the questions and the answers, then writes about the interview. You can find interviews in magazines and newspapers. Interviews are common on television and radio programs, too. Interviews can tell you about the personal experiences of people you might never meet.

You may come across other kinds of writing that might be called personal narrative. One kind is a **testimonial**. A person giving a testimonial is telling you his or her own views and opinions about something. This kind of writing often tries to persuade you to do something — to vote for a particular candidate, for instance. A well-known person, such as a senator, might state, "I'm voting for Jane Smith for governor because she's the best candidate." You are supposed to think that if the senator is voting for Jane Smith, then you should, too.

Celebrities in the fields of entertainment or athletics are often asked to give testimonials. They might try to convince you to buy a certain product. Advertisers want you to think that if your favorite baseball player uses XYZ toothpaste, then you should use it, too.

A personal narrative is a story or a statement about an experience told by a person who was there. A personal narrative may entertain you, inform you, or persuade you. Reading a personal narrative can make you feel that you have been a part of the author's experience.

Jean is a young American who loves the United States even though she lives in China. Read to find out how that viewpoint gets Jean into trouble.

What makes this account of childhood events a personal narrative?

Homesick

by Jean Fritz

In my father's study there was a large globe with all the countries of the world running around it. I could put my finger on the exact spot where I was and had been ever since I'd been born. And I was on the wrong side of the globe. I was in China in a city named Hankou, a dot on a crooked line that seemed to break the country right in two. The line was really the Yangtse River, but who would know by looking at a map what the Yangtse River really was?

Orange-brown, muddy mustard-colored. And wide, wide, wide. With a river smell that was old and came all the way up from the bottom. Sometimes old women knelt on the riverbank, begging the River God to return a son or grandson who may have drowned. They would wail and beat the earth to make the River God pay attention, but I knew how busy the River God must be. All those people on the Yangtse River! Coolies hauling water. Women washing clothes. Houseboats swarming with old people and young, chickens and pigs. Big crooked-sailed junks with eyes painted on their prows so they could see where they were going. I loved the Yangtse River, but, of course, I belonged on the other side of the world. In America with my grandmother.

Twenty-five fluffy little yellow chicks hatched from our eggs today, my grandmother wrote.

I wrote my grandmother that I had watched a Chinese magician swallow three yards of fire.

The trouble with living on the wrong side of the world was that I didn't feel like a *real* American. Actually, I was American every minute of the day, especially during school hours. I went to a British school and every morning we sang "God Save the King." Of course the British children loved singing about their gracious king. Ian Forbes stuck out his chest and sang as if he were saving the king all by himself. Everyone sang. Even Gina Boss who was Italian. And Vera Sebastian who was so Russian she dressed the way Russian girls did long ago before the Revolution when her family had to run away to keep from being killed.

But I wasn't Vera Sebastian. I asked my mother to write an excuse so I wouldn't have to sing, but she wouldn't do it. "When in Rome," she said, "do as the Romans do." What she meant was, "Don't make trouble. Just sing." So for a long time I did. I sang with my fingers crossed but still I felt like a traitor.

Then one day I thought: If my mother and father were really and truly in Rome, they wouldn't do what the Romans did at all. They'd probably try to get the Romans to do what *they* did, just as they were trying to teach the Chinese to do what Americans did. (My mother even gave classes in American manners.)

So that day I quit singing. I kept my mouth locked tight against the king of England. Our teacher, Miss Williams, didn't notice at first. She stood in front of the room, using a ruler for a baton, striking each syllable hard as if she were making up for the times she had nothing to strike.

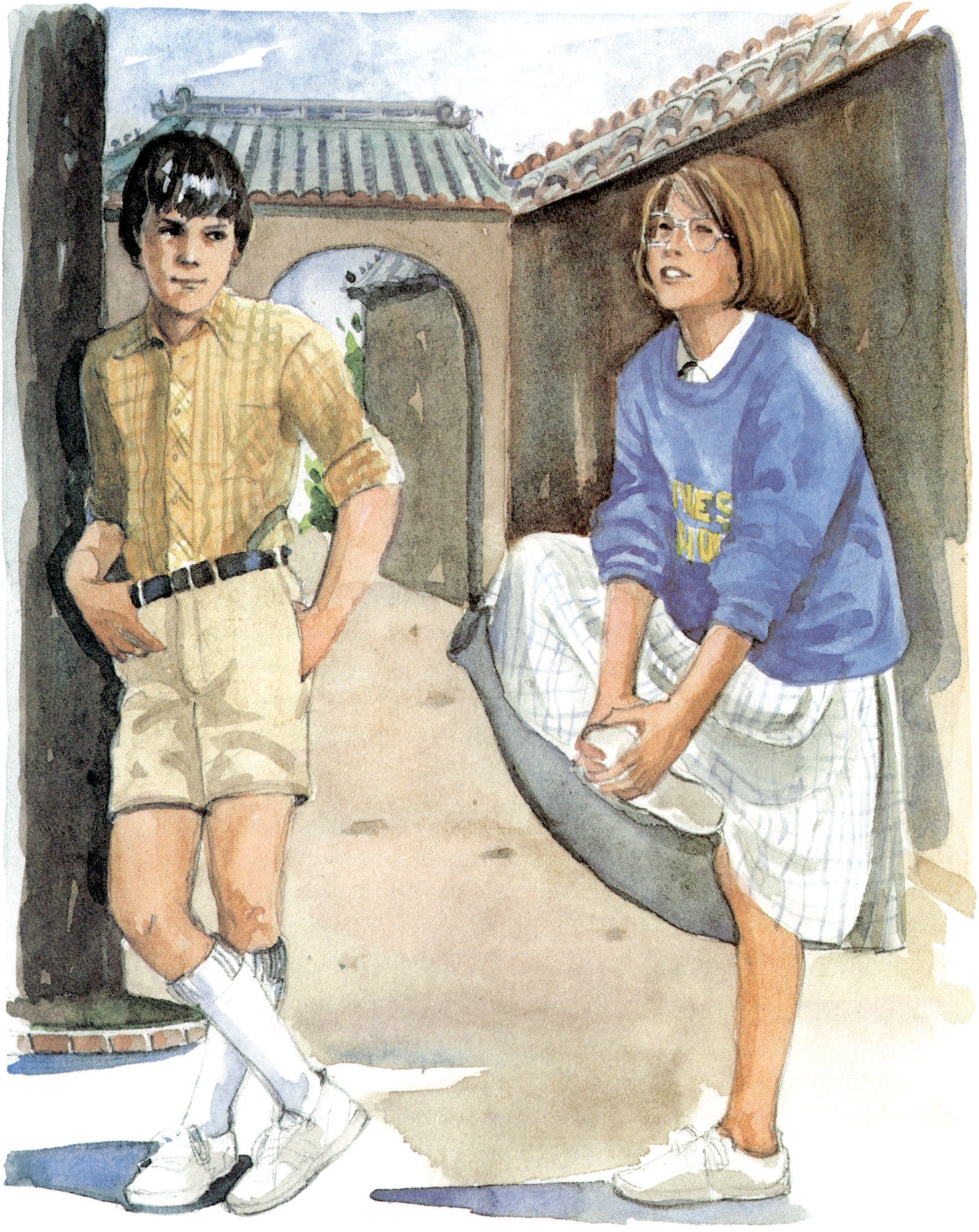

"Make him vic-tor-i-ous," the class sang. It was on the strike of "vic" that Miss Williams noticed. Her eyes lighted on my mouth and when we sat down, she pointed her ruler at me.

"Is there something wrong with your voice today, Jean?"

"No, Miss Williams."

"You weren't singing."

"No, Miss Williams. It is not my national anthem."

"It is the national anthem we sing here," she snapped. "You have always sung. Even Vera sings it."

I looked at Vera with the big blue bow tied on the top of her head. Usually I felt sorry for her but not today. At recess I might even untie that bow, I thought. Just give it a yank. But if I'd been smart, I wouldn't have been looking at Vera. I would have been looking at Ian Forbes and I would have known that, no matter what Miss Williams said, I wasn't through with the king of England.

Recess at the British School was nothing I looked forward to. Every day we played a game called Prisoner's Base, which was all running and shouting and shoving and catching. I hated the game, yet everyone played except Vera Sebastian. She sat on the sidelines under her blue bow like someone who had been dropped out of a history book. While everyone was getting ready for the game, I was as usual trying to look as if I didn't care if I was the last one picked for a team or not. I was leaning against the high stone wall that ran around the schoolyard. I was looking up at a little white cloud skittering across the sky when all at once someone tramped down hard on my right foot. Ian Forbes. Snarling bulldog face. Heel grinding down on my toes. Head thrust forward the way an animal might before it strikes.

"You wouldn't sing it. So say it," he ordered. "Let me hear you say it."

I tried to pull my foot away but he only ground down harder.

"Say what?" I was telling my face please not to show what my foot felt.

"*God save the king.* Say it. Those four words. I want to hear you say it."

Although Ian Forbes was short, he was solid and tough and built for fighting. What was more, he always won. You had only to look at his bare knees between the top of his socks and his short pants to know that he would win. His knees were square. Bony and unbeatable. So of course it was crazy for me to argue with him.

"Why should I?" I asked. "Americans haven't said that since George the Third."

He grabbed my right arm and twisted it behind my back.

"Say it," he hissed.

I felt the tears come to my eyes and I hated myself for the tears. I hated myself for not staying in Rome the way my mother had told me.

"I'll never say it," I whispered.

They were choosing sides now in the schoolyard and Ian's name was being called—among the first as always.

He gave my arm another twist. "You'll sing tomorrow," he snarled, "or you'll be sorry."

As he ran off, I slid to the ground, my head between my knees.

Oh, Grandma, I thought, why can't I be there with you? I'd feed the chickens for you. I'd pump water from the well, the way my father used to do.

It would be almost two years before we'd go to America.

I was ten years old now; I'd be twelve then. But how could I think about *years*? I didn't even dare to think about the next day. After school I ran all the way home, fast so I couldn't think at all.

Our house stood behind a high stone wall. I flung open the iron gate and threw myself through the front door.

"I'm home!" I yelled.

Then I remembered that it was Tuesday, the day my mother taught an English class at the Y.M.C.A. where my father was the director.

I stood in the hall, trying to catch my breath, and as always I began to feel small. It was a huge hall with ceilings so high it was as if they would have nothing to do with people. Certainly not with a mere child, not with me — the only child in the house.

Lin Nai-Nai, my amah, was the only one around, and of course I knew she'd be there. It was her job to stay with me when my parents were out. As soon as she heard me come in, she'd called, "Tsai loushang," which meant that she was upstairs. She might be mending or ironing but most likely she'd be sitting by the window embroidering. And she was. She even had my embroidery laid out, for we had made a bargain. She would teach me to embroider if I would teach her English. I liked embroidering: the cloth stretched tight within my embroidery hoop while I filled in the stamped pattern with cross-stitches and lazy daisy flowers. The trouble was that lazy daisies needed French knots for their centers and I hated making French knots. Mine always fell apart, so I left them to the end. Today I had twenty lazy daisies waiting for their knots.

Lin Nai-Nai had already threaded my needle with embroidery floss.

"Black centers," she said, "for the yellow flowers."

I felt myself glowering. "American flowers don't have centers," I said and gave her back the needle.

Lin Nai-Nai looked at me, puzzled, but she did not argue. We were good friends, so I didn't know why I felt so mean.

She shrugged. "English lesson?" she asked, smiling.

I tested my arm to see if it still hurt from the twisting. It did. My foot too. "What do you want to know?" I asked.

We had been through the polite phrases—Please, Thank you, I beg your pardon, Excuse me, You're welcome.

"If I meet an American on the street," she asked, "how do I greet him?"

I looked her straight in the eye and nodded my head in a greeting. "Sewing machine," I said. "You say, 'Sew-ing ma-chine.' "

She repeated after me, making the four syllables into four separate words. She got up and walked across the room, bowing and smiling. "Sew Ing Ma Shing."
   Part of me wanted to laugh at the thought of Lin Nai-Nai maybe meeting Dr. Carhart, our minister, whose face would surely puff up, the way it always did when he was flustered.

But part of me didn't want to laugh at all. I didn't like it when my feelings got tangled, so I ran downstairs and played Chopsticks on the piano. Loud and fast. When my sore arm hurt, I just beat on the keys harder.

Then I went upstairs to my room (the blue room) and began *Sara Crewe*. Now there was a girl, I thought, who was worth crying over. I wasn't going to think about myself. Or Ian Forbes. Or the next day. I wasn't. I wasn't.

And I didn't. Not all afternoon. Not all evening. Still, I must have decided what I was going to do because the next morning when I started for school and came to the corner where the man sold hot chestnuts, the corner where I always turned to go to school, I didn't turn. I walked straight ahead. I wasn't going to school that day.

I walked toward the Yangtse River. This part near the river was called the Mud Flats. Sometimes it was muddier than others, and when the river flooded, the flats disappeared underwater. But today the river was fairly low and the mud had dried so that it was cracked and cakey. Most of the men who lived here were out fishing, some not far from the shore, poling their sampans through the shallow water. Only a few people were on the flats: a man cleaning fish on a flat rock at the water's edge, a woman spreading clothes on the dirt to dry, a few small children. But behind the huts was something I had never seen before. Even before I came close, I guessed what it was. Even then, I was excited by the strangeness of it.

It was the beginnings of a boat. The skeleton of a large junk, its ribs lying bare, its backbone running straight and true down the bottom. The outline of the prow was already in place, turning up wide and snub-nosed, the way all junks did. I had never thought of boats starting from nothing, of taking on bones under their bodies. The eyes, I supposed, would be the last thing added. Then the junk would have life.

The builders were not there and I was behind the huts where no one could see me as I walked around and around, marveling. Then I climbed inside and as I did, I knew that something wonderful was happening to me. I was a-tingle, because suddenly I knew that the boat was mine. No matter who really owned it, it was mine. Even if I never saw it again, it would be my junk sailing up and down the Yangtse River. My junk seeing the river sights with its two eyes, seeing them for me whether I was there or not. Often I had tried to put the Yangtse River into a poem so I could keep it. Sometimes I had tried to draw it, but nothing I did ever came close. But now, *now* I had my junk and somehow that gave me the river too.

I thought I should put my mark on the boat. Perhaps on the side of the spine. Very small. A secret between the boat and me. I opened my schoolbag and took out my folding penknife that I used for sharpening pencils. Very carefully I carved the Chinese character that was our name. Gau. (In China my father was Mr. Gau, my mother was Mrs. Gau, and I was Little Miss Gau.) The builders would paint right over the character, I thought, and never notice, but I would know. Always and forever I would know.

For a long time I dreamed about the boat, imagining it finished, its sails up, its eyes wide. Someday it might sail all the way down the Yangtse to Shanghai, so I told the boat what it would see along the way because I had been there and the boat hadn't. After a while I got hungry and I ate my egg sandwich. I was in the midst of peeling an orange when all at once I had company.

A small boy, not more than four years old, wandered around to the back of the huts, saw me, and stopped still. He was wearing a ragged blue cotton jacket with a red cloth, pincushion-like charm around his neck which was supposed to keep him from getting smallpox. Sticking up straight from the middle of his head was a small pigtail which I knew was to fool the gods and make them think he was a girl. (Gods didn't bother much with girls; it was boys that were important in China.) He walked slowly up to the boat, stared at me, and then nodded as if he'd already guessed what I was. "Foreign devil," he announced gravely.

I shook my head. "No," I said in Chinese. "American friend." Through the ribs of the boat, I handed him a segment of orange. He ate it slowly, his eyes on the rest of the orange. Segment by segment, I gave it all to him. Then he wiped his hands down the front of his jacket.

"Foreign devil," he repeated.

"American friend," I corrected. Then I asked him about the boat. Who was building it? Where were the builders?

He pointed upriver. "Not here today. Back tomorrow."

I knew it would only be a question of time before the boy would run off to alert the people in the huts. "Foreign devil, foreign devil," he would cry. So I put my hand on the prow of the boat, wished it luck, and climbing out, I started back. To my surprise the boy walked beside me. When we came to the end of the street, I squatted down so we would be on the same eye level. "Good-bye," I said. "May the River God protect you." For a moment the boy stared. When he spoke, it was as if he were trying out a new sound.

"American friend," he said slowly.

When I looked back, he was still there, looking soberly toward me.

The time, according to the Customs House clock, was five after two, which meant that I couldn't go home for two hours. I wandered up and down the streets, in and out of stores. I weighed myself on the big scale in the Hankow Dispensary and found that I was as skinny as ever. I went to the Terminus Hotel and tried out the chairs in the lounge. At first I didn't mind wandering about like this. Half of my mind was still on the river with my junk, but as time went on, my junk began slipping away until I was alone with nothing but questions. Would my mother find out about today? How could I skip school tomorrow? And the next day and the next? Could I get sick? Was there a kind of long lie-abed sickness that didn't hurt?

I arrived home when I planned, opened the door, and called out, "I'm home!" Cheery-like and normal. But I was scarcely in the house before Lin Nai-Nai ran to me from one side of the hall and my mother from the other.

"Are you all right? Are you all right?" Lin Nai-Nai felt my arms as if she expected them to be broken. My mother's face was white. "What happened?" she asked.

Then I looked through the open door into the living room and saw Miss Williams sitting there. She had beaten me home and asked about my absence, which of course had scared everyone. But now my mother could see that I was in one piece and for some reason this seemed to make her mad. She took me by the hand and led me into the living room. "Miss Williams said you weren't in school," she said. "Why was that?"

I hung my head, just the way cowards do in books.

My mother dropped my hand. "Jean will be in school tomorrow," she said firmly. She walked Miss Williams to the door. "Thank you for stopping by."

As soon as Miss Williams was gone and my mother was sitting down again, I burst into tears. Kneeling on the floor, I buried my head in her lap and poured out the whole miserable story. My mother could see that I really wasn't in one piece after all, so she listened quietly, stroking my hair as I talked, but gradually I could feel her stiffen. I knew she was remembering that she was a Mother.

"You better go up to your room," she said, "and think things over. We'll talk about it after supper."

I flung myself on my bed. What was there to think? Either I went to school and got beaten up. Or I quit.

After supper I explained to my mother and father how simple it was. I could stay at home and my mother could teach me. My mother shook her head. Yes, it was simple, she agreed. I could go back to the British School, be sensible, and start singing about the king again.

I clutched the edge of the table. Couldn't she understand? I couldn't turn back now. It was too late.

So far my father had not said a word. He was leaning back, teetering on the two hind legs of his chair, the way he always did after a meal, the way that drove my mother crazy. But he was not the kind of person to keep all four legs of a chair on the floor just because someone wanted him to. He wasn't a turning-back person so I hoped maybe he would understand. As I watched him, I saw a twinkle start in his eyes and suddenly he brought his chair down slam-bang flat on the floor. He got up and motioned for us to follow him into the living room. He sat down at the piano and began to pick out the tune for "God Save the King."

A big help, I thought. Was he going to make me practice?

Then he began to sing:

320

"My country 'tis of thee,
Sweet land of liberty, . . ."

Of course! It was the same tune. Why hadn't I thought of that? Who would know what I was singing as long as I moved my lips? I joined in now, loud and strong.

"Of thee I sing."

My mother laughed in spite of herself. "If you sing that loud," she said, "you'll start a revolution."

"Tomorrow I'll sing softly," I promised. "No one will know." But for now I really let freedom ring.

Then all at once I wanted to see Lin Nai-Nai. I ran to her room.

"It's me," I called through the door and when she opened up, I threw my arms around her. "Oh, Lin Nai-Nai, I love you," I said. "You haven't said it yet, have you?"

"Said what?"

"Sewing machine. You haven't said it?"

"No," she said, "not yet. I'm still practicing."

"Don't say it, Lin Nai-Nai. Say 'Good day.' It's shorter and easier. Besides, it's more polite."

"Good day?" she repeated.

"Yes, that's right. Good day." I hugged her.

The next day at school when we rose to sing the British national anthem, everyone stared at me, but as soon as I opened my mouth, the class lost interest. All but Ian Forbes. His eyes never left my face, but I sang softly, carefully, proudly. At recess he sauntered over to where I stood against the wall.

He spat on the ground. "You can be glad you sang today," he said. Then he strutted off as if he and those square knees of his had won again.

And, of course, I was glad.

Discuss the Selection

1. Why did Jean refuse to sing "God Save the King" in school? What trouble did she get into because of her refusal?
2. What did Jean do on the day she skipped school? Give a brief account of Jean's day.
3. What do you think of Jean's decision not to sing? What might you have done if you were in her place?
4. How did Jean's father help her solve the problem of singing "God Save the King" in school?
5. How had Jean misled her amah, Lin Nai-Nai? Find the words at the end of the story that indicate Jean was sorry she had misled her.

Apply the Skills

A personal narrative is a story about a personal experience. It is told from the viewpoint of the person who had the experience.

"Homesick" is a personal narrative. Answer the following questions about the story.

1. Who told the story in "Homesick"?
2. What makes this story a personal narrative?
3. How might this story be different if it were told by Jean's mother?

Think and Write

Prewrite

[Note cards:]
- Jean skips school.
- Jean refuses to sing "God Save the King" in school.
- A bully threatens Jean.
- Jean's father helps her find a solution to her problem.

Each note card above describes a major event from "Homesick." Make note cards describing two other major events from the story. Then arrange all the note cards in order to make a list of important story events.

Compose

Use your list to write a plot summary of "Homesick." Remember that a plot summary includes only the most important events from a story. Your summary might begin with this sentence: *Jean, a young American girl, lives in China with her parents.*

Revise

Read your summary. Have you included only the most important story events? Are the events presented in the correct order? Does your summary give readers a brief but accurate description of the events in the story? If not, revise your work.

Saying Yes

by Diana Chang

"Are you Chinese?"
"Yes."

"American?"
"Yes."

"*Really* Chinese?"
"No . . . not quite."

"*Really* American?"
"Well, actually, you see . . ."

But I would rather say
yes

Not neither-nor,
not maybe,
but both, and not only

The homes I've had,
the ways I am

I'd rather say it
twice,
yes

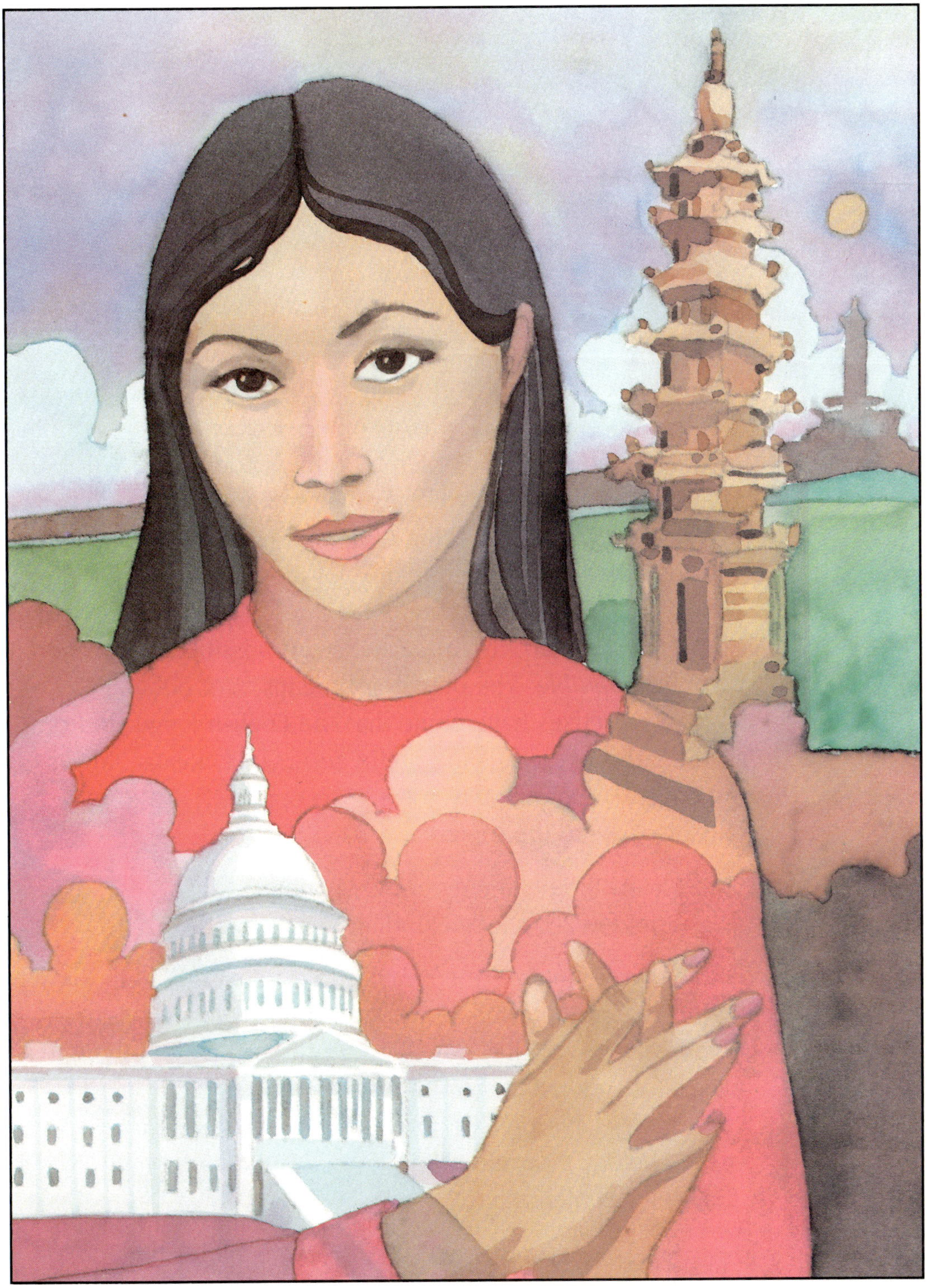

Vocabulary Study

Prefixes

A **prefix** is a word part that is added to the beginning of a word. A prefix may be one or more syllables. Each prefix has a meaning of its own. When a prefix is added to a word, the meaning of the prefix changes the meaning of the word.

If you know the meaning of a word, and the meaning of the prefix, you can often figure out the meaning of the new word. For example, the prefix *im-* means "not." When you put the prefix *im-* in front of the word *possible*, you make the word *impossible*. The new word means "not possible."

Many prefixes have come into the English language from Latin. One of these is the prefix *anti-*. *Anti-* means "against" in Latin. The prefix *anti-* means "to oppose," or "to go against." Read the sentence below:

> At the beginning of every winter you should put antifreeze in a car's radiator.

The word *antifreeze* combines the prefix *anti-* with the word *freeze*. *Anti-* means "to go against," so *antifreeze* means "to go against freezing." Antifreeze is something that keeps a car's radiator from freezing.

Another Latin prefix is *ante-*. The prefix *ante-* means "to come before." Look for the word with the prefix *ante-* in the following sentence:

> The senator waited in the antechamber before she entered the President's office.

The word *antechamber* combines the prefix *ante-* with the word *chamber*. You may know that the word *chamber* is a synonym for *room*. *Ante-* means "to come before." An antechamber is "a room that comes before" or "a room near a main room."

Look for the word with a prefix in each of the sentences that follow. Use what you know about the prefixes and the rest of the sentence to help you figure out what each word means.

1. The environmental group planned an antipollution campaign to clean up the river.
2. The dinosaurs antedate large mammals.
3. The secretary asked us to wait in the anteroom.
4. One mouse was very antisocial and stayed away from the other mice.
5. The doctor told me to put antiseptic on the cut to kill germs.

Which word means "to come or happen before"?
Which word means "to reduce or eliminate pollution"?
Which word means "a substance to prevent infection"?
Which word means "a room leading to a larger room"?

As you read, look for prefixes in unfamiliar words. Use the prefix to help you figure out what the word means.

On a trip to China, Jean sees the country from the viewpoint of someone who has lived there. Read the story to find out how the trip makes Jean feel about her own past.

As you read the story, notice how prefixes change the meanings of words.

China Homecoming

by Jean Fritz

Jean at age 8

When I was a child, my parents were always talking about "home." They meant America, of course, which sounded so wonderful I couldn't understand why they had ever left it. Why had they traveled halfway around the world to China to have me and then just stayed on, talking about "home"? Somehow, living on the opposite side of the world as I did, I didn't feel like a real American.

But maybe when I was twelve years old, I told myself, I'd begin to feel like a real American. Twelve years old was the beginning of growing up, so perhaps I would change.

The day before my twelfth birthday I asked my mother what the chances were, but, as usual, she was impatient with my American feelings. "You have always been a real American," she said.

"Not born and bred," I said.

"Well, being twelve isn't going to make any difference."

And she was right.

It took me a long time to feel like a real American. Even after we came back to America when I was thirteen, I didn't feel as American as I thought I should. Not as American, I imagined, as my cousin Charlotte must feel. After all, she didn't have anything in her head but American thoughts and pictures.

But not me. As soon as I was asleep, off I'd rush to the Yangtse River. I didn't do anything on the river; I just looked at it, letting the orange-brown foreverness of it flow past and, it seemed, even flow through me. As hard as I was trying to grow up American, I could not let China go.

Eventually I did come to feel American, but only after I had grown up and married Michael, a born-and-bred American, and had two born-and-bred American children, David and Andrea. And most important, I could not feel that I truly belonged to my country until I had waded into history and stretched my own American experience into the past.

Still, all the time I was growing up and even after I was grown up, the Yangtse River hovered on my horizon. Wide-eyed junks stared at me as they sailed past, as if they were trying to remember who I was. When I was in high school, I wrote in my diary, "If somehow, sometime I do not go back to China, I will never forgive myself." About the same time I wrote the first poem I had ever written without rhyme. It was on a Saturday morning; I wrote it, sitting up in bed, still in my pajamas. I was excited because almost as soon as I had started I felt that I was not writing the poem at all; it was writing me. When I had finished, I took it downstairs to read to my mother.

I began my poem and ended it with the same line: "It will not be the same when I go back."

Somewhere between the two lines I began to cry. I was surprised at myself. I had never cried over poetry before, especially my own, which always sounded better in my head than it did after it reached the paper. This poem, however, made it right to the paper as if it had skipped the poky in-between business of writing altogether. But what surprises me now is that I said "when" I go back to China. Not "if."

Over and over again I pictured myself walking the streets of Hankow, pointing out places of interest to an imaginary friend of the future. "And that's where I went to school," I'd say, wondering if the red brick British school would look as big and hateful to me now as it did then. "And there's the Customs House." I couldn't imagine Hankow without its Customs House tower guarding the waterfront, its clock ticking off the minutes through good times and bad.

My mother and father and I kept China alive through the language too. Many Chinese phrases had long ago settled so comfortably into our family conversation that we never thought of using the English equivalents. "Xiaosyin," we'd say when we wanted to warn one another to be careful. And if I had a cold and was sniffling instead of blowing my nose, my mother would tell me to "kai bitzi." There were dozens of such everyday expressions that kept the two parts of my life linked together, reassuring me that my childhood hadn't been just made up.

But when much later my father and mother died and I wanted to talk about old times in Hankow, there was not one single person I could talk to. It was scary. It was as if the story I had been telling myself over and over was beginning to evaporate into thin air.

There was only one thing I could do. I could write it all down quickly before it slipped away. Once it was in black and white between the covers of a book, it would be safe. So I wrote *Homesick: My Own Story*, but when I had finished, I didn't write "The End," the way I usually do after I've put down the last word.

This wasn't the end. I knew now I had to go back to China, not only to see what, if anything, was left in Hankow from my own story but to get to know the city as it is now. And to find out if at last I could call it my hometown.

Michael and I finally received permission from the Chinese Embassy. And the night before we were to leave, David and Andrea, grown up now, gave us a farewell party. They were as excited about our plans as we were, so it was a happy time. And then Michael and I were off on our adventure.

When we landed in Hong Kong, we were at last in China but not the China I wanted. I wasn't in the real China until I stepped on the train bound for Hankou (which is the way Hankow is spelled now). And there on the back of every train seat was

A pagoda in Hankou

a lace antimacassar. Of course! I had forgotten Chinese train seats had always worn lace over their shoulders as if they were dressed up to go out. Yes, I was back now.

And when I looked out the window of the moving train, time simply collapsed. Had I been here fifty years ago, five hundred years ago, maybe two thousand years ago — the scene would have been the same. Peasants in wide straw hats. Blue-shirted farmers with their trousers rolled up to their knees wading in rice paddies. Lazy water buffaloes with their curling, half-moon horns, looking as if they had been designed especially for China, where gates are so often moon-shaped, roofs curved, and small bridges humped in the middle. If I went behind the scene and talked to the people, I knew they would each have stories of how times had changed. But from the train window the people seemed as if they had always been there.

"Oh, Michael," I said, "I'm so happy."

By the time we reached the railroad station, my long-smoldering excitement suddenly burst into flame.

"Look," I pointed out to Michael. "There's the sign. It says HANKOU." It seemed wonderful to me; everything seemed wonderful.

A young woman who was to be our guide and interpreter found us and directed us to a waiting car.

"You are going to stay at the Shengli Hotel," she said in perfect English. "It was once a bank, built in the 1930's. Were you here then?"

"No, I left in 1928." I was so busy looking as we made our way, honking through the busy streets, I could barely talk.

After a few minutes she glanced back at me. "Well," she said, "does Hankou seem different?"

"Better, oh, much better. It's all Chinese now as it should be. And the people do not look as poor."

But there were so many of them. The city had always been crowded, I knew that.

The guide turned to me and smiled. "Perhaps you would rather not go directly to the hotel. Is there any place you would rather go first?"

"I'd like to go to the riverfront," I said. We traveled across the city and came out at the downriver end of the waterfront road, just where I wanted to be. And yes, the Customs House was still there. I hadn't realized how much I'd wanted it to be there until I saw it. Nor how much I wanted the clock to be running. It was, faithful as ever.

When we got back in the car and as we drove down the road, I noticed a riverfront park. Of course I wanted to go in. Inside there was a grove of trees, a jungle gym, concrete slabs on which men played cards. Michael wandered about, taking pictures, but I went straight to the mud flats which stretched down to the docks and to the river. Except for sampans (long rowing boats), all the boats were modern-looking — launches, steamers, cargo boats, tugboats, flatboats. No wide-eyed junks now. No forest of masts as there had once been. But Hankou was obviously still a trading center, its river linking together three-fourths of the country.

Standing at the edge of the mud flats, I let myself sink into the scene until suddenly I felt the whole map of China around me. And I was at its very center. In the middle. I could feel the four points of the compass — north, south, east, west — radiating from where I stood. The Chinese live close to the compass, planning their gardens, building their houses with the compass always in mind. Inside the palace at the Forbidden City, for instance, all shadows point north at noon. I'd like to look at the floor of my house and tell the time by the shadows.

I was still admiring the river, thankful that there were no foreign gunboats as there had once been, when I heard a small excited voice behind me.

"Waigwo ren! Waigwo ren!" the voice shouted. "Foreigner! Foreigner!"

Foreigner. Well, at least I wasn't a foreign devil, I thought. I turned and saw a three- or four-year-old boy in blue shorts and yellow shirt pointing at me as he ran to an older woman. His grandmother, I suppose. She was dressed the old-fashioned way in the same kind of blue cotton jacket and trousers that my amah, Lin Nai-Nai, had always worn.

I walked toward the little boy and his grandmother. "I'm an American," I told them.

The woman smiled. "You speak Chinese!"

I hadn't been aware of it but I really had started speaking Chinese. "I speak a little," I said, "but I speak poorly."

"You speak well." Chinese are always polite.

By this time a group was gathering around me. Even with so many tourists, Chinese are still curious about foreigners; perhaps they are simply looking for clues to the outside world. But I was a Chinese-

Jean back in Hankou

speaking foreigner, worthy of special attention.

"I was born and raised in Hankou," I told the group. "I have come back." The grandmother repeated the news loudly as if the others couldn't hear or understand.

"We give you welcome," she said.

"Yes, welcome, welcome." The whole crowd was smiling as if they were proud of me.

"How old are you?" I was taken aback at the grandmother's question, but I would soon learn that most conversations start this way.

Not used to broadcasting my age, I spoke quietly. "Sixty-seven," I said.

"Sixty-seven!" she shouted to the crowd.

"How old are *you*?" I asked.

"Sixty-four." The grandmother seemed pleased that I had returned the question. Chinese are proud to be old. She patted me on the arm as if we were friends.

"When did you leave China?" someone called.

"Fifty-five years ago."

I told them that I'd been thirteen when I left China and that my father had worked at the Y.M.C.A.

I was doing all right, I told myself. I grinned at Michael who was taking pictures of us all.

When we got back in the car,

334

Michael squeezed my hand. "Happy?" he asked.

I nodded.

"Feel like a stranger?"

"I can't tell yet. I'm still just trying to believe it."

The next day I felt like an excavator, digging up bits and pieces of my own history. Only fifty-five years, to be sure — not long in terms of Hankou's history but pretty long in terms of my own.

After a week and a half in Hankou we still had not come across my old house. We had driven along many streets in the section of the city where my house had been, but I felt sure I hadn't passed it. My address had been #2 Rue de Paris, but people no longer knew the old names of the streets. Perhaps my memory was not so good after all, I thought. Or perhaps the house wasn't there.

One afternoon, I told our driver I thought I'd had enough sight-seeing for the day. "I'm tired," I said. "Let's go back to the hotel." We turned up a one-way street parallel to the river street we normally took. I hadn't been on it before, yet it looked strangely familiar. Surely I had been here before.

Then suddenly I saw it. My house.

"Stop!" I cried. "Oh, stop! There's my house!"

It looked exactly the same. I jumped out of the car, Michael behind me. Somehow I wanted to explain to the present occupants who I was without my words traveling secondhand through the interpreter; I went to the front door and knocked.

A nice-looking man of about thirty-five answered my knock, and I told him I had once lived in this house. Oh, I had practiced just how I would say it. Over and over again in America I had practiced. And now as I repeated the line, I felt like a character in a fairy story who has at last found the missing treasure.

Before I had even finished my speech, the man called to his sister to put the kettle on for tea. Then he flung open the door. It might still have been my hallway and I might just have come from school.

And the staircase. I couldn't take my eyes off the staircase. It was those very steps, I told myself, that I had run up and down so many times; my father, too. He always took steps two at a time. And the bannister. The fingerprints were invisible, but they were still there.

For a moment I couldn't move. The past had swallowed me up.

By this time the man who had met us at the door had introduced

Jean's old school

himself. He was Mr. Zhang, a high school teacher, and he knew some English. He and his wife and son lived in our old living room; his sister and her family lived in our dining room, and across the hall his parents lived in my father's study. Upstairs, the bedrooms were occupied by various uncles and aunts.

We went into his sister's quarters, our old dining room for tea. Although there was a double bed and a crib in it now, a two-burner stove, a small table, a chest of drawers, and a few straight chairs, the room itself had not been changed. Nor, as far as I could see, had any room in the house. In spite of the crowded conditions, everything was neat and clean.

"Is the house still cold in the winter?" I asked.

"Very cold."

We talked like old friends.

When I left the house I looked across to where my old church had once been. Yes, it was still there, but it had changed. No fancy entranceway now; no stained-glass windows. I went to the car to tell the interpreter that I would just run across the street to see my old church.

"But you are tired," the driver reminded me.

"Not now," I said. "Oh, not now."

"You see," I told Michael later, "I didn't make it all up. It wasn't a dream. I was really here. And I remembered it right."

"And now you're back."

"*Really* back," I agreed.

Now that I knew where my house was, I thought I could find the British School I had attended. I gave the driver directions — now right, now left, and although I recognized no landmarks along the way, we came out right. There was no danger I wouldn't know the school when I saw it. How could I forget? Indeed, as I got out of the car, I half expected to see my old enemy, Ian Forbes, waiting to beat me up as he had every day. I had few happy memories of the place. Yes, I had enjoyed being the duchess in the school's production of *Alice in Wonderland*. And I had liked reciting poetry. Still, my teacher, Miss Williams, had had to spoil it by writing on my report card, "Jean recites well but with too much expression."

On the side of the building, a granite stone was still marked HANKOW PRIVATE SCHOOL. I spoke to the doorkeeper. "I went to this school," I said. "What is the building used for now?"

It was a rest home for geologists.

Our interpreter had to translate this answer for me and even then it seemed strange. Were geologists people who became especially tired? But the doorkeeper said we could come in and look around.

I didn't have to think twice about which door led to my classroom. I walked right up and knocked. Two rumpled-up geologists came to the door and then scurried away as soon as they were told who I was. Inside were two single beds draped with mosquito nets, two desks, two chairs. That was all, yet the room seemed full. How had it ever held our whole class, twelve of us, and our desks and Miss Williams too?

Michael took my picture on a chair in the middle of the room where my desk had once been. I smiled because it suddenly struck me as funny that after fifty-five years I could suddenly be mad at Ian Forbes and Miss Williams all over again.

The day finally came when the interpreter reminded us that we had only three more days. I didn't need reminding; I knew only too well.

"Tomorrow you will have a free morning," she said. "And I have a surprise for you."

"On the last night that you are here, there will be a banquet for you. The Secretary General of the People's Government is giving it. Because you are Friends of China."

As soon as we were upstairs in our room, Michael put his arm around me. "How about that?" he asked.

I shook my head in wonder. "How about it?"

On our last day, we ended the afternoon with a visit to a museum across the river. In it was a room memorializing the siege of Wuchang when the army attacked the city, the last stronghold of a local warlord. The siege lasted from September 15 to October 10, 1926, and of course I had been here then.

Our guide here was full of figures — the size of the armies, the number of dead, and when she came to a cannon that had been fired against the city, she passed it casually.

"Oh yes," she said, "this was a small cannon that was used."

I stopped. Putting my hand on the cannon, I suddenly felt my eyes fill up.

"It was placed on the hill, wasn't it?"

She looked at me in surprise. "Yes. How did you know?"

"I was here. I heard it." And of course I had. Booming. Booming. Booming. It wasn't just memory that was swelling up in me. It was

The Yangtse River

a feeling that had been growing for the last few days. I'd had no words for it before, but I had them now.

China was not only, as it had always been, part of me. *I was part of China.* Of course I had only been a girl; I'd played no personal part. All the same, I'd been born in China, lived here, watched the river rise and fall, seen the moon come and go, waited out wars. I had a place, a small place in the long unwritten part of China's long history. I held tight to the cannon, knowing that I would never again have trouble answering the question "Where is your hometown?" Of course it was Hankou. Where else would it be?

Back at the hotel, we dressed for the banquet. We were to eat in a private dining room on an upper floor of the hotel. When we stepped off the elevator, the Secretary General and members of the Foreign Affairs Bureau were there to meet us. The Secretary General, who was also president of a local university, was a tall, thin, handsome man dressed in an impeccably tailored jacket. He looked kind and wise, just the way a Chinese scholar should look.

"Our dinner is to be a small family affair," he said as he led us into the dining room. "This is the best way for friends to say good-bye."

Jean at the testimonial dinner given for her by the Secretary General

Although the party was small, the food was anything but meager: eel, seaweed soup, mandarin fish, preserved duck eggs, duck meat wrapped in pancakes, a fungus dish for dessert (sweet and delicious). Dish after dish appeared before us. I have never seen Chinese eat together without showing enjoyment, without laughter, without frequent rising to clink glasses and make toasts. I, too, should propose a toast soon, I thought, but as I looked around the table, I knew I could not say what I was feeling.

Oh, I wanted life to be kind to these people. That's what I wanted to say. I wanted the government to be steady and safe and caring. I wished they could all speak openly. And all the young people I'd met who felt caught in too tight a pattern — I wanted them to fulfill themselves as well as work for their country and help move it ahead. I worried about China.

But I said none of this. I stood, raised my glass, and said what also lay in my heart. I spoke of my pride in the city and my happiness in seeing China's progress. I gave the Secretary General a copy of my book, *Homesick*, which he said would go on the shelves of his college library.

In turn, he had gifts for us. A brown and white porcelain vase, tall and graceful. "When you look at this," he said, "you must think of your hometown, Hankou."

In addition, he gave me my personal "chop," a marble seal with the characters of my name on the bottom. On the top a tiny elephant trumpeted with trunk upraised. Chinese use their chop when they sign their letters, documents, paintings, and poetry. I would press mine into the jar of red paste that had come with it, then stamp the characters (Gau Qing—my maiden name) on whatever paper I wanted to sign.

Before I had a chance to express my thanks, the Secretary General said he had an announcement to make. He raised his glass to me. "I now declare that you are an honorary citizen of Hankou, your hometown."

I could scarcely take in the words, but I could see that everyone was standing and smiling at me.

I smiled back. Raising my glass high, I clinked the Secretary General's glass and in turn clinked each glass at the table.

"You do not have a citizen, honorary or otherwise," I said, "more proud of her citizenship."

After dinner when all the goodbyes had been said, Michael and I walked down to the river. I took my place in the middle of the compass —north, south, east, west fanning out around me. Overhead, a lopsided moon presided over China as it always had.

"There is an old Chinese saying," I told Michael. "The moon shines brightest on your hometown."

"Do you think it's true?"

"Maybe. If your hometown is Hankou." Happy as I was, I heard myself sigh.

"You're going to be sorry to leave, aren't you?" Michael asked.

"Yes, I hate to leave China," I admitted. "It hasn't been long enough."

Still, when I thought of America on the other side of the world, I knew I wouldn't be sorry to be back. It had taken me a long time to make America feel like home. Besides, I had work to do.

As soon as I got back, I had to start writing. I wouldn't rest until I had my China homecoming down on paper. Safe between the covers of a book. And when I'd finished writing, I'd stamp the paper with my own seal. Just as any Chinese would do at the end of a story.

Discuss the Selection

1. What did Jean's trip to China make her realize about her past and the history of China?
2. What happened to Jean between the time she moved back to America and the time she returned to China? Write a brief summary of the events.
3. Which part of Jean's return trip to China did you find most interesting? Why?
4. What response did Jean finally decide she would give if asked the question "Where is your hometown?" Why would she answer this way?
5. Find the part of the story that told about Jean's old house. How had it changed?

Apply the Skills

A prefix can change the meaning of a word. The prefix *ante-* means "before." The prefix *anti-* means "against."

Define the underlined word in each of the following sentences.

1. Jean Fritz's "Homesick" antedates "China Homecoming."
2. Jean waited nervously in the small anteroom before she entered the huge banquet hall.
3. The Chinese people certainly were not antisocial when they met Jean Fritz.

Think and Write

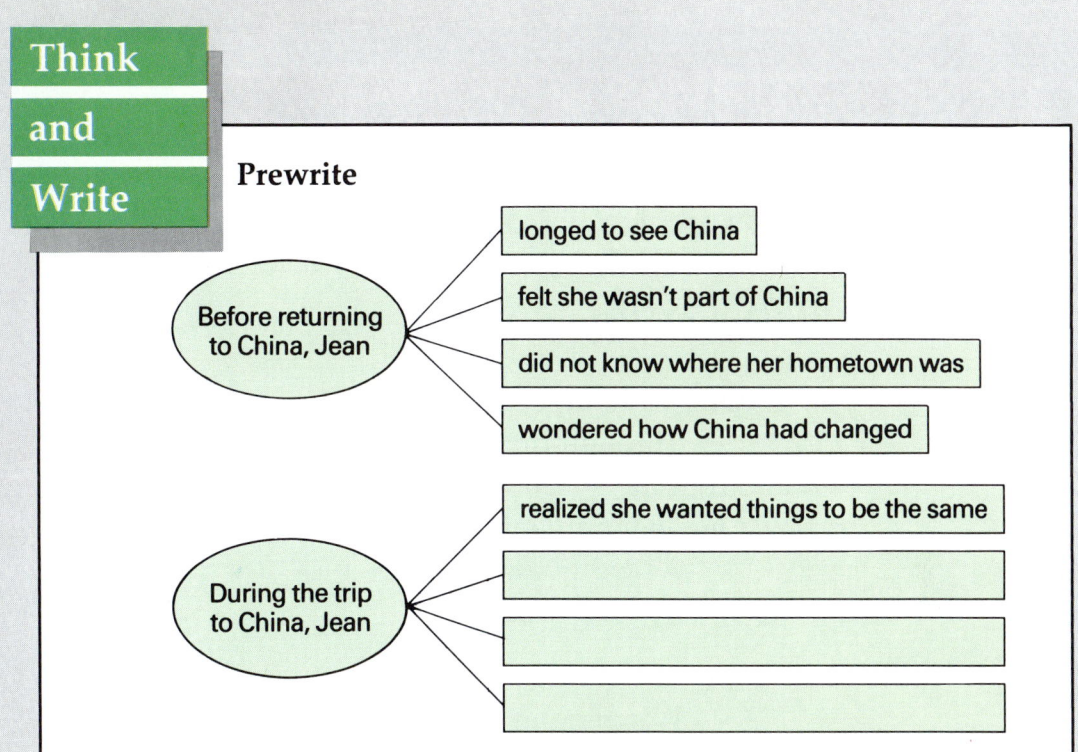

Prewrite

Before returning to China, Jean
- longed to see China
- felt she wasn't part of China
- did not know where her hometown was
- wondered how China had changed

During the trip to China, Jean
- realized she wanted things to be the same
-
-
-

The top half of the diagram above lists some of the ways Jean Fritz felt before she returned to China for a visit. The bottom half lists one way Jean felt during her trip to China. Think about how Jean felt during her visit. Then copy and complete the bottom half of the diagram.

Compose

Use the diagram to help you compose two paragraphs. In the first paragraph, describe Jean's feelings before she returned to China. Then write a second paragraph contrasting those feelings with the way she felt during the trip. Your first paragraph might begin in this way: *Before Jean returned to China for a visit, she longed to see that country again.*

Revise

Read your paragraphs. Do they include all of the information on the diagram? If not, revise your work.

343

The Fallow Deer at the Lonely House

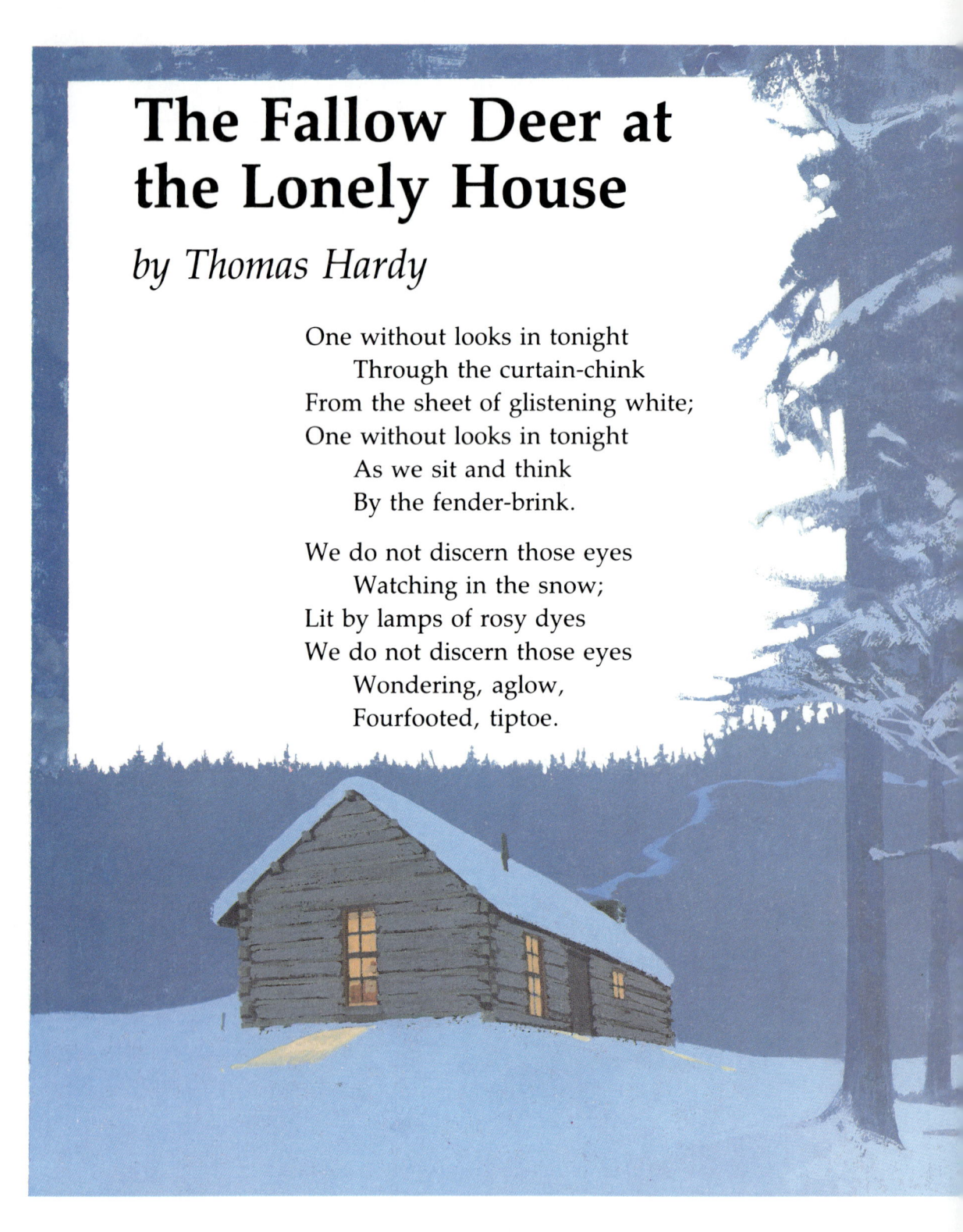

by Thomas Hardy

One without looks in tonight
    Through the curtain-chink
From the sheet of glistening white;
One without looks in tonight
    As we sit and think
    By the fender-brink.

We do not discern those eyes
    Watching in the snow;
Lit by lamps of rosy dyes
We do not discern those eyes
    Wondering, aglow,
    Fourfooted, tiptoe.

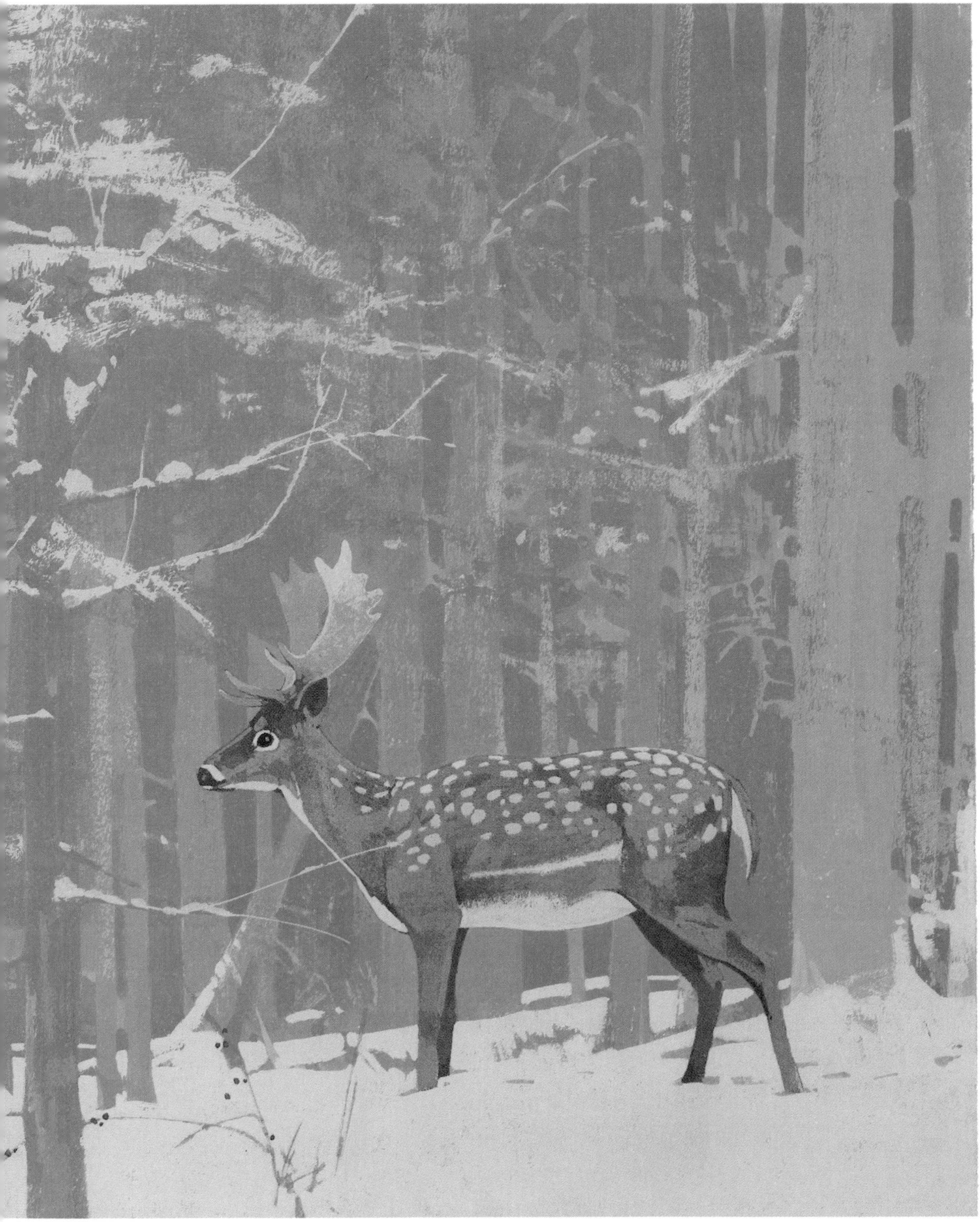

Comprehension Study

Fact and Opinion

The ability to distinguish between fact and opinion helps a reader evaluate and judge material critically. A **fact** is something that is true and can be proved. The statement "The price of an ounce of gold rose thirty-three cents yesterday" is a fact. It can be proved by checking figures in a newspaper or by listening to a news report.

An **opinion** is the way a person feels about a topic or an issue. It cannot be proved. Opinions can be based on a person's emotions, or feelings. They can be based on facts. Opinions may or may not be true. The statement "I think that the price of gold is too high" is an opinion. The speaker is expressing an opinion, but the opinion is based on the fact that the price of gold has been rising.

Certain words can be clues to whether a statement is a fact or an opinion. Words such as *guess, feel, hope, seem,* and *think* are often used when someone states an opinion.

Read the pair of sentences below. Decide which sentence states a fact and which expresses an opinion.

> Gymnastics was the most exciting event in the Summer Olympic Games.
> Athletes competed in synchronized swimming for the first time in the 1984 Summer Olympics.

The first sentence is an opinion. This speaker thought gymnastics was exciting. The opinion is based on the speaker's feelings about how exciting gymnastics was. Notice that none of the clue words mentioned above were used. You can tell this statement is an opinion because it cannot be proved. Some people may agree with the author about the excitement of gymnastics, but others may have a different opinion.

In the example, the second sentence is a fact. It can be checked to see if it is true or not. It is a statement that can be proved.

Opinions Based on Facts

You will find that authors often put statements of fact and opinion in the same selection. You need to be able to tell which statements are facts and which ones are opinions. This will help you make judgments about the selection.

Read the following paragraph. Look for statements of fact—statements that can be proved—and statements that tell the author's opinions.

> Of all the things I saw in China, the most impressive was the Great Wall. The Great Wall of China is almost 4,000 miles long. It is 25 feet tall and 15 feet wide at the top. Parts of the wall are over 2,000 years old. It is beautiful to see the wall wind around mountains and across the borders of deserts through northern China.

The first and the last statements of the paragraph cannot be proved. They are the author's opinions about the beauty and the impressiveness of the wall. All of the other statements are facts. You could check an encyclopedia to prove that each of these statements is true. The author has used both facts and opinions to tell about the Great Wall.

347

Judging an Author's Opinion

When you read an author's opinion, do you have to agree with it? No, of course you don't. You have to judge what the author says and decide whether you agree or not. Perhaps the author does not present *enough* facts to convince you to agree. Perhaps the facts given are *not strong enough* to make you agree. Or, perhaps you feel that the author has only given *one side* of the issue.

The following paragraph states the author's opinion about broccoli. Before you read, decide what opinions you have about broccoli.

Broccoli is a terrific vegetable. It is very high in vitamins A and C. Both the flowers and the tender stems can be eaten. Broccoli is delicious when cooked and served with butter or cheese sauce. Broccoli is especially good served raw in salads or with dip.

The author presented some facts about broccoli along with his or her opinions. Did you like broccoli before you read the paragraph? If you did, you might agree with the author's opinions. If you did not like broccoli before you read the paragraph, did the author cause you to change your mind?

Leading You to an Opinion

An author's opinion might not be stated in a selection. The selection may contain just a set of facts. You can often tell what the author's opinion is from the *way* the author presents the facts. You can also tell what opinion the author is trying to lead you, the reader, to have.

In the paragraph that follows, the author does not state an opinion. See if you can tell what the author's opinion is and what the author wants you to think.

> Tropical rain forests provide homes for many treasures of the plant and animal world. Rain forests also give us valuable foods, chemicals, and medicines. There are many other important resources in them that have not yet been discovered. But farming, logging, and mining are destroying these precious rain forests. Only wise conservation programs can save them for our future.

The author has given you many facts about rain forests. You could prove each statement to be true. The author did not state his or her opinion directly, but you can tell what the author's opinion is. Words such as *treasures, valuable, important, precious, only,* and *wise* tell you that the author thinks rain forests are important enough to be saved through conservation. You can also tell what opinion the author wants you to form. Does the author want you to think that rain forests should be preserved? Yes, this is the opinion the author wants you to form. All of the facts the author has stated support this opinion.

When you can tell the difference between a fact and an opinion, you will be able to judge the information you read. You will be able to make your own decisions about a topic.

Textbook Application: Fact and Opinion in Social Studies

Most textbook authors try to present only the facts about a subject. However, sometimes an author will state an opinion or will explain another person's opinion. Phrases such as "he thought" or "they felt" will tell you that a statement is someone's opinion.

Fact and Opinion in Social Studies

The selection that follows is from a social studies book. It explains some of the things that Marco Polo found in China in 1275. Most of the selection is fact, but some statements tell how Marco Polo felt about the things he saw. As you read, decide whether the statements are fact or opinion.

Which sentence in this paragraph tells what Marco Polo's opinion was?

Are there any opinions expressed in this paragraph?

> The Great Wall was one of the things that impressed an Italian visitor to China in A.D. 1275. He was Marco Polo, one of the first Europeans to spend much time in China. Marco Polo was amazed by the things he saw there.
>
> While Europe was still in the Middle Ages, the Chinese had a brilliant and well-organized empire. Chinese cities such as Beijing bustled with trade and art. Polo learned that the Chinese had a mail service. More than 200,000 riders on horseback delivered letters along the Great Wall. Chinese boats called

junks carried goods about 1,000 miles along the Grand Canal, which linked Beijing with Hangchou. It had been built 600 years earlier.

Marco Polo also commented on other Chinese inventions, such as gunpowder and the compass. He marveled that the Chinese were using paper money. It was far easier to use than the heavy metal coins of Europe. Chinese houses were heated with coal. In some areas the Chinese used coal to heat bath water at a time when few Europeans ever bathed.

—The World Past and Present,
Harcourt Brace Jovanovich

> **What can you infer about Marco Polo's opinion from the facts in this paragraph?**

As you read textbooks, remember that you may find statements of opinion. When you can tell fact from opinion, you will be able to judge information for yourself. You will be able to decide whether you agree with the author or not.

In these letters, a boy learns about his family from his father's viewpoint. Read the letters to find out how this family makes dreams come true.

Letters are a form of personal narrative. As you read these letters, notice how the author includes his thoughts and feelings.

Letters to a Black Boy

by Bob Teague

As a football player at the University of Wisconsin, Bob Teague was so popular that people wanted him to run for public office. Instead, after college he became a newspaper reporter and then a newscaster for a major television network.

Teague started writing letters to his son, Adam, when Adam was only ten months old. Teague wanted his son to know about his family when he grew up and how they had faced their problems. Teague wrote about himself and about Adam's mother, the "Taw Lady," as the ten-month-old called her. His letters also told family stories about his relatives, especially his Aunt Letty.

By publishing the letters, Teague sent them not only to his son but to any family with problems to overcome.

Dear Adam,

I was a bit miffed today by your response to me when the Tall Lady—a nickname your mother may never lose—went shopping and left us alone. No matter what games I thought up, you made it clear that you would not be happy till she returned.

Every five minutes, it seemed, you would crawl to the front door. "Taw Lady? Taw Lady?" was the only question you could ask. You would stay at the door—a questioning look on your face—until I opened it to prove that she was not just beyond it in the hallway. I also tried to explain that she had gone to the store. But you had no idea of what your daddy was driving at. We must have repeated that routine a dozen times.

Anyway, new fathers are sensitive about things like that. It makes them feel useless.

Not that I don't understand your point of view. Daddies are seldom there when you need them. They always seem to be off somewhere. Mothers, on the other hand, are dependable. They have patience for the hundred tiny details so important to your sense of well-being. I felt exactly the same about the only mother I ever knew, Aunt Letty.

When my real mother died giving birth to me, Aunt Letty, her sister, dropped whatever she was doing in Detroit. She came to live with my daddy and me in Milwaukee. I never did find out what it was she left behind. Her reasoning, I gathered years later, was that to know might have given me a feeling of guilt, or of being in her debt.

Whatever it was, Aunt Letty seemed to have no regrets. She plunged into the job of helping a black infant to grow up. She stayed with us until I went away to college at seventeen.

By then she had taught me what I still regard as the most important lesson a black boy has to learn. She convinced me that life was much larger than the limits put on us for the color of our skins. She taught me that I must keep in mind that my world is bigger than the boundaries of the ghetto. She taught me that the world has pains and pleasures, beauty and ugliness, victories and defeats that all people everywhere come to know. She taught me to dream beyond my blackness.

Years later, she taught the whole family how to make a common dream come true.

During the Thanksgiving Day recess of my sophomore year in college, she invited—no, she ordered—the whole family to dinner. By then, she had won her master's degree. She was teaching at a small teachers' college. My daddy and I drove three hundred miles in his 1937 Chevrolet to Detroit.

When we arrived at Aunt Letty's four-room apartment on Twelfth Street in the ghetto, the others were already there. I met fourteen strangers—relatives I had never seen before. But I felt our kinship immediately. Three of the men and two of the women—my daddy's brothers and sisters—reminded me of him. There was also something in their faces—eyes, noses, and chins—that looked like me. Two other women—my mother's sisters—looked like the pictures of mother that my daddy kept. Although all my aunts and uncles had children, I was the only nonadult present. Aunt Letty had told the others to leave their kids at home. She had told them that this was to be an important meeting. I was flattered that she regarded me, at eighteen, as a man.

Aunt Letty had stuffed three turkeys for the dinner. Her dining room was not big enough for the herd she had invited. We served ourselves from the table. Then we filled the chairs, the stools, and the couch in the living room. Some of us wound up sitting on the floor.

During the meal, there was much reminiscing among my daddy and his brothers. They had not seen one another for nearly twenty years. I gathered from their talk that their daddy—my grandfather Claybourn—had been a tough old codger when they were boys together in Tennessee. Almost every story ended with "and then Poppa Claybourn whupped me till I couldn't sit down." Laughter. I was glad that my daddy remembered those "whuppings." It explained why he had spanked me less than a dozen times when I was a boy. As a rule, he had punished me by taking away privileges, such as movies on Saturday mornings at the Princess Theater.

Finally, when we began eating dessert—sweet potato pie—Aunt Letty made a little speech.

"This is the first time we've been together as a family. I hope it won't be the last. The thing that prompted me to call you all together was a letter I got a few months ago from James there. He wanted to know if there was anything I could do to help his son Raymond get to college. In case you haven't heard, Raymond wants to be an airline pilot."

She paused. Some of her sisters and brothers-in-law caught their breaths and groaned sympathetically.

"I know what you're thinking," Aunt Letty went on. "It's a terribly big dream for a young black man to have in Tennessee. But I say why not? I say Raymond ought to have his chance to follow his dream. I say that's what living is all about. I say chances are that boy will wind up in a foundry just like his father unless he gets that chance. And I say all the children in this family—the girls, too—should have their chance. Now none of us at the moment can afford to send anybody to college. It's terribly expensive. But if we stick together as a family, we can send them all, one or two at a time. Confucius say,

'What one man find impossible, seventeen men and women find simple.' " Aunt Letty is fond of crediting the most unlikely wisdom to Confucius.

She went on to explain her idea for a fund. Each branch of the family would contribute to the fund every year. It would guarantee college for every child who dreamed of going. She didn't bother asking for a vote. She could tell from the looks on our faces—and from the tears in the women's eyes—that she was providing the answer to many prayers.

Dear Adam,

This weekend it was your turn to meet the tribe — twenty years after your daddy's introduction.

Those fifteen friendly strangers who almost smothered you with affection are kinfolk — uncles, aunts, and cousins on your daddy's side of the family. You will meet them again and again over the years. As a rule, no children are brought to our annual reunions. So they went overboard for you. They were longing for their own youngsters hundreds of miles away in Wisconsin, Michigan, Illinois, Indiana, and Tennessee.

Why are children left out of our family reunions?

Mainly because the purpose of the gathering is to plan what we can do for all the youngsters in our tribe. We discuss money, job contacts, or special arrangements for projected trips. We even transfer household items from a branch of the family that no longer needs them to the branch that needs them most. Your playpen and the clothes you have outgrown will soon be going to Tennessee.

As I've said before, this tradition began about twenty years ago. It was started by that round-faced gray-haired woman who held you on her lap more than anyone else, Aunt Letty. She's the leader of our tribe. She is also my favorite aunt. Aunt Letty is sixty-two years old now, though she doesn't look it. In her spare time she runs a free school in the Detroit ghetto, where she lives by choice. She encourages black youngsters and helps them with their studies. "There are new opportunities opening up all the time," Aunt Letty is fond of saying. "But Confucius say, 'Opportunity empty if no one prepared to seize it.'"

Aunt Letty always speaks her mind. Confucius is her way of softening the impression that she is giving orders. None of us in the tribe is fooled, however. Aunt Letty

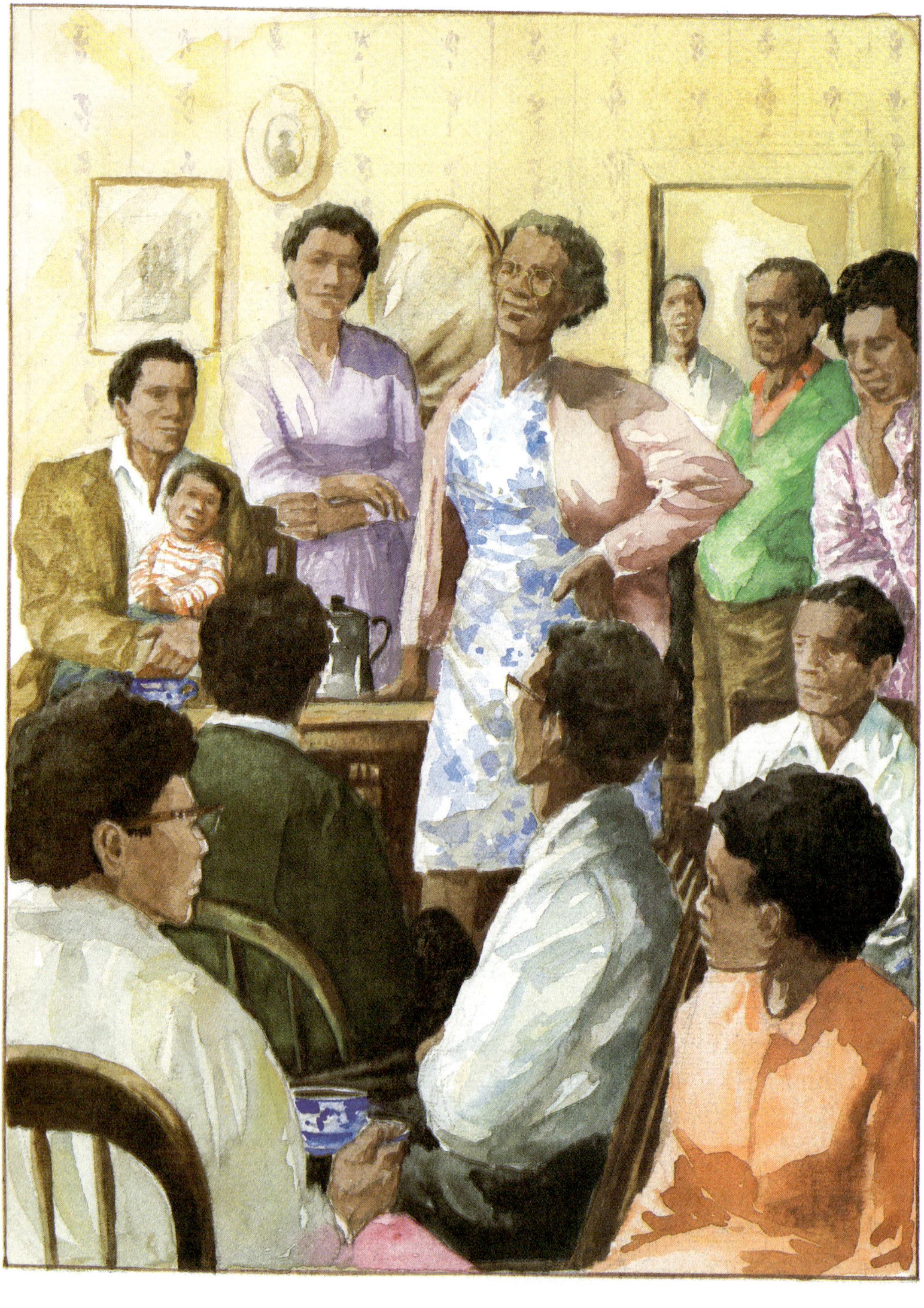

gives the orders, all right. Her orders are always wise. We obey the best we can. In the family assistance program that she started, each one of us gives ten percent of his or her yearly income after taxes. The money goes into a fund, run by Aunt Letty. She spends as much as is necessary to send the tribe's children to college. She invests the rest as she sees fit, and the profits are added to the fund.

This weekend she announced when all of us were together that some of us would have to give a bit more. "Confucius say, 'When cost of living go up, cost of college go into orbit.'"

She explained that the extra assessment was necessary because two more youngsters in the tribe would be starting college next fall. She peered over her glasses. She looked first at me, then at Uncle Mark, and finally at Cousin Raymond. Uncle Mark is a lawyer in Nashville. Cousin Raymond, the first to benefit from the fund, is an airline pilot who lives in Chicago. Our incomes are far above others in the family.

"How much more does Confucius say we should give this time, Aunt Letty?" Cousin Raymond asked with a smile.

Aunt Letty smiled back and focused on him over her glasses. "Confucius say, 'Fifteen hundred too much, five hundred not enough, but one thousand each just right.'"

The three of us sighed, along with our wives. Then we wrote the checks.

Discuss the Selection

1. How did the author's family make dreams come true for family members?
2. How did Adam's family assistance program begin? Briefly summarize its beginnings.
3. How did you feel about Aunt Letty? Would you like her to be your aunt? Explain your answer.
4. How did the family help Cousin Raymond? What was the outcome of their assistance?
5. On what page did you learn what Aunt Letty's relationship was to the author? Find that part of the story and read it.

Apply the Skills

A personal narrative is a story of an experience that is told by the person who had the experience. The person telling the story includes his or her thoughts and feelings about the experience.

Look through "Letters to a Black Boy" to find sentences that tell how Adam's father felt about the experience of being invited to the first reunion, about his new-found relatives, and about Aunt Letty's idea for a fund.

Think and Write

Prewrite

Aunt Letty's Actions	Cause of Her Actions
Aunt Letty comes to live with Bob Teague.	Bob's mother, her sister, has died.
Aunt Letty wants the family to start a fund for the children.	
	Extra money is needed to send two more children to college.

The left-hand side of the chart above lists some of the actions that Aunt Letty took for the good of her family. The right-hand side of the chart lists the causes of these actions. Think about Aunt Letty's actions in the story and about what caused them. Then copy and complete the chart.

Compose

Pretend you are a member of Aunt Letty's family. Write a personal letter to a friend explaining what Aunt Letty has done for her family and why she did these things. Include the information from the chart in your letter. Be sure to add the date, a closing, and a signature. You might begin the letter in this way:

Dear ____,
   I went to visit Aunt Letty today. She's a very special member of our family.

Revise

Read your letter. Check to be sure that you dated the letter and that you ended the letter with a closing followed by a signature.

Study Skills

Propaganda Techniques

Sometimes writers want to convince you to do something or to persuade you to their point of view. This kind of writing is called propaganda. **Propaganda** is an effort to persuade people to support certain ideas.

Forms of Propaganda

There are many kinds of propaganda. One kind is **advertising**. Advertisers want to convince you to buy their products. They try to make you think their product is better than others. You have seen this type of propaganda on TV and in magazines.

Editorials are another kind of propaganda. They can be found in newspapers and on TV. An editorial gives an opinion about something. The person who writes an editorial tries to persuade people who read it to agree with that opinion. Most newspapers have an editorial page. On this page you may find an editorial stating an editor's thoughts about a topic. You may also find editorial cartoons and letters to the editor stating people's opinions.

The cartoon on the next page might be found on an editorial page. The cartoon is about taxes. "Everyperson" stands for the average taxpayer. The boulder stands for the taxes Everyperson pays. There is a heavy tax burden on Everyperson's back that is about to crush him.

In this editorial cartoon, the artist wants people to agree that for most taxpayers, today's taxes are too great.

A small newspaper might print the following editorial:

Save the Forests

Local builders have revealed plans to build apartments on what is now forest land. This is the last undeveloped land in our city. We are against their plans.

Destroying the forests will destroy the balance of nature. Wildlife will be forced to flee, and will most likely die because their homes will be gone. Our forests must be preserved to protect the land and save trees that would take many years to replace.

New apartments will also overload existing services. The builders have not disclosed plans to build new support services, such as schools, stores, and roads.

The writer of this editorial is against the building of new apartments. Several reasons are given: Wildlife will die, forests will be destroyed, and new apartments will overload existing services.

Slanted Writing and Loaded Words

A person who writes propaganda wants to convince you to support an idea or an action. The writer can do this in different ways. One way is to use **slanted writing**.

In slanted writing, a writer uses only those facts that will support his or her idea. In the editorial about saving the forests, the writer gives many reasons why new apartments would be bad. Since the writer is against the building of new apartments, the editorial uses only facts that support that point of view. The writer did not offer any reasons why new apartments might be good.

Sometimes writers use **loaded words** to make people respond. Loaded words often appeal to people's emotions. They try to slant people's opinions to support something or to take a stand against it.

Look back at the editorial about the forests. Words such as *destroy, flee,* and *die* are loaded. They help to create a picture of animals running for their lives. They slant people's opinions against new apartments.

The Panthers

**SLEEK, SWIFT, BOLD
ONLY FOR THOSE WHO DARE —**

The sign at the bottom of the previous page advertises a new car. Strong words such as *sleek, swift, bold,* and *dare* appeal to the reader's emotions. Suppose the sign had said, "For sale — fast new car." It might catch someone's eye for a short time, but those words would not be likely to hold someone's attention.

**For hair smooth as silk, shiny, fresh and clean —
Use Glossy Shampoo**

This advertisement for shampoo uses many loaded words. Can you identify them?

People should read propaganda very carefully. They should use it to form their *own* opinions. Propaganda is neither good nor bad. It is a persuasive tool.

> *In her stories, Yoshiko Uchida tries to help readers understand her viewpoints about people everywhere. What are these viewpoints?*
>
> *As you read the selection, think about what parts are fact and what parts are opinion.*

Yoshiko Uchida: From Japan to America, With Love

by Bernice E. Cullinan

Yoshiko Uchida likes to write books for young people about young people. She wants them to know that human beings are alike all over the world, with similar joys and hopes. Whether she writes about Japan, Japanese-Americans, or Americans, Yoshiko Uchida writes about the positive things in life.

Uchida was born in Alameda, California, and grew up in Berkeley. Both of her parents were immigrants from Japan. Following the Japanese custom of that time, their marriage was arranged. Her father came to the United States to work. Her mother came to the U.S. a few years later to marry. She never saw the man she was going to marry until she arrived. The arranged marriage was a successful one. Uchida remembers her parents as loving and sensitive.

Uchida writes about this Japanese marriage custom in one of her books, *A Jar of Dreams*. Like Uchida, the book's main character, Rinko, has parents whose marriage was arranged by a go-between. Uchida expresses her own feelings about the custom through Rinko's words. "I've always wondered how Mama could do such a thing. I mean, leave behind her entire family and sail to a foreign country to marry a man she had never seen before. I know I'd never do a thing like that. But Mama said that's what a lot of Japanese women did in those days."

Yoshiko Uchida remembers her childhood with mixed emotions. As a young girl, she always liked to draw and write. She recalls going to the backyard of her house where there was a hammock strung between a peach and an apricot tree. Sitting in the hammock, she would write her stories on the back of old wrapping paper. The ideas for these stories came from her Japanese home and heritage. Her parents and visiting relatives told Japanese folktales that were not known in the United States.

Uchida had some bad memories of her school years. For a while, she felt that she did not fit in. She could not adjust to being one of only a few Japanese-Americans in her school, to being different.

Some of these feelings are shared by the characters in her books. Rinko's feelings of not fitting in in *A Jar of Dreams* are based on Uchida's own memories. Rinko says, "I felt ashamed of who I was and wished I could shrink right down and disappear into the sidewalk. There are a few girls in my class at school who make me feel that way too . . . They talk to each other, but they talk over and around and right through me like I was a pane of glass. And that makes me feel like a big nothing. Some days I feel so left out . . . I hate having a name like Rinko Tsujimura that nobody can pronounce or remember. And more than anything, I wish I could be just like everybody else."

Yoshiko Uchida writes about Japanese-American children who have experiences similar to her own. This is the subject that she knows best. She also knows that anyone, not just Asian-Americans, can feel as

Yoshiko Uchida, aged 10, with her parents, her grandmother, and her older sister (seated)

she did. Anyone can feel alienated — alone and without friends.

Through characters like Rinko, Uchida helps readers understand the feelings of all young people, whether they're members of a minority group or not. Rinko could be any young person when she says, "I don't know why I can't speak up in class. I certainly can make myself heard when I'm at home. And when I'm having conversations with people inside my head, I'm always speaking up, telling them what I think in a loud, firm voice.

"But in school it's different. If you feel like a big nothing and don't like who you are, naturally you don't speak up in a loud, firm voice. You don't talk to other people either, unless they talk to you first."

After graduating from the University of California, Uchida continued her education and received a master's degree from Smith College in Massachusetts. Then she was awarded a special grant to go to Japan and collect folktales and stories for children's books. She remained in Japan for several years. When she returned to New York she began writing books containing these Japanese stories. She wanted American children to become familiar with the marvelous tales she had heard in Japan. She even illustrated some of the stories.

Uchida made the stories that had been told and retold to Japanese children meaningful to American children too. She wants American children to read about Japanese children, and to come to respect differences in other people's customs and culture. By preserving these stories, she hopes to give young Asian-Americans a sense of their past and a sense of pride in their background.

Yoshiko Uchida received a Distinguished Service Award from the University of Oregon in 1981 for having "helped to bring about a greater understanding of the Japanese-American culture."

Whether she retells traditional Japanese folktales or writes about Japanese-American children, Yoshiko Uchida is a gifted storyteller. She writes about how much alike people are beneath the surface, regardless of where they were born or what they look like. She shows that people everywhere all have the same basic feelings. She teaches that people should care for each other in many ways. It is this valuable lesson that makes Yoshiko Uchida's writing so special.

Discuss the Selection

1. What are some of the viewpoints that Yoshiko Uchida tries to convey in her writing?
2. How and where did Uchida learn the Japanese stories and folktales that she writes about?
3. Reread the passages that show how Rinko, the main character in *A Jar of Dreams*, feels. Do you think Uchida has written about how young people really feel? Explain your answer.
4. How did Uchida feel about school when she was young? Why did she feel this way?
5. People think that Uchida's writing is special. Find the parts of the selection that show this.

Apply the Skills

In writing, an author often uses facts as well as opinions. Facts are true and can be proved. Opinions are based on thoughts and feelings and cannot be proved.

Identify each of the following sentences from the selection as either fact or opinion.

1. Uchida was born in Alameda, California, and grew up in Berkeley.
2. It is these valuable lessons that make Yoshiko Uchida's writing so special.
3. Yoshiko Uchida is a gifted storyteller.
4. Yoshiko Uchida received a Distinguished Service Award from the University of Oregon in 1981.

Think and Write

Prewrite

```
                Information Summary
Name: _____
Birthplace and Family: _____
_____
Her Early Years: _____
_____
Her Writing and Her Views: _____
_____
Awards and Honors: _____
```

Imagine that you have been chosen to introduce Yoshiko Uchida to an audience to whom she will speak. Introductions of speakers briefly summarize the highlights of the life and work of the speaker. To gather information for your introduction, copy the chart above and complete it with information from the selection about Yoshiko Uchida.

Compose

Use the information on your chart to write a brief introduction for Yoshiko Uchida. Remember to include the highlights of Uchida's life and work. Try to keep your introduction brief and interesting. You may wish to end your introduction with a sentence similar to the following: *And now, without further delay, our speaker and favorite writer, Yoshiko Uchida.*

Revise

Read your introduction. Is it interesting? Is it brief? Does it summarize the information in your chart? If not, revise your work.

Comprehension Study

Author's Purpose and Viewpoint

Authors have different purposes, or reasons, for writing. A writer may create a story in order to **entertain** readers. An author may write to **inform**, or tell facts about something. Some writers write in order to **criticize**, or express their opinions. Others want to **persuade** their readers to think or act in a particular way.

To Entertain

Most of the stories and books that you read were written to entertain you. The author felt that he or she had an interesting story to tell. Whether you like funny stories, scary stories, or exciting stories, you read the kinds of stories and books you enjoy. This kind of reading is entertaining.

To Inform

In the following paragraph, the author tells the reader about campfire safety.

> To build a campfire first find a clear spot, away from trees or structures. Clear the ground down to the soil. Use dead twigs and branches to start the blaze. Keep the fire small. When you are finished using the campfire, douse the flames completely. Before leaving the campsite, make sure the fire is totally out.

The purpose of this paragraph is to inform the reader. This kind of writing rarely calls on the reader to form an opinion or to make judgments.

To Criticize

In the following paragraph the writer's purpose is to criticize or express an opinion about a new movie.

> Ron William's new movie, *Danger at Dawn*, is a thriller. He's created a masterpiece of suspense — no sooner does the plot twist than it unexpectedly turns again. From opening to closing credits, the audience sits on the edges of their seats. The actors are convincingly real and the special effects are great!

It is clear that this writer liked *Danger at Dawn*. The writer's critical opinion is positive, or favorable, toward the movie. By reading this review and others, a movie viewer can form his or her own opinion of the movie, and then decide whether to see it.

To Persuade

An author may want to convince readers to feel a certain way or to act a certain way. This author writes to persuade the reader. Read the following example. What is the author trying to persuade you to feel and do?

> Building a waste treatment facility in Glen Oaks will decrease the value of our homes. The serene, suburban atmosphere will be destroyed by the rumbling of heavy trucks down our peaceful streets. Foul odors will force us indoors. Do you want this to happen? If not, join your neighbors to fight this proposed construction.

The author of that paragraph is against the building of a waste treatment plant. The author tries to persuade the reader to oppose the proposed construction.

Author's Viewpoint

In order to understand what you read, it is helpful to be able to determine what the author thinks and feels about the subject. An author may have strong feelings about a particular topic. These feelings can determine how the author writes about the topic. The author bases his or her viewpoint on facts, emotions, and past experiences.

Often an author does not state his or her viewpoint. A reader must infer, or form ideas about, the author's viewpoint from what is stated and the way it is stated. Read the following paragraph to determine the author's viewpoint.

Water is a precious resource. It is up to each person to waste as little of it as possible. People should ask themselves what they can do to help. If everyone does his or her part to save water, there will be no water shortages.

It is this writer's viewpoint that everyone must take measures to save water. As you read, you can form your own opinion of the author's view. Your opinion is based on your experiences, your background, and what you already know about the topic.

Read the following paragraph to find the author's viewpoint.

> Larry Nicolletti is the best, most qualified candidate for senator. His record in the state legislature shows that he has worked hard for his constituents over the years. He has been a fine representative and would be an even better senator.

In this paragraph, the author strongly supports Larry Nicolletti as a candidate for senator. Although the author refers to Mr. Nicolletti's record, specific things he has done are not mentioned. You may either agree or disagree with this author's opinion. A stronger argument could be built for or against this candidate if more specific facts were given.

As you read, try to figure out what the author's viewpoint is. This will help you decide why the author wrote the selection. Knowing the author's viewpoint and the author's purpose will help you make up your own mind about what you read.

Textbook Application: Author's Purpose and Viewpoint in Health

Most textbooks are written to teach or inform you about a topic. The author tries to present information that will be interesting to read and easy to understand. You read a textbook to find out about the topic.

The following selection is taken from a health book. The sidenotes will help you understand the author's purpose. Does the author have a viewpoint?

> **Here the author is explaining about one kind of medicine. What facts are given?**

> **Look for facts about another kind of medicine. What is the author's purpose in giving these facts?**

> **The author has a definite viewpoint about taking medicines. What is it?**

Two Kinds of Medicine

Some medicines can be used only with a doctor's order, or **prescription**. These medicines are **prescription medicines**. Only a doctor can decide who should use these medicines and when and how they should be used. Prescription medicines are prepared by a health worker called a **pharmacist**. Pharmacists work in hospitals and drugstores.

Some medicines can be bought without a prescription. These are called **over-the-counter**, or **OTC**, **medicines**. Most OTC medicines are used to treat minor health problems. OTC medicines include cold pills, cough syrups, and pain pills. They are sold in drugstores and in some food stores.

How to Use Medicines Safely

You should never take a medicine unless a parent or doctor tells you to. Even then, you should always take a medicine exactly as directed. Every medicine comes with directions that tell the proper way to use it.

Directions for using an OTC medicine are printed on the label that comes with it. Additional directions are sometimes included on an extra sheet of paper inside the medicine package. Look for the answers to these questions as you read the directions: Who should take the medicine? What symptoms should the medicine be used to relieve? What is the **dosage**, or correct amount of the medicine, that should be taken at one time? How often should the medicine be taken? What are the possible side effects of the medicine? Make sure you can answer these questions before you take any medicine.

Prescription medicines also have labels that give directions for using the medicine safely. The name of the doctor who wrote the prescription and the name of the person who should take the medicine are printed on the label. If your name is not on the label, do not take the medicine.

— *HBJ Health,*
Harcourt Brace Jovanovich

> This paragraph explains how to use OTC medicines. What is the author's purpose in this explanation?

> This is an explanation of how to use prescription medicines safely. What is the author's purpose in providing this information? Did the author accomplish this purpose?

Whenever you read, you make judgments about what you read. A good reader thinks about what the author's purpose for writing and viewpoint are. Thinking about these things will help you to make your own judgments about what you read.

A sharp eye and a quick mind are important in the Wild West. Read to find out how Opie keeps from being fooled.

Authors write to inform, to persuade, to give an opinion, and to entertain. Why did the author write "The Ghost on Saturday Night"?

The Ghost on Saturday Night

by Sid Fleischman

There's nothing bashful about a tule fog. It'll creep inside your clothes. It'll seep through the window cracks and get right into bed with you.

When I got home from the schoolhouse on Tuesday, there wasn't a wisp of fog. I lived with my Great-Aunt Etta, and she was waiting for me.

"Opie," she said. "How would you like chicken for supper?"

"Yes, *ma'am!*" I said.

"Splendid. I've got the chicken. You go pluck it."

I gave a groan. She gave me the chicken. She had a way of foxing me into doing pesky chores like that.

I sat myself on the chopping stump and began to pull feathers. I passed the time thinking up names for my horse. I already had a list a mile-and-a-half long.

I didn't own a horse — yet.

But I had one promised. Aunt Etta had struck a bargain with me. When I earned enough money to buy a good saddle, she'd buy a good horse to fit under it.

The trouble was I was only ten and kind of runty in size. The older, bigger boys seemed to get all the after-school jobs around town.

"Wild Charlie," I said aloud. I liked the sound of that. I could see myself galloping across the meadow on Wild Charlie. But when I looked up, I couldn't see the meadow. Or the trees. Or the barn. And before long I couldn't even see the chicken in my hands.

A tule fog had sprung up.

My heart gave a mighty leap. There was saddle money to be made in a good thick fog! I had already saved $2.11. But I needed heaps and heaps of money—$17.59 exactly.

I guess there's nothing thicker and wetter than a ground-hugging California tule fog. Aunt Etta was always saying not to stand in one too long. You'd grow webbed feet.

I felt my way back to the house and handed the bird to Aunt Etta.

"I'll be back for supper," I said.

"Don't you get lost," she said. "That tule is so thick you'll need a compass to cross the road."

"Yes, ma'am."

I lifted my feet for town. I guess I was the only boy in Golden Hill who'd gone into the fog business. I'd gotten the idea from Aunt Etta herself.

Even in the thickest tule she was sure-footed as a mountain goat. She knew every brick, every post, and every building by heart. So did I. I could streak through town with my eyes shut.

I passed one end of the old Horseshoe Mine tunnel. I couldn't see it, but I knew it was there because of the dip in the road. Before long I reached the hotel hitching rack. I crossed the dirt street and counted forty-seven strides. That brought me to Muldoon's General Store.

"Any special errands you want run, Mr. Muldoon?" I asked. He was one of my best tule customers.

"Opie," he said, "if that fog gets any thicker, you'd be able to drive a nail into it and hang your coat. Think you can find the barbershop?"

"Yes, sir."

He filled a can with lamp oil, and I set out to deliver it. I turned the corner and kept going until I reached the livery stable. I knew it by the smell. Then I crossed the street. When I sniffed hair tonic, I knew I was at Ed Russell's barbershop.

It turned out there was a stranger in town. Mr. Russell had just finished cutting his hair.

"Opie," he said, "you could do this gentleman a service if you scouted him back to the hotel."

"Be pleased to," I said.

That stranger was a big man and uglier than homemade soap. He clasped my shoulder with one hand as I led him out along the wooden sidewalk. That hand of his was cold. It felt like ice melting on my shoulder.

He followed along behind me without saying a word.

I didn't say much either. He was kind of scary. But when we passed the bank, I said, "You ever hear of anyone buying a horse with a penny?"

He didn't answer.

"Well, sir, that's what my Great-Aunt Etta is going to do," I added.

He wasn't interested—that was clear. So I didn't tell him it was an 1877 Indian-head penny. Rare as a hen's tooth, that date. And mighty valuable. She had Mr. Whitman, the banker, keep it in his safe.

"Here we are, sir," I said. We reached the hotel porch. He lifted that freezing claw of his off my shoulder. I was glad to be rid of him. But I hoped I would be a nickel closer to my saddle.

He dug in his vest pocket. He handed me a card. And he disappeared through the door.

I was sorely disappointed. He was not only big and ugly; he was stingy too. What did I want his card for?

It was kind of hard to read in the fog. The sun was giving off about as much light as an orange cat. But as I held it closer I saw that it wasn't a calling card. It was a ticket of some sort.

> Admit Two
>
> Compliments of Professor Pepper

Admit two to what? Not a word about that. I might have thrown it away if I hadn't been so puzzled. I jammed it into my back pocket and went about my fog business.

By the time I reached home, I had the jingle of thirty-five cents in my pocket. I hoped the tule fog would hang on for weeks.

But it lifted around noon the next day. And all over town signs had been tacked up.

Professor Pepper! I could still feel the chilly clasp of his hand on my shoulder.

I ran home and showed my ticket to Aunt Etta.

"He gave it to me himself!" I said.

"Who did?"

"Professor Pepper. He's a famous ghost-raiser!"

She looked at me over the tops of her glasses. "What on earth is a ghost-raiser?"

"Haven't you seen the signs? He's going to raise the ghost of Crookneck John on Saturday night. Right here in Miners' Union Hall."

THE GHOST IS COMING!

See the ghost of Crookneck John!

Famous Outlaw
Murderer
Bank Robber
Thief & Scoundrel

Hung three times before he croaked!

The Genuine Ghost

Brought back by Professor Pepper, the famous ghost-raiser. Don't miss this event. Startling! Educational! Ladies welcome. No children under twelve allowed.

Miners' Union Hall
50 cents Admission

Saturday Night
8 p.m. sharp

"Poppycock," Aunt Etta said.

"The signs say so. The genuine ghost too."

"I'll believe that when I see it," she snorted.

"But they won't let me in," I said.

"Why not?"

"I'm not old enough."

Aunt Etta stared at me. I didn't have to tell her how much I wanted to have a peek at the ghost of Crookneck John. She could see that for herself.

"Well, I'm old enough for both of us," she said. "We'll go."

"But Aunt Etta—"

"You don't think I'd visit a spook show *alone*, Opie. We'll see it together. That's that. Leave it to me."

Saturday morning arrived at last.

Then it was Saturday afternoon.

Then it was Saturday night.

Aunt Etta put on her hat, and we set out for the Miners' Union Hall.

We climbed the wooden stairs to the hall. A toad-faced man stood at the door. He was taking folks' money and tossing it into a box.

When he saw me, he shook his head. "That boy ain't old enough to be twelve," he said.

"Correct," Aunt Etta said.

"Then he can't go in."

"Nonsense," she said.

"Ma'am, that ghost will scare him skinny."

"He's already skinny."

"Then his hair will turn white," the man said.

"Horsefeathers, sir." She handed him my ticket from Professor Pepper himself. "Will you kindly read that."

"It says admit two."

Aunt Etta straightened to her full height. "Exactly. I'm *one* and he's *two*. And the ticket orders you to *admit* us. Step aside, sir, before I call the sheriff."

That man turned white at the mention of the sheriff.

"Come along, Opie," Aunt Etta said.

We breezed right through the door. Oh, she was clever as forty crickets, my Great-Aunt Etta.

The hall was long and shadowy. Two oil lamps burned and smoked right in front of the curtain. That's all the light there was.

We took chairs near the front and waited. Before long all the chairs were taken. And folks were standing along the walls.

We could hear noises behind the curtain. There were creaking sounds. And sawing sounds. And hammering sounds.

"Maybe it's the ghost," I said.

Aunt Etta shook her head. "Crookneck John was an outlaw—not a carpenter."

We waited. And waited some more. At ten minutes to nine, Professor Pepper stepped through the curtains.

"I will ask you not to scream out," he announced in a deep voice.

"Moonshine," Aunt Etta whispered.

Professor Pepper took a grip on the lapel of his black frock coat. "What you will see tonight is stranger than strange. Odder than odd. Aye, a dead man deader than dead will walk among you. A cutthroat, he was. Bank robber. The most feared outlaw of the century!"

I began to scrunch down in my chair. I couldn't help it.

"Hung once, he was," Professor Pepper went on. "Hung twice, he was. Hung three times! Aye, that's how he came to be known as Crookneck John."

Professor Pepper lowered his heavy brows. "I would advise the faint-hearted to leave before the ghost-raising begins."

He paused. Everyone seemed to look at everyone else. "Now, then, I must have absolute silence!" said Professor Pepper. He clapped his hands sharply.

The curtains parted.

A pine coffin was stretched across two sawhorses. It looked old and rotted, as if it had been dug out of the ground.

"Aye, the very box holding the bones of Crookneck John," the professor declared. "The coffin is six feet long. Crookneck John was almost seven feet. Buried with his knees bent up, he was."

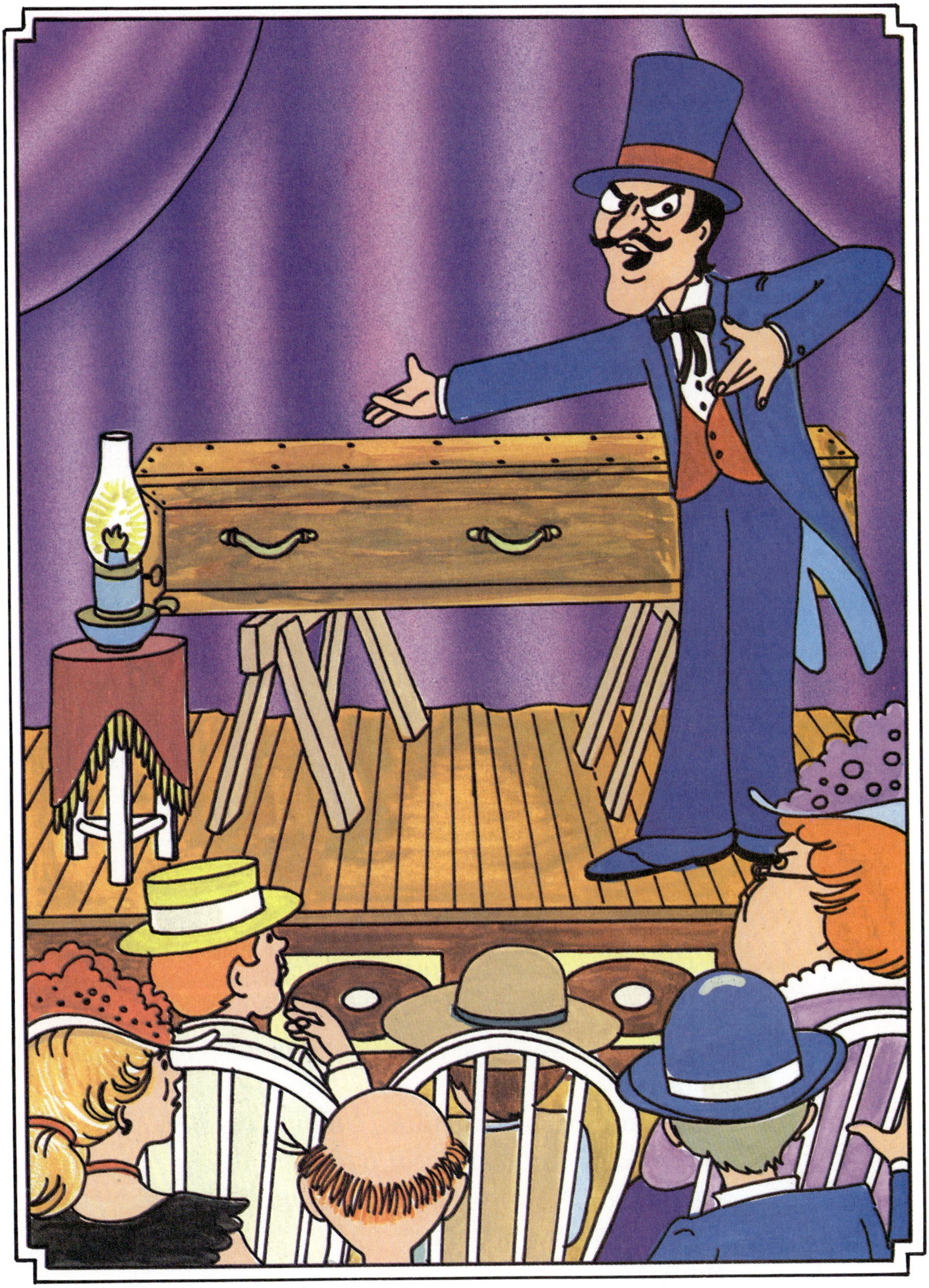

Then Professor Pepper clapped his hands again. His assistant, the toad-faced man, appeared and blew out the two oil lamps. Pitch darkness closed in on the hall.

For a moment, I don't think anyone took a breath.

Professor Pepper's voice came rolling out through the blackness.

"Crookneck John," he called. "I have your bones. Is the spirit willing to come forth, eh? Give a sign."

Silence. All I could hear was my own heart beating. Then there came a hollow rap-rap-rapping from the pine box.

"Aye, I hear the knock of your big knuckles, Mr. Crookneck John. Now rise up. Rise up your bones and stretch your legs, sir."

My eyes strained to see through the darkness.

A minute went by. Maybe two or three. When Professor Pepper spoke again, he was getting impatient.

"Rise up, you scoundrel! Ashamed to show your crooked neck to these honest folks, eh? This is Professor Pepper himself speaking. I won't be made a fool of, sir!"

Seconds ticked away. Then a minute or two. Professor Pepper became as short tempered as a teased snake.

"Rise up, I say!" he commanded. "I've a hanging rope in my hand! Aye, and I'll string you up a *fourth* time!" And then there came a creaking of wood. And a groaning of nails. My neck went cold and prickly. *The lid of that pine coffin was lifting!*

"I can't make out a thing," Aunt Etta said.

Suddenly the snarl went out of Professor Pepper's voice. "No! No!" he gasped. "Down! Back, sir! Not the rope!" Gurgling sounds escaped from his throat. "Help! Help! The lamps. Light the la—!"

I was sitting so straight by then that I must have shot up six inches taller. The toad-faced man struck a match to the nearest lamp.

The air lit up. And there, against the curtain, staggered Professor Pepper. A noose was pulled tightly around his neck.

The lid of the coffin stood open.

Professor Pepper clawed at the rope around his throat and caught a breath. "Save yourselves!" he croaked. "Run for your lives! Lock your doors! Shut your windows! Stay off the streets! The Crookneck Ghost is loose!"

"Come on, Aunt Etta!" I said.

She was calm as an owl at midnight. "Sit where you are."

The hall emptied in a whirlwind hurry. Even the toad-faced man was gone.

There was no one left but Professor Pepper and us.

"Madam," he said. He'd freed himself of the rope and was hammering the lid back on the coffin. "Your lives are in terrible danger!"

"Pish-posh," she answered. "I'll expect you to refund everyone's money, sir."

At that, he banged his thumb with the hammer, "What!"

"Other folks paid at the door to *see* a ghost. They have been flimflammed."

"Really, Madam!"

"*I* didn't see a ghost. *Opie* didn't see a ghost. No one *saw* that ghost of yours."

He stopped shaking the pain out of his thumb. "Unfortunately, Madam, my assistant appears to have flown for his life. And with the box full of money. Why, it wouldn't surprise me if we find him with his neck broke and robbed by that thieving ghost."

"Pay up, sir," was all Aunt Etta would say. "Come along, Opie."

"Hold on," Professor Pepper said with sudden politeness. "I've been nearly strangled. Aye, short of breath I am. Perhaps that lad will help me carry the coffin downstairs."

"What on earth for?" Aunt Etta said.

"Why, Crookneck John must return to his dry bones before the crow of dawn, Madam. That's the way of ghosts, you know. I'll have the burying box moved to the jailhouse. He'll wake up behind bars, the scoundrel! Aye, with the money, if he has it."

Then he turned an eye on me. "I'll reward you for your trouble, lad. Cash money."

It wouldn't be much if I knew him, but cash money was saddle money.

Aunt Etta could read my thoughts. "I've seen enough play-acting for one night," she said. "It's past my bedtime. I'm going home, Opie."

"I won't be long," I said.

That pine box was heavy. I didn't think dry old bones could weigh so much. Then I reminded myself that Crookneck John had been seven feet tall.

The moon was rising and full.

When we struggled down to the foot of the stairs, Professor Pepper's breath gave out.

"This'll do, lad," he said. "Oh, I should have known better than to raise the Crookneck Ghost on a full moon night. Turns him wild."

Then he dug in his coat pocket and handed me a coin. A mighty small one.

"Run home fast as you can, hear? Make sure that fine lady of yours is safe. I'll manage for myself."

"Much obliged for the cash money," I said politely. But I could tell from the feel it was only a cent piece.

I didn't run home. I wasn't worried about Aunt Etta. She'd said it was all play-acting. Professor Pepper *himself* could have done the rap-rap-rapping on the coffin. And he could have tied the noose around his *own* neck.

I wasn't even past the hotel when the moon faded out of the sky. The tule fog was creeping back.

I gave the cent piece a flip in the air and caught it. I put it in my pocket and then took it out again. Awfully clean and shiny, I thought, as if it had never been in use. Like Aunt Etta's rare Indian-head penny in the bank safe.

There was just enough moonlight left to make out the date.

My breath caught. It was an 1877 Indian-head cent.

It appeared to be Aunt Etta's very own penny, I thought. The penny was going to buy a horse to fit under my saddle!

But how had it come to be in Professor Pepper's coat pocket?

Just then I heard the snort of a horse and the creaking of wagon wheels.

"Bah! This fog's so thick I couldn't find my nose with both hands and a lantern."

I knew that voice. It belonged to Professor Pepper's assistant.

"I'm not interested in your nose, idiot!" It was the snarl of Professor Pepper himself. "Find the road. And quick before this town has the law on us."

The law? Suddenly I knew the only way Aunt Etta's rare cent could have gotten into the professor's pocket.

He'd robbed the bank!

I had to do something. I felt my way along the hotel hitching post until I could make out the faint glow of their wagon lamp.

"Stop, sir!" I called out. "You're heading straight into a tree. Need help?"

"Help indeed!" said Professor Pepper. "Where's the road out of town, eh?"

Then he paused.

"Don't I know that voice?"

I was having a time to keep my teeth from clacking now. "Yes, sir," I said. "I'm Opie. I scouted you from the barbershop to the hotel in a thicker fog than this."

"Well, take that nag by the nose and lead us out of here. When Crookneck John wakes up in the jailhouse, he'll be after my blood."

More play-acting, I thought! Oh, he was full of tricks. He'd scared folks into staying off the streets while he got away. But he hadn't counted on the tule fog.

Or me. An idea had already sprung into my head.

I led the horse and wagon step by step along the road; toward home. When I came to the dip, I stopped. We were at one end of the old Horseshoe Mine.

"There's a big tunnel on the left, sir. About two miles long. It's kind of a short cut through the fog."

"Aye, a short cut would please me!" The professor laughed.

A moment later they went clattering into the mine tunnel.

I was in such a hurry to reach Mr. Whitman's house that I must have barked my shins six times and run into a wall at least once.

Mr. Whitman owned the bank. I showed him Aunt Etta's 1877 one-cent piece. I told him I thought Professor Pepper had robbed the safe. And we went for the sheriff.

Sure enough, the bank safe was empty.

"But the walls of the bank are solid stone," Mr. Whitman said. "How did he get in?"

I had already noticed bits of sawdust. I looked up. The sheriff looked up.

"Yup," he said. "Professor Pepper cut through the floor of the Miners' Union Hall upstairs. Probably let himself down with the rope and up again. Then hammered the wood back into place."

I remembered hearing hammer sounds behind the curtain during the long wait for the show to start.

"And he must have hoped we'd believe it was the Crookneck Ghost who'd robbed the bank," the sheriff said. "Well, Professor Pepper can't have got far in this fog."

"Not far at all," I said. "He's in Horseshoe Mine."

"The Horseshoe Mine! Doesn't he know it makes a perfect horseshoe and comes out about forty feet from the jailhouse?"

"No, sir," I said. "I didn't tell him that."

The end of the tunnel was dark as a sack of black

cats. The sheriff waited. His three deputies waited. And I waited too.

Before long we could hear the echo of horse's hooves. My heart began to beat a little faster. The glow of lantern appeared like a firefly deep in the tunnel.

The sheriff lifted his shotgun and nodded to his deputies. "Get ready, boys. The rest of you stay back."

The wagon lantern grew larger and brighter. Then I could see Professor Pepper himself—chuckling and singing.

But when he saw the law waiting for him, he gave a gasp and a groan.

"Great jumping hop-toads!" he cried out. He grabbed the reins and tried to turn the wagon around. But the mine shaft wasn't wide enough.

The sheriff charged forward and caught the horse by the halter.

"That will do, gents," he said. "Welcome back to Golden Hill. Easy, now, or you'll end up buckshot ghosts."

"Thunder and lightning," the professor snarled. "We've been outfoxed!"

His helper was still clutching the box full of flimflam money. The deputies led them away, together with Professor Pepper.

The sheriff climbed onto the wagon and called to me.

"Opie. Did you say this coffin was uncommon heavy?"

"Yes, sir."

"Hold the lantern."

As I held the lantern, he pried off the lid. There were no bones in the pine box at all.

It was full of money. The stolen bank money.

The sheriff looked through his reward posters.

"Sorry, Opie," he said finally. "There's no reward offered for Professor Pepper. You do deserve one."

"That's all right," I said. "I got Aunt Etta's penny back for her. Rare as a hen's tooth, that penny. She's going to buy me a horse with it someday."

Mr. Whitman was sitting nearby counting the stolen money. He looked up. "A horse," he said. "Well, a horse has got to have something on it."

When I got home from school on Monday, a saddle was waiting for me in the parlor. The whole room smelled of fresh leather.

"Aunt Etta," I said, "That's the finest looking saddle I *ever* saw!"

"Not much use without a horse under it," she said. "I've already plucked a chicken for supper. If you've got nothing better to do we could go looking for your horse."

"Yes, ma'am!"

"You might start thinking up a name."

"Aunt Etta," I said. "I've got a list a mile-and-a-half long."

Discuss the Selection

1. How did Opie's sharp eye and quick mind keep him from being fooled?
2. How did Opie trap Professor Pepper?
3. What feelings do you think Opie had about Professor Pepper when he first met him?
4. How did Opie get the horse and saddle at the end of the story?
5. How important is the tule fog to the action of the story? Find the parts of the story that would be different if the fog hadn't been there.

Apply the Skills

The reason why an author writes a story or an article is called the author's purpose. Authors write to instruct, to state an opinion, to criticize, to persuade, and to entertain.

"The Ghost on Saturday Night" was written to entertain you. What part of the story do you think was the most entertaining? Explain why you think so.

Think and Write

Prewrite

Who?
What?
When?
Where?
Why?
How?

News articles include the answers to these six basic news-gathering questions: Who? What? When? Where? Why? and How? They begin with the most important information.

Think about Professor Pepper's robbery of the bank. Copy the chart above and fill it in with information from the story about the bank robbery.

Compose

Use the information from the chart to write a news article about the bank robbery. Give your article a headline that explains what it is about.

Revise

Read your news article. Did you include the answers to all of the questions on the chart? Is the most important information at the beginning of the article? If not, revise your work.

Literature Study

Point of View

All stories are written from a certain point of view depending on how the story is narrated, or told. Authors choose to tell their stories from two basic points of view: first-person or third-person.

In a **first-person** point of view, the author has a character in the story tell what happens. All the other characters, as well as the action in the story, are presented through what this one character sees or hears.

The views of a first-person narrator are one-sided. For example, suppose two characters run in a race. One character wins; the other loses. Because each character's experience is different, each will tell the story of the race differently.

One way to recognize the first-person point of view is to look for first-person pronouns, such as *I, me, mine, we, us,* and *ours*. You'll find these first-person pronouns in the telling of the story and in the dialogue.

A story written from the **third-person** point of view is told by a narrator who is *not* a character in the story. A third-person narrator is someone totally outside the story who tells us the thoughts of the characters and what happens to them. You can recognize the third-person point of view by the use of third-person pronouns, such as *he, she, his, her, they, them,* and *their*.

If the third-person narrator relates what happens to several characters, this is called the **omniscient**, or all-knowing, point of view. An omniscient narrator can tell us what all of the characters feel and think.

Sometimes an author chooses a third-person point of view but concentrates on one character's feelings and thoughts. This is called **limited third-person** point of view. When the limited third person is used, we learn more about one character in a story than we do about the other characters.

Let's return to the race example. Told from a limited third-person point of view, the story might read as follows:

> Sean was three feet behind Tracy as they rounded the last curve. Sean knew he couldn't catch Tracy now. His heart sank. He watched hopelessly as Tracy sprinted toward the cheering crowds at the finish line.

Told from an omniscient point of view, the same story would include both characters' experiences and feelings:

> Tracy didn't know how far ahead she was as she sprinted toward the finish line. Her legs felt as if they were lighter than air. Sean lumbered behind in second place. He knew he couldn't win now. His heart was heavy with disappointment and defeat.

Each point of view gives a reader a different outlook. Knowing how different points of view are used helps you better understand and appreciate a story.

Author Profile

Robert C. O'Brien

Robert C. O'Brien is the pen name for Robert Leslie Conly. At a very young age, Conly created imaginary worlds for himself, but he did not begin to share his imaginary worlds with readers until he was in his late forties.

Conly had always been involved in the publishing world. He worked as an editor and writer for magazines and newspapers, such as *National Geographic, Newsweek, Washington Times Herald* and *Pathfinder*. The book *The Silver Crown* was the beginning of his career as a writer of children's stories.

Shortly after finishing his first book, Conly started on *Mrs. Frisby and the Rats of NIMH*. He started the book in November of 1967 and by March of 1968 had completed only two chapters. He was not sure whether he should continue this book. At this time, he had been reading a book called *The Immense Journey* by Loren Eiseley. This book was about prairie dogs and how millions of years ago they were ahead of humans in the race toward dominance. It also discussed evidence that prairie dogs' ancestors drove our ancestors out of the prairies and into the woods. This book, along with other readings, made Conly wonder about survival and what the world would be like if people were eliminated by means of war or pollution and only rats were survivors. This kind of thinking led to the book *Mrs. Frisby and the Rats of NIMH*. Conly stated, "I suppose it's a rather grim idea to serve as a background for a children's book. But once I got it started, the rats took charge, and they turned out to be much saner and pleasanter than we are."

Mrs. Frisby and the Rats of NIMH won six awards, including the Newbery Medal. The author's other books include *A Report from Group 17*, another story involving scientific research, and *Z for Zachariah*, the story of two survivors after a nuclear war.

During the author's speech accepting the Newbery Medal, he revealed his reasons for writing books for children. He stated that his ideas were not always for children, but he enjoyed writing for children, "because children like a straightforward, honest plot—with a beginning, a middle, and an end: a problem, an attempt to solve it, and at the end a success or a failure."

In the next selection, there is a problem which the characters try to solve. Whether there is success or failure at the end will be left up to you, the reader, to decide.

This story is told from the viewpoint of someone who was a subject in a scientific experiment. Read the story to find out who the subject was and what experiment he was taking part in.

As you read the story, think about point of view. Notice the words that the author uses to indicate who is telling the story.

Mrs. Frisby and the Rats of NIMH

by Robert C. O'Brien

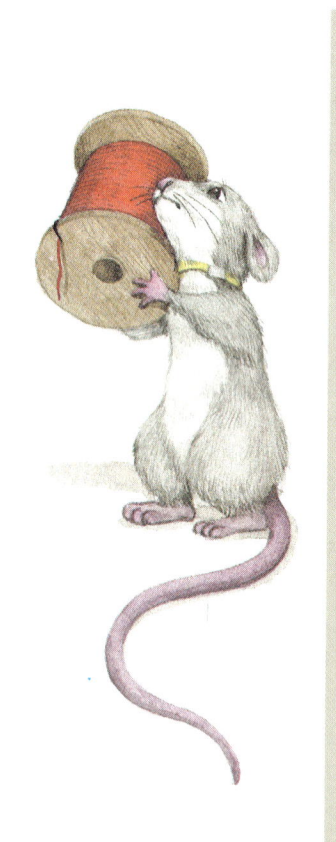

A mouse named Mrs. Frisby knew about the group of rats living on the same farm as she did, but she never had much to do with them. Then one day she met one rat named Nicodemus who told her their story.

It all started one night when Nicodemus and his friend Jenner went to a certain market to eat. They noticed a truck with the letters NIMH on it parked nearby. As the rats began to eat, people jumped out of the truck and began catching them in nets. Then the people emptied the nets into a cage in the truck and drove away. The rats were unloaded from the truck at NIMH—the National Institute of Mental Health—divided into A, B, and C test groups, and placed in individual wire cages. Three people—Dr. Schultz, Julie, and George—were to be their teachers for three years. Nicodemus continued to explain his story.

During the days that followed, our lives fell into a pattern, and the reason for our captivity gradually became clear. Dr. Schultz was a neurologist—that is, an expert on brains, nerves, intelligence, and how people learn things. He hoped, by experimenting on us, to find out whether certain injections could help us learn more and faster. The two younger people working with him, George and Julie, were graduate students in biology.

"Watch always," he told them, "for signs of improvement, faster learning, quicker reactions in Group A as compared to Group B, and both as compared to the control group."

My own training began on the day after the first injections. It was George who did it; I suppose Julie and Dr. Schultz were doing the same test on other rats. He took my cage from the shelf and carried it to another room, similar to the first one but with more equipment and no shelves of cages in it. He placed the cage in a slot against the wall, slid open the end, opened a matching door in the wall—and I was free.

Or so I thought. The small doorway in the wall led into a short corridor, which opened, or seemed to, directly onto a green lawn. I could see it clearly, and behind it some bushes, and behind them a street—all outdoors, and nothing but air between me and them. Furthermore, I could smell the fresh outdoor breeze blowing in. Were they letting me go?

I made a dash toward the open end of the corridor—and then jumped back. I could not go on. About two feet from my cage (still open behind me) there was something dreadfully wrong with the floor. When I touched my feet to it, a terrible, prickling feeling came over my skin; my muscles cramped, my eyes blurred, and I got instantly dizzy. I never got used to that feeling—no one ever does—but I did experience it many times and eventually learned what it was: electric shock. It is not exactly a pain, but it is unbearable.

Yet, I was in frenzy to reach that open lawn, to run for the bushes, to get away from the cage. I tried again—and jumped back again. No use. Then I saw, leading off to the left, another corridor. I had not noticed it at first because I had been looking so eagerly at the open end of the one I was in. The second one seemed to stop about five feet away in a blank wall. Yet there was a light there; it must turn a corner. I ran down it, cautiously, not trusting the floor. At the end I turned right—and there was the lawn again, another opening. I got closer that time; then, just as I thought I was going to make it—another shock. This was repeated over and over; yet each time I seemed to get a little closer to freedom.

But when I finally reached it and the grass was only a step away, a wire wall snapped down in front of me, another behind me; the ceiling opened above me; and a gloved hand reached and picked me up.

A voice said, "Four minutes, thirty-seven seconds." It was George.

I had, after all my running through the corridors, emerged into a trap only a few feet from where I had started, and through a concealed opening up above, George had been watching everything I did.

I had been in what is called a maze, a device to test intelligence and memory. I was put in it many times again, and so were the others. The second time I got through it a little faster because I remembered — which corridors had electric floors and which did not. The third time I was still faster; and after each trial George (or sometimes Julie, sometimes Dr. Schultz) would write down how long it took. You might ask: Why would I bother to run through it at all if I knew it was only a trick? The answer is: I couldn't help it. When you've lived in a cage, you can't bear *not* to run, even if what you're running toward is an illusion.

There were more injections and other kinds of test, and some of these were more important than the maze, because the maze was designed only to find out how quickly we could learn, while some of the others actually taught us things — or at least led up to actual teaching.

All of these activities helped to pass the time, and the weeks went by quickly, but they did not lessen our longing to get away. I wished I could see my mother and father and run with my brother to the marketplace. I know all the others felt the same way; yet it seemed a hopeless thing. Still, there was one rat who decided to try it anyway.

He was a young rat, probably the youngest of all that had been caught, and by chance, he was in the cage next to mine; I might mention that like Jenner and me, he was in the group Dr. Schultz called A. His name was Justin.

It was late one night that I heard him calling me, speaking softly, around the wooden partition between our cages. Those partitions generally kept all of us from getting to know each other as well as we might have done and discouraged us from talking much to one another; it was quite hard to hear around them, and of course you could never see the one you were talking to. I think Dr. Schultz had purposely had them made of some soundproof material. But you *could* hear, if you and your neighbor got in the corners of the cages nearest each other and spoke out through the wire front.

"Nicodemus?"

"Yes?" I went over to the corner.

"How long have we been here?"

"I don't know. Several months—I think, but I have no way to keep track."

"I'm going to try to get out."

"Get out? But how? Your cage is shut."

"Tomorrow we get injections, so they'll open it. When they do, I'm going to run."

"Run where?"

"I don't know. At least I'll get a look around. There might be some way out. What can I lose?"

"You might get hurt."

"I don't think so. Anyway *they* won't hurt me."

By *they* he meant Dr. Schultz and the other two. He added confidently, "All these shots, all the time they've spent—we're too valuable to them now. They'll be careful."

That idea had not occurred to me before, but when I thought about it, I decided he was right. Dr. Schultz, Julie, and George had spent most of their working hours with us for months; they could not afford to let any harm come to us. On the other hand, neither could they afford to allow any of us to escape.

Justin made his attempt the next morning. And it did cause a certain amount of excitement but not at all what we expected. It was Julie who opened Justin's cage with a hypodermic in her hand. Justin was out with a mighty leap, hit the floor (about four feet down) with a thump, shook himself, and ran, disappearing from my view, heading toward the other end of the room.

Julie seemed not at all alarmed. She calmly placed the needle on a shelf, then walked to the door of the laboratory and pushed a button on the wall. A red light came on over the door. She picked up a notebook and pencil from a desk near the door and followed Justin out of my sight.

A few minutes later, Dr. Schultz and George entered. They opened the door cautiously and closed it behind them. "The outer door is shut, too," said Dr. Schultz. "Where is it?"

"Down here," said Julie, "inspecting the air ducts."

"Really? Which one is it?"

"It's one of the A group, just as you expected. Number nine. I'm keeping notes on it."

Obviously the red light was some kind of warning signal, both outside the door and in — "laboratory animal at large." And not only had Dr. Schultz known one of us was out, but he had expected it to happen.

". . . a few days sooner than I thought," he was saying, "but so much the better. Do you realize . . ."

"Look," said Julie. "He's doing the whole baseboard — but he's studying the windows too. See how he steps back to look up?"

"Of course," replied Dr. Schultz. "And at the same time he's watching us too. Can't you see?"

"He's pretty cool about it," said George.

"Look," said Julie, "A-9 has made a discovery. He's found the mice."

George said, "See how he's studying them."

"Probably," said Dr. Schultz wryly, "he's wondering if they're ready for their steroid injections, too. As a matter of fact, I think the G group is. They're doing almost as well as A group."

"Should I get the net and put him back?" George asked.

"I doubt you'll need it," Dr. Schultz said, "now that he's learned he can't get out."

But they were underestimating Justin. He had learned no such thing.

Of course, Justin did not escape that day, nor even that year. When they—Julie—put on a glove and went to pick him up, he submitted meekly enough, and in a short time he was back in his cage.

Yet he had learned some things. He had, as Julie noticed, looked at the air ducts—the openings along the wall through which warm air flowed in winter, cool air in summer—and he had studied the windows. Mainly he had learned that he could, occasionally at least, jump from his cage and wander around without incurring any anger or injury. All of this, eventually, was important. For it was Justin, along with Jenner, who figured out how to get away. I had a part in it too. But all that came later.

I won't go into details about the rest of our training except for one part of it that was the most useful of all. But in general, during the months that followed, two things were happening.

First, we were learning more than any rats ever had before and were becoming more intelligent than any rats had ever been.

The second thing could be considered, from some points of view, even more important—and certainly more astonishing—than the first. Dr. Schultz (you will recall) had said that a new series of injections might increase our life span by double or more. Yet even he was not prepared for what happened. Perhaps it was the odd combination of both the old and new injections working together—I don't know, and neither did he. But the result was that as far as he could detect, in the A group the aging process seemed to stop almost completely.

Apparently (though we seldom saw them) the same thing was happening with the G group, the mice who were getting the same injections we were.

Dr. Schultz was greatly excited about this. "The short life span has always been a prime limiting factor in education," he told George and Julie. "If we can double it, and speed up the learning process at the same time, the possibilities are just enormous."

The one important phase of training began after weeks of really hard work. One of the first and simplest of these exercises was a picture, a clear photograph, of a rat. I suppose they felt sure we would know what that was. This picture was shown on a screen, with a light behind it. Then, after I had looked at the picture and recognized it, a shape flashed on the screen under it—a sort of half circle and two straight lines, not like anything I had seen before. Then the voice began:

"Are. Are. Are."

It was Julie's voice, speaking very clearly, but it had a tinny sound; it was a record. After repeating "are" a dozen times or so, that particular shape disappeared and another one came on the screen, still under the picture of the rat. It was a triangle, with legs on it. And Julie's voice began again:

"Ay. Ay. Ay."

When that shape disappeared, a third one came on the screen. This one was a cross. Julie's voice said:

"Tea. Tea. Tea."

Then all three shapes appeared at once, and the record said:

"Are. Ay. Tea. Rat."

You will already have recognized what was going on: They were teaching us to read. The symbols under the picture were the letters R-A-T. But the idea did not become clear to any of us, for quite a long time. Because, of course, we didn't know what reading *was*.

Oh, we learned to recognize the shapes easily enough, and when I saw the rat picture, I knew straight away what symbols would appear beneath it. I even learned that when the photograph showed not one but several rats, a fourth shape would appear under it — a snaky line — and the sound with that one was "ess — ess — ess." But as to what all this was *for*, none of us had any inkling.

It was Jenner who finally figured it out. By this time we had developed a sort of system of communication, a simple enough thing, just passing spoken messages from one cage to the next. Justin, who was still next to me, called to me one day, "Message for Nicodemus from Jenner. He says it is important."

"All right," I said, "what's the message?"

"Look at the shapes on the wall next to the door. He says to look carefully."

My cage, like Jenner's and those of the rest of A group, was close enough to the door so I could see what he meant: Near the doorway there was a large, square piece of white cardboard fastened to the wall—a sign. It was covered with an assortment of black markings to which I had never paid any attention (though they had been there ever since we arrived).

Now, for the first time, I looked at them carefully, and I soon grasped what Jenner had discovered.

The top line of black marks on the wall were instantly familiar: R-A-T-S; as soon as I saw them, I thought of the picture that went with them; and as soon as I did that, I was, for the first time, reading. Because, of course, that's what reading is: using symbols to suggest a picture or an idea. From that time on, it gradually became clear to me what all these lessons were for, and once I understood the idea, I was eager to learn more. I could scarcely wait for the next lesson and the next. The whole concept of reading was, to me at least, fascinating. I remember how proud I was when, some months later, I was able to read and understand that whole sign. I read it hundreds of times, and I'll never forget it:

RATS MAY NOT BE REMOVED FROM THE LABORATORY WITHOUT WRITTEN PERMISSION. And at the bottom we could read the word: NIMH.

But then a puzzling thing came up, a thing we're still not sure about even now. Apparently Dr. Schultz, who was running the lessons, did not realize how well they were succeeding. He continued the training, with new words and new pictures every day; but the fact is, once we had grasped the idea and learned the different sounds each letter stood for, we leaped way ahead of him.

I'm sure Dr. Schultz had plans for testing our reading ability. I could even guess, from the words he was teaching us, what the tests were going to be like. For example, he taught us *left, right, door, food, open, close,* and so on. It was not hard to imagine the test: I would be placed in one chamber, my food in another. There would be two doors and a sign saying: "For food, open door at right," or something like that. Then if I—if all of us—moved unerringly toward the proper door, he would know we had read and understood the sign.

As I said, I'm sure he planned to do this, but apparently he did not think we were ready for it yet. I think maybe he was even a little afraid to try it; because if he did it too soon, or if for any other reason it did not work, his experiment would be a failure. Dr. Schultz wanted to be very sure, and his caution was his undoing.

Justin announced one evening around the partition, "I'm going to get out of my cage tonight and wander around a bit."

"How can you? It's locked."

"Yes. But did you notice, along the bottom edge, there's a printed strip?"

"What does it say?"

"I've been trying to read it the last three times they brought me back from training. It's very small print. But I think I've finally made it out. It says: To release door, pull knob forward and slide right."

"Knob?"

"Under the floor, about an inch back, there's a metal

thing just in front of the shelf. I think that's the knob, and I think I can reach it through the wire. Anyway, I'm going to try."

I heard a scuffling noise, a click, and scrape of metal, and in a matter of seconds I saw his door swing open. It was as simple as that—when you could read.

"Wait," I said.

"What's the matter?"

"If you jump down you won't be able to get back in. Then they'll know."

"I thought of that. I'm not going to jump down. I'm going to climb up the outside of the cage. It's easy. I've climbed up the inside a thousand times. Above these cages there's another shelf, and it's empty. I'm going to walk along there and see what I can see. I think there's a way to climb to the floor and up again."

"Why don't I go with you?" My door would open the same way as his.

"Better not this time, don't you think? If something goes wrong and I can't get back, they'll say it's just A-9. But if two of us are found outside, they'll take it seriously. They might put new locks on the cages."

He was right, and you can see that already we both had the same idea in mind: that this might be the first step toward escape for all of us.

And so it was. By teaching us how to read, they had taught us how to get away.

Justin climbed easily up the open door of his cage and vanished over the top with a flick of his tail. He came back an hour later, greatly excited and full of information. Yet, it was typical of Justin that even excited as he was, he stayed calm, he thought clearly. He climbed down the front of my cage rather than his own, and spoke softly; we both assumed that by now the other rats were asleep.

"Nicodemus? Come on out. I'll show you how." He directed me as I reached through the wire bars of the door and felt beneath it. I found the small metal knob, slid it forward and sideward, and felt the door swing loose against my shoulder. I followed him up the side of the cage to the shelf above. There we stopped. It was the first time I had met Justin face to face.

He said, "It's better talking here than around that partition."

"Yes. Did you get down?"

"Yes."

"How did you get back up?"

"At the end of this shelf there's a big cabinet — they keep the mouse cages in it. It has wire mesh doors. You can climb up and down them like a ladder."

"Of course," I said. "I remember now." I had seen that cabinet many times when my cage was carried past it. For some reason, perhaps because they were smaller, the mice were kept in cages-within-a-cage.

Justin said, "Nicodemus, I've found a way to get out."

"You have! How?"

"At each end of the room there's an opening in the baseboard at the bottom of the wall. Air blows in through one of them and out through the other. Each one has a metal grid covering it, and on the grid there's a sign that says: LIFT TO ADJUST AIR FLOW. I lifted one of them; it hangs on hinges, like a trap door. Behind it, there is a thing like a metal window; when you slide it wide open, more air blows in. But the main thing is that it's easily big enough for us to walk through and get out."

"But what's on the other side? Where does it lead?"

"On the other side there's a duct, a thing like a square metal pipe built right into the wall. I walked along it, not very far, but I can figure out where it must go. There's bound to be a duct like it leading to every room in the building, and they must all branch off one main central pipe — and that one has to lead, somewhere, to the outside. Because that's where our air comes from. That's why they never open the windows. I don't think those windows *can* open."

He was right, of course. The building had central air conditioning; what we had to do was find the main air shaft and explore it. There would have to be an intake at one end and an outlet at the other. But that was easier said than done, and before it was done, there were questions to be answered. What about the rest of the rats? There were twenty of us in the laboratory, and we had to let the others know.

So, one by one, we woke them and showed them how to open their cages. We did not attempt to leave that night, but went together and looked at the metal grid Justin had discovered, and made plans for exploring the air ducts. Jenner was astute at that sort of thing; he could clearly foresee problems.

"With a vent like this leading to every room," he said, "it will be easy to get lost. When we explore, we're going to need some way of finding our way back here."

"Why should we come back?" someone asked.

"Because it may take more than one night to find the way out. If it does, whoever is doing the exploring must be back in the cage by morning. Otherwise Dr. Schultz will find out."

Jenner was right. It took us about a week. What we did, after some more discussion, was to find some equipment: first, a large spool of thread in one of the cabinets where some of us had seen Julie place it one day. Second, a screwdriver—because, as Jenner pointed out, there would probably be a grill over the end of the airshaft to keep out debris, and we might have to pry it loose. We hid these in the duct, a few feet from the entrance. We could only hope that they would not be missed, or that if they were, we wouldn't be suspected.

Justin and two others (one of whom is named Arthur) were chosen as the exploration party. They had a terrible time at first: Here was a maze to end all mazes; and in the dark they quickly lost their sense of direction. Still they kept at it, night after night, exploring the network of shafts that laced like a cubical spider web through the walls and ceilings of the building. They would tie the end of their thread to the grid in our laboratory and unroll it from the spool as they went. Time and time again they reached the end of the thread and had to come back.

"It isn't long enough," Justin complained. "Every time I come to the end, I think, 'If I could just go ten feet farther . . .'"

And finally, that's what he did. On the seventh night, just as the thread ran out, he and the other two reached a shaft that was wider than any they had found before, and it seemed, as they walked along it, to be slanting gently upward. But the spool was empty.

"You wait here," Justin said to the others. He had a hunch. The air coming through the shaft had a fresher smell where they were, and it seemed to be blowing harder than in the other shafts. Up ahead, he thought he could hear the whir of a machine running quietly, and there was a faint vibration of the metal under his feet. He went on. The shaft turned upward at a sharp angle, and then, straight ahead, he saw it: a patch of lighter-colored darkness than the pitch black around him, and in the middle of it, three stars twinkling. It was the open sky. Across the opening there was, as Jenner had predicted, a coarse grill.

He ran toward it for a few seconds longer and then stopped. The sound of the machine had grown suddenly louder, changing from a whir to a roar. It had obviously shifted speed; an automatic switch somewhere in the building had turned it from low to high, and the air blowing past Justin came on so hard it made him gasp. He braced his feet against the metal and held on. In a minute, just as it had begun roaring, the machine returned to a whisper. He looked around and realized it was lucky he had stopped; by the dim light from the sky he could see that he had reached a point where perhaps two dozen air shafts came together like branches into the trunk of a tree. If he had gone a few steps farther, he would never have been able to distinguish which shaft was his. He turned in his tracks, and in a few minutes he rejoined his friends.

We had a meeting that night, and Justin told all of us what he had found. He had left the thread, anchored by the screwdriver, to guide us out. Some were for leaving immediately, but it was late, and Jenner and I argued against it. We did not know how long it would take us to break through the grill at the end. If it should take more than an hour or two, daylight would be upon us. We would then be unable to risk returning to the laboratory and would have to spend the day in the shaft—or try to get away by broad daylight. Dr. Schultz might even figure we had gone and trap us in the air shaft.

Finally, reluctantly, everyone agreed to spend one more day in the laboratory and leave early the next night.

Then, just as we were ending our meeting, a new complication arose. We had been standing in a rough circle on the floor of the laboratory, just outside the two screen doors that enclosed the mice cages. Now, from inside the cabinet, came a voice:

"Nicodemus." It was a clear but plaintive call, the voice of a mouse. We had almost forgotten the mice were there, and I was startled to hear that one of them knew my name. We all grew quiet.

"Who's calling me?" I asked.

"My name is Jonathan," said the voice. "We have been listening to your talk about going out. We would like to go too, but we cannot open our cages."

Justin was studying the cabinet intently.

"Why not?" he said. "If we can get the doors open."

Someone muttered, "They will slow us down."

"No," said the mouse Jonathan. "We will not. Only open our cages when you go, and we will make our own way. We won't even stay with you, if you prefer."

"How many are you?" I asked.

"Only eight. And the cabinet doors are easy to open. There's just a simple hook, halfway up."

"The cages open the same way as yours," said another mouse, "but we can't reach far enough to unlatch them."

"All right," I said. "Tomorrow night, as soon as Dr. Schultz and the others leave, we'll open your cages, and you can follow the thread with us to get out. After that, you're on your own."

"Agreed," said Jonathan, "and thank you."

"And now," I said, "we should all get back to the cages. Justin, please hook the doors again."

The next day was terrible. I kept expecting to hear Dr. Schultz say, "Who took my screwdriver?" And then to hear Julie add, "My thread is missing too." That could have happened and set them to thinking—but it didn't, and that night, an hour after Julie, George, and Dr. Schultz left the laboratory, we were out of our cages and gathered, the whole group of us, before the mouse cabinet. Justin opened its doors, unlatched their cages, and the mice came out.

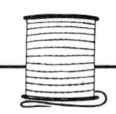

They looked very small and frightened, but one strode bravely forward.

"Nicodemus?" he said to me. "I'm Jonathan. Thanks for taking us out with you."

"We're not out yet," I said, "but you're welcome."

We had no time for chatting. The light coming in the windows was turning gray; in less than an hour it would be dark, and we would need light to figure out how to open the grill that was at the end of the shaft.

We went to the opening in the baseboard.

"Justin," I said, "take the lead. Roll up the thread as you go. I will bring up the rear. No noise. There's sure to be somebody awake somewhere in the building. We don't want them to hear us." I did not want to leave the thread where it might be found: The more I thought about it, the more I felt sure Dr. Schultz would try to track us down.

Justin lifted the grid, pushed open the sliding panel, and one by one we went through. As I watched the others go ahead of me, I noticed for the first time that one of the mice was white. Then I went in myself, closing the grid behind me and pushing the panel half shut again, its normal position.

With Justin leading the way, we moved through the dark passage quickly and easily. In only fifteen or twenty minutes we had reached the end of the thread; then, as Justin had told us it would, the shaft widened; we could hear the whir of the machine ahead, and almost immediately we saw a square of gray daylight. We had reached the end of the shaft, and there a terrible thing happened.

Justin—you will recall—had told us that the machine, the pump that pulled air through the shaft, had switched from low speed to high when he had first explored through there. So we were forewarned, but the forewarning was no use at all, not so far as the mice were concerned.

We were approaching the lighted square of the opening when the roar began. The blast of air came like a sudden whistling gale; it took my breath and flattened my ears against my head, and I closed my eyes instinctively. I was still in the rear, and when I opened my eyes again, I saw one of the mice sliding past me, clawing uselessly with his small nails at the smooth metal beneath him. Another followed him, and still another, as one by one they were blown backward into the dark maze of tunnels we had just left. I braced myself in the corner of the shaft and grabbed at one as he slid by. It was the white mouse. I caught him by one leg, pulled him around behind me, and held on. Another blew face-on into the rat ahead of me and stopped there; it was Jonathan, who had been near the lead. But the rest were lost, six in all. They were simply too light; they blew away like dead leaves, and we never saw them again.

In another minute the roar stopped, the rush of air slowed from a gale to a breeze, and we were able to go forward again. I said to the white mouse, "You'd better hold on to me. That might happen again."

He looked at me in dismay. "But what about the others? Six are lost! I've got to go back and look for them."

Jonathan quickly joined him. "I'll go with you."

"No," I said. "That would be useless and foolish. You have no idea which shaft they were blown into, nor even if they all went the same way. And if you should find them, how would you find your way out again? And suppose the wind comes again? Then there would be eight lost instead of six."

The wind did come again, half a dozen times more, while we worked with the screwdriver to pry open the grill. Each time we had to stop work and hang on. The two mice clung to the grill itself; some of us braced ourselves behind them, in case they should slip. And Justin, taking the thread with him as a guideline, went back to search for the other six. He explored shaft after shaft to the end of the spool, calling softly as he went—but it was futile. To this day we don't know what became of those six mice. They may have found their way out eventually, or they may have died in there. The opening was there in the grill for them, just in case.

The grill. It was heavy metal, with holes about the size of an acorn, and it was set in a steel frame. We pried and hammered at it with the screwdriver, but we could not move it. It was fastened on the outside; we couldn't see how. Finally the white mouse had an idea.

"Push the screwdriver through the grill near the bottom," he said, "and pry up." We did and the metal bent a fraction of an inch. We did it again, prying down, then left, then right. The hole in the grill was slightly bigger, and the white mouse said, "I think that's enough." He climbed to the small opening and, by squirming and twisting, he got through. Jonathan followed him; they both fell out of sight, but in a minute Jonathan's head came back in view on the outside.

"It's the sliding bolt," he said. "We're working on it." Inside we could hear the faint rasping as the two mice tugged on the bolt handle, working it back. Then the crack at the base of the grill widened; we pushed it open, and we were standing on the roof of NIMH, free.

Discuss the Selection

1. From whose viewpoint was this story told? In what kind of scientific experiment was this character a subject?
2. How did the rats manage to escape from captivity?
3. How did you feel when Nicodemus described his experiences and frustrations in the maze?
4. How was learning to read useful to the rats?
5. Only by working together did the rats and mice manage to escape. Find the part of the story that shows how the two groups helped each other.

Apply the Skills

A story told from the first-person point of view is told from the point of view of a character in the story. The character explains his or her own thoughts or feelings, but not the thoughts or feelings of other characters.

Find the parts of the story what tell how Nicodemus feels about trying to reach freedom. Are Jenner's feelings about escape also described?

Thinking About "Viewpoints"

In this unit, you've read stories that represent many different viewpoints. You viewed China through the eyes of a young Jean Fritz, who yearned to return to America. Then you met an older Jean Fritz, anxious to visit China, her real home. Through letters, you got to know Bob Teague's Aunt Letty, whose viewpoint united an entire family. And you experienced a scientific experiment from the viewpoint of one of its subjects, a rat named Nicodemus.

The authors of the stories in this unit shared their viewpoints — their ideas and their feelings — with you. Did the views of these authors strengthen any of your views? Did the authors introduce you to new views and ideas? Did their ideas help to change any of your views about the world around you?

Each author had his or her own viewpoint, just as you do. Viewpoints are important, for they help to make each of us a unique person.

1. In "Homesick" and "China Homecoming," Jean Fritz was homesick for different places. What place was she homesick for in each story? Why was she homesick for two different places?

2. All people feel strongly about their homes, wherever those homes may be. What characters in this unit's stories have strong feelings about home? How do they show their feelings?

3. In "Letters to a Black Boy," you learned how the members of Adam's extended family united to help others achieve their dreams. How did family members help each other in other selections?

4. Pretend you could interview the main character in the story "Mrs. Frisby and the Rats of NIMH" or in "Homesick." List five questions you might ask that character.

5. "The Ghost on Saturday Night" and "Mrs Frisby and the Rats of NIMH" were told from the first-person point of view. Choose one of these stories and explain how it might have been different if it had been told from another character's point of view.

6. Some of the characters in this unit's stories had viewpoints that changed. Choose one of these characters and explain how his or her viewpoint changed.

7. Think about the people you have met in these selections. Which person would you like to know better? Explain your answer.

Read on Your Own

My Black Me edited by Arnold Adoff. Dutton. Twenty-five poets write fifty ways of being "my black me."

The Secret of the Andes by Ann Nolan Clark. Viking. A young Inca boy, raised on an isolated mountain, becomes curious about the mysteries of the world below—and the mystery of his own life.

The Ghost on Saturday Night by Sid Fleischman. Little, Brown. Opie tells how he uncovers the mystery of a runaway ghost and helps the sheriff catch some tricky characters.

Homesick by Jean Fritz. Putnam. Living with her parents in China, ten-year-old Jean Fritz finds herself homesick for her own country, the America she "sees" only in her grandmother's letters and in stories.

China Homecoming by Jean Fritz. Putnam. The homesickness that brought Jean Fritz to America in 1927 returns 55 years later—this time *for* China. She travels across the ocean once more, in search of the China of her childhood.

The Lilith Summer by Hadley Irwin. The Feminist Press. A young girl and an elderly woman, paid to keep each other company for a summer, begin their relationship with mixed feelings. When they invent a private language, a bond starts to form between them.

And Now Miguel by Joseph Krumgold. Crowell. Miguel, the middle brother in a family of shepherds, is determined to leave boyhood behind and follow the older shepherds on the yearly sheep drive into the mountains of New Mexico.

Ben and Me by Robert Lawson. Dell. The story of Ben Franklin, as told by a mouse who lives and writes in Franklin's fur hat.

North to the Orient by Anne Morrow Lindbergh. Harcourt Brace Jovanovich. This is the story of Anne Lindbergh's flight, with her husband, Charles, north beyond Alaska to the Far East.

Mrs. Frisby and the Rats of NIMH by Robert C. O'Brien. Atheneum. The exciting tale of a group of rats made superintelligent by scientific experiments and how they help a farmyard mouse, Mrs. Frisby.

Dreamers and Doers by Norman Richards. Atheneum. This book traces automobile and airplane tires, the rocket ship, the light bulb, the photograph, and the movie camera back to the notebooks of the scientists who invented them.

The Alfred Summer by Jan Slepian. Macmillan. The four-member Brighton Beach boat-building brigade — two of them with handicaps — band together to cross the waters of a difficult summer.

Dragonwings by Laurence Yep. Harper & Row. At the time of the San Francisco earthquake, a Chinese immigrant, Windrider, builds a flying machine with the help of Moon Shadow, his son.

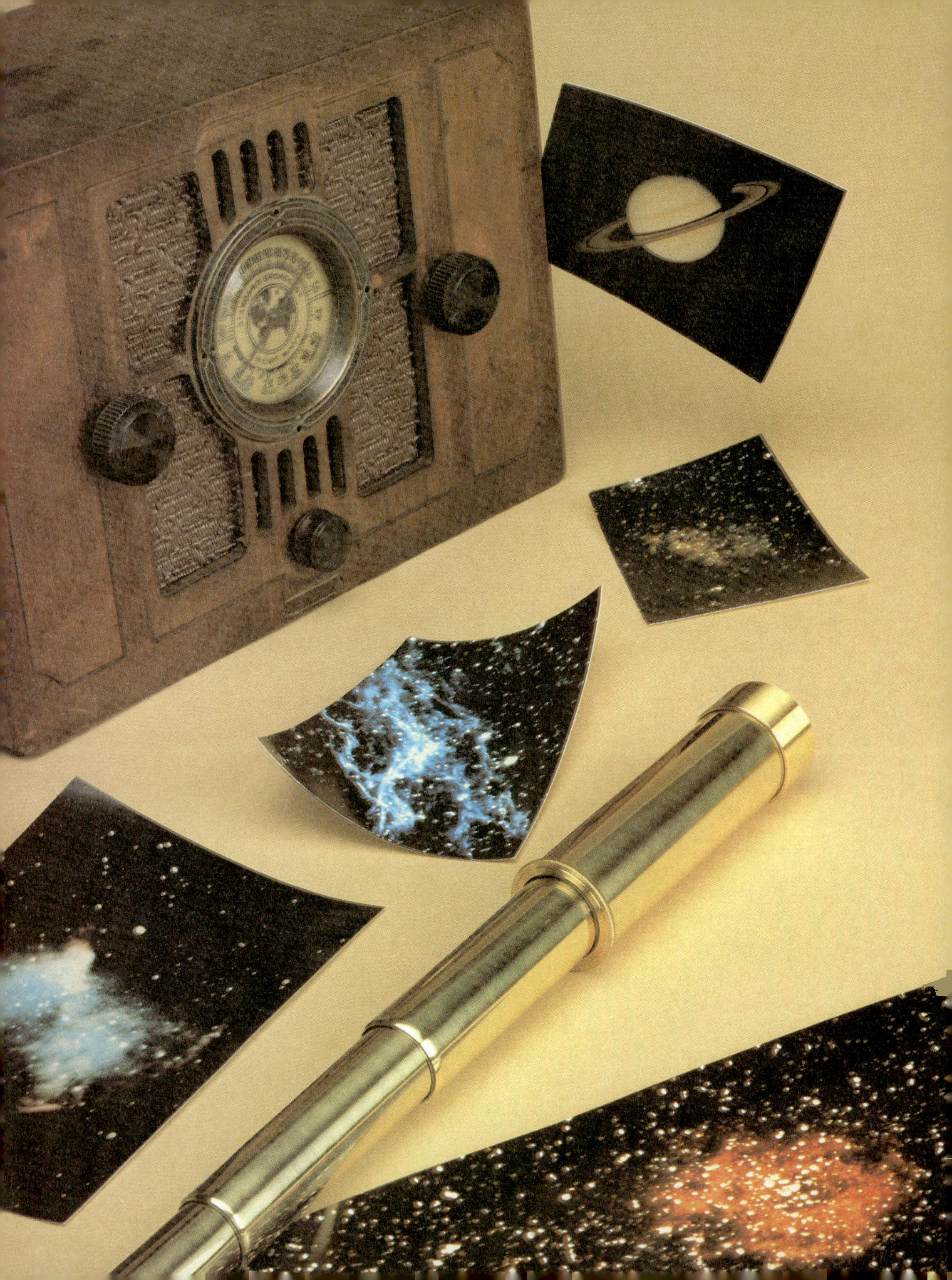

Unit 4
Tomorrows

What do you imagine that the future will be like? Will rocket-like space cars zoom along elevated highways? Or will they clutter the skies? Will you be able to travel back in time and visit ancient lands? Will you travel to strange planets in distant galaxies? Will you rub elbows with robots on moving sidewalks? Will you live in bustling underground or underwater cities? The world of tomorrow is a world of the imagination. We don't know for sure what it will be like. We can only imagine.

Just as we dream about life hundreds of years from now, people in the past imagined what life would be like today. Some of their visions have turned into reality; some have not. The old stories about life forms on Mars have recently been disproved by space probes to the red planet. Some dreamers of the past — inventors and scientists — worked to make their visions for the future come true. They helped shape today's world. Others will take their place to shape tomorrow's world.

The selections in this unit all contain visions of the world of tomorrow. They describe everything from life in future worlds to space travel.

The world of tomorrow belongs to all of us. Maybe after reading these stories, you'll have a clearer vision of how you want that world to be.

Literature Study

Science Fiction

Science fiction is fantasy about science and about the future. A science fiction story often describes places, events, and characters that are not like anything in our world. For example, think about the planet Krypton, a movie about the future, and the characters R2-D2 and C3PO. These creations are all from stories that are science fiction.

Science fiction writers often take what is known about science now and imagine, or guess, how advances in technology will change things in the distant future. Their guesses are often very accurate. For instance, rockets, submarines, body-part transplants, moon landings, robots, and talking computers were all imagined long ago. These things were all ideas dreamed up by science fiction writers. They were dreamed up long before they became today's scientific reality.

Science fiction deals with the possible developments of science in the future. In fact, it often starts where science leaves off. For example, scientists today have not figured out how to travel faster than the speed of light to cross the great distances of space between planets. At today's relatively slow speed of space travel, a space ship in a realistic story would take many years to reach the planets in our solar system. But a space ship in a science fiction story has no speed limits. For these ships, travel to other planets in galaxies outside our solar system is an everyday trip.

Keeping one step ahead of science today is not easy for the writers of science fiction. Scientists have only recently found out that no life exists on Mars or Venus. So you're not likely to find any Martians or Venusians in the science fiction being written today. In fact, the more we find out about our solar system, the more science fiction writers turn to other solar systems as settings for their work.

Read the following paragraph from a science fiction story.

> Ambassador Caldwell's first visit to the galaxy's outermost planet, Dipon, went well. She was met by an official Diponite, who greeted her enthusiastically. Ambassador Caldwell was confused at first about which of the Diponite's hands to shake. But then she remembered her training classes back on Earth. She politely reached for the second hand from the right. She knew she would have to be careful not to insult these sensitive creatures during this important peacekeeping visit.

This paragraph is set in a future time when humans are traveling to distant planets and meeting strange-looking aliens. But notice that Ambassador Caldwell is doing something we do here now on Earth; she is politely meeting new people. Science fiction stories are sometimes very realistic. It is only the futuristic settings of these stories that make them science fiction.

Science fiction has always been popular because we are curious about the future. We wonder what tomorrow's world will be like. Science fiction is especially popular today. Science is changing our world faster than at any other time in history. If we want to know how far science can take us, we can look to science fiction.

Not all science fiction stories take place in space. Read to find out what a futuristic voyage through the human body accomplishes.

As you read, think about elements of science that make this story science fiction.

Fantastic Voyage

by Isaac Asimov

Scientist Jan Benes has developed a process called miniaturization. He can reduce people in size and keep them that way for a short time. Benes has an accident and a blood clot forms on his brain. The clot must be removed, but operating would be too dangerous.

The other scientists decide to try something they have never done before. They miniaturize four men and a woman to microscopic size. A doctor injects the group, in their submarine *Proteus*, into Benes's bloodstream. Their mission: Reach Benes's brain and remove the clot in 60 minutes. They have only a small amount of time left. Soon they will begin to deminiaturize. The trip through the bloodstream is not an easy one: Every defense the body has against invaders—even friendly ones—comes after the *Proteus*. A team of doctors and nurses in the operating room are monitoring their progress. Carter and Reid are watching through a window overlooking the operating room.

"Where are they now?" asked Carter.

"I'm not positive yet, but they seem to be headed for the inner ear. I'm not sure that I approve of that," said Reid.

"Why not?" Carter glanced quickly at the time-recorder. It read 27.

"It will be difficult. We'll have to watch out for sound."

"Why?"

"The ear reacts to sound; the cochlea vibrates. If the *Proteus* is anywhere near it, it will vibrate, too, and it may vibrate to pieces."

Carter leaned forward in his seat, staring at Reid's calm face. "Why are they going there, then?"

"I suppose because they think that's the only route that will get them to their destination fast enough. We have no way of telling since their radio is broken."

Carter asked, "Are they in there yet? In the inner ear, I mean?"

"Just about," said Reid.

"Do the people down there in the operating room understand about the necessity for silence?"

"They won't be in the ear long."

"They'll be in it long enough. Listen, you tell those people down there . . . no, too late to take a chance. Get me a piece of paper and call in someone from outside. Anyone."

An armed security man came in and saluted.

Carter had scribbled on the paper in block letters: SILENCE! ABSOLUTE SILENCE WHILE PROTEUS IS IN EAR.

"Take this," he said to the security man. "You go down into the operating room and show it to each person. Make sure each one looks at it. Don't make any noise; don't say one word. Do you understand?"

"Yes, sir," he said.

"Go ahead. Hurry. And take off your shoes. Walk into that room on stocking feet."

They watched from the observation room, counting the interminable seconds until the stockinged soldier walked into the operating room. From doctor to nurse to doctor he went, holding up the paper. Person after person nodded grimly. None budged from his or her spot. For a moment, it seemed a mass paralysis had gripped everyone in the room.

"Obviously they understand," said Reid.

"Now, listen," said Carter. "You get in touch with the various people at controls. No buzzers must sound, no bells, no gongs, nothing. For that matter, no flashing lights. I don't want anyone to be startled into as much as a grunt."

"They'll be through in a few seconds."

"Maybe," said Carter, "and maybe not. Hop to it."

Reid hopped to it.

The *Proteus* had entered a wide region of pure liquid. Except for a few antibodies flashing by, now and then, there was nothing to be seen except the glitter of the ship's headlights.

"We're in the cochlear duct," said Michaels. "Inside the little spiral tube in the inner ear that does our hearing for us. This one does Benes's hearing for him. It vibrates to sound in different patterns. See?"

It was almost like a shadow in the fluid, a huge, flat shadow whipping past them.

"It's a sound wave," said Michaels.

"Does that mean someone is talking?" asked Cora.

"Oh, no. If someone were talking or making any real sound this thing would heave like an earthquake. Even in absolute silence, though, the cochlea picks up sounds; the distant thud of the heartbeat, the rasp of blood working through the tiny veins and arteries of the ear, and so on. Didn't you ever cup your ear with a shell and listen to the sound of the ocean? What you're listening to mainly is the magnified sound of your own ocean, the blood stream."

Grant said, "Will this be dangerous?"

Michaels shrugged. "No worse than it is — if no one talks."

Duval asked, "Why are we slowing? Owens!"

Owens replied, "Something's wrong. The engine is choking off and I don't know why."

There was the slowly intensifying sensation of being in a down-dropping elevator as the *Proteus* settled lower in the duct. They hit bottom with a slight jar.

Owens said anxiously, "The engine is overheating and I had to stop it. I think . . ."

"What?"

"It must be those reticular fibers. They must have blocked the intake vents."

"Can you blow them out?" asked Grant, tensely.

Owens shook his head. "Not a chance. Those are intake vents. They suck inward."

"Well, then, there's only one thing to do," said Grant. "It has to be cleaned off from the outside." With furrowed brow, he began to clamber into his diving outfit.

Cora was looking anxiously out the window. She said, "There are antibodies out there. What if they attack?"

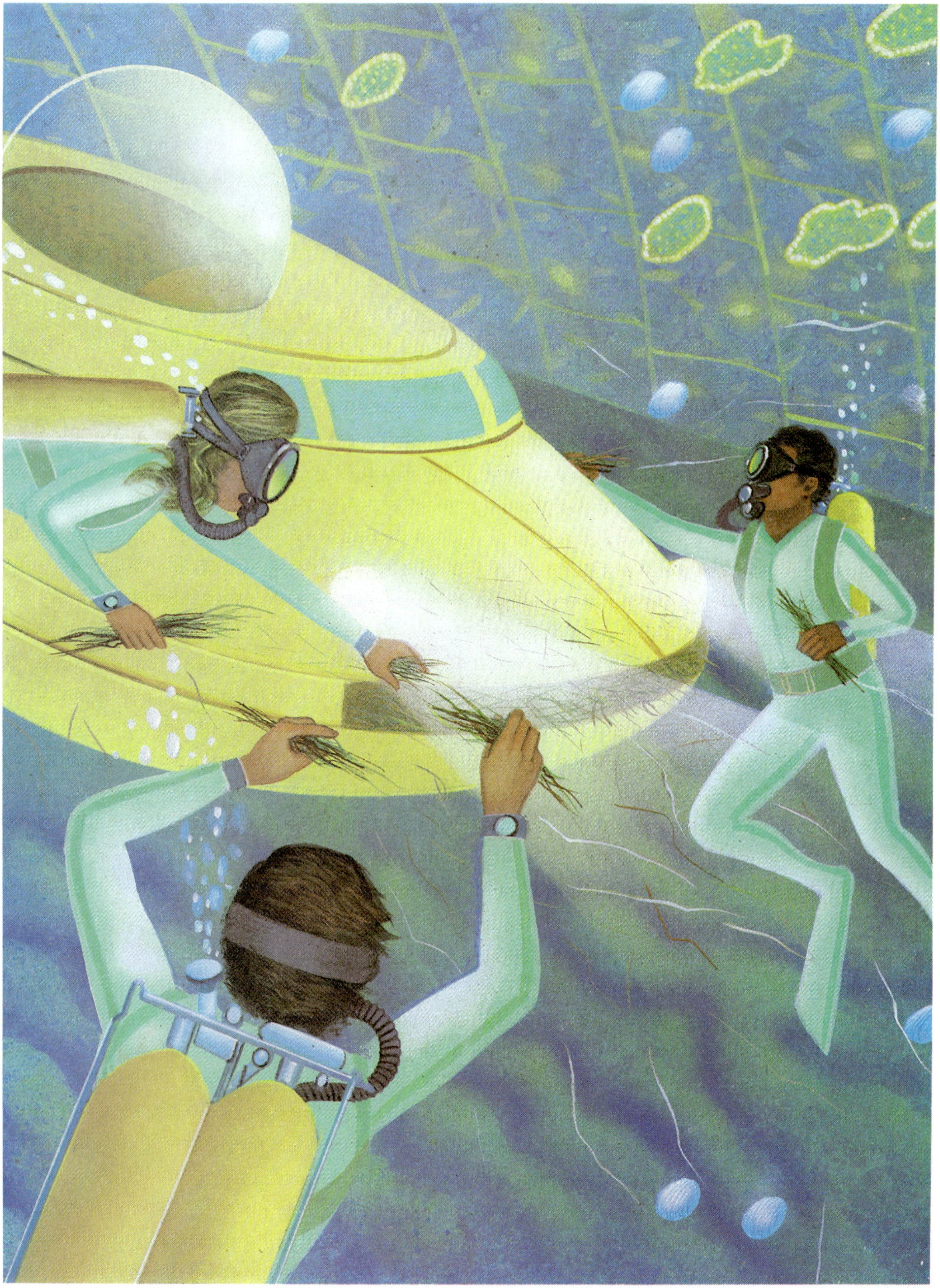

"Not likely," said Michaels, reassuringly. "They're not sensitized to the human shape. And as long as no damage is done to the tissues themselves, the antibodies probably will remain passive."

Grant dropped out the hatch of the ship, landing on the wall of the cochlear duct. He looked ruefully at the ship. It was not the clean, smooth metal it had been. It looked furry, shaggy.

He propelled himself toward the bow of the ship. Owens was quite correct. The intake valves were choked with fibers.

Grant seized a double handful and pulled. They were difficult to get loose. Many broke off at the surface of the vent filters.

Michaels's voice reached him over his small receiver. "How long will it take you? We've got a 26 reading on the time-recorder."

"It's going to take me quite a while." Grant yanked desperately, but the fibers seemed to fight back.

Within the ship, Cora announced tensely, "I'm going out to help him." She seized her diving suit.

"All right," Michaels said, "I will, too. Owens had better stay at the controls."

Soon the three of them were wiggling about the ship's bow, desperately snatching at the fibers, pulling them loose, letting them drift away in the slow current.

Cora said, "We're making it."

"But we're in the cochlea a lot longer than we had expected to be." Michaels replied, "At any moment, some sound . . ."

"Be quiet," said Grant irritably, "and finish the job."

Carter made as if to tear his hair and then held back. "No, no, no, NO!" he cried. "They've stopped again."

"Why do you suppose they've stopped?" asked Reid.

"I don't know," answered Carter. "All I do know is that we have only twenty-four minutes left."

"The longer they stay in the inner ear," Reid said, "the more nearly certain it will be that someone will make a sound — sneeze or something."

"You're right," Carter said. "Call in that messenger."

The security man entered again.

Carter said, "You still have your shoes off? Okay. Take this down and show it to one of the nurses."

The message read: COTTON AT BENES'S EARS.

Carter watched through the control window as the security man entered, hesitated a moment, then moved with quick, gingerly steps to one of the nurses.

She smiled, looked up at Carter and made a circle of her thumb and forefinger.

"It will deaden the noise," said Reid. "It won't stop it."

"It's better than nothing," responded Carter.

The nurse slipped off her own shoes and was at one of the tables in two steps. Carefully, she opened a fresh box of absorbent cotton and unrolled two feet of it.

She pulled off a fistful in one hand. It didn't come readily. She pulled harder. Her hand went flying outward, striking a pair of scissors on the table.

It skittered off the table, striking the hard floor. The nurse's foot flew desperately after it, clamping down upon it hard, but not until after it had given out one sharp, metallic clang.

The nurse's face reddened into a look of deathly horror. Carter crumpled into his chair.

Owens turned on the engine of the *Proteus* and gently checked the controls. He said, "It looks good. Are you all set out there?"

Grant's voice sounded in his ear. "Nothing much left. Get ready to move. We're coming in."

And at that moment, the universe seemed to heave. Owens seized a panel for support and held on desperately, listening to a distant thunder.

Below, Duval held on desperately.

Outside, Grant felt himself flung high in the air as though caught in the grip of a huge tidal wave. He flipped over and over and plunged into the wall on the cochlear duct. Grant knew that the wall was responding with rapid vibrations to some sharp sound.

Cora had been holding on to a projection of the *Proteus* at the moment the vibration had struck. Instinctively, her grip tightened and for a moment she rode the *Proteus* as though it were an insanely bucking bronco. The breath was jerked out of her and her grip was torn away. She went skidding across the floor of the membrane on which the ship had been resting.

The ship's headlights caught the path ahead of her and though she tried in horror to brake her motion it was quite useless.

She was heading, she knew, for a section of the organ of Corti, the basic center of hearing. Within the organ were the hair cells — fifteen thousand of them. They vibrated according to the pitch and loudness of the sound waves in the inner ear.

Cora saw them — a series of tall, graceful columns, moving first one way and then another as though a wave were rippling over them. Cora went skidding and spinning. Finally she managed to grab one of the hair cells. She heard someone calling her. Then she screamed, "Help! Everybody! Help!"

The first devastating shock had passed and Owens was bringing the *Proteus* under control. The sound had been sharp and quick dying. That alone saved them.

"We had better leave," said Duval. "Get the others in."

Owens called, "Michaels! Grant! Peterson!"

"Coming in," responded Michaels.

"Wait," called Grant. "I don't see Cora."

He called, "Cora! Where are you?"

Her voice replied, "I'm caught among the hair cells."

"Where are they? Michaels, where are the hair cells?"

Grant could make out Michaels approaching the ship from another direction.

Michaels shouted, "This way! Owens, follow me! We'll need the light."

Grant followed Michaels's quickly moving figure and saw the columns ahead.

"I see her," said Grant, pointing. "Cora! Move your arms so I can be certain."

She waved.

"All right. I'm coming to get you. We'll have you back in a shake and a half."

Cora waited and felt a touch at her knees, the faintest and gentlest sensation, like that of a fly's wing brushing against her. She looked toward her knee but saw nothing. There was another touch near her shoulder, then still another.

Quite suddenly, she made them out, just a few. They looked like little balls of wool — antibodies. It was almost as though they were testing her, deciding whether she

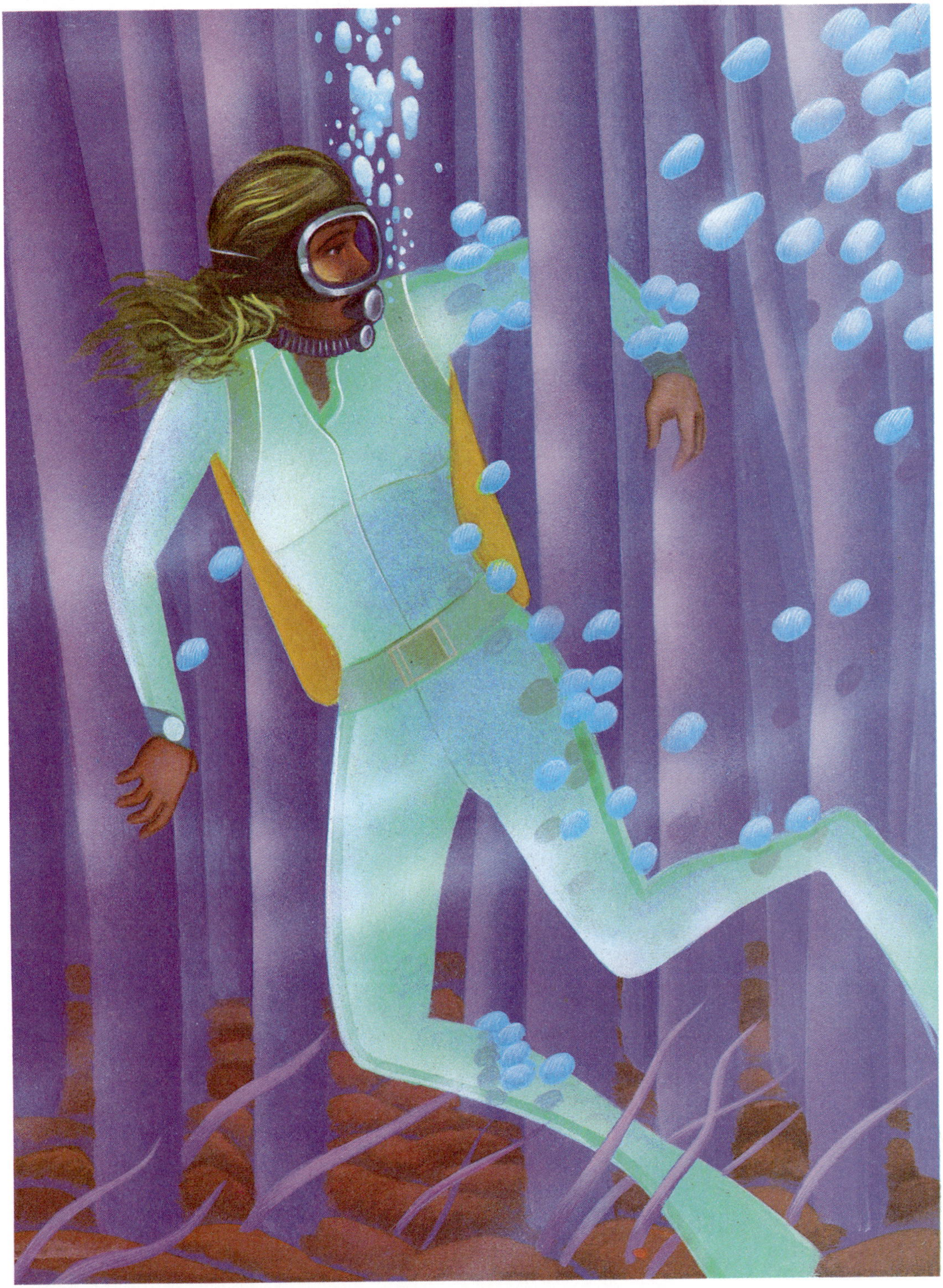

were harmless or not. There were only a few, but more were drifting toward her.

She screamed, "Come quickly. Antibodies all about."

An antibody had touched her elbow and was clinging there. She shook her arm. The antibody did not shake loose. Another joined it, the two fitting together neatly, filaments interlaced.

"Antibodies," muttered Grant.

Michaels said, "She must have done enough damage to surrounding tissue to spark their appearance."

Grant could see them swarming about her like a cloud of tiny fruit flies.

He said, "Michaels, get back to the sub. One person is enough to risk. I'll get her out of here somehow. If I don't, it will be up to the three of you to get whatever's left of us back into the ship. We can't be allowed to deminiaturize here, whatever happens."

Michaels hesitated, then said, "Take care," and turned, hastening back to the *Proteus*.

Grant continued to plunge toward Cora.

"Let's get out of here, Cora," he panted.

He was pulling desperately at her oxygen cylinders, which had cut into a column and stuck. Cora's ankle was caught between two fibers and he strained them apart. "Now, let's go!"

They started moving away. Cora's body was fuzzed with clinging antibodies but the bulk were left behind. Then they began to follow; first a few, then many, then the entire growing swarm.

Cora's back was half-covered by a mosaic of the woolballs. A few were now beginning to attach themselves to Grant's body.

"Faster, Cora!"

They sped toward the waiting *Proteus*.

Grant's hand clutched at the wheel of the hatch, while the signal light flashed redly about it.

Cora cried out, "They're coming! Let's get into the hatch."

Grant looked back. They were finding their way, sensing their presence. Chains of them were coming toward them. The light turned green. He whirled at the wheel, desperately.

The antibodies were all about them, but making chiefly for Cora. Grant pulled the hatch door open, thrust Cora into it, antibodies and all, and squeezed in after her. The hatch barely held both.

He pushed forcefully against the hatch door while antibodies continued to pour in. The door closed but hundreds of them clogged the door at the end. He managed to turn the wheel that locked the door in place. Hundreds of antibodies filled the space. They formed a solid band around Cora.

"They're tightening, Grant," she said.

Grant hammered at the inner door.

"I . . . I . . . can't brea . . ." gasped Cora.

The door opened. Duval's hand seized Cora's arm and pulled her in. Grant followed.

They both started pulling the antibodies off Cora. A strand tore, then another, then still another.

Grant said, "It's easier now. Just brush them off."

Duval added, "They're designed to work in body fluid, of course. Once they're surrounded by air, the molecular attractions alter in nature."

Cora was breathing in deep, shuddering gasps.

"Are you all right, Peterson?" asked Duval.

Cora took a deep breath and said, with an effort but in a steady voice, "Quite all right."

"We've got to get out of here. We have practically no time left," said Owens.

In the control room, the television receivers seemed to spring back into life. "General Carter..."

"Yes, what now?"

"They're moving again, sir. They're out of the ear and heading rapidly for the clot."

"They survived!" He looked at the time-recorder, which read 12. "Twelve minutes. Can they still make it, Reid?"

Reid was crumpled in his chair, looking miserable. "They can make it. They can even get rid of the clot, maybe. But I don't know if we can get them out in time."

"They're reaching the base of the brain, sir," came the word.

Michaels was back at his chart. Grant was near him.

"Is that the clot here?"

"Yes," said Michaels.

"It looks way off. We only have twelve minutes."

"It's not as far as it looks. We'll have clear sailing now."

Carter had his jacket off and his sleeves rolled up. "In the brain?" he said.

Reid rubbed his eyes. "Practically at the clot. They've stopped."

Carter looked at the time recorder, which read 9.

He said, "Think they'll make it?"

Reid shook his head. "No, I don't."

"We've entered the brain itself," announced Owens, with controlled excitement.

He doused the ship's lights and all of them looked forward in a moment of wonder.

Michaels said, "Look ahead."

He pointed. They were in the blood stream again. The red corpuscles (bluish in color) drifted without any definite motion. Up ahead was a shadow.

The *Proteus* came to a halt. For an instant or two, there was silence. Then Owens said quietly, "That's our destination, I think."

Duval nodded. "Yes. The clot."

Michaels smiled wearily. "It's too late." He pointed to the time-recorder, which was just making the slow, slow change from 7 to 6. He said, "You couldn't possibly perform the operation in time to allow us to get to the removal point in the jugular. Even if you succeed in the removal of the clot, we'll end by deminiaturizing right here and killing Benes."

"Hold it," interrupted Grant, angrily. "Owens, how long will it take us to get to removal point?"

Owens answered faintly, "Two minutes!"

"That leaves us four minutes. Maybe more. Mightn't it take longer to deminiaturize than we're counting?" continued Grant.

Duval replied, "It might take a minute or two, if we're lucky."

"All right," said Grant, "We've got four minutes, plus maybe two minutes extra. That's six of our long, time-distorted minutes. Get going, Duval."

Duval said, "Get the laser, Peterson." Both were in their swim suits by now.

"Owens, operate the hatch for them," said Grant. Duval and Cora disappeared into the hatch.

They swam quickly in the direction of the clot; he carrying the laser, she the power unit.

"If we can break up the clot and relieve the pressure without touching the nerve itself," muttered Duval, "we will be doing well. Let's see now."

He maneuvered for position, raised the laser, and pressed the laser trigger. For the barest moment, a thin beam of light flashed into being. For that moment, the clot had stood out in the brilliance of the laser beam and a line of small bubbles formed and marked out its path.

Cora said, excitedly, "It's working, Dr. Duval. A whole dark area is lighting up."

Grant was swimming up to them. "How's it coming, Duval? We have less than three minutes."

Duval was aiming the laser beam in short bursts at quick intervals.

Grant said, "I think we've just about had it, Doctor. Time's gone."

"I'm just about done. The clot has crumbled away. Just one portion. Ah . . . Mr. Grant, the operation has been a success."

"And we've got maybe three minutes to get out, maybe two. Back to the ship, now . . ."

"If we follow the optic nerve, we can make it to the eye in a minute or less," said Duval.

"How much time do we have left?" asked Cora.

Duval said, "None! I think we're beginning to deminiaturize now. In a minute or so we'll be large enough to attract the attention of a white cell."

"Deminiaturizing? Now? I don't feel it."

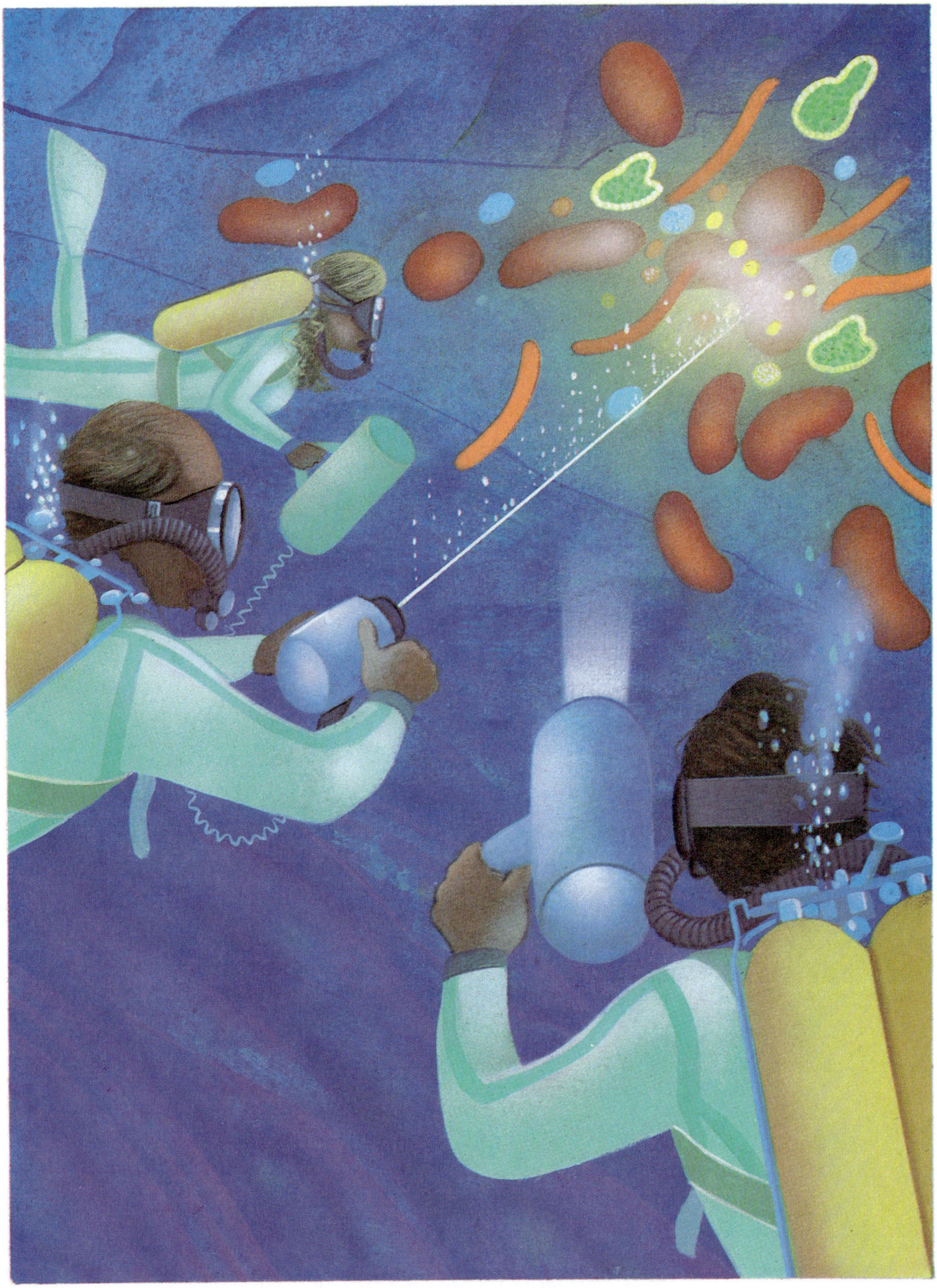

"You won't. But the surroundings are slightly smaller than they've been. Let's go!"

"It's too late for them to get out now," said Reid.

A message came through from the operating room: EEG data indicates Benes's brain action is being restored to normal.

Carter yelled, "Then the operation is a success."

The time-recorder moved to 0 and a loud alarm went off. Its shrill jangle filled the entire room with the clang of doom.

Reid raised his voice to be heard. "We've got to take them out."

"It will kill Benes."

"If we don't take them out, that will kill Benes, too."

Carter seemed to shrink. "Give the order," he said.

Reid went to the transmitter. "Remove the *Proteus*," he said quietly. Then he went to the window overlooking the operating room.

The surgical team gathered around Benes's head. Carter and Reid watched from above. Carter's depression was deepening by the moment.

It was over. All for nothing. All for nothing. All for . . .

"General Carter! Sir!" The sound was urgent. The man's voice was cracking with excitement.

"Yes?"

"The *Proteus*, sir. It's moving."

Carter yelled, "Stop surgery!"

Each member of the surgical team looked up in startled wonder.

"Where's it heading?" shouted Carter.

"Along the optic nerve, sir."

Carter turned fiercely on Reid. "Where does that go? What does it mean?"

Reid's face lit up. "It means an emergency exit I hadn't thought of. They're heading for the eye and out through the tear duct. They may make it. Get a microscope slide, someone. Carter, let's get down there."

The optic nerve was a bundle of fibers, each like a string of sausages.

"Everything's definitely getting smaller. Do you notice that?" asked Owens.

Grant nodded. "I sure do."

"We only have seconds to go," said Duval.

"We're in the eye now. We're only the width of a teardrop from safety," announced Grant.

"Through here and we'll be in the tear duct," said Duval.

They went through the membranous wall. "We're out," cried Duval with a controlled excitement. "We're out of the body!"

Duval said, "This is the cornea. The other wall is the lower eyelid. We've got to get far enough away to deminiaturize fully without hurting Benes, and we only have seconds to do it in."

Up above, many feet above (on their still tiny scale), was a horizontal crack. "Through there," said Duval.

"The ship's on the surface of the eye!" came the triumphant shout.

"All right," said Reid. "Right eye."

A technician leaned closer with the microscope slide at Benes's closed eye. A magnifying lens was in place.

454

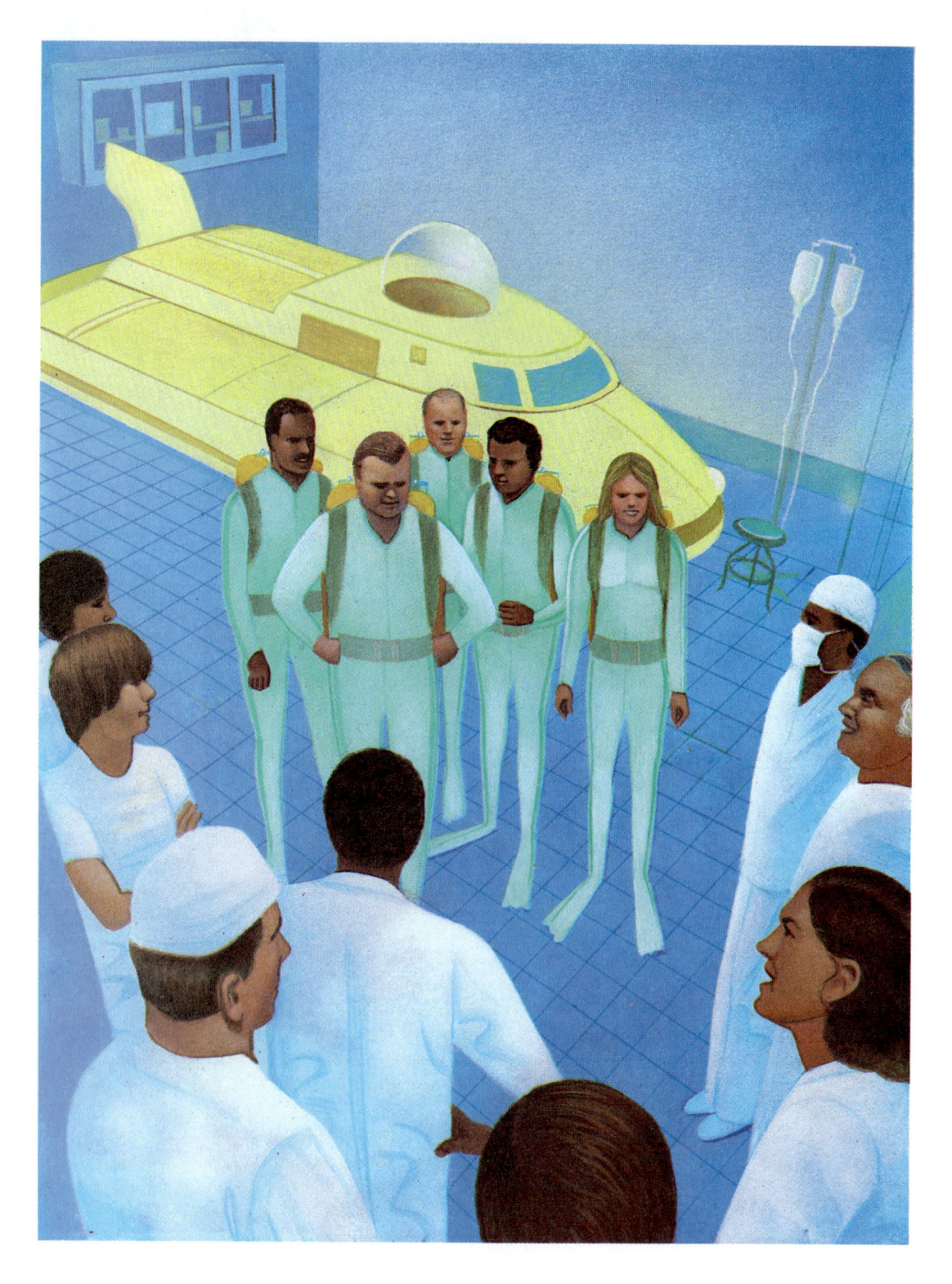

Slowly, the lower eyelid was gently pulled down.

"It's there," said the technician in hushed tones. "Like a speck of dirt."

Skillfully, he placed the slide to the eye. A tear with the speck in it squeezed onto it. Everyone backed away.

Reid warned, "Something that is large enough to see is going to get much larger very quickly. Scatter!"

The technician, torn between hurry and the necessity for gentleness, placed the slide down on the floor of the room, then backed away at a quick trot.

The nurses wheeled Benes on the operating table quickly through the door and, with startling speed, the speck on the slide grew to full size.

The submarine was there, where nothing had been a moment before.

Reid gasped, "Eight seconds to spare!"

A short while later Benes's eyes were open. He tried to smile.

A nurse whispered anxiously, "Only a minute, now. He doesn't know what's happened, so don't say anything."

"I understand," said Grant.

To Benes, in a low voice, he said, "How are you?"

Benes tried again to smile. "I'm not sure. Very tired. I have a headache and my right eye hurts, but I seem to have survived."

"Good!"

"It takes more than a knock on the head to kill a scientist," said Benes. "All that mathematics makes the skull as hard as a rock, eh?"

"We're all glad of that," said Cora, gently.

And then he did smile.

Discuss the Selection

1. What does the voyage of *Proteus* accomplish?
2. Why were the crew members of *Proteus* short of time when they got to the brain?
3. When the *Proteus* was in Benes's ear, absolute quiet was essential. How did you feel when the operating room nurse accidently knocked the scissors onto the floor?
4. How did the crew of *Proteus* manage to remove the clot and get out of Benes's body with so few minutes remaining on the time-recorder?
5. General Carter felt at times hopeful and at other times hopeless about the mission. Find parts of the story that show his changing moods and the reasons for them.

Apply the Skills

Science fiction has certain characteristics. "Fantastic Voyage" contains many of the elements that make a piece of writing science fiction. Make a list of five things that helped you to identify this story as science fiction.

Think and Write

Prewrite

Operating Room	Body
1. Carter sends the note for absolute silence.	1. *Proteus* stops to clean out its vents.
2. A nurse knocks a pair of scissors off the tables.	2. Cora Peterson is attacked by antibodies.
3.	3.
4.	4.

All of the action in "Fantastic Voyage" takes place in two settings. One setting is the internal environment of Benes's body. The other is the operating room and observation area. Copy and complete the chart by describing two more events that took place in each setting.

Compose

Using the information from the completed chart, write one paragraph that summarizes the story from the point of view of someone in the operating room. Then write a second paragraph that summarizes the story from the point of view of someone on *Proteus*.

Revise

Read your paragraphs. Make sure that each paragraph contains a different point of view.

In this science fiction story, Ray Bradbury tells us about our world in 1928 through the eyes of the children of tomorrow. Read the story to find out what the Time Children think about our world.

As you read, look for parts of the selection that indicate that the story is science fiction.

Time in Thy Flight

by Ray Bradbury

A wind blew the long years away past their hot faces. The Time Machine stopped.

"Nineteen hundred and twenty-eight," said Janet. The two boys looked past her.

Mr. Fields stirred. "Remember, you're here to observe the behavior of these ancient people. Be inquisitive, be intelligent, observe."

"Yes," said the girl and the two boys in crisp khaki uniforms. They wore identical haircuts, had identical wristwatches, sandals, and coloring of hair, eyes, teeth, and skin, though they were not related.

"Shh!" said Mr. Fields.

They looked out at a little Illinois town in the spring of the year. A cool mist lay on the early morning streets. Far down the street a small boy came running in the last light of the marble-cream moon. Somewhere a great clock struck 5 A.M. far away. Leaving tennis-shoe prints softly in the quiet lawns, the boy stepped near the invisible Time Machine and cried up to a high dark house window.

The house window opened. Another boy crept down the roof to the ground. The two boys ran off with banana-filled mouths into the dark cold morning.

"Follow them," whispered Mr. Fields. "Study their life patterns. Quick!"

Janet and William and Robert ran on the cold pavements of spring, visible now, through the slumbering town, through a park. All about, lights flickered, doors clicked, and other children rushed alone or in gasping pairs down a hill to some gleaming blue tracks.

"Here it comes!" The children milled about before dawn. Far down the shining tracks a small light grew seconds later into steaming thunder.

"What is it?" screamed Janet.

"A train, silly, you've seen pictures of them!" shouted Robert.

And as the Time Children watched, from the train stepped gigantic gray elephants, steaming the pavement with their mighty waters, lifting question-mark nozzles to the cold morning sky. Cumbrous wagons rolled from the long freight flats, red and gold. Lions roared and paced in boxed darkness.

"Why — *this* must be a — circus!" Janet trembled.

"You think so? Whatever happened to them?"

"Like Christmas, I guess. Just vanished, long ago."

Janet looked around. "Oh, it's awful, isn't it?"

The boys stood numbed. "It sure is."

Men shouted in the first faint gleam of dawn. Sleeping cars drew up, dazed faces blinked out at the children. Horses clattered like a great fall of stones on the pavement.

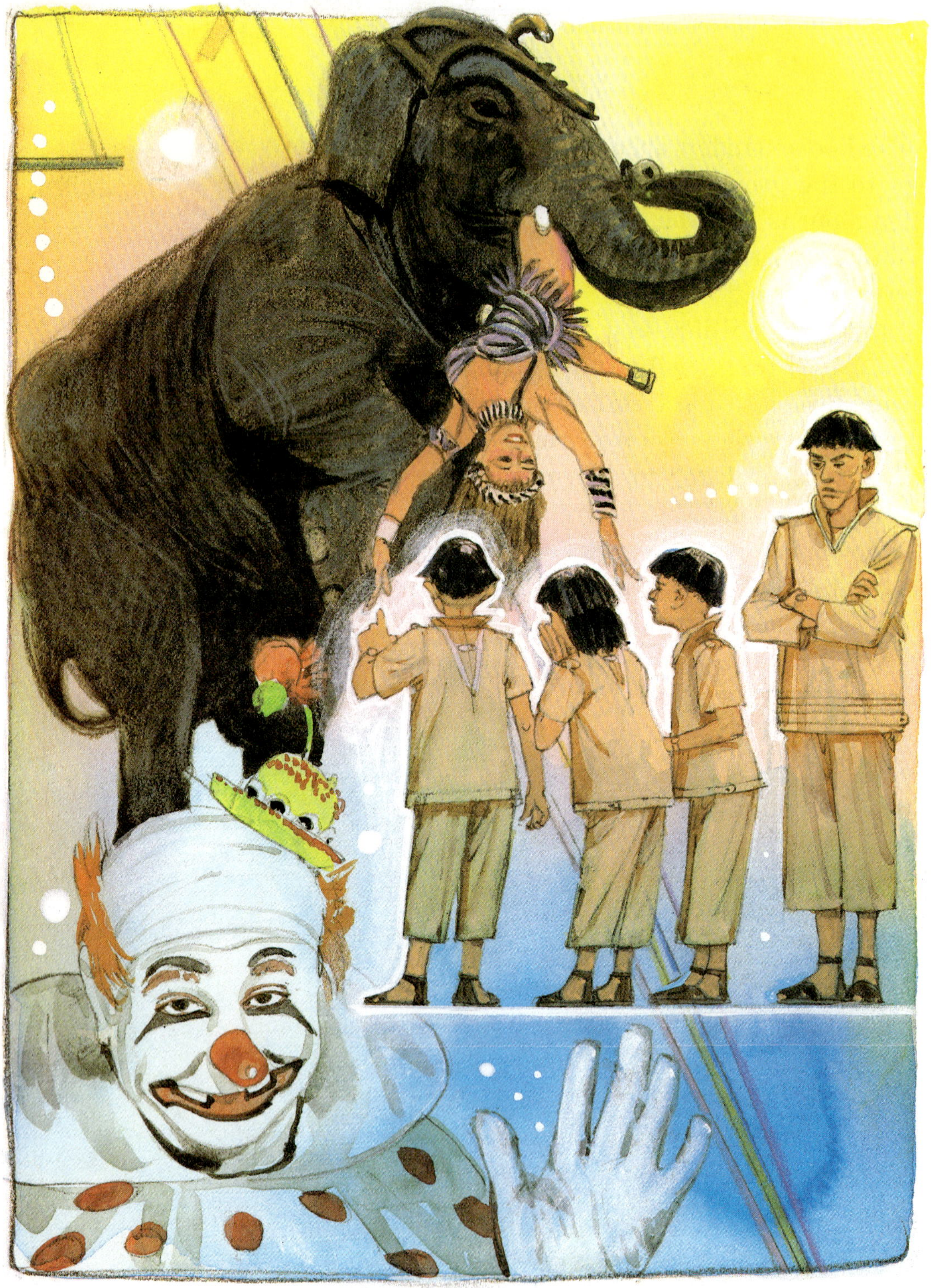

Mr. Fields was suddenly behind the children. "Disgusting, barbaric, keeping animals in cages. If I'd known this was here, I'd never let you come see. This is a terrible ritual."

"Oh, yes." But Janet's eyes were puzzled. "And yet, you know, it's like a nest of maggots. I want to study it."

"I don't know," said Robert, his eyes darting, his fingers trembling. "It's pretty crazy. We might try writing a thesis on it if Mr. Fields says it's all right . . ."

Mr. Fields nodded. "I'm glad you're digging in here, finding motives, studying this horror. All right — we'll see the circus this afternoon."

"I think I'm going to be sick," said Janet.

The Time Machine hummed.

"So that was a circus," said Janet, solemnly.

The trombone circus died in their ears. The last thing they saw was candy-pink trapeze people whirling while baking powder clowns shrieked and bounded.

"You must admit psychovision's better," said Robert slowly.

"All those nasty animal smells, the excitement." Janet blinked. "That's bad for children, isn't it? And those older people seated with the children. Mothers, fathers, they called them. Oh, that *was* strange."

Mr. Fields put some marks in his class grading book.

Janet shook her head numbly. "I want to see it all again. I've missed the motives somewhere. I want to make that run across town again in the early morning. The cold air on my face — the sidewalk under my feet — the circus train coming in. Was it the air and the early hour that made the children get up and run to see the train come in? I want to retrace the entire pattern.

Why should they be excited? I feel I've missed out on the answer."

"They all smiled so much," said William.

"Manic-depressives," said Robert.

"What are summer vacations? I heard them talk about it." Janet looked at Mr. Fields.

"They spent their summers racing about like idiots, beating each other up," replied Mr. Fields seriously.

"I'll take our State Engineered summers of work for children anytime," said Robert, looking at nothing, his voice faint.

The Time Machine stopped again.

"The Fourth of July," announced Mr. Fields. "Nineteen hundred and twenty-eight. An ancient holiday when people blew each other's fingers off."

They stood before the same house on the same street but on a soft summer evening. Fire wheels hissed, on front porches laughing children tossed things out that went bang!

"Don't run!" cried Mr. Fields. "It's not war, don't be afraid!"

But Janet's and Robert's and William's faces were pink, now blue, now white with fountains of soft fire.

"We're all right," said Janet, standing very still.

"Happily," announced Mr. Fields, "they prohibited fireworks a century ago, did away with the whole messy explosion."

Children did fairy dances, weaving their names and destinies on the dark summer air with white sparklers.

"I'd like to do that," said Janet, softly. "Write my name on the air. See? I'd like that."

"What?" Mr. Fields hadn't been listening.

"Nothing," said Janet.

"Bang!" whispered William and Robert, standing under the soft summer trees, in shadow, watching, watching the red, white, and green fires on the beautiful summer night lawns. "Bang!"

October.

The Time Machine paused for the last time, an hour later in the month of burning leaves. People bustled into dim houses carrying pumpkins and corn shocks. Skeletons danced, bats flew, candles flamed, apples swung in empty doorways.

"Halloween," said Mr. Fields. "The acme of horror. This was the age of superstition, you know. Later they banned the Grimm Brothers, ghosts, skeletons, and all that claptrap. You children, thank God, were raised in an antiseptic world of no shadows or ghosts. You had decent holidays like William C. Chatterton's Birthday, Work Day, and Machine Day."

They walked by the same house in the empty October night, peering in at the triangle-eyed pumpkins, the masks leering in black attics and damp cellars. Now, inside the house, some party children squatted telling stories, laughing!

"I want to be inside with them," said Janet at last.

"Sociologically, of course," said the boys.

"No," she said.

"What?" asked Mr. Fields.

"No, I just want to be inside. I just want to stay here. I want to see it all and be here and never be anywhere else. I want firecrackers and pumpkins and circuses. I want Christmases and Valentines and Fourths, like we've seen."

"This is getting out of hand," Mr. Fields started to say.

But suddenly Janet was gone. "Robert, William, come on!" She ran. The boys leaped after her.

"Hold on!" shouted Mr. Fields. "Robert! William, I've got you!" He seized the last boy, but the other escaped. "Janet, Robert — come back here! You'll never pass into the seventh grade! You'll fail, Janet, Bob — *Bob*!"

An October wind blew wildly down the street, vanishing with the children off among moaning trees.

William twisted and kicked.

"No, not you, too, William, you're coming home with me. We'll teach those other two a lesson they won't forget. So they want to stay in the past, do they?" Mr. Fields shouted so everyone could hear. "All right Janet, Bob, stay in this horror, in this chaos! In a few weeks you'll come sniveling back here to me. But I'll be gone! I'm leaving you here to go mad in this world!"

He hurried William to the Time Machine. The boy was sobbing.

"Don't make me come back here on any more Field Excursions ever again, please, Mr. Fields, please —"

Almost instantly the Time Machine whisked away toward the future, toward the underground hive cities, the metal buildings, the metal flowers, the metal lawns.

"Good-bye, Janet, Bob!"

A great cold October wind blew through the town like water. And when it had ceased blowing it had carried all the children, whether invited or uninvited, masked or unmasked, to the doors of houses which closed upon them. There was not a running child anywhere in the night. The wind whined away in the bare treetops.

And inside the big house, in the candlelight, someone was pouring cold apple cider all around, to everyone, no matter *who* they were.

Discuss the Selection

1. What were some of the things the Time Children thought about the world of 1928?
2. How was the Time Machine able to move about in time without being seen by the people of the town?
3. What do you think the Time Children would notice and comment about if they were to visit your world today?
4. What was life like for the Time Children in the future?
5. At what point in the story does Janet's attitude about our world change? Find that passage.

Apply the Skills

Science fiction stories sometimes describe scientific advances that in our world are impossibilities. Readers can identify stories as science fiction by recognizing these scientific advances.

Identify some of the scientific advances of the future that are described in this story.

Think and Write

Prewrite

World of 1928	World of the Time Children
mothers and fathers	no parents
	holidays like Machine Day
	underground hive cities
	metal flowers and lawns
	state engineered summers of work

The world that the Time Children lived in was very different from the world of 1928 which they visited. The chart above compares the two worlds. Copy and complete the chart with details from the story.

Compose

Write a paragraph contrasting the world of 1928 with the world of the Time Children. Use the information on your chart and other examples from the story in your paragraph.

Revise

Read your paragraph. Did you contrast each item in the world of 1928 with one from the world of the Time Children?

Vocabulary Study

Multiple Meanings

Would it surprise you to know that there are over forty different meanings for the word *set*? There are many words in the English language that have multiple meanings. Even though a word may look and sound the same, it can have different meanings in different sentences. Read the following sentences.

> Ryan realized that a high grade in science would allow him to participate in the school science fair.
>
> The hill's steep grade prevented my friend Miko from planting a vegetable garden.

Although the word *grade* looks and sounds the same in both sentences, it has different meanings. In the first sentence, *grade* means "a score or mark showing merit for work done." In the second sentence, *grade* means "an angle, or a tilt."

You probably already know the meaning of the word *grade* as it is used in the first sentence. But how do you decide the correct meaning of an unfamiliar word that has several meanings? You use what you know about the other words in the sentence to figure out the word's meaning. This is known as using context clues. In the second sentence, the words *steep* and *hill's* are clues that tell you that the word *grade* has something to do with the slope and tilt of the land.

The word *block* can mean "to prevent or stop" or "a solid piece of material with flat sides." Which meaning is correct for the word *block* in the next sentence?

A cornerstone is a concrete block that may be filled with memorabilia from the era in which a building was constructed.

In this sentence, *block* means a "solid piece of material with flat sides." What context clues helped you to figure out the meaning? The words *concrete* and *filled* helped you to determine the correct meaning in the sentence.

Match the meanings of the following boldface words with the sentences below them.

bay
- **a.** a chestnut-colored horse
- **b.** an inlet of the sea

1. The crew docked the ship in the bay.
2. Michael's beautiful bay earned a first place ribbon in jumping.

current
- **a.** the flow of electricity through a wire
- **b.** now in effect

3. The electrician shut off the current before starting work.
4. This department store carries only current styles.

case
- **a.** a particular instance or example
- **b.** an action or lawsuit in a court of law

5. The defense lawyer presented her case to the judge.
6. This incident is clearly a case of mistaken identity.

Remember to use context clues to help you figure out an unknown word's meaning. When you have difficulty figuring out the meaning from context clues, use a dictionary. Knowing how to figure out word meanings can help you to improve your understanding of what you read.

The narrator of this story meets a man who is able to make great plans for the future. Read the story to find out how that man influences his tomorrows.

As you read the story, look for words that have more than one meaning.

Saturn Rising

by Arthur C. Clarke

Yes, that's perfectly true. I met Morris Perlman when I was about twenty-eight. I met thousands of people in those days, from presidents downward.

When we got back from Saturn, everybody wanted to see us, and about half the crew took off on lecture tours. I've always enjoyed talking, but some of my colleagues said they'd rather go to Pluto than face another audience. Some of them did.

My beat was the Midwest. The first time I ran into Mr. Perlman — no one ever called him anything else, certainly never Morris — was in Chicago. The agency always booked me into good, but not too luxurious, hotels. That suited me. I liked to stay in places where I could come and go as I pleased.

It's all a long time ago now, but I must have been lecturing at the University. I was having breakfast in the coffee shop when a slightly built, middle-aged man dropped into the seat on the other side of the table. He nodded a polite good morning, then gave a start of surprise as he recognized me. (Of course, he'd planned the encounter, but I didn't know it at the time.)

"This is a pleasure!" he said. "I was at your lecture last night. How I envied you!"

I gave a rather forced smile. I'm never very sociable at breakfast, and I'd learned to be on my guard against cranks, bores, and enthusiasts. Mr. Perlman, however, was not a bore—though he was certainly an enthusiast, and I suppose you could call him a crank.

He looked like any average, fairly prosperous businessman. I assumed that he was a guest like myself. The fact that he had attended my lecture was not surprising. It has been a popular one, open to the public, and of course well advertised over press and radio.

"Ever since I was a kid," said my uninvited companion, "Saturn has fascinated me. I know exactly when and how it all started. I must have been about ten years old back in the nineteen-fifties. I used to sit for hours trying to grasp the fact that this incredible object, with its silver rings spinning around it, wasn't just some artist's dream, but actually existed. It was a world, in fact, ten times the size of Earth.

"At that time I never imagined that I could see this wonderful thing for myself. I took it for granted that only the astronomers, with their giant telescopes, could ever look at such sights. But then, when I was about fifteen, I made another discovery — so exciting that I could hardly believe it."

"And what was that?" I asked.

"I found that any fool could make a high-powered astronomical telescope in his own kitchen, for a few dollars and a couple of weeks' work. It was a revelation. Like thousands of other kids, I borrowed a copy of Ingalls's *Amateur Telescope Making* from the public library and went ahead. Tell me, have you ever built a telescope of your own?"

"No. I'm an engineer, not an astronomer. I wouldn't know how to begin the job."

"It's incredibly simple, if you follow the rules. You start with two disks of glass, about an inch thick. I got mine for fifty cents from a ship chandler's. They were porthole glasses that were no use because they'd been chipped around the edges. Then you cement one disk to some flat, firm surface. I used an old barrel, standing on end.

"Next you have to buy several grades of emery powder, starting from coarse, gritty stuff and working down to the finest that's made. You lay a pinch of the coarsest powder between the two disks and start rubbing the upper one back and forth with regular strokes. As you do so, you slowly circle around the job.

"You see what happens? The upper disk gets hollowed out by the cutting action of the emery powder. As you walk around, it shapes itself into a concave, spherical surface. From time to time you have to change to a finer grade of powder. And you have to make some simple optical tests to be sure that your curve's right.

"Later still, you drop the emery and change to rouge, until at last you have a smooth, polished surface that you can hardly credit you've made yourself. There's only one more step, though that's a little tricky. You still have to silver the mirror and turn it into a good reflector. This means getting some chemicals made up at the drugstore and doing exactly what the book says.

"I can still remember the kick I got when the silver film began to spread like magic across the face of my little mirror. It wasn't perfect. But it was good enough. I wouldn't have swapped it for anything on Mount Palomar.

"I fixed it at one end of a wooden plank. There was no need to bother about a telescope tube, though I put a couple of feet of cardboard around the mirror to cut out stray light. For an eyepiece I used a small magnifying lens I'd picked up in a junk store for a few cents. Altogether, I don't suppose the telescope cost more than five dollars, though that was a lot of money to me when I was a kid.

"We were living then in a rundown hotel my family owned on Third Avenue. When I'd assembled the telescope, I went up on the roof and tried it out, among the jungle of TV antennas that covered every building in those days. It took me a while to get the mirror and eyepiece lined up, but I hadn't made any mistakes and the thing worked. As an optical instrument it was probably lousy. After all, it was my first attempt. But it magnified at least fifty times. I could hardly wait until nightfall to try it on the stars.

"I'd checked with the almanac and knew that Saturn was high in the east after sunset. As soon as it was dark I was up on the roof again, with my crazy contraption of wood and glass propped between two chimneys. It was late fall, but I never noticed the cold, for the sky was full of stars. And they were all mine.

"I took my time setting the focus as accurately as possible, using the first star that came into the field. Then I started hunting for Saturn. I soon discovered how hard it was to locate anything in a reflecting telescope that wasn't properly mounted. But presently the planet shot across the field of view. I nudged the instrument a few inches this way and that — and there it was.

"It was tiny, but it was perfect. I don't think I breathed

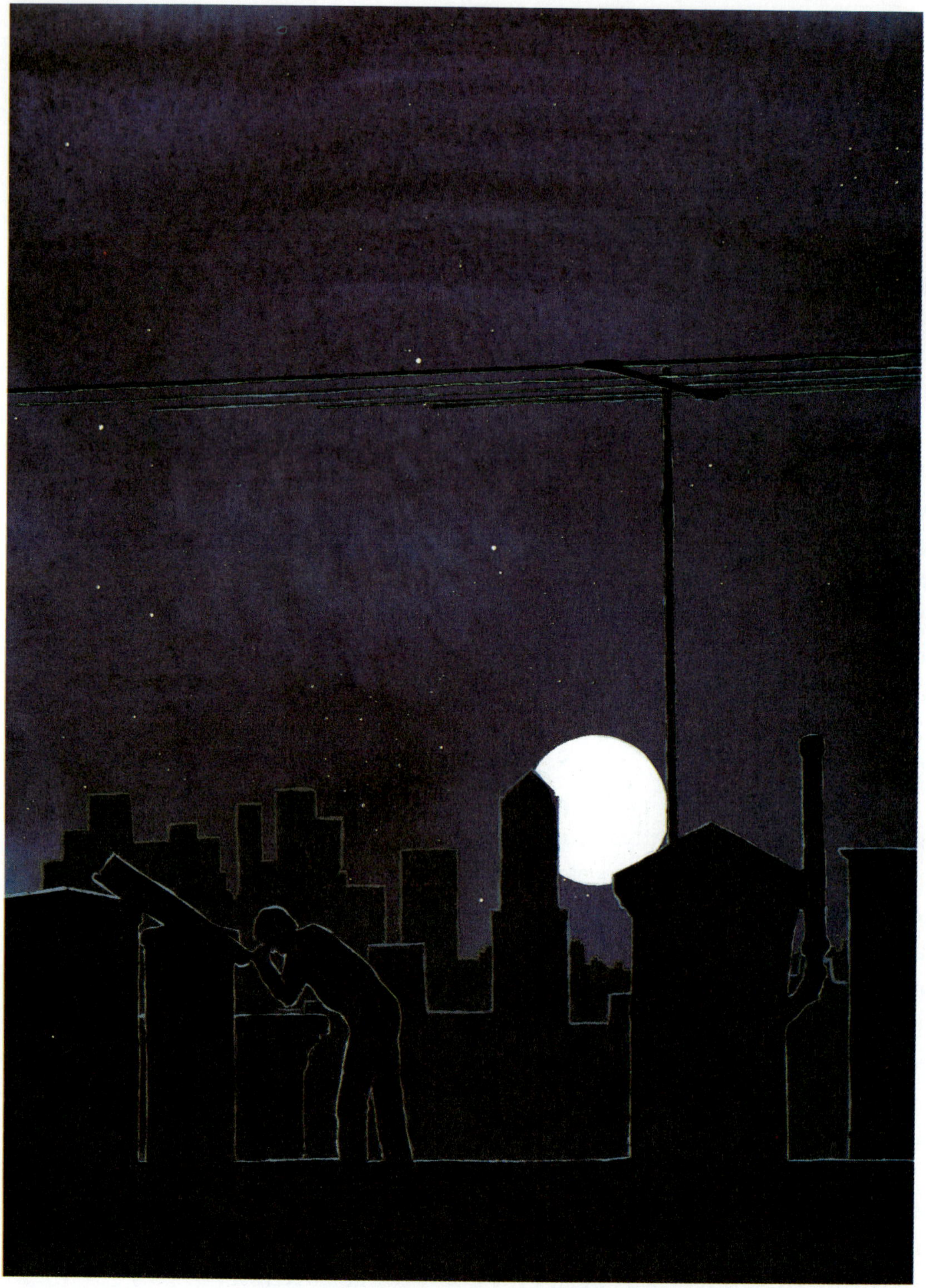

for a minute. I could hardly believe my eyes. After all the pictures, here was the reality. It looked like a toy hanging there in space, with the rings slightly open and tilted toward me. Even now, forty years later, I can remember thinking, It looks so *artificial*! There was a single bright star to the left of it, and I knew that was Titan."

He paused, and for a moment we must have shared the same thoughts. For to both of us Titan was no longer merely the largest moon of Saturn — a point of light known only to astronomers. It was the fiercely hostile world upon which *Endeavour* had landed. There three of my crew mates lay in lonely graves, farther from their homes than any of humankind's dead had ever rested before.

"I don't know how long I stared, straining my eyes and moving the telescope across the sky in jerky steps as Saturn rose above the city. I was a billion miles from New York, but presently New York caught up with me.

"I told you about our hotel. It belonged to my mother, but my father ran it — not very well. It had been losing money for years. All through my boyhood there had been continuous financial crises. My father must have been half crazy with worry most of the time. I had quite forgotten that I was supposed to be helping the clerk at the reception desk . . . .

"So Dad came looking for me, full of his own cares and knowing nothing about my dreams. He found me stargazing on the roof.

"He wasn't a cruel man. He couldn't have understood the study and patience and care that had gone into my little telescope or the wonders it had shown me during the short time I had used it. I don't hate him anymore.

But I'll remember all my life the splintering crack of my first and last mirror as it smashed against the brickwork."

There was nothing I could say. My initial resentment at this interruption had long since changed to curiosity. Already I sensed that there was much more to this story than I'd heard so far. And I'd noticed something else. The waitress was treating us with great respect — only a little of which was directed at me.

My companion toyed with the sugar bowl while I waited in silent sympathy. By this time I felt there was some bond between us, though I did not know exactly what it was.

"I never built another telescope," he said. "Something else broke besides that mirror — something in my heart. Anyway, I was much too busy. Two things happened that turned my life upside down. Dad walked out on us, leaving me the head of the family. And then they pulled down the Third Avenue El."

He must have seen my puzzled look, for he grinned across the table at me.

"Oh, you wouldn't know about that. But when I was a kid, there was an elevated railroad down the middle of Third Avenue. It made the whole area dirty and noisy. The Avenue was a slum district of pawnshops and cheap hotels like ours. All that changed when the El went. Land values shot up, and we were suddenly prosperous. Dad came back quickly enough, but it was too late. I was running the business. Before long I started moving across town — then across country. I wasn't an absent-minded stargazer anymore. I gave Dad one of my smaller hotels, where he couldn't do much harm.

"It's forty years since I looked at Saturn, but I've never

forgotten that one glimpse. Last night your photographs brought it all back. I just wanted to say how grateful I am."

He fumbled in his wallet and pulled out a card. "I hope you'll look me up when you're in town again. You can be sure I'll be there if you give any more lectures. Good luck, and I'm sorry to have taken so much of your time."

Then he was gone, almost before I could say a word. I glanced at the card, put it away in my pocket, and finished my breakfast, rather thoughtfully.

When I signed my check on the way out of the coffee shop, I asked, "Who was that gentleman at my table? The boss?"

The cashier looked at me strangely. "I suppose you *could* call him that," she answered. "Of course he owns this hotel, but we've never seen him here before. He always stays at the Ambassador, when he's in Chicago."

"And does he own *that*?" I said. I'd already suspected the answer.

"Why, yes. As well as —" and she rattled off a whole string of others, including the two biggest hotels in New York.

I was impressed and also rather amused. It was now obvious that Mr. Perlman had come here with the deliberate intention of meeting me. It seemed a roundabout way of doing it. I knew nothing then of his shyness and secretiveness. From the first, he was never shy with me.

Then I forgot about him for five years. During that five years, I made my second trip.

We knew what to expect this time and weren't going completely into the unknown. There were no more worries about fuel, because all we could ever use was waiting for us on Titan. We just had to pump its methane atmosphere into our tanks, and we'd made our plans accordingly. One after another, we visited all the moons, and then we went into the rings . . .

There was little danger, yet it was a nerve-racking experience. The ring system is very thin, you know — only about twenty miles in thickness. We descended into it slowly and cautiously, after having matched its spin so that we were moving at exactly the same speed. It was like stepping onto a carrousel a hundred and seventy thousand miles across . . .

But a ghostly kind of carrousel, because the rings aren't solid and you can look right through them. Close up, in fact, they're almost invisible. The billions of separate particles that make them up are so widely spaced that all you see in your immediate neighborhood are occasional small chunks, drifting very slowly past. It's only when you look into the distance that the countless fragments merge into a continuous sheet, like a hailstorm that sweeps around Saturn forever.

That's not *my* phrase, but it's a good one. For when we brought our first piece of genuine Saturnian ring into the air lock, it melted down in a few minutes into a pool of muddy water. Some people think it spoils the magic to know that the rings — or ninety percent of them — are made of ordinary ice. But that's a stupid attitude. They would be just as wonderful, and just as beautiful, if they were made of diamond.

When I got back to Earth, in the first year of the new century, I started off on another lecture tour. It was only a short one, for now I had a family and wanted to see as much of it as possible. This time I ran into Mr. Perlman

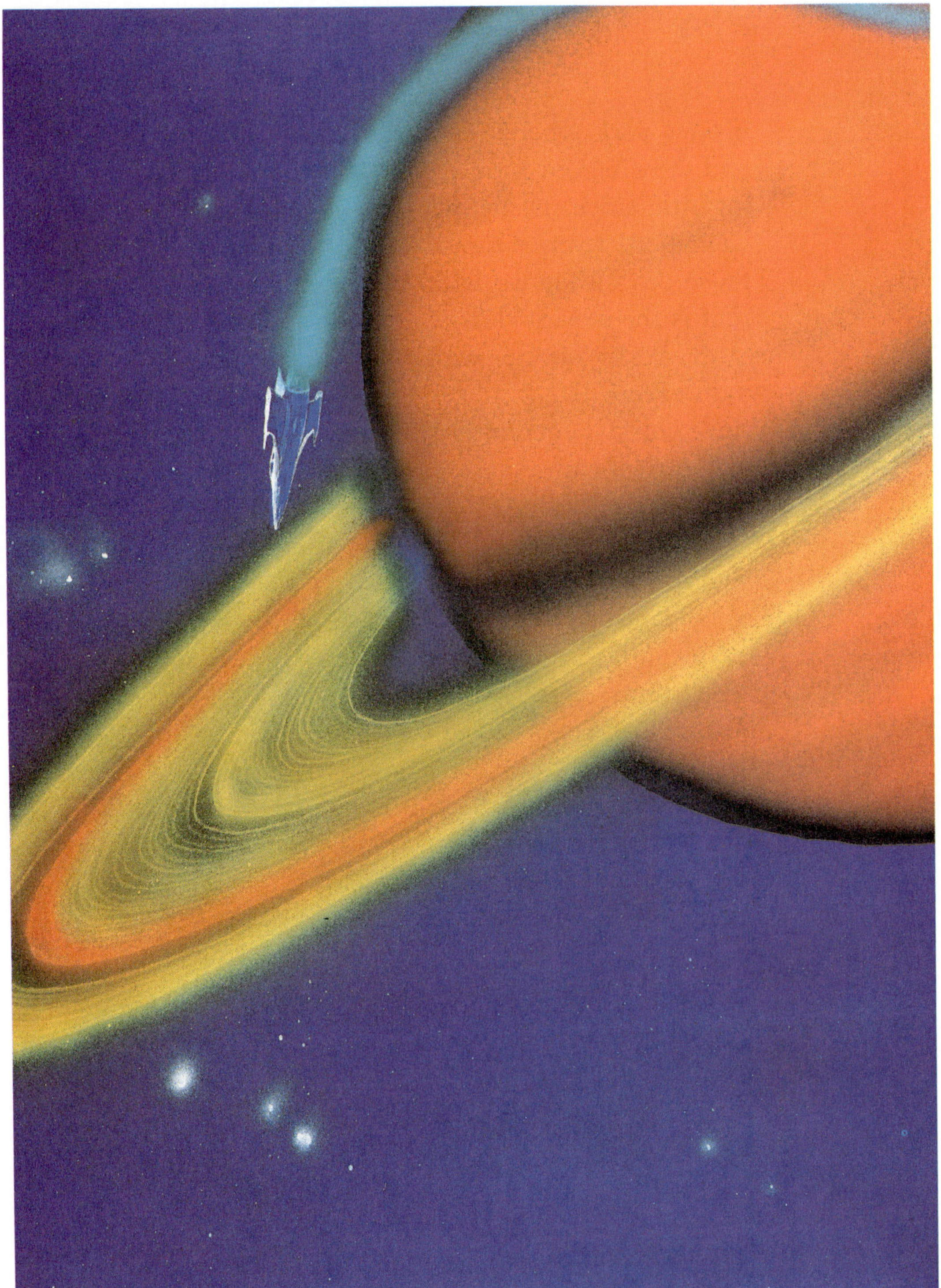

in New York, when I was speaking at Columbia University and showing our movie, "Exploring Saturn." (A misleading title since the nearest we'd been to the planet itself was about twenty thousand miles. No one dreamed, in those days, that we would ever go down into the slush that is the closest thing Saturn has to a surface.)

Mr. Perlman was waiting for me after the lecture. I didn't recognize him, for I'd met about a million people since our last encounter. But when he gave his name, our meeting all came back, so clearly that I realized he must have made a deep impression on my mind.

Somehow he got me away from the crowd. Half an hour later we were having a superb dinner in an exclusive restaurant (his, of course). It was a wonderful meal.

Now all the facts and photos gathered by the two expeditions to Saturn were available to everyone, in hundreds of reports and books and popular articles. Mr. Perlman seemed to have read all the material that wasn't too technical. What he wanted from me was something different. Even then, I put his interest down to that of a lonely aging man, trying to recapture a dream that had been lost in youth. I was right, but that was only a fraction of the whole picture.

He was after something that all the reports and articles failed to give. What did it *feel* like, he wanted to know, to wake up in the morning and see that great, golden globe with its scudding cloud belts dominating the sky? And the rings themselves, what did they do to your mind when they were so close that they filled the heavens from end to end?

You want a poet, I said, not an engineer. But I'll tell you this. However long you look at Saturn, and fly in and out among its moons, you can never quite believe it. Every so often you find yourself thinking, A thing like that *can't* be real. And you go to the nearest view port, and there it is, taking your breath away.

You must remember that, altogether apart from our nearness, we were able to look at the rings from angles and vantage points that are quite impossible from Earth, where you always see them turned toward the sun. We could fly into their shadow. And then they would no longer gleam like silver. They would be a faint haze, a bridge of smoke across the stars.

And most of the time we could see the shadow of Saturn lying across the full width of the rings, eclipsing them so completely that it seemed as if a great bite had been taken out of them. It worked the other way, too. On the day side of the planet, there would always be the shadow of the rings running like a dusky band parallel to the equator and not far from it.

Above all — though we did this only a few times — we could rise high above either pole of the planet and look down upon the whole stupendous system, so that it was spread out beneath us. Then we could see that instead of the four visible from Earth, there were at least a dozen separate rings, merging one into the other. When we saw this, our skipper made a remark that I'd never forgotten. "This," he said — and there wasn't a trace of flippancy in the words — "is where the angels have parked their halos."

All this, and a lot more, I told Mr. Perlman in that little but oh-so-expensive restaurant just south of Central Park. When I'd finished, he seemed very pleased, though he was silent for several minutes. Then he said, about as casually as you might ask the time of the next train at your local station, "Which would be the best satellite for a tourist resort?"

When the words got through to me, I nearly choked. Then I said, very patiently and politely (for after all, I'd had a wonderful dinner), "Listen, Mr. Perlman. You know as well as I do that Saturn is nearly a billion miles from Earth — more than that, in fact, when we're on opposite sides of the sun. Someone worked out that our round-trip tickets averaged seven and half million dollars apiece. And believe me, there was no first-class accommodation on *Endeavour I* or *II*. Anyway, no matter how much money he had, no one could book a passage to Saturn. Only scientists and space crews will be going there, for as far ahead as anyone can imagine."

I could see that my words had absolutely no effect. He just smiled, as if he knew some secret hidden from me.

"What you say is true enough *now*," he answered, "but I've studied history. And I understand people, that's my business. Let me remind you of a few facts.

"Two or three centuries ago, almost all the world's great tourist centers and beauty spots were as far away from civilization as Saturn is today. What did — oh, Napoleon, let's say — know about the Grand Canyon, Victoria Falls, Hawaii, Mount Everest? And look at the South Pole. It was reached for the first time when my father was a boy, but there's been a hotel there for the whole of your lifetime.

"Now it's starting all over again. *You* can appreciate only the problems and difficulties, because you're too close to them. Whatever they are, people will overcome them, as they've always done in the past.

"For wherever there's something strange or beautiful or novel, people will want to see it. The rings of Saturn are the greatest spectacle in the known universe. I've always guessed so, and now you've convinced me. Today it takes a fortune to reach them, and those who go there must risk their lives. So did the first people who flew but now there are a million passengers in the air every second of the day and night.

"The same thing is going to happen in space. It won't happen in ten years, maybe not in twenty. But twenty-five is all it took, remember, before the first commercial flights started to the moon. I don't think it will be as long for Saturn . . .

"I won't be around to see it, but when it happens, I want people to remember me. So where should we build?"

I still thought he was crazy, but at last I was beginning to understand what made him tick. And there was no harm in humoring him, so I gave the matter careful thought.

"Mimas is too close," I said, "and so are Enceladus and Tethys. Saturn just fills the sky, and you think it's falling on top of you. Besides, they aren't solid enough. They're nothing but overgrown snowballs. Dione and Rhea are better. You get a magnificent view from both of them. But all these inner moons are so tiny. Even Rhea is only eight hundred miles across, and the others are much smaller.

"I don't think there's any real argument. It will have to be Titan. That's a good sized satellite. It's a lot bigger than *our* moon and very nearly as large as Mars. There's a reasonable gravity too — about a fifth of Earth's so your guests won't be floating all over the place. And it will always be a major refueling point because of its methane atmosphere, which should be an important factor in your calculations. Every ship that goes out to Saturn will touch down there."

"And the outer moons?"

"Oh, Hyperion, Iapetus, and Phoebe are much too far away. You have to look hard to see the rings at all from Phoebe! Forget about them. Stick to good old Titan. Even if the temperature is two hundred below zero, and ammonia snow isn't the sort of stuff you'd want to ski on."

He listened to me very carefully. If he thought I was making fun of his impractical, unscientific notions, he gave no sign of it. We parted soon afterward. It must have been fifteen years before we met again. He had no further use for me in all that time. But when he wanted me, he called.

I see now what he had been waiting for. His vision had been clearer than mine. He couldn't have guessed, of course, that the rocket would go the way of the steam engine within less than a century, but he knew *something* better would come along. It was not until they started building fusion plants that could warm up a hundred square miles of a world as cold as Pluto that he got in contact with me again.

He was a very old man and dying. They told me how rich he was, and I could hardly believe it. Not until he showed me the elaborate plans and the beautiful models his experts had prepared with such remarkable lack of publicity.

He sat in his wheelchair like a wrinkled mummy, watching my face as I studied the models and blueprints. Then he said, "Captain, I have a job for you. . . ."

So here I am. It's just like running a spaceship, of course. Many of the technical problems are identical. And by this time I'd be too old to command a ship, so I'm very grateful to Mr. Perlman.

There goes the gong. If you are ready, I suggest we walk down to dinner through the Observation Lounge.

Even after all these years, I still like to watch Saturn rising — and tonight it's almost full.

Discuss the Selection

1. How did Perlman's plans affect the narrator's future?
2. What event in Perlman's boyhood began his fascination with Saturn?
3. Do you think that building a tourist resort on Titan was a good idea? Why or why not?
4. Why did Mr. Perlman think that building a hotel on Titan was a good idea?
5. When did you first begin to think that Perlman wanted more from the narrator than just a pleasant conversation about Saturn? Find that part of the story and reread it.

Apply the Skills

Many words have more than one meaning. Clues to the meaning of a word in a sentence can often be found by using context clues.

Read the sentences below and choose the correct definition for each underlined word.

1. My beat was the Midwest.
    a. a route regularly walked or covered
    b. a throbbing, as of a heart
2. I'd learned to be on my guard against cranks.
    a. handles that transmit motion by turning
    b. persons with strong and unreasonable feelings about something
3. For wherever there's something strange, or beautiful, or novel, people will want to see it.
    a. a fiction book
    b. unusual

Think and Write

Prewrite

Sights
1. Saturn's eleven moons
2.
3.
4.

Activities
1. rocket snowmobiling
2. low-gravity skiing
3.
4.

The chart above describes some of the things you could see and do if you were visiting Mr. Perlman's hotel on Titan. Copy the chart and complete it with other sights and activities. Remember, this hotel is in the future, so you can use your imagination as well as the information given in the story.

Compose

Imagine that you are staying in Mr. Perlman's hotel. Write a friendly letter to someone on Earth, describing the things you are seeing and doing. Include the sights and activities from your chart. You might want to begin your letter as follows:

> Dear ____,
> *This has been a great vacation!*

Revise

Reread your letter. Did you begin your letter with a friendly greeting? Did you end with a closing? If not, revise your work.

Post Early for Space

by Peter J. Henniker-Heaton

Once we were wayfarers, then seafarers, then airfarers;
   We shall be spacefarers soon,
Not voyaging from city to city or from coast to coast,
But from planet to planet and from moon to moon.

This is no fanciful flight of imagination,
No strange, incredible, utterly different thing;
It will come by obstinate thought and calculation
And the old resolve to spread an expanding wing.

We shall see homes established on distant planets,
Friends departing to take up a post on Mars;
They will have perils to meet, but they will meet them,
As the early settlers did on American shores.

We shall buy tickets later, as now we buy them
For foreign vacations, reserve our seat or berth,
Then spending a holiday month on a moon of Saturn,
Look tenderly back to our little shining Earth.

And those who decide they will not make the journey
Will remember a son up there or a favorite niece,
Eagerly awaiting news from the old home-planet,
And will scribble a line to catch the post for space.

489

Comprehension Study

Predict Outcomes

After you have begun reading a story, you may be able to figure out how it will end. Events that have already taken place, the way characters behave, and what characters say may give you clues to what will happen later. Making informed guesses about what will happen is called **predicting outcomes**.

Before making any prediction, it is important to think about the events that have already taken place. Thinking about past events can help you to make sensible predictions. Read the following paragraph and decide which choice below is the best prediction for what might happen next.

Captain Flagg stared out the observation window. The ship was quickly approaching the mysterious orange planet. Something about the planet's strange color made the captain uneasy. Why wasn't the planet on the galactic maps? He could bypass the unusual place. No one would realize that it existed. However, his mission was to explore new planets with his crew. He sighed as he lifted his communicator and asked the engineer to prepare the landing craft.

Which of the following are events that might happen?

1. The captain will fly by the planet.
2. The captain will take a landing craft to explore the orange planet.
3. The captain will receive a message from his commander.
4. Something terrible will happen on the orange planet.

Is choice 1, *The captain will fly by the planet,* a good prediction based on the paragraph? No, because the paragraph says that the captain's mission was to explore new planets and that the captain had the landing craft prepared. Is choice 2 a good prediction? Yes, it seems likely that the captain will take a landing craft to explore the orange planet. The paragraph says nothing about a message to the captain from his commander. So choice 3 is not a good prediction. What about choice 4, *Something terrible will happen on the orange planet?* This prediction is a probable one. The sentence *Something about the planet's strange color made the captain uneasy* might cause you to predict that something bad will probably happen.

Sometimes the illustrations in a story contain clues that can help you to make predictions about what will happen next. Look at the details in this picture. Then select the sentence that best predicts what will happen next.

a. The reporter will probably take a vacation after finishing her work.

b. The reporter will probably read over the story she is typing.

c. The reporter will probably take a break for lunch.

Since the reporter in the picture is typing, the best prediction is choice **b**, *The reporter will probably read over the story she is typing*. There are no clues in the picture to suggest that the reporter will take a vacation when she finishes her work, so choice **a** is not a sensible prediction. The clock says 4:30, so it is probably too late in the day for the reporter to take a break for lunch. This tells you choice **c** is not a likely outcome.

Read this passage and make a prediction about what might happen as a result of the events. Look for clues to support your prediction.

> This year, the weather has been a problem for farmers. Heavy rains in the spring made planting difficult. Then more rains washed away the seeds that farmers were finally able to plant. Planting more seeds was almost impossible because the soil had turned to mud. After such a wet spring, a dry summer brought no improvement in growing conditions. The farmers are worried. Never have they experienced such a horrible season.

Based on the passage, which of the following predictions might you make?

  a. This year's harvest will be late.
  b. Farmers will earn a lot of money this year.
  c. This year's harvest will be a poor one.

Choice **c**, *This year's harvest will be a poor one*, is the correct prediction. Three clues from the passage helped you make the correct prediction. The first clue was the information that heavy rains washed away the seeds. The second clue was the mention of a very dry summer. The last sentence of the passage, *Never have they experienced such a horrible season*, also tells you that there will not be a good crop to harvest.

It is fun to try to predict what is going to happen in a story and then to read to find out if your prediction was correct. As you make predictions, you should remember three things. First, a set of events might have several possible outcomes. Second, a prediction states only what *might* happen — what really happens could be quite different from what you predict. Third, when you make a prediction you have to use all of the clues from a story as well as your own experience.

Textbook Application: Predicting Outcomes in Science

You already know that the details in a story can be used as clues to help you figure out what will happen next. When you read textbooks, you can use the information in them to make predictions, too.

The following passage is taken from a science textbook. Read each paragraph. The sidenotes will help you use the information given to make predictions.

What might happen if electric wires were to get hot? Can you predict that the author is going to tell you ways to keep this from happening?

What are two things you could predict might cause an overload of electrical circuits?

Do you think people have found a way to prevent fires caused by short circuits?

Fuses and Circuit Breakers

The wiring in your home is covered by rubber or plastic insulation. One reason, as you know, is to prevent electric shock. Yet another reason is heat. Whenever current runs through a wire, heat is produced. The rubber or plastic around the wire keeps the outside of the insulation from getting too hot.

The wires in your home can usually carry a great deal of current without becoming too hot. Sometimes people plug too many appliances into a socket. If the wires are old or damaged, the heat may burn through the insulation. There is an **overload** of current in the wire. The walls may begin to heat up from the hot wires. The results can be deadly.

If an electric cord becomes damaged, the two wires in the cord may touch each other and a **short circuit** is produced. Much more heat than normal builds up in the wires. A short circuit can cause a serious fire very quickly. Since the short circuit could be inside the walls, you may not be able to tell if the wires are heating up until it's too late.

How can we protect ourselves from fires due to short circuits or overloads? Many homes are protected by **fuses**. The current that enters a home goes through the fuses first. Look at a new fuse. Can you see a thin strip of metal? When there is a short circuit or overload, the thin strip of metal quickly melts. The connection between the current and the wires in the house is then broken. The current stops flowing. The fuse protects you before any damage can occur.

> A fuse protects a home from short circuits and overloads. What should you do if a fuse "blows" or melts?

Many homes have **circuit-breaker** switches instead of fuses. Each circuit breaker is connected to some of the wires in the house. If there is a short circuit or overload, the circuit-breaker switch turns to the off position immediately. Again, the electric current is stopped. When the overload is corrected, you can flick the switch back on and the current flows again. Circuit breakers are more convenient than fuses, since they do not have to be replaced.

> If the lights suddenly go off in one room, what would you guess has happened? What problems should you look for?

—*HBJ Science, Brown,*
Harcourt Brace Jovanovich

Good readers make predictions as they read. Then they use the information they read to evaluate whether their predictions were correct. As you read textbooks, remember to use the information given to make predictions. You may have to revise your predictions as you discover new information. Making predictions and revising those predictions will help you remember and understand what you read.

In the world of tomorrow, space travel may be an everyday thing. Read to find out what aspects of life on the Space Shuttle are like everyday life on Earth.

As you read, try to predict whether you would enjoy flying on the Space Shuttle.

Let's Take a Trip into Space

by Don Dwiggins

Flying in a Space Shuttle is much like flying in a big airplane. One main difference is weightlessness. And you take off straight up from the launch pad, on top of a storm of fire and smoke. You're strapped in your seat lying head down. But you wear a comfortable flight suit, not a big space suit. A helmet finishes the outfit.

As your Shuttle rises faster and faster, it picks up speed smoothly. The gravity increases to 3 g and your body weight increases three times. If you weigh 100 pounds on Earth, for a brief moment you'll weigh 300 pounds. (A "g" is the force or pull of Earth's gravity on your body at sea level.) Your heart may beat faster for a while, until the excitement of the launch passes. Then you can relax and look out the window at Earth, hundreds of miles below.

Every 90 minutes in orbit you'll see a new sunrise and sunset. The cabin air you breathe is just like back on Earth. But you'll get a surprise when you start to move around. Instead of weighing 100 pounds or 300 pounds, you'll weigh nothing at all!

Riding in orbit at about 17,500 miles an hour, you are weightless. If you bend down to pick up something, you may end up doing somersaults. So you'll use the handholds with suction cups.

Eating is different in space. Your fork and spoon will drift off the table if you aren't careful. Crumbs will float upward, a danger if you inhale them. And spilled water doesn't drip down. It, too, floats up. Tiny balls of water will stick to the wall and spread like glue.

To make sure you eat well, there's a menu of more than 100 different kinds of food. Much of it is dried. There are cereals, vegetables, eggs and fruit, steak and shrimp. There are 20 kinds of beverages, also dried. But there is no orange juice or whole milk. When water is added to them, the orange crystals turn to "rocks." Milk floats around in lumps and tastes bad in space. But on a six-day flight, you can eat a different meal three times a day every day.

The Shuttle has an oven, hot and cold water taps, trays, silverware, and wet and dry wipes. To fix a meal you take out the plastic-wrapped pouch marked for the day and meal — Day 2, Meal A. For dried foods, you inject the right amount of water through a needle. Foods to be heated are placed in the oven. Food trays have magnets on them.

At the table you'll eat standing up, held in place by suction cups on your shoes. Table manners are important in space. Eat slowly, with no sudden moves that could make your food float away. And take small bites.

After supper it's time to turn in for a good night's sleep. Across the mid-deck is a two-tier bunk. A third sleeper can stretch out underneath. A fourth can sleep standing up. There's no sense of up or down in zero gravity. You could sleep standing on your head, for that matter.

Each bed is a padded board with a fireproof sleeping bag. You crawl into your bag and zip it up. Then you fasten the straps around you. The hard board you sleep on feels as soft as a mattress.

To stay healthy in space, you need exercise. Step on a small treadmill, adjust the straps, and jog to music from a tape deck. Turn on an airduct to keep cool. If you don't, you'll need a vacuum cleaner to get the sweat off your skin. Sweat sticks, like any water drops in zero gravity.

There are no showers on a Shuttle. Instead, you'll take a sponge bath. The water and liquid soap stick to your skin. So you wash with one cloth and use another to rinse yourself.

Your personal kit contains items such as extra clothing, toothbrush and toothpaste, a comb, and a nail clipper. Your nails grow slowly in space. So you'll only need to trim them once a month.

One big problem is motion sickness caused by weightlessness. More than 30 percent of Shuttle astronauts have suffered from it, with dizziness, nausea, cold sweats, headaches, and drowsiness. It lasts only about three days. Space doctors say it may be because of the difference between what your eyes and your inner ears tell the brain. In weightlessness, the parts of the ear that help with balance are upset.

Long Shuttle flights cause muscles and bones to wear down somewhat. The heart grows slightly smaller, too. This is because there is no gravity. Exercising on the treadmill creates the resistance the body is used to on Earth. Future Space Stations will need some sort of artificial gravity to keep people healthy. But for normal Shuttle flights of a week to a month, the space environment is relatively safe.

When it's time to return to Earth, you'll strap yourself down again. But first you put on a special pair of pants, called an anti-gravity suit. This prevents you from blacking out on the return from weightlessness to Earth gravity. The Shuttle commander will flip the ship around tailfirst and fire rockets to slow down. Then the commander turns the Shuttle end-for-end again to begin entering the atmosphere.

Computers take over to get the Shuttle ready for letdown. Air friction blocks out all contact with the ground. Very high heat raises the temperature of the Shuttle's nose and leading edges to more than 3000° F. But special tiles on the outside keep the Shuttle safely cool.

After the flight path and speed are set, the Shuttle is lined up with the landing site. The approach starts at 333 miles an hour. The descent path is seven times as steep as that of a commercial airplane. There is no motor noise because the Shuttle lands like a glider, without engines. At about 1,750 feet, the nose is pulled up to slow down. The Shuttle lands at over 200 miles an hour.

The commander or the autopilot makes the landing. The 100-ton craft touches down gently, rolling to a stop in about 8,000 to 9,000 feet. It's been a perfect flight!

Discuss the Selection

1. What aspects of flying on the Space Shuttle are like everyday life on Earth?
2. Describe how you eat on the Space Shuttle.
3. Earth can be seen from the Shuttle windows. How do you think you would feel about looking down on the Earth from so far up in space?
4. What are some of the problems encountered by humans during space flights?
5. What causes motion sickness in space? Find the part of the selection that tells you.

Apply the Skills

This selection describes some of the problems humans have when traveling in space. Think about some of the problems you might have on a long space mission. Predict what future space vehicles will have in them to solve these problems.

Think and Write

Prewrite

Weightlessness	
Advantages	**Disadvantages**
1. easy to turn somersaults	1. requires eating carefully
2.	2.
3.	3.
4.	4.

What would it be like to be weightless in space? As you reread the selection "Let's Take a Trip into Space," think about the advantages and disadvantages of weightlessness. Copy the chart above. Complete it with a list of advantages and disadvantages. You can list some of your own, too.

Compose

Using the information on your chart, write two paragraphs. In the first paragraph, describe the advantages of being weightless. In the second paragraph, describe the disadvantages. Be sure to include a topic sentence for each paragraph. Your first topic sentence might be this: *There are many advantages to being weightless.*

Revise

Read your paragraphs. Have you listed all the advantages in the first paragraph and all the disadvantages in the next? If not, revise your work.

Study Skills

Tables and Schedules

Tables

A **table** is a type of chart that organizes related numbers. It displays information in a clear, easy-to-read manner. The way a table is arranged makes it easy to find and use information.

The table that follows shows the amount of grain grown by several countries. Notice that the table has four columns and that each column has a label at the top. The first column contains the names of the countries. The second column shows the amount of corn grown by each country. What information is displayed in the third and the fourth columns?

Grain Production (millions of tons)			
Country	**Corn**	**Wheat**	**Rice**
China	31	37	115
India	5	22	61
Soviet Union	12	84	—
United States	118	49	5

You use a table by reading across the rows and by reading down the columns. Suppose you want to know how much wheat is produced in India. Read down the "country" column until you find the name India and then move your finger across the row until you reach the "wheat" column. You should find the number 22. The number 22 doesn't seem like a very substantial amount of wheat for a nation as large as India. Look back at the title at the top of the table. Beneath the words *Grain Production*, you will see the words *millions of tons*. When you combine the number 22 with the knowledge that the number listed represents millions of tons, you discover that India grew 22 million tons of wheat. Use this method to find out how much rice was produced in the United States.

When numbers are arranged in a table, it makes it easy to compare numerical facts. Which country produced the most corn? Which country produced the most wheat? Which country produced more rice, India or China?

You can also use tables to make inferences. How much rice did the Soviet Union produce? No number appears in the table. Doesn't the Soviet Union grow rice? Rice grows where the climate is warm and the rainfall is bountiful. What can you infer about the Soviet Union from this information?

Schedules

Schedules are special tables that list times or dates. Bus, train, and airplane schedules give the times of arrivals and departures of the various forms of public transportation. Movie and television schedules tell when a performance will start. Some schedules also list the dates on which certain events will take place. The schedule below is part of a movie schedule that might appear in a local newspaper.

Theater	Rating	Movie	Time
Alton	★	My Friend the Robot	7:00, 9:15
Beauford	★★★	Special Seasons	6:00, 9:00
Center City	★★★★	The Golden Statue	8:20, 10:00
Lewiston	★★	Invaders from Other Planets	2:55, 5:35, 8:15
Tanmont	★★★	Silver Spurs	7:40, 9:45

The column on the left contains the names of local movie theaters in alphabetical order. The stars indicate how the movie was rated by a critic. The highest rating a movie can receive is four stars. Which film listed received the highest rating? The name of the film is in the next column. Then the times that a movie is shown are listed. The movies are shown in the afternoon and evening. A matinee is a movie shown in the afternoon. Which movie has a matinee showing? At what time is it shown? The matinee of *Invaders from Other Planets* is scheduled for 2:55 in the afternoon. Have you seen other types of movie and television schedules?

Other kinds of tables and schedules tell you about arrivals and departures of public transportation. Knowing how to read these schedules can help you make informed decisions about which train, bus, or airplane to take. On the next page is a section of a train schedule that could be used by persons traveling between Fairmont, Milton, and Rainsville.

TO FAIRMONT		
Leave Rainsville	**Arrive Milton**	**Arrive Fairmont**
6:10	6:58	7:25
7:20	—	8:18
7:52	8:45	9:15
8:30	9:30	10:00
9:25	10:05	10:37
10:30	11:25	11:55
12:10	1:10	1:45
12:56	1:45	2:20
1:45	2:36	3:10

This schedule contains a list of the trains going to Fairmont each weekday. The portion of the schedule that is shaded indicates P.M., or trains that travel after 12 o'clock noon.

Suppose that you live in Rainsville and that you must be in Fairmont for an important meeting at 11:30 A.M. Which train will allow you to arrive at your destination in plenty of time for the 11:30 meeting? Look at the column labeled "Arrive Fairmont." As you read down the list of arrival times, you will discover that one train arrives at 10:37, and the next train arrives at 11:55. If you take the 11:55 train you will be too late to attend your meeting. Therefore, you will have to take the train that arrives at 10:37. Put your finger on 10:37 and move back across the row until you reach the Rainsville column. What time will you have to leave Rainsville in order to reach Fairmont at 10:37? You will have to plan to be on board the train in Rainsville before its 9:25 departure.

Think about the tables and schedules that you have used. Knowing how to read tables and schedules helps you find the information you need quickly and easily.

When Tom Edison was young, he spent a lot of time asking "Why?" He used the answers to his questions to invent things that would improve the quality of life in the world of tomorrow. What does Tom do in this play to earn himself a job and the better tomorrows it will bring?

As you read, can you predict what will happen to Tom?

Tom Edison and the Wonderful "Why"

by Faye Parker

The action of the play takes place in and around the little town of Port Huron, Michigan, during the early 1860's.

The Cast

Jim MacKenzie, a telegrapher
Thomas Alva Edison, a boy of fourteen or fifteen
Tanny Edison, Tom's younger sister
Elvira Snivet, Tom's teacher
Muley O'Toole, a conductor on the railroad
Arvine Stevenson, Miss Snivet's favorite pupil
Why, a Pixie, part of all our dreams
Mrs. Nancy Edison, Tom's mother
Jamie MacKenzie, a small child or doll

SCENE 1
Before the Curtain

(Sound of steam engine, wheels, and whistles as Why magically appears, his lights twinkling.)

Why: There's a boy on a train that whistles through the night. You know his name? It's Edison, Thomas Alva. For months now he's been selling peanuts to the passengers who travel through Michigan. He works hard, and he keeps asking "Why?" That's one reason I like him, because he likes me. My name is Why, you know. Of course I only belong in dreams and nobody cares much about them, except me, I guess. *(train whistle)* Tom's on that train right now and do you know what he's got in the baggage car with him? A laboratory and a printing press. You know something else? He's got ideas. If you want to take the word of a dream person like me, I'd say he's got ideas that will be very important to people about 125 years from now. People like you, I mean. Like that idea of his about moving pictures. Who knows? Maybe someday people will see moving pictures and cartoons and plays right in their own homes. Or do you think that's a crazy idea?

For Tom and for me, this is 1860. Tom has probably sold every bag of double-jointed peanuts by now and is working in his laboratory. I *hope* he'll ask "Why?" so I can get to see him. *(train whistle)* Do you hear that whistle? Sounds like it's calling him, doesn't it? If you can make a noise like that whistle, maybe he'll hear it and we'll find him working at his test tubes, thinking of something that may mean a lot to you someday. *(plaintive)* Woo-woo! Woo-woo! Woo-woo! *(conducts whistle imitation and slips off as the curtain opens on next scene)*

507

SCENE 2

(Interior of the baggage car of the Port Huron-Detroit train. One side of the car has an open door through which we see an evening landscape, which gives us the impression that we are in a moving train. Tom stands working at a workbench to the left in the car. At right is an old-fashioned hand printing press and an opening which leads to the passenger cars. The whistle sounds once again. Tom imitates it and laughs.)

Tom: That whistle means we're heading for Mt. Clements now. I wonder what Jim MacKenzie will think when I tell him I've got the Morse Code worked out just about to perfection? Woo! Woo! (*as code*)

Muley: (*from offstage*) Tom! Tom! (*coming in*) A lady up in the second car wants some homemade fudge. (*Tom starts out.*) Now, get yourself back in here and wait 'till I've given you the whole of your orders!

Tom: (*comes back*) Yes, Mr. O'Toole.

Muley: Charlie, the engineer, wants to see a copy of this week's paper you wrote and printed. He didn't believe me when I told him Abraham Lincoln was elected President.

Tom: But he was, Muley. I mean, Mr. O'Toole.

Muley: (*testily*) I know he was, but you know Charlie — he won't believe it unless he sees it.

Tom: But I sold every paper I printed about the election.

Muley: Then print another copy.

Tom: (*going to press and putting paper in*) All right. (*He takes it out. Muley reaches for it.*) Better not touch it yet. Your fingers will get all smudgy and black from the ink.

Muley: Take it to Charlie. His hands will get the paper all smudgy and black from coal.

Tom: (*seriously*) It's the carbon in coal that makes his hands black and makes the ink black, too. There's carbon in lamp black, too, and I've got an idea about that. (*He picks up basket and runs off.*)

Muley: (*looking after Tom, mimicking him*) I've got an idea about this! I've got an idea about that! (*at lab, opening bottles and sniffing*) Why can't I do experiments in my spare time, Mr. O'Toole? (*sniffs one, grimaces*) Phew! I've got an idea about *that*? What's the lad doin' messing around with these smelly bottles? You'd think he'd be satisfied makin' all that money printin' his paper. He must sell those papers to at least six hundred customers. (*at press, studying type*) Sure comes as a surprise to Elviry Snivet and me when we saw how nice that Tom can write up a story. She was right to kick him out of school, though. He near drives me crazy with his ideas and his questions, questions, questions! (*picks up oil lamp*) Wonder what he's got this lamp all apart for.

Tom: (*running back on*) What do you think I just thought of, Mule . . . Mr. O'Toole?

Muley: (*startled, hastily puts lamp down*) I don't care what you've thought of Tom Edison. You just keep the corks tight in these bottles or you'll have the whole train smelling like dead Lake Michigan mackerel in the broilin' sun.

Tom: Beg pardon? I didn't hear you very well. My ears are . . .

Muley: Quit worrying about your ears and tend to your job.

Tom: (*puts basket down and goes to lab shelf*) Yes, sir, it's just that I had such a good idea I had to tell someone.

Muley: Tell it to the bottles, or to the stars out there. It's too late for me to stand around listenin' to nonsense. I'm goin' into the passenger car and rest my achin' feet. (*He starts off.*) You just mind you keep the corks in them bottles. (*He leaves.*)

Tom: (*picks up lamp and looks at it*) I really think it could work. I really do. (*on knees*) If I wound some kind of wire or filament through the carbon, it might hold the electrical spark and keep it glowing. (*He leans against shelves, still holding the unlighted lamp. He yawns and speaks to the lamp.*) That idea, my dim little chimney, is going to take a lot of work, a lot of experimenting. You're just a messy old oil lamp, but you're better than a candle and someday (*yawn*) when I'm not quite so sleepy (*yawn*) I'm going to try to find a way to make a light, as small as you, be as bright as a thousand candles. But (*very sleepy*) that's going to take about ten per cent inspiration and ninety per cent perspiration. (*He dozes off. Only the sounds of the wheels are heard as lights dim and Why music sounds softly under. Why appears in the baggage car door.*)

Why: (*softly*) Tom? Tom. (*Tom, deeply asleep, turns over.*) Tom, I want to talk to you.

Tom: (*asleep*) O.K., Mr. O'Toole. I'll get busy.

Why: (*at Tom's side, waves his arm causing lamp to light brightly; Tom rubs his eyes and looks*) Look!

Tom: How in the world did you do that? How did you make the light so bright?

Why: I didn't really. You're dreaming, remember? And people like you who have ideas when they're awake, can sometimes see them come true in their dreams.

Tom: Is this what they mean about having dreams come true!

Why: You had to do some wide-awake dreaming to have it happen, Tom.

511

Tom: (*as lights dim again*) I wonder what it would be like in about a hundred years to be able to walk into an auditorium and see things with light like that. (*blackout by now, as Tom lights candle*) This is what it's like now, but just imagine what could happen. (*Why raises arms and house lights come on; Why lowers arms, house lights go off; footlights come on; he gestures to light positions as borders, etc., come on and off in spectacular series.*) Blue lights! Red lights! Bright, bright white lights! All of them turned on and off by magic. No matches, no smoky wicks! Just wonderful, wonderful light! (*Lights black out and Why's costume shimmers and glows.*)

Why: When you grow up, you'll have to work on that.

Tom: (*as lights slowly come up in car door*) Oh, I will!

Why: Why?

Tom: Because I've just got to find out the answer to so many things.

Why: Like some of the other things you've been thinking about?

Tom: Yes, like that silly idea I had about a way to keep sounds so we could hear them again.

Why: You mean you think there's a way to save a sound so people could hear it over again?

Tom: Why not, Why? If President Lincoln makes a speech, wouldn't it be nice to save it so that everyone could hear his voice sometime later?

Why: How would you manage to do that?

Tom: Like this: I'd have a little thing I could talk into . . .

Why: Let's name it a microphone!

Tom: All right. Well, I'd pick it up and I'd say: "Mary had a little lamb, its fleece was white as snow. And everywhere that Mary went, the lamb was sure to go."

Why: Then, you'd turn a switch and what would happen?

Tom: This! (*pantomimes turning switch, sound playback of "Mary had a little lamb"*)

Why: That was your own voice!

Tom: Saying what I just said!

Why: Wouldn't it be wonderful if you could do that with *mine*?

Tom: The people who have never heard a violin . . .

Why: Could hear a *whole symphony orchestra*! (*music soars under and holds*) Microphones, phonograph records, electric light, moving pictures, all of them will change people's lives a lot!

Tom: (*sleepily*) Phonographs, microphones. (*sits sleepily*) You do know a lot of funny words . . . (*yawns*) . . . I never heard so many funny words . . . (*voice trailing off*)

Why: (*as his lights dim and he disappears*) Keep asking questions, Tom. Good luck. (*Lights go back to normal; Tom is asleep as before.*)

Muley: (*from off*) Next stop Mt. Clements! Five minutes to Mt. Clements Depot.

Tom: (*wakens and jumps up*) Mt. Clements already? How'd the time pass so quickly? I must have slept longer than I thought. (*picks up his basket*) I'd better get busy or Muley will . . . (*starts out the door, bumps into Muley who is coming in*) OOPS! I'm sorry, Mr. O'Toole, I was just . . .

Muley: You were just trying to knock the breath out of me, that's what! (*sniffs and advances to lab shelf*) And you left the corks out of these bottles. (*He lunges at Tom, who ducks, making him grab air, lunges again and misses. Tom gets to the lab, picks up a bottle to recap it, just as Muley grabs his arm, making the container fall. Flash-*

pot explosion goes off at spot. They both back away.) Now you've done it! You set the train on fire!

Tom: Jumpin' Jehosephat! I've done it again! (*frantically trying to put out the fire*) I'm sorry. I'm so sorry.

Muley: Well, Thomas Alva Edison, this cooks your goose! (*thrusting bottles into Tom's arms*) Take your smelly chemicals and your double-jointed peanuts! (*picking him up bodily*) This is the last I want to see of you! (*throws Tom, who rolls across the apron as the curtains slowly close enough to hide the lab*) Here's your coat! And your hat! And you can pick up the rest of your things anywhere between here and the Mt. Clements station! (*throwing coat, hat, etc., with lines*) And this is what I think of your ideas! (*Curtains close as crashing glass sounds behind them and train sounds fade in the distance.*)

Tom: (*alone on apron, gets up and walks slowly with coat slung over his shoulder; picks up broken bottle*) Why'd he have to knock it out of my hand? People are going to think I'm a firebug. Now everybody's going to think I'm addled for sure. (*trudges slowly off*)

SCENE 3

(*Outside the Port Huron station. We see Tanny carrying an armful of papers. She is walking fast, paying no attention to Arvine's voice from off.*)

Arvine: Tanny! Tanny Edison! Hey, wait up! (*dashes on, overtakes her and stops her*)

Tanny: Please get out of my way, Arvine. I've got work to do.

Arvine: Selling Tom's papers for him, huh? I heard he lost his job on the railroad.

Tanny: How did you find out?

Arvine: Muley O'Toole told Miss Snivet and Miss Snivet told the whole school.

Tanny: (*darkly*) You might know. (*starts walking*) Tom didn't need that old job anyway. He fixed up his printing press and he's selling lots of newspapers.

Arvine: That's not what I've been hearing. I've been hearing that his papers aren't worth two cents now that he can't get to Detroit and get the news. My father says there's talk of war with the South and Tom didn't print a word about it in last week's paper.

Tanny: He's busy studying telegraphy. That's what he really wants to do.

Arvine: Telegraphy! Poo! He's always been talking about that! James Mitchell is still bragging about the telegraph system Tom put up between his house and yours.

Tanny: Why shouldn't he? I'll just guarantee that there aren't two other boys in the whole wide world who can operate their own telegraph system from one house to another.

Arvine: Go ahead and brag your head off about Tom and his telegraph. There ain't a real telegraph operator in the world who'd ever give your addled brother a job!

MacKenzie: (*enters from RR station speaking over his shoulder to someone inside*) I'll be back in a few minutes, dear. Have a nice visit with Mrs. Corliss. The baby will probably sleep for another hour.

Mrs. Mac: (*from inside depot*) It looks like rain, Jim. Better hurry back. (*MacKenzie strides to stage right, tips his hat to Arvine and Tanny who are down left. Tom, looking defeated for him, comes on right. Tom lights up at the sight of his friend.*)

Tom: Good morning, Mr. MacKenzie. It's good to see you again!

Mac: I'm glad to see you too, Tom. I wanted to tell you how sorry I am about what's happened.

Tom: I guess it wouldn't do a bit of good to tell you it was an accident.

Mac: (*kindly*) If you say it was, I believe you, Tom. But accident or no, a lot of damage was done to that baggage car.

Tom: If you'd just give me a chance to work for you, Mr. MacKenzie, I'd pay back every nickel.

Mac: (*still kind but firm*) I'm afraid there's no place for you with the railroad, Tom. Muley O'Toole reports that you did some strange carryin' on in that baggage car. That's why I'm here today. I've come to talk with him and have a look at that burned-up car. I've got to estimate the damage.

Tom: (*earnestly*) It isn't burned up, Mr. MacKenzie, honest. I got the fire out before Muley threw me off the train. There wasn't much damage, again, honest.

Tanny: (*unable to contain herself*) There was plenty of damage done to Tom. He's all bruised up and his coat's a mess and . . . and every single experiment — every single thing in his laboratory is — ruined!

Mac: I'm sorry to hear that.

Arvine: I'm not. (*to Mac*) It's good riddance to bad rubbish! You don't know Tom Edison the way I do. He's always spending his money on what he calls "experiments," and all they ever do is get people into trouble.

Tom: You're not going to listen to him, are you, Mr. MacKenzie!

Mac: (*hand on Tom's shoulder*) It's Mr. O'Toole I'll have to listen to, Tom. He's the conductor and we both work for the railroad.

Tanny: (*heartbroken*) You'll only hear one side of the story from him.

Mac: I have an appointment with Mr. O'Toole. I've got to keep it.

Arvine: And I've got an appointment down to the river to go fishin'. I'm goin' to keep it. (*skips off*)

(*Tom, crushed, starts off right. Mac goes to him and pats his shoulder.*)

Mac: We'll always be friends, Tom. Why don't you go into the depot and say hello to my wife and baby? (*as Tom hesitates*) They'd like to meet you.

Tom: Oh, is the baby here? I'd like to see him. (*going into depot*)

Muley: (*from off*) Get the horse shod by tonight, Smitty. I'm takin' Elvira Snivet for a buggy ride and I don't want any trouble with the horse. (*comes on*) Oh, here you are, Mr. MacKenzie. (*They shake hands.*) You didn't waste much time gettin' up here to look at the damage, did you?

Mac: I'm always on the job when it comes to railroad property, Mr. O'Toole. And I've got a special interest in young Tom Edison.

Muley: You won't be so interested when you see what he's done. I'll have to show you right away. (*sound of train approaching*) My train's comin' in. We'll have to hustle.

Snivet: (*enters*) Oh, Mr. O'Toole, there you are. I was afraid I'd miss you.

Muley: Evenin' Elvira. This is Mr. MacKenzie, here.

Snivet: Charmed to meet you Mr. MacKenzie, I'm sure. Mr. O'Toole always refers to you so admiringly.

Mac: Thank you, Ma'am.

Tanny: (*at fence, screaming*) There's a baby on the train track! He doesn't even know the train is coming.

Mac: (*running to her side*) It's my little Jamie! (*then runs off stage*)

Snivet: He's going to be killed!

Muley: The train can't stop!

Tanny: I can't look!

Muley: (*Stops dead, staring as we see Tom dash past upstage side of fence as train approaches. Tom jumps out of the way, the child in his arms as train screeches to a stop.*) Did you see that? The boy grabbed that baby right out from under the very wheels of the locomotive (*dazedly shaking head*) One more inch and the cowcatcher would have killed them both.

Tanny: Tom saved the baby! Oh, Tom saved the baby!

Muley: (*confused*) He did that. He almost got himself killed, but he saved that baby all right.

Mac: (*bursts out of station door with a year-old child clutched to his chest*) He's all right. He's safe. (*hugging child*) Oh, Jamie, you'll never know how lucky you are.

Tanny: Tom saved him, didn't he, Mr. MacKenzie?

Mac: (*warmly*) Indeed he did, Miss Edison. Indeed he did. Tom! Tom, come out here, if Mrs. MacKenzie will let you go.

Tom: (*breathlessly comes out*) Jamie's all right, isn't he? I might have hurt him picking him up so fast.

Mac: He's all right. He's fine. He's living and breathing thanks to you. (*Baby whimpers.*)

Tanny: Isn't he sweet?

Tom: He's crying a little.

Tanny: He looks all right.

Mac: He is all right. After all the excitement, he wants to be back on his mother's lap. (*as he moves into the station with the baby*) . . . where he belongs. I'll be right back.

(*Thunder rumbles in the distance and flashing lights suggest an oncoming storm.*)

Tom: Looks like there's going to be a storm.

Tanny: Oh, Tom! How can you talk about the weather after what you just did?

Mac: (*enters from depot*) Tom, Mrs. MacKenzie and I are so grateful. We'll never be able to repay you for what you did.

Tom: Aw, Mr. MacKenzie, anybody would have —

Mac: You risked your life for our Jamie, young man, and I'm going to do the only thing I can do for you.

Tanny: (*eagerly*) Are you going to give him back his job?

Mac: I'm going to do better than that. I'm going to see to it that he gets a job as a telegrapher on the Detroit-Port Huron Railroad.

Tom: You don't really mean it, Mr. MacKenzie! You can't be serious.

Mac: I was never more serious, Tom. Now, come into the depot and say good-bye to Mrs. MacKenzie. You, too, Tanny. And hurry; we've only a minute or two before our train pulls out. (*Thunder and lightning off as the happy youngsters follow MacKenzie into the depot.*)

Snivet: Well! Did you ever! Did you hear what Mr. MacKenzie said, Muley? Addled Thomas Edison saved a baby's life so he's going to become a telegrapher — a mere troublesome boy getting a position of importance — and with the same railroad you work for.

Muley: (*incensed*) He'll have a better job than I've got, the young pipsqueak! He'll be the boss of me! I have one question to ask you, Elvira Snivet: (*marching to depot door*) Why did you have to go and kick Thomas Alva Edison out of school? (*He exits leaving the door swinging in Elvira's face, then pokes head out again.*) Now he'll be the boss of me! (*exits*)

(*Train whistle up under threatening storm sounds. We see the train pull out as Snivet waves and goes to the bench. Tom and Tanny come out exuberantly.*)

Tom: He really did mean it, Tanny!

Tanny: Isn't it wonderful? And won't you surprise them when they find out you already know all about the Morse code!

Tom: Dot-dot-dot-dash-dash! I'll send those signals out along the telegraph and people far away from me will feel nearer.

Tanny: Won't Mother be proud! She always said you were smart.

Snivet: (*rising with dignity*) Your mother didn't have to answer your silly questions all day in school.

Tanny: Miss Snivet!

Tom: We didn't know you were . . .

Arvine: (*bursts on as thunder and lightning come nearer, then skids to a stop pointing in terror off*) The bridge — (*much gulping*) the bridge!

Tom: What about the bridge?

Snivet: Tell us, Arvine. Don't just stand there gasping and gulping.

Arvine: The railroad bridge — it's — Oh, it's awful!

Tanny: What's awful about it?

Arvine: It's washed away! It rained so hard and the river got so high it just toppled over. It isn't there anymore!

Snivet: (*swooning*) You mean the railroad bridge is out? Has the train crossed it yet?

(*Mounting hysteria*)

Arvine: No, the train's going to run right into the river!

Tanny: The MacKenzies are on that train with their dear little baby.

Arvine: They'll all be killed.

Tom: Now wait a minute, everybody. The train stops at Magatt's Junction to pick up the milk. It won't get to the bridge for, well, about five minutes.

Arvine: The fastest horse in town couldn't get there that soon!

Snivet: They haven't a chance, not a chance. OHHHhhh! (*keeps it up*)

Tanny: They'll all be drowned. It's the most terrible thing I ever heard of.

Tom: Is that old engine still back of the depot, Arvine?

Arvine: Yes, but we can't get it started. The wheels are being fired.

Tom: We don't need to make it run. We've got to get the steam up so I can make the whistle blow. Come on! (*He dashes through the depot; Arvine follows.*)

Tanny: He's going to try to signal the train in Morse code.

Snivet: (*wringing her hands*) What good will that do? We're helpless. Utterly, completely, heartbreakingly helpless!

Tanny: Don't talk like that, Miss Snivet. I can't bear it.

Snivet: The train is roaring toward the river right now. (*Suddenly a loud whistle shrieks from above depot: Dot-Dot-Dot-Dash Dash-Dash — Dot-Dash-Dash-Dot.*)

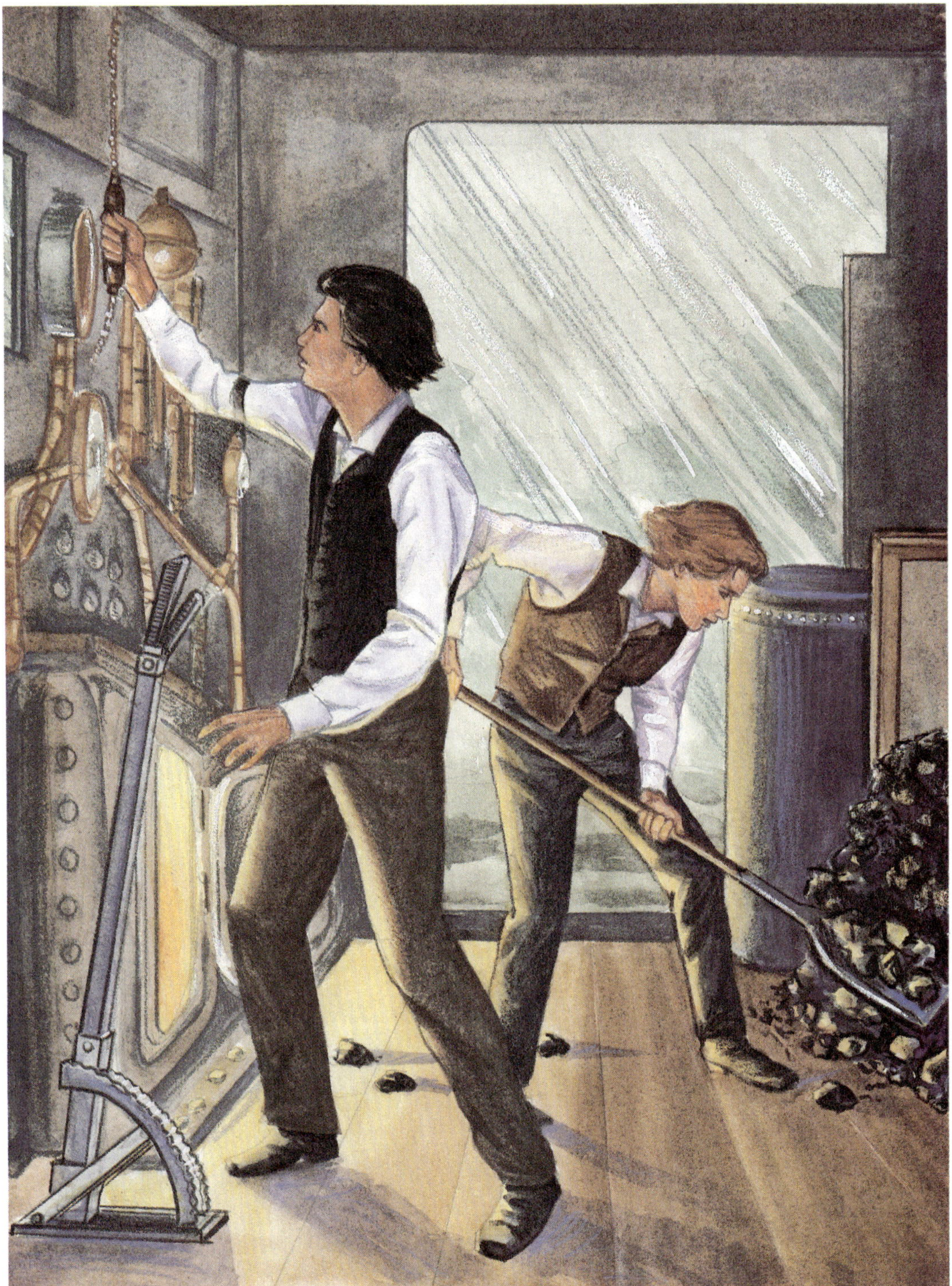

Tanny: (*with train whistle cue*) Tom's sending a signal. He made the whistle spell stop.

Snivet: (*daring to hope*) Do you . . . do you think they'll be able to hear it?

Arvine: (*bursts out of door as whistle continues*) We got the steam up and Tom's sending a code message now.

Snivet: Oh, Arvine, do you think they'll hear it?

Arvine: It's loud enough, but how could anybody know what it means?

Tanny: Mr. MacKenzie's on that train, don't forget. He's a real telegrapher.

Snivet: Oh, how I hope he hears it.

Arvine: I hope he understands.

Mrs. E: (*entering*) What's the matter? What's wrong?

Arvine: The bridge is out and the train is heading for the river.

Mrs. E: Where's Tom?

Snivet: He's sending signals, trying to stop the train!

Tanny: Listen! Listen, everybody! Tom's told them the bridge is out and he's stopped signalling.

(*There is complete silence for a beat, before a coded whistle is heard in the distance.*)

Tanny: (*repeating*) S . . . A . . . F . . . E. They've stopped in time!

Mrs. E: Thank heaven!

Tom: (*comes back on, limp*) I got through to them! Mr. MacKenzie must have heard me.

Tanny: (*runs to him and hugs him*) Oh, Tom. How did you ever think of it?

Arvine: (*sits*) Whew! I thought that whole train was done for.

Mrs. E: Oh, son! What might have happened to those people but for you!

Arvine: The way Tom had me shovelin' coal there I thought I'd fall flat on my face!

Tom: We had to get the steam up fast, Arvine. You sure made a good fireman. I never could have stopped that train without you.

Tanny: (*runs and flings arms around Arvine*) Oh, Arvine, thanks. I'm sorry if I ever was mean to you.

Arvine: (*overwhelmed and embarrassed*) Awwww! I just shoveled the coal.

Tanny: (*to Snivet*) Have you heard? Tom's got a job.

Arvine: He'll be the boss of Aloysious O'Toole!

Tom: I'll be a real telegrapher! My new job begins tomorrow.

Mrs. E: It will be the beginning of good things. You are a boy with ideas, Tom. You've got a wonderful future.

Tom: (*as music sneaks under and lights dim*) I hope you're right.

Why: (*mysterious, on public address system as all but Tom turn away in tableau*) Tom! Tom!

Tom: (*in single spot, looks up and out*) Yes, Why, I can hear you!

Why: Don't ever stop asking questions, Tom, and remember (*symphonic theme swells up under these lines and through to curtain*) electric light . . . phonograph records . . . moving pictures! All these wonderful ideas will come true some day if you keep asking "Why!"

Tom: I will, Why. I will! (*Music comes up as Tom stands center stage.*)

CURTAIN

Discuss the Selection

1. A job would make Tom's tomorrows better. What did Tom do to earn himself a job?
2. Why was Muley O'Toole upset after Tom was promised a telegrapher's job?
3. How did you feel when Muley fired Tom from his job on the railroad?
4. What important idea was "Why" trying to teach Tom?
5. When did you first begin to realize that Tom's bad luck was going to change? Find that part of the play and reread it.

Apply the Skills

Good readers use the clues in what they read to predict what will happen. You probably predicted that Tom would save the baby and the train in the play. Use clues from the play to predict what happens after the play ends. Answer the following questions.

1. How will Muley O'Toole and Elvira Snivet probably react when they see Tom again? What clues from the play helped you to make your prediction?
2. How will the MacKenzies treat Tom when they return to Port Huron? What clues from the play helped you make your prediction?

Think and Write

Prewrite

Critic's Notes About the Play

The Play Itself:
  Plot — exciting _____

  Characters — interesting, very lifelike _____

The Production:
  Scenery and Lighting — _____

  Acting — _____

Imagine that you are a theater critic seeing "Tom Edison and the Wonderful 'Why'" onstage. Your task is to write a review of the play and of the production (how it was put on) for publication. Think about the play. Then copy and complete the chart above with your notes about the imaginary play you have attended.

Compose

Use your notes to write a review of the play. In two paragraphs, state your opinions about the quality of the play itself and the quality of the production. Use details from the play to support your opinions. Be sure to begin each paragraph with a good topic sentence.

Revise

Read your review. Did you use details from the play to support your opinions? Did you include topic sentences? If not, revise your work.

Comprehension Study

Sequence

The events in a story take place in a certain order. We call the order in which the events happen the **sequence of events.** Remembering the sequence of events in a story will help you understand the story.

Clue words often help you decide the order in which events happen. Words such as *first, next, then, after that,* and *finally* can be clues to the sequence of events. Read the paragraph that follows and pay attention to the words that indicate the order in which things happen.

> Several months before the marathon, Tara began to train. First, she put herself on a special diet. Then, she started exercising daily in a gym. She also began running a mile or more each day until, after several weeks, she was running ten miles per day. A week before the race, Tara took time off from work to train for eight hours a day. Finally, Tara felt that she was fully prepared to run in the marathon.

To prepare for this race, Tara had to do things in a certain order, or sequence. For example, she could not train eight hours on the first day she exercised; she had to gradually build up the amount of time she spent training each day. The words *first, then, after several weeks,* and *finally* show the sequence or order of Tara's preparations.

Sometimes events take place at approximately the same time. Read the following paragraphs to find out about the steps involved as the Chin family planned and built a house.

> Before the Chins began to build their dream house, they had to make several types of arrangements. They had to select a location where they wanted to construct the house. They also had to hire an architect to help them draw up the plans. Since they weren't going to build the house themselves, they had to hire a contractor who would do the actual building.
>
> After they settled these items, construction began. First, the land was cleared and leveled. Next, a large hole was excavated and concrete was poured for the foundation. The wooden frame for the house was constructed on the foundation. Then, electrical wires, gas lines, and water pipes were installed. Finally, after the walls were up, the Chins began to plan the finishing touches they would add to make the house their home.

The first paragraph lists several steps that had to be completed before the house could be built. The Chins may have found the land first, then had the plans drawn up. Or, they may have had the plans for the house drawn up before they found the right land. If you were asked to tell what the Chins did first, you would have to name all of the steps described in the first paragraph.

What are some of the steps that followed in sequence when the Chins built their house? The sequence of steps included clearing the land, pouring the foundation, and building the house. Did you find the clue words *first, next, then,* and *finally?*

When you follow directions or prepare a recipe, you must always follow a certain sequence. You should always read the whole set of directions or the whole recipe before you begin. This way, you can plan ahead and keep the sequence of steps in mind as you work. It is a good idea to have the directions or the recipe nearby to check from time to time. This paragraph tells how to change a flat tire. As you read, try to remember the steps in order.

First, remove the spare tire, the jack, and the lug wrench from the trunk of your car. Place a block of wood or a rock in front of the tire that is diagonally across from the flat to keep the car from rolling. Begin by using the lug wrench to loosen the nuts that bolt the flat tire to the wheel. Carefully jack up the car. With the wrench, remove the nuts. Next, remove the flat tire and replace it with the spare tire. Fasten the nuts securely before you lower the car. Then, tighten the nuts again. Finally, replace your tools in the trunk, take away the block of wood from the tire, and you're ready to drive away.

These sentences tell some of the steps involved in changing a flat tire. Put them in the correct sequence.

- **a.** Put the tools away in the trunk.
- **b.** Carefully jack up the car.
- **c.** Remove the flat tire from the wheel.
- **d.** Take the spare tire, jack, and lug wrench out of the trunk.
- **e.** Lower the car.
- **f.** Put on the spare tire.

Look for clue words such as *first, next, later, following that,* and *finally* to help you determine the sequence of events in a story. When you understand the sequence of events, you will be able to better understand what you read.

Textbook Application: Sequence in Social Studies

Authors of textbooks try to present information in a way that will be easy for you to understand. They often describe events in the order in which they happened. This makes the events easier to remember. For instance, when a scientific process is explained, the steps are usually described in order. This sequence is important for a complete understanding of the process.

The following paragraphs are taken from a social studies textbook. As you read them, pay attention to the sequence of events. Look for clue words to help you.

> **Notice how events are told in time order. Look for the clue words *beginning, led by, first, later,* and *during*. What do these words tell you?**

Beginning in the 1500's Western nations gained colonies in Southeast Asia. Led by the Portuguese, they came first for the precious spices of the "Indies." Spain later sent missionaries to convert the Philippines. Dutch traders won control of the islands of Indonesia. During the nineteenth century, the English occupied Burma and the Malay Peninsula, which contains Malaysia and part of Thailand. The French took over much of Vietnam and Kampuchea. Everywhere the Europeans set up plantations, where natives worked for low wages. Raw materials went back to Europe to be turned into finished goods. Raw materials are natural resources, such as wood, that can be made into useful products. Southeast Asian cities, such as Singapore, became centers of European culture.

Japan was the next nation to invade Southeast Asia. In search of raw materials for its growing industries, Japan in the 1930's began its campaign to take over the South Pacific. During World War II its armies conquered the Philippines, Indonesia, and most of Southeast Asia as far west as Burma. At first, many national leaders welcomed the Japanese for freeing Asia from European rule. Soon, however, most people realized that the Japanese military brought harsh rule. Many Southeast Asians joined the fight against Japan.

Once they had helped defeat the Japanese, nation after nation demanded freedom. Some nations succeeded quickly. The Philippines gained independence from the United States in 1946. Burma became free of England in 1948. In some places more fighting was necessary. Four years of war were needed to free Indonesia from the Dutch. It took many years of bloodshed before France agreed to an independent Vietnam in 1954.

— *The World: Past and Present,* Harcourt Brace Jovanovich

> **What is the clue word in the first sentence? How did national leaders feel about the Japanese at first? How did they feel later?**

> **When did the nations of Southeast Asia demand their freedom? Which country gained its freedom first? Which country gained its freedom last? How can you tell?**

As you read textbooks, look for clues to the sequence of events. This can help you keep the information about events in order in your mind. Putting events and information in sequence will help you remember what you read.

Tomorrow a robot might drive a car or cook a meal for you. Read this selection to find out how robots are used today.

Are robots used in space? As you read the selection, look for a description of their introduction into space. What is the sequence of events involved in their introduction?

The Electronic Revolution: Robots

by Nigel Hawkes

If you saw a typical robot you might not be too impressed. It would probably be nothing more than a mechanical arm with a tool such as a paint-sprayer at the end — not at all like the "tin men" you see in science fiction movies.

Real robots are tools that make our work easier. People have been using machines like this ever since the first factories were built. The big difference between robots and other machines, however, is that robots are run by computers.

A robot is a machine that was made to imitate certain human actions. A robot does not have to look like a human being. But it must be able to do its tasks automatically. The word "robot" was first used by the Czech writer Karel Capek. In a play he called *Rossum's Universal Robots,* Capek wrote about an army of industrial robots that became too clever and took over the world. Capek made up the word "robot" from the Czech word *robota,* which means "forced work." Since Capek wrote this play, there have been many science fiction books and movies that tell about robots taking over the world.

Robot Workers

Today we may not worry much about robots taking over the world. But some people do worry about robots taking over people's jobs. Robots can work 24 hours a day, without taking breaks or having to rest at all. For many routine jobs they can do a better job than human beings. They do not make mistakes. On the other hand, robots help people by doing boring, repetitive work for them.

A robot works on a piano in a Japanese factory.

A robot arm places a circuit in a new computer board.

Robots Today

Perhaps the most famous robots in science fiction are C3PO and R2-D2, the mechanical heroes of the film *Star Wars*. Robots like C3PO, which look like people, are called androids.

Real robots don't look anything like people. The only parts of a human body that have been copied are the arm and hand. This is because most practical jobs robots are needed for are done with the hands. Like a human arm, a robot's arm can swivel, sweep, move sideways, and bend at the shoulder, elbow, and wrist. Usually, they are fitted with a simple gripper that acts like a hand.

Programming a Robot

A robot knows what to do by following instructions from a microprocessor. This is a kind of tiny electronic computer. The microprocessor contains a few simple instructions that tell the robot how to do the job at hand. When there is a new job to be done, it can be given new instructions by reprogramming it.

The same robot can do many different jobs. Most machines, such as the machines you may find in your kitchen, can do only one job. One robot can be used to put together, weld, and paint the frames of a washing machine. But between each stage, the tools carried by the robot's "hand" have to be changed. For each job, its "memory" must also be reprogrammed with fresh instructions.

A robot arm spray-paints a truck.

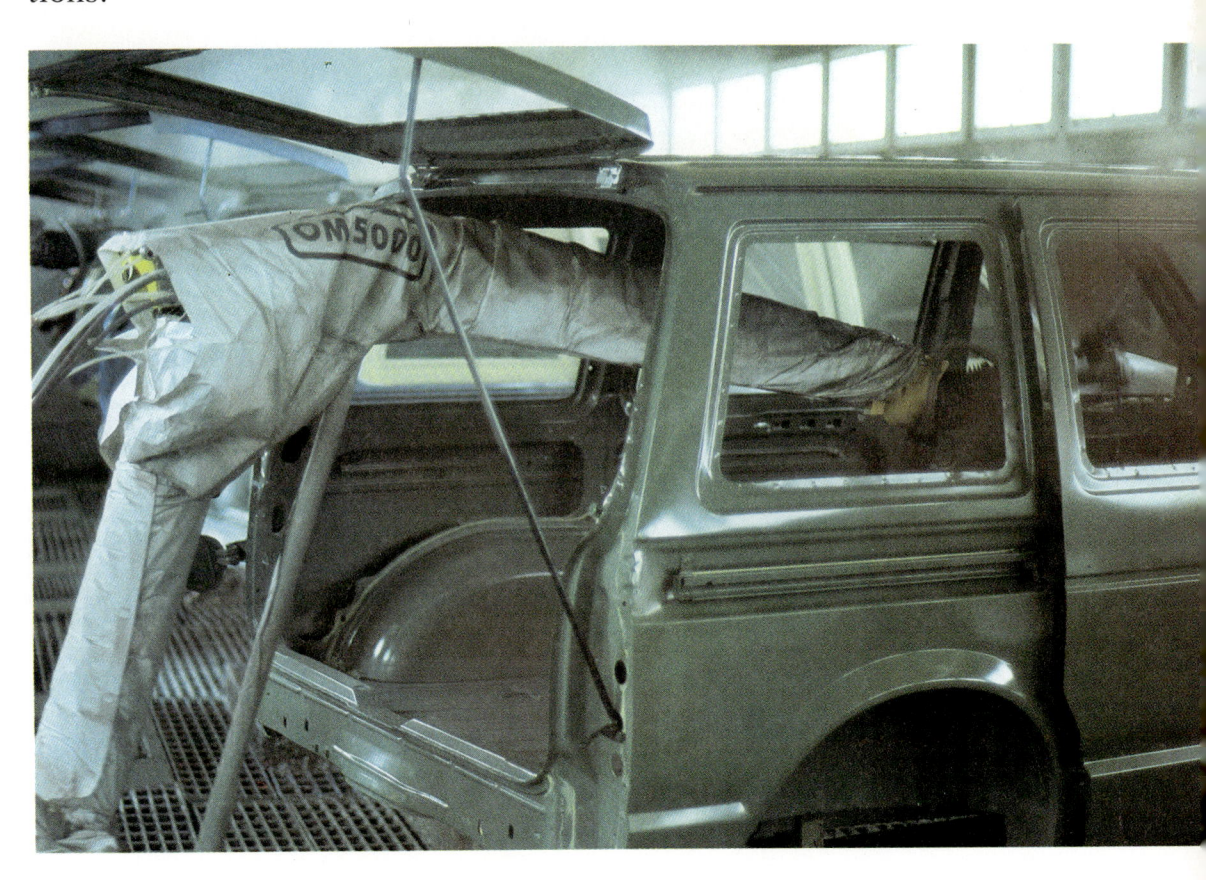

Instructing a Robot

There are two ways of telling a robot what to do. The easiest way to do this is to guide the machine through all the moves it has to make. The robot's computer stores these movements in its memory so that the robot can repeat them in exactly the same way every time. Another way is to use a keyboard to punch detailed instructions into the robot's memory.

Robot arms welding in a car plant.

Industrial Robots

Robots are very good for performing repetitive jobs which are simple and do not need human knowledge. In factories, they are used for painting, for picking things up and putting them onto the production line, and for welding pieces of metal together, particularly for car bodies. Robots never tire of doing these jobs, so the quality is just as good every time. And unlike a person, a robot never loses concentration. Its work is just as good at the end of the day as it is at the beginning.

Robots are good for doing these kinds of jobs for other reasons. When a new model of a car is being introduced, the same production line can be used. The robots are simply reprogrammed to put in the new parts. This is much easier and cheaper than building a new production line. Robots are also fast. At one car production plant in Detroit, 50 robots replaced 200 welders — and increased the number of cars that were made.

Robots in Transportation

Robots may not be as clever or as able to do as many different things as human beings can, but they make mistakes far less often. So there are advantages in using robots to fly planes, drive trains, and maybe one day even drive cars. Some airplanes are already flown by robots known as automatic pilots. At takeoff and landing a human pilot takes over, ready to deal with any unforeseen circumstances that may arise. Robots cannot deal with the unexpected.

Space Robots

Robots can work well in outer space because they do not need air, food, heat, or most of the things people need to stay alive. The Soviet Union's exploration of the moon, which included landing two moon vehicles that traveled around the lunar surface, was all done by remote control robot landers. The United States sent astronauts to the moon instead, but it sent a robot, called Viking, to land on the planet Mars. One reason for this was that the distance to Mars was too far for people to travel. The Viking lander took eleven months to reach Mars, whereas it takes astronauts only three days to reach the moon.

One day soon, robots may be sent into orbit to repair the many satellites that are used for communications, navigation, and weather forecasting. Launched from a space shuttle, the robot spacecraft could carry tools and spare parts, just like a car repair service on Earth.

Viking's robot arm probes the surface of Mars.

An astronaut repairing a malfunctioning satellite. In the future, this task might be performed by robots.

Intelligent Robots?

Robots in the near future will probably be able to see. Their eyes will be TV cameras, which would "look" around them and send back pictures to the robot's "brain." This will make robots much more useful to people. A seeing robot will be able to pick out the parts it needs, in the right order, and then put them together to make a finished product. It will identify parts that do not work properly and reject them. This is a job which only people can do now.

The final challenge is to make robots that can not only do and see but think as well. Such machines are still a long way in the future. Scientists are already working on the possibility. Thinking robots could do many jobs which today's robots are not able to do. They could learn from experience and use logic to solve problems. There are already computer programs that can solve real-life problems for farmers, doctors, and scientists. Perhaps some time in the next century, we will have intelligent robots to run our homes and offices.

Discuss the Selection

1. How are robots used in our world today?
2. What is the difference between machines and robots?
3. What advantages do you think there would be in having robots in your home?
4. Why is outer space a better working environment for robots than for people?
5. Find sentences in the selection that support this statement: *Intelligent robots are a real possibility for the future.*

Apply the Skills

Real events happen in a certain order. This order is called the sequence of events. Use information given in the selection to describe the sequence of events involved in the introduction of robots into space. Use the following words as a guide.

1. First,
2. Next,
3. In the future,

Think and Write

Prewrite

Today's Robots	Your Robot
Description	**Description**
1. mechanical arms	1.
2. mechanical hands	2.
3. microprocessor controlled	3.
4. not human looking	4.
Uses	**Uses**
1. paint washing machines	1.
2. explore space	2.
3. weld metal parts	3.
4. fly planes	4.

The first column above describes today's robots. Imagine a robot of your own. Copy the second column. Complete it with notes that describe your robot and give a few of its uses.

Compose

Use your notes to write a paragraph about your imaginary robot. Be sure to describe your robot and tell about its uses. Begin your paragraph with a topic sentence.

Revise

Read your paragraph. Did you describe your robot? Did you tell about its uses? Reread your topic sentence. Is it a good statement of your paragraph's main idea?

People often make predictions about what the world of tomorrow will be like. Read to find out how accurate one man's predictions were.

As you read, think about the sequence of new developments through history.

Predictions from 1900

by John Elfreth Watkins, Jr.

Imagine someone at the turn of the century being able to predict what life would be like now. In 1900 a young journalist named John Elfreth Watkins, Jr., did just that. At that time women did not have the right to vote, the telephone was not widely used, and cars called "horseless carriages" were rare. Also, the Wright brothers had not yet flown their plane at Kitty Hawk, radio broadcasts had not started, and motion pictures were just beginning to roll.

Watkins got his ideas about what life would be like in the year 2000 after talking with experts in many fields. Then he published his predictions in a magazine in December 1900. The surprising thing about Watkins's predictions is not how many he got wrong, but how many he got right!

Here is part of Watkins's original article. The information that follows it tells how accurate his predictions were.

1. By the year 2000, there will be from 350 million to 500 million people in America. Nicaragua will ask to become a state after the great canal is finished. Mexico will be next.

2. A college education will be free to every man and woman. There will be several great national universities. Some students will be given free board, free clothing, and free books. Doctors will visit the public schools. They will give children free eyeglasses, free dental care, and free medical care of every kind. During vacations, children will be taken on trips all over the world. Good manners, social behavior, and housekeeping will be taught in the schools.

3. Americans will be one to two inches taller. The increase in height will be because of better health care, changes in food, and athletics. Americans will live for fifty years instead of thirty-five. Everyone will live in the suburbs. The trip from home to the office will take only a few minutes. It will cost only a penny.

4. Very few medicines will be swallowed. Drugs will be given through the skin. Doctors will be able to see through the skin. They will be able to see a living heart and take pictures of any part of it. This work will be done with rays of invisible light.

5. Everyone will walk ten miles a day. Gymnastics will begin in the nursery. Toys and games will be designed to strengthen the muscles. Exercise classes will be given in all schools. Every school, college, and community will have a gymnasium. A person who cannot walk ten miles at one time will be thought to be a weakling.

6. People will be able to see around the world. There will be cameras connected to screens at the ends of electrical circuits, thousands of miles apart. Americans will be able to see such things as the coronations of kings in Europe. The instrument bringing these pictures to people's doors will be connected to a giant telephone. Thus, actors or speakers will be heard as they are seen.

7. Hot and cold air will be turned on to change the temperature of a house. This will be done just as we now turn on hot or cold water. This cool air and heat will come to houses in the same way that gas or electricity come to us now. Getting up early to build the furnace fire will become an old-fashioned job. Homes will have no chimneys, because no smoke will be created within their walls.

8. Cars will cost less than horses do today. Farmers will own automobile wagons and automobile plows. A one-pound motor in one of these vehicles will do the work of a pair of horses or more. Children will ride in automobile sleighs in winter. Cars will replace every horse vehicle now known. There will be automobile ambulances and automobile street cleaners. The horse will become a rare sight.

9. There will be airships, but they will not be able to compete with cars and ships for passengers or freight. Some airships will carry people and goods. Others will be used by scientists to observe the earth from high above it.

10. There will be no street cars in large cities. All "hurry traffic" will be below or high above the ground. In most cities people will travel on subways. Subways will be reserved for express trains. Cities will become free from all noises.

11. There will be no mosquitoes, flies, or roaches. Window screens will not be needed. People will get rid of the mosquitoes by draining all stagnant pools. Swamp lands will be filled in. Still water streams will be chemically treated. Since horses will no longer be found in cities, the number of house-flies will be reduced.

How Accurate Were Watkins's Predictions?

1. There were about 235 million people living in the U.S. in 1984. If we add the number of people in Mexico and Central America, the total is about 335 million. The "great canal" is the Panama Canal.

2. Several billion dollars of scholarship and loan money are available for college students each year. But the free college Watkins predicted has not come to pass. The only free medical care given in public schools are tests of eyesight and hearing.

3. For exactly the reasons Watkins states, Americans are about 4 inches taller than they were in 1900. In 1900, the average lifetime was 47 years (not 35 as Watkins wrote). Today it is 74 years. Many, but by no means all, people have moved from the cities to the suburbs since 1900. But transportation to the city costs a lot more than a penny!

4. So far, no one has found a way to do away with pills and liquid medication. However, many medicines today are given by injection and some are even

applied using bandage-like patches. Just as Watkins predicted, X-rays, CAT scanners, lasers, and electron microscopes have enabled doctors to see into the human body.

5. Americans today are very concerned with health and exercise. Most schools have gymnasiums and require students to take part in gym classes. Many people exercise regularly. It's anybody's guess how many of us could walk ten miles at one time. Could you?

6. Satellites high above the earth send TV signals around the world. So we can "see around the world," but not in exactly the way Watkins predicted.

7. Modern heating systems do let us turn heat and air conditioning on and off. But fireplaces and chimneys are still popular in many homes.

8. The automobile has replaced the horse. However, a car's engine strength is still given as "horsepower." Can you think of anything that resembles Watkins's "automobile sleigh"?

9. In 1900, Watkins probably was thinking about blimps when he wrote about "airships." He probably never imagined the large jet airplanes of today. Watkins was right in predicting high-flying observation airships, though he most likely did not have today's satellites in mind.

10. Watkins correctly guessed the use of subways in our cities. But, unfortunately, cities are still very noisy places.

11. Also, mosquitoes, flies, and roaches are still with us. It is a good thing that we did not fill in all our swamps. We have learned that swamp lands are important to our ecology.

Discuss the Selection

1. Which of Watkins's predictions were accurate?
2. What did Watkins predict about future Americans' health and health care?
3. Which of Watkins's predictions would you like to see come true? Which ones are you glad didn't come true?
4. Choose one of Watkins's inaccurate predictions. Suggest why it did not come true and why he made the wrong prediction.
5. Find the prediction that comes close to guessing that television will be invented.

Apply the Skills

Many things have led up to the scientific advances being made today. For example, personal computers could be invented only after three things were developed: first, vacuum tubes; next, transistors; and finally, microchips. Match Watkins's predictions on the left with the developments on the right that had to happen first.

Watkins's Predictions
1. airships observe the earth
2. people are taller
3. cars are abundant and cost less than horses

Earlier Developments
a. mass production
b. airplanes
c. better food and health care

Think and Write

Prewrite

Transportation	
Today	**Tomorrow**
1. walking	1.
2. bicycling	2.
3.	3.
4.	4.
5.	5.

Think about all of the ways you and your friends use to get around — besides being driven in a car. Copy the chart above. Complete the left column by listing all the ways you get around. Then imagine how young people one hundred years from now will get around. List those ways on the chart under the heading Tomorrow.

Compose

Use the list on the Tomorrow side of your chart to write a paragraph making predictions about how young people one hundred years from now will get around. Include details in your predictions that will help readers understand what you're describing.

Revise

Read your paragraph. Have you included enough details to make your predictions clear? If not, revise your work.

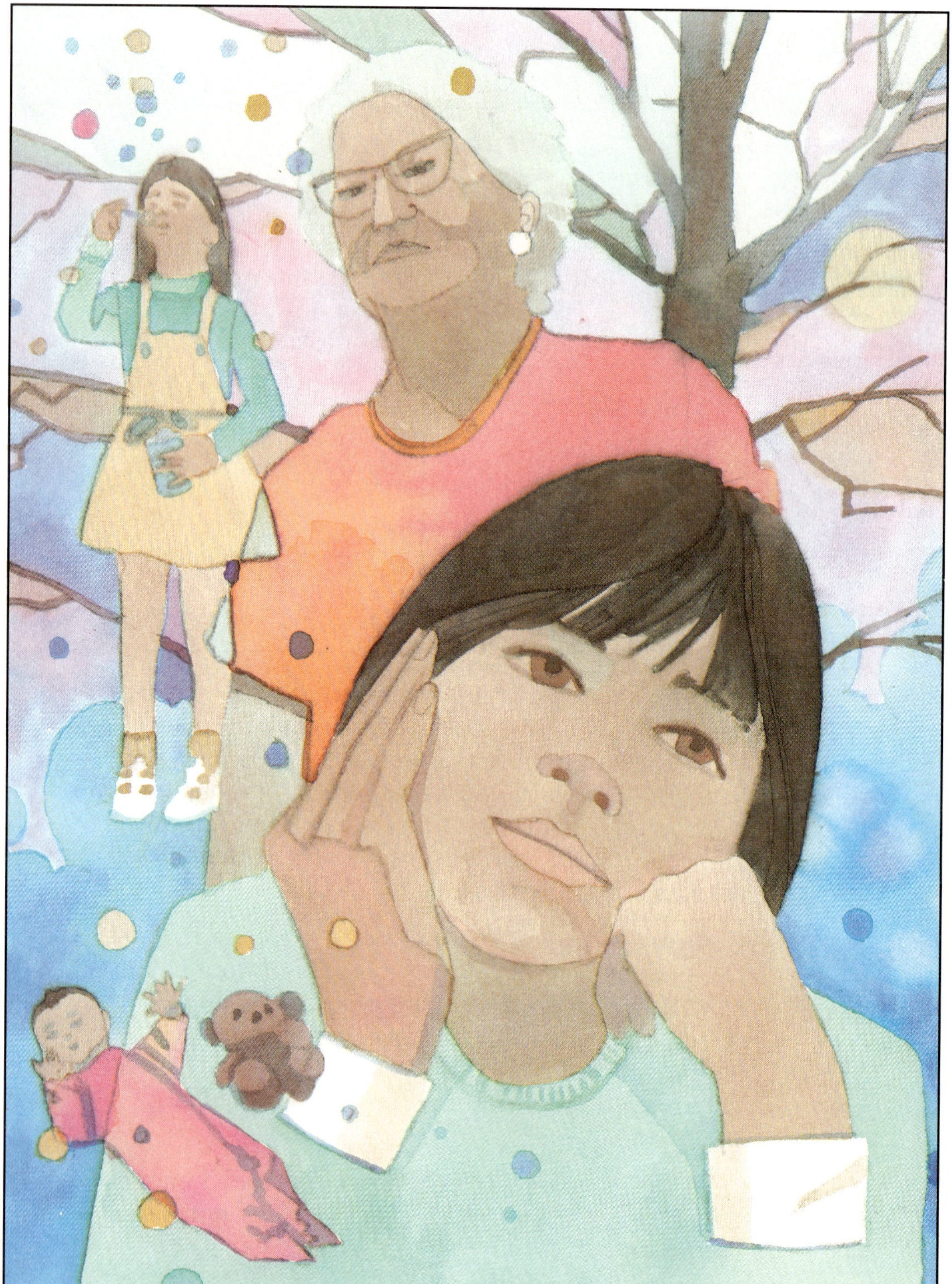

The Yesterdays and the Tomorrows

by Hal Borland

No year stands by itself,
any more than any day stands alone.
There is the continuity of all the years
in the trees,
the grass,
even in the stones on the hilltops.
Even in man.
For time flows like water,
eroding and building,
shaping and ever flowing;
and time is a part of us,
not only our years, as we speak of them,
but our lives,
our thoughts.
All our yesterdays are summarized in our now,
and all the tomorrows are ours
to shape.

> *Don Madden's illustrations are sure to entertain people of all ages for many tomorrows to come. Read this selection to learn how the artist created the right look for Incognito Mosquito.*
>
> *As you read the selection, notice the order in which events took place in Don Madden's life.*

Meet Don Madden
by Barbara Reeves

Don Madden is a very talented artist who illustrates books for young people. He is best known for the lively cartoon style that he uses in his drawings. In addition to illustrating books, Madden has drawn cartoons for magazines and advertisements. He has even written and illustrated a book of his own.

Don Madden was born in Cleveland, Ohio, but he didn't live there long. His family moved to the East Coast when he was young. They lived in Atlantic City, New Jersey, and Philadelphia, Pennsylvania. After high school, Madden attended the Philadelphia Museum College of Art. He received his formal training in art there. Later he taught drawing and design to art students at the college.

For a while, Madden lived in New York City. One of the things he enjoyed most about the city was the Museum of Natural History. He lived very close to the museum and made frequent trips there. But even the Museum of Natural History was not enough to keep Don Madden in the city. After ten years of city life, he decided to retreat to a calmer life in the country.

Don Madden and friends
(Don Madden is the one in the middle)

    Now Madden lives in an old farmhouse in northern New York State. He shares the house and surrounding land with his wife, his children, a cat who chases bats, and a dog. Madden enjoys gardening and raising geese.

    Like many artists, Don Madden does most of his work at home. He gets assignments from his agent, a person who helps him find jobs that are best suited for his style of illustration. He completes the assignments at home, handling the details by telephone or through the mail. Madden especially enjoys illustrating books for young people. His love for this type of illustration shows in his finished work.

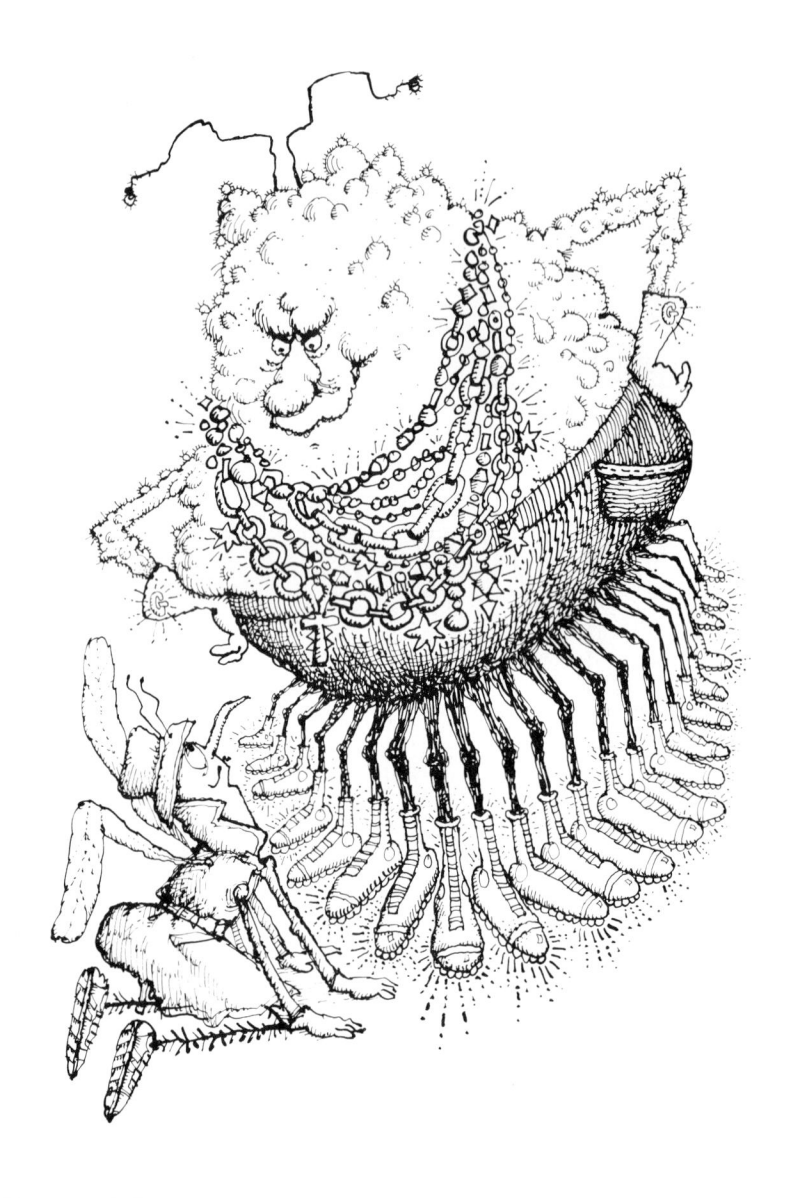

Goldfungus and Incognito, from Incognito Mosquito Flies Again.

    Some of the most entertaining parts of the book *Incognito Mosquito: Private Insective* are Don Madden's humorous illustrations. Creating illustrations that fit a particular book takes time and hard work. Before he drew the illustrations for *Incognito Mosquito: Private Insective*, Madden read the final manuscript of the book. He had to imagine the character of Incognito Mosquito and decide what the character should look like, based on the author's description. Madden drew seven preliminary versions of Incognito. Then the author studied them and selected the one that was to become the Incognito Mosquito that appears in the book. After that decision was made, Don Madden had to be sure that the basic character of Incognito Mosquito was consistent in all of the illustrations he drew for the book.

Madden especially likes the character of Incognito Mosquito. Incognito reminds him of detective characters from old radio and television shows. He likes the way the clever detective sometimes makes mistakes but is smart enough to overcome them.

Dirty Harry and his Gang, from Incognito Mosquito, Private Insective.

Bug ballet from Incognito Mosquito Flies Again.

    Creating the right look for Incognito Mosquito was only part of the work involved in illustrating the book. Madden also had to create many other strange and interesting insects to represent the characters that Incognito Mosquito meets in his investigations. Madden read the author's words carefully to be sure he was giving the characters just the right look — and the right number of arms and legs!

    Incognito Mosquito: Private Insective is only the first in a series of books about Incognito Mosquito that Don Madden has illustrated. Madden's amusing drawings can also be found in the second Incognito Mosquito book, and he is busy working on the illustrations for a third.

Madden is also enthusiastic about a book which he wrote and illustrated himself. The main character is Wartville Wizard, a man who leads a fight to stop people from littering. The idea for the book came to Madden when he saw people littering the highways and countryside near his home. Disturbed by what he had seen, he decided that one of the best ways to fight littering was to write a book about it.

Don Madden's drawings entertain people of all ages. It is children and young people, however, who especially seem to enjoy his humorous and wonderfully imaginative characters.

Discuss the Selection

1. What steps did Madden have to complete to create the right look for Incognito Mosquito?
2. Explain why Don Madden is able to do his work at home.
3. Do you think an artist's life and work are attractive? Why or why not?
4. How did Madden react when he saw people littering the highways and countryside near his home?
5. What phrases and sentences from the selection suggest that Don Madden is happy living in the country? Find those parts of the selection.

Apply the Skills

Events that occur in a person's lifetime happen in a certain order. Most stories also present events in a certain order.

The sentences below tell about events in Don Madden's life. Use the selection about Don Madden to put the events in the correct order.

1. Don Madden attended college in Philadelphia.
2. Madden moved to northern New York.
3. Madden lived in New York City for ten years.
4. Madden lived in Atlantic City when he was young.
5. Don Madden was born in Cleveland, Ohio.

Think and Write

Prewrite

Short Story Summary
Something annoying:
Story setting:
Story characters:
Story problem:
Story solution:

Don Madden wrote and illustrated a book in response to something that annoyed him — people littering. His book has a main character who leads the fight to stamp out littering.

Think about something that annoys you. Then imagine a short story about it. Copy the chart above. Complete it with information about your story.

Compose

Using the information on your chart, write a short story. Be sure to state the story's setting and to describe the main characters vividly. Make sure that there is a solution to the story's central problem.

Revise

Read your story. Did you clearly state the problem and the solution? Can you add words that will make the description of your main character more vivid?

Literature Study

Setting

The **setting** of a story is where and when the story takes place. Details in a story provide clues to help you figure out the setting.

As you read the following paragraph from the beginning of a story, notice the many details it provides about the setting.

> Randy saw the shore slowly slip away. Soon it would be gone from view. As she lazily stretched out on the deck, she saw sea gulls spiraling in the blueness overhead and diving into the water looking for food. The sun's hot rays beat down upon her and the waves gently rocked her to sleep.

The setting of this story is not directly stated. Context clues in the paragraph help you figure out where the story is set. Words such as *shore, deck, sea gulls,* and *waves* tell you that Randy is on a boat leaving the shore. When is the story set? The phrases *blueness overhead* and *sun's hot rays beat down upon her* are clues that let the reader know that it is late morning or early afternoon. In some stories you have to use picture clues, in addition to context clues, to help you determine the setting.

Some authors state the settings of their stories directly. This sentence is a simple statement of the setting: "At 12:30 P.M., Randy fell asleep on the deck of her boat." The reader of this sentence would immediately know what the story's setting is. However, the descriptive details in the paragraph make it much more interesting to read.

Setting plays an important part in creating the **mood** of a story. Mood is the general feeling that an author tries to convey in a piece of writing. Writers create a certain mood by choosing carefully the words that characters say or by describing a setting in a certain way. For example, in the paragraph about Randy, is the general mood conveyed one of anxiety, of anger, or of peacefulness? Words like *lazily stretched* and *gently rocked* help suggest that the story's mood is one of peacefulness.

Read the paragraph below. Use clues about the setting to help you decide what the paragraph's mood is.

> I paused at the bottom of the rotted steps and peered through the darkness at the ramshackle old house. Its tower was silhouetted against the full moon. Soft noises — moans and creaking — began to fill the freezing air. Was it just the wind?

What words would you use to describe the mood of this paragraph? The words *eerie, creepy,* or *scary* might be used to describe the mood. What words help to convey this mood? Words like *rotted, peered, ramshackle, full moon, moans,* and *creaking* all help to create the paragraph's mood.

In your reading, look carefully for clues that will help you figure out the setting and the mood. Determining a story's setting and mood will help you to understand and enjoy what you read.

Author Profile

Virginia Hamilton

"I think I dream writing," Virginia Hamilton says. "Writing is who I am." This does not mean that she thinks writing is the most important thing in the world, though. Hamilton thinks that living and finding out about life are the most important things. A writer, she says, must not "forget or fear to look at life."

Many of Virginia Hamilton's books seem to grow directly out of her own life, like branches from a tree. Like herself, many of her characters are from Ohio.

Even for those characters who are from big cities or Caribbean islands or future worlds, the problems they face and overcome are related to the problems she or people she knows have faced and overcome.

Virginia Hamilton was born in Yellow Springs, Ohio. She says it was "a home for the descendants of abolitionists and fugitive slaves." Hamilton's own mother was the daughter of one of those slaves. Yellow Springs was once a haven for them. It was a station on the "underground railroad," the trail of hiding places slaves used to follow to freedom.

Her award winning book, *The House of Dies Drear*, is set in a house that was once such a hiding place.

Hamilton learned from her family, that "life must be freedom." A bright and sensitive child, she was given freedom to go off and discover what there was to find. What she found was her mother's side of the family. "My mother's people were warm-hearted, generous to the sick and landless, and fond of telling tales about one another and even their ancestors.

"My Uncle King told the best tall tales. But my own mother could take a slice of fiction floating around the family and polish it into a saga. So could my father. Having come from a Creole family that wandered the face of this country and Canada, he was always a traveling man, if only in his mind."

Life, Hamilton believes, travels in a circle. A daughter can repeat her father's journeys by traveling in her mind. When she was a girl, Hamilton was afraid of the dark. She would calm herself by listening to her father play his mandolin. He disliked the dark as much as she and tried to conquer it by playing music. Lying in bed, she tried to conquer her fear by imagining different characters, what she calls "the endless parade of figures that tramped across the reaches of my mind."

That parade of characters has tramped right into her books. Hamilton has received many awards for her work. They include two Newbery medals for the best children's book of the year and the Edgar Allan Poe award for best children's mystery of the year.

Today, married and raising her own children, Hamilton often writes late at night during the hours that used to frighten her. One night, as you are about to read in the next story, she wrote about a family in Ohio and a terrifying time when — if the radio could be believed — people thought that Martians had landed.

Someday we may be able to travel from planet to planet. Someday we may have visitors from outer space. Read to see what Willie Bea wanted to do when she thought the Martians had landed.

The year is 1938. There is no television, only radio and movies. Notice how important the setting is in the story.

Willie Bea and the Time the Martians Landed

by Virginia Hamilton

On Halloween night in 1938, the actor Orson Welles read a play called *War of the Worlds* on the radio. This play was in the form of a radio broadcast describing an invasion by creatures from Mars. For people living on farms and in small towns in 1938, the radio was the only source of news. Many thought that the play was a real news flash. They were sure that the earth was really being invaded by Martians. Panic gripped parts of the country.

Virginia Hamilton has taken this real-life event and created a fictional story about twelve-year-old Willie Bea and her family in Ohio. As the story opens, Willie Bea and her younger sister and brother have dressed up for Halloween. They are ready to show off their costumes, when they hear something strange downstairs.

There was a commotion downstairs. For a minute Willie Bea couldn't tell what was going on. Everybody was talking at the same time. It sounded like somebody was hurt bad or something, moaning and crying. It was a woman, sounding scared to death.

"What's the matter, what's happened?" they heard Willie Bea's mama say.

"You have an accident with the car?" they heard her papa ask.

"It's awe-fel! It's jus' aw-awe-fel!" they could hear the woman cry, in bitter anguish.

"What?" whispered Willie Bea.

The moaning, crying voice sounded familiar.

"What?" whispered Bay Sister.

"Shhhh!" said Willie Bea. Carefully, she crept farther down the stairs. She had Bay Sister by the hand and she knew Bay Sister would take Bay Brother's hand without her having to tell her.

She decided whoever was upset in the living room would feel better once she saw their wonderful costumes: two ghosts and one hobo.

"It's the end of ev-ree-thing!" the woman cried. "Oh, my heaven, it's awe-fel, it's aw-awe-fel!"

"Aunt Leah!" said Willie Bea.

"Aunt Leah?" said Bay Sister.

Willie Bea eased them down onto the landing. The landing was lighted by the glow from the living-room lamps. She pulled Bay Sister, who pulled Bay Brother, behind her. She wanted the three of them in their costumes to just sort of flow into view. Just to appear there, like Halloween phantoms.

"The Gobble-uns are here!" Willie Bea announced, in as good a voice as a radio announcer. She always said that about Gobble-uns on Halloween. They stood there, the three of them as dressed up, as frightening as they could be.

No one heard Willie Bea. No one was listening. For the living room was a crazy, mixed-up scene. Willie Bea froze on the landing, taking it all in with Bay and Bay Sister. The three of them were poised there in silence, unmoving.

A tall, very good-looking man stood in the middle of the living room. Not her father. The man had on a greatcoat of dark wool. He'd unbuttoned the coat and flung it open. He had on a dark felt hat that matched the coat. Its crown was dented from front to back, with a stiff brim turned up slightly on the sides. Willie Bea glimpsed a gorgeous tuxedo suit of clothes under the man's coat. Suit jacket with satin lapels. A white dress shirt with goldlike buttons. There was a satin bow tie. The man had on a handsome gold chain draped across his chest. Willie Bea knew there would be a watch in the man's watch fob. The gent's shoes were white, and black on the shiny top front and the sides of the heels.

"Mr. Hollis, do sit down, won't you?" Willie Bea's mama was saying.

But the man, Mr. Hollis, couldn't sit down. For hanging on his shoulder, being held in an almost standing position, was wonderful Aunt Leah. What in the world is she doing here? wondered Willie Bea.

Aunt Leah had on a full-length, to-the-floor, silky black, honest-to-goodness evening gown. It was the first evening gown Willie Bea had ever seen on anybody outside of the ladies in the movies. Aunt Leah had on a necklace of glistening pearls that came down to her waist and were tied

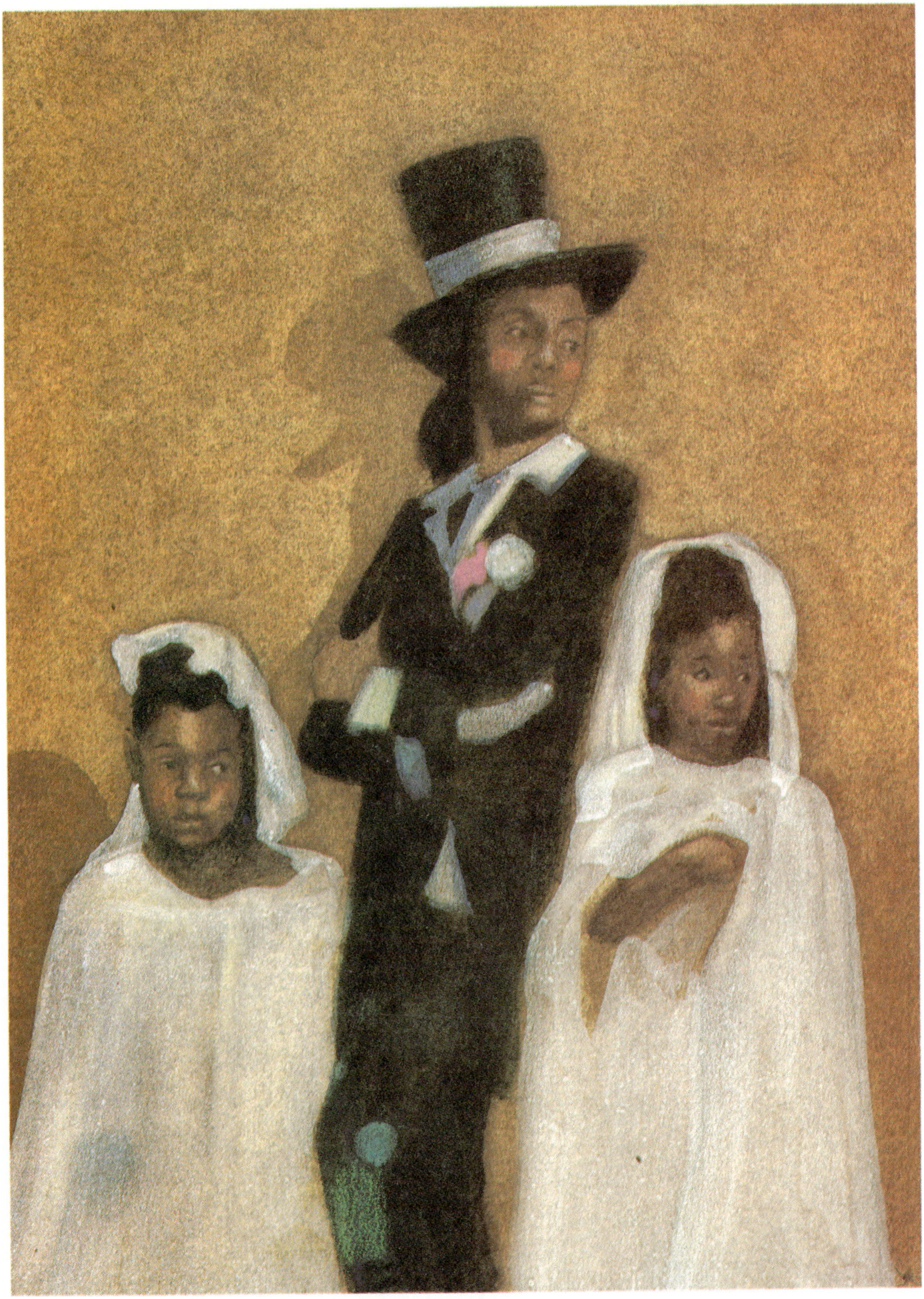

in a pearly knot halfway down. She had on gold, low-cut dress shoes with very high heels. Her hair was piled high on her head, with curls that cascaded down on each side at her temples. A cluster of pearls decorated her earlobes. Her face was rouged and powdered to perfection. Willie Bea didn't know how any one person could be so perfectly beautiful in so many different ways as was Aunt Leah.

But now Aunt Leah was crying and moaning. Mr. Hollis supported her with one strong arm around her waist. He half-carried Aunt Leah across to the radio. He rapidly turned the dial, trying to find something. You could hear garbled voices going in and out of hearing very quickly. Mr. Hollis took his fist and pounded the top of the radio.

"Now, here, don't do that!" said Willie Bea's father. He looked shocked. "That won't help anything. Tell me what you are looking for."

"It's the world," said Mr. Hollis in a thin, tenor voice. "She called me after she heard it, but I'd already left to come for her."

"What?" Willie Bea's papa was saying. "The world? You mean there is a war?"

"The world," murmured poor Aunt Leah. She clung to Mr. Hollis, eyes tightly closed. Her silk-stockinged legs seemed weak and trembly. "It's all over," she cried. "Heard it on the radio. The world. *The-world-is-coming-to-an-end!*"

Aunt Leah's legs buckled completely. It was then that Aunt Leah fainted dead away.

There was silence in the living room. Just the sound of the radio, down very low with its static and its whistling. Willie Bea's papa had stopped fiddling with it. Not one station would come in clearly. Her father ran his hand rapidly through his hair a couple of times. Then he gave up on the radio, which he knew to have a weak tube, and turned back to the women on the couch. He stood there, lost in thought, staring at them.

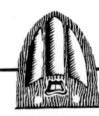

Willie Bea's mama and Aunt Leah were on the couch. Mr. Hollis was sitting on the piano bench.

"She comin' to now," Mr. Hollis said in his odd, high voice. He glanced from Aunt Leah to Willie Bea's papa. "She'll tell you now. She's comin' to."

A moment ago, Willie Bea and Bay and Bay Sister had crept into the room. All three of them squeezed into the overstuffed easy chair facing the couch, surrounded by the heady scent of roses. That was the fragrance of the smelling-salts mixture in the bottle that Willie Bea's mama waved under Aunt Leah's nose.

"Uh-nuh, uh-nuh," moaned Aunt Leah with each pass of the bottle. She came to in stages. The first stage of coming to was an anguished look that contorted Aunt Leah's face. Willie Bea's mama had her arm around her sister.

After the look had passed and her features relaxed, Leah's eyebrows knitted together. Her lips parted and her eyes fluttered wide open. She didn't look around, she looked straight into Willie Bea's face.

"They've come. They landed," Aunt Leah said.

"What, Leah?" said Willie Bea's mama.

"Oh, its awful!" said Aunt Leah, and she began to cry. "Martians!" she said. "From the planet Mars! Landed right there in the state of New Jersey!"

"Now, Leah!" said Willie Bea's mother. She looked alarmed, but very doubtful.

"I'm tellin' you, I heard it on the radio," said Aunt Leah. "It was on the radio!"

They were silent that time. All of them. For if it came over the radio, if it was one of those sudden news bulletins, like urgent messages from on high, then it had to be true.

"Leah, are you sure?" said Willie Bea's papa. He stood before the couch, his hands deep in his pants pockets.

"Listen here," Aunt Leah said. She began to shape the air in front of her with her hand as she spoke. "This radio announcer," she began, "starts out sayin' that, incredible as it seems, some strange *beings* have landed in the New Jersey farmlands. And that they are the first of an *invading army* from the planet Mars!" Aunt Leah looked around at all of them.

They were speechless—Willie Bea's mama and her good papa. Staring at Aunt Leah, tongue-tied. It was too much for Leah to be making up, their looks seemed to say.

Willie Bea felt her heart leap into her mouth.

"Now a battle was fought," Aunt Leah continued. "The government sent our army of seven thousand men to fight this monster machine full of invaders out of Mars."

When she could, Aunt Leah spoke again. "One hundred and twenty of our army soldiers survived. One hundred and twenty, that's all! And the rest, fallen all over the battlefield, some place called Grover Mill or somethin'. They were crushed and trampled by the monster. Burned by the heat ray."

"Heat ray!" said Willie Bea's papa. He looked off then, gazing at the walls, as if some distant light had smacked him between the eyes. "It was awful," said Aunt Leah. "It went on and on. The announcer breaking in on the shows, don't you see? See, the Martians have plowed through the whole state of New Jersey. They're goin' into New York City!" She paused and took a deep breath.

"And then the radio announcer was standin' on the rooftop," said Aunt Leah. "Sayin' he was seein' the Martians, tall as skyscrapers. They waded across the Hudson River into New York City. They lifted their metal hands!"

Ever so slowly, Aunt Leah's hands rose higher in the air. Willie Bea and Bay and Bay Sister were statues, stunned and tongue-tied.

"This is the end now, he said," said Aunt Leah. She stared at them earnestly. "He said, the announcer said, smoke comes out, black smoke driftin' over the city. People in the streets see it now. Said they are running toward the East River, New York. Running away from it. Thousands of people dropping in the river like rats." Aunt Leah's shoulders shook. "It reaches the Time Square, New York City. People tryin' to get away, but it's no use! Said they're fallin' like flies."

As if in a dream, Willie Bea saw Aunt Leah's pearl necklace glisten and shimmer in the light. She was aware she was holding her breath a moment, for fear Aunt Leah would stop talking. Willie Bea had to know everything she could about the Martians.

"The poor announcer," Aunt Leah moaned, holding her head as though it ached. "He's the one I usually listen to, I think. And he just shut off right then. He went dead on the air. The Martians and their machines have just taken over everything. Oh. Oh! Who's to say they haven't already landed here?"

"Now, now," said Willie Bea's mama, patting Aunt Leah.

"After that, I didn't listen again," Aunt Leah went on. "I just wanted to come here, be with everybody." She smiled wanly. Her chin trembled.

Willie Bea's papa stood there, wondering what to do.

"Don't have a telephone," he said absently. "If I did, I could put in a call to Officer Bogen downtown, although I don't know what good that would do."

Before anyone could say anything or do anything, the front door opened. It swung in ever so slowly, as if the black night had pressed too hard and had pushed it open. Willie Bea's papa jumped back and spun around, facing the door. Mr. Hollis moved back on the piano bench and his elbows hit the piano keys. A great, discordant noise rose from the piano and spread around them. Willie Bea in the chair had her back to the door. She couldn't move. Neither could Bay Sister. But Bay Brother dived down into Willie Bea's lap. He scooted over, his face and head hidden under her arm.

Willie Bea shivered, thoughts paralyzed, as a stream of cold fell over the chair and down her neck.

"Hey, now, don't upset yourselves. It's just me." Uncle Jimmy's voice. Willie Bea went limp with relief.

"I heard," he said, nodding at the radio. "Papa says, come on over home. Everybody's there now but y'all."

Uncle Jimmy cleared his throat importantly. "They've seen them lyin' low over by the Kelly farm," he said.

Suddenly, fear in the room was the shape of a poison snake. Coiled. Rattles shaking.

"They're great big," Uncle Jimmy said, his voice low. "Gleamin' eyes," he said. "V-shaped mouths. Big as trees. Big as houses. Tall as a standpipe, I heard—eighty foot high. Over there at the Kelly farm, on the north of town."

Willie Bea's mama said, "We're going over home. Willie Bea, come on. Bay Sis."

Willie Bea's papa turned off the radio, turned out all but one light, and they left the house.

All over town, in other towns, in cities, the Martians landed. And everywhere, fearing for their lives, the people panicked.

It was a chill night, all right, an uncomfortably cool night.

"It's airish out," Willie Bea's mama said, starting across the road to over home. "Nobody goes out of Grand's house tonight."

Willie Bea realized she would have to find a way out of Grand Wing's house this night. The Kelly farm was the reason she had to get out. What Uncle Jimmy had said about the Martians.

Martians! Tall as trees! V-shaped mouths! If she could just see them, talk to them.

Perhaps they were frightened, she thought. That was why they had used the heat ray. More than likely, they were lost and had to land. Ran out of gasoline on their way back home. That could be it.

Willie Bea knew where the Kelly farm was. Owned by Kellys. The very name filled her with the mystery of such people. Rich landholders. They brought their harvested grain through town in wagons pulled by tractors. She certainly had heard of them.

She knew the general location of the Kelly farm, that is. She had never been in that direction away from home. Willie Bea knew her way downtown and her end of town well. But rarely did she venture to the far side of town, or beyond the town. Girls her age just didn't wander over there. And it was hard getting around if you had no automobile in the family and no bicycle.

Over home. They came in and the din in the front room was something awful. It spilled down the hallway and into the kitchen. Babies squalling. Young'uns Bay Brother's age were hollering and shrieking. Noise, movement, as more and more folks gathered. They all came with something to add about the Martian invasion.

She could feel fear. Some grown folks over home were afraid. It was in the way they looked around over their shoulders at the bay windows. They kept watching the front door like they expected it to fly open. To reveal a dreaded monster thing from Mars framed there in the doorway.

There was always a clump of men bent low over the radio console. Turning the dial back and forth, one of them would bob up and down, saying, "Shhh! Shhh! We can't hear!"

Oh, the fear all around was almost a shape that Willie Bea could touch.

Right before her eyes, there was Toughy Clay staring.

"Where'd you come from?" Willie Bea said.

"I'm just here!" Toughy yelled back, happy as could be to be part of noise and action. "Guess what?"

"What?"

"They landed at the Kelly farm," Toughy said.

"I know that," Willie Bea said. To hear Toughy say it made her cold and still inside. It was all true.

"Well, you don't know this," he said. "I saw one. Great big Martian man."

"You . . . *what?*" Willie Bea said, barely able to get the words out.

Toughy nodded. Looked away. "It crunched down behind a tree. Hidin', I guess. But it was bigger 'n any old tree. Its fire eyes were in its chest. That's why it thought it was hidin' behind the tree. 'Cause the tree just came up to its chest, where the eyes were."

"What were they doing?" she said, shivering.

"Nothin', *they*," Toughy said. "I only saw this one Martian, just scrunched down near the Kelly place. Great big, house-size. Silo-high."

"Ohhh!" Willie Bea said, and sat down hard in a straight chair. She hadn't known the chair was there. But she was glad it was. For her legs simply gave way under her.

Then she whispered, "Come on!"

"Where we goin'?" Toughy wanted to know. They crossed the Dayton road and walked in shadows, dark shades of night among the trees around Willie Bea's house. They raced for the barn.

Just inside the door there was a light bulb. Willie Bea pulled its chain, and a dim light came on. "Just a minute," she whispered, "we'll be out of here."

They could hear the hogs beyond the closed door. Willie Bea bent over and got her stilts. "Help me," she called. Toughy Clay came slowly over. "You can use Bay Sister's," she told him. "They're just as tall as mine."

"What're you doin', Willie Bea?" Toughy said.

"Don't you see?" she said. "We can *stride* right on over to the Kelly farm on these!"

"Oh, no," he whispered, and hung his head.

She looked at him. "You know the way. You have been there?" she asked him.

He nodded, but he did not look up.

"Then let's go!" she said.

Toughy wouldn't think of refusing Willie Bea. After all, she was inviting him. Most of the time he seemed to get on her nerves. And it was his own fault he had talked about the Kelly farm. He had no one to blame but himself for that kind of lie. It had just slipped out—a Martian man!

Resignedly, he followed her over to the porch, where they could get on their stilts. Toughy helped Willie Bea first. Then, when she was on her stilts, she steadied his stilts while he fixed his feet.

"You go first," Willie Bea told him when they were ready. "You know the way."

"All right, Willie Bea," he said softly. There was no point in arguing. He did know the way over there, no lie. And moving, scared, was probably a whole lot better than standing still, scared to death.

"Hope we don't run into nuthin'," he said under his breath.

They strode the dark world, stilting. Willie Bea and Toughy Clay were out in the countryside. They were along roads, and through the fields whenever it was possible for them to get over fences.

The velveteen night and the distant, cold stars were what they could see traveling with them. They imagined they were alone on earth. Willie Bea could feel the loneliness in her heart and soul, and more than once she wished she was home. Why'd I start this journey? she wondered.

Toughy Clay didn't dare turn around to check their backs, for fear he would see something beyond belief and fall. "You ever think what's gonna happen if one of us falls off these stilts?" he whispered loudly to Willie Bea.

But she was thinking hard, and when she answered, it was not about one of them falling. She said, "Maybe that Mars is falling down. They say it's red and *mean*, boy!"

Wonder what is really going on, she thought. And if the United States army can't stop the spacemen, what will happen to us? And why come everything is so awful quiet all around? She felt strange, as if they were being watched.

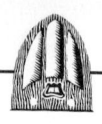

Her hands and face were cold now. So cold! Out here where there were only cornfields, the cold seemed to sift down from the sky into the ground and come up again. Willie Bea longed to stop and just take stock of things. Her muscles were mighty sore, holding on so tightly to the stilts. Her fingers cramped her, and her legs were stiff and chilled. They were starting to ache.

"Maybe we oughtn't to come out here," she said softly. All was so still around them. "Toughy, maybe we ought to just go back."

Toughy strode ahead of her. They crossed onto a narrower gravel strip with fields on either side. Gravel was tricky beneath their stilts. Willie Bea saw that there was no fence on either side of the gravel road.

"This is a private road," Toughy told her.

"Whose private?" she asked him.

"It's the Kelly private," Toughy said. "Cuts right through the corn, and they own it. Can say who walk and stride on it, too." Toughy had never been on the Kelly road before. But he recognized it from the years of stories he had heard about the farm.

"Are we that close? Keep your voice down," she whispered.

Toughy stood, shifting back and forth to keep his balance.

"Where'd you see the monster?" Willie Bea asked.

Toughy shifted uneasily on his stilts. He cleared his throat, about to tell his lie again, when Willie Bea said, "Come on! We'll follow the road closer."

It was deep, dark going, and their stilts made grating sounds on the gravel. Noise, a deep rumbling, was coming out of the ground. Willie Bea couldn't hear herself breathe, or think.

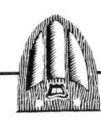

"What's that?" she hollered at Toughy.

"Don't know. Can't tell where it is or what it is!"

It was getting closer. Willie Bea thought she saw something. Like the blackest night moving.

"You see that?" she thought she yelled. Her mouth moved, but she couldn't hear what came out. "Toughy!" she screamed.

"Willie Bea!" he was screaming back. "Willie Bea!"

Now they could guess what the noise was. The great black dark that moved was one of the monsters. It was a rolling, ear-splitting, outlandish alien. And huge.

The thing must have turned a corner in front of them from behind the house, somehow. It had turned toward them and they saw its evil eye.

An awful, white, wicked, round eye. It could have been its heat ray, but it didn't hurt them. It was just blinding.

The great black dark came straight for them. And another huge blackness came on behind it. Giants as tall as houses, tall as trees, on the move.

Another one came after the second. Two of them marching, rolling behind the first. They spread out to the left of the first one. Their blinding eyes outlined the first one. Illuminated it for Willie Bea to see plainly that it was a deadly, monstrous alien.

"It's true! It's an invasion!" Toughy was yelling. "Run. Run, Willie Bea!"

Willie Bea couldn't hear him. She couldn't move. She was transfixed by the monsters. The first one's neck wasn't in the center of its body, where it should have been. It was on the right side of it! The long neck was like a wide stovepipe jutting out of its side. Its head that fitted on its neck was *all* V-shaped.

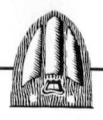

The white eyes of the monsters coming on held her hypnotized. She thought she told them, "Turn off your rays. Don't fight. We only want to be friends!"

"Willie Bea, we'd better get back. You coming with me?"

The first monster was now to the left side of the road. Its head on the side, on its long neck, was coming right at her.

"Oh, no, I can't go back with you!" she told it.

The second monster was passing along beside the gravel road. Willie looked up at its head.

"No! Get away!" she hollered.

Then she was backing away from the third monster. She thought its light was bearing down. "You leave me be!" She flailed her arms backward and one stilt leg slipped in the gravel. She twisted, trying to untangle herself from the foot wedges. She was falling. She saw the last monster's head turn in her direction. Its light was full on her. It was coming for her.

Willie Bea, falling. She hit the ground, falling hard. Something struck her a glancing blow on the forehead.

All went dark for Willie Bea. The dark filled with glowing comets and stars. Great planets of Venus and Mars. All such colors of worlds, pumpkin yellow and orange in a Halloween universe.

Willie Bea opened her eyes on an alien standing over her. She thought she saw its V-shaped mouth: "Willie Bea! Are you hurt?"

"No. I won't go back with you either," she told it. "I like my own world."

"You hit your head. It knocked you silly," the alien said.

Willie Bea's head started hurting. Suddenly, she felt cold all over. She saw a great light. It was upon her and the someone who stood over her.

582

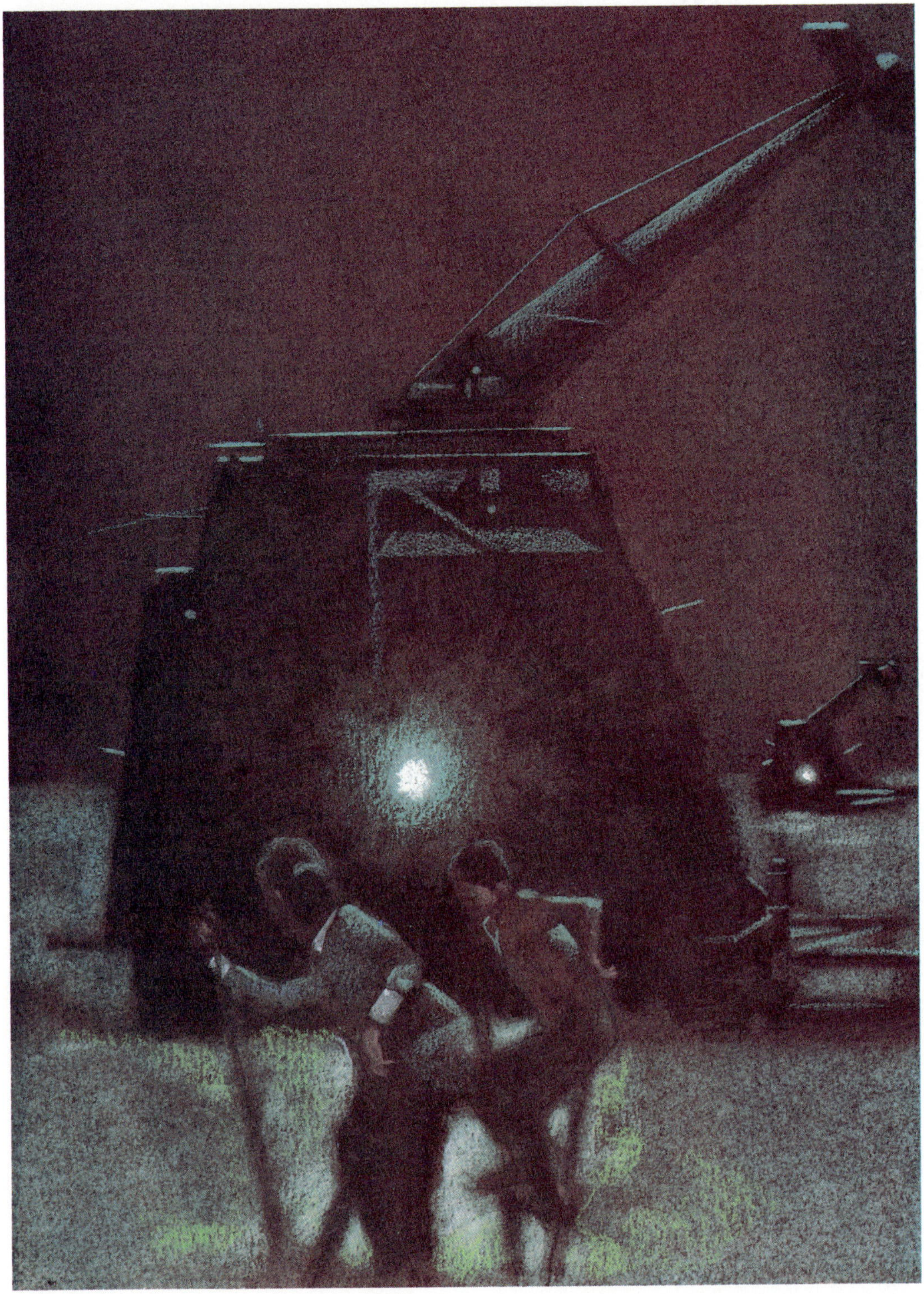

"Where . . . ?" was all she could think to say.

She heard fast footfalls on the gravel. She lifted her head and was blinded by the white monster-light. The monster made its roaring sound, but it wasn't moving now.

"What happened?" it hollered, sounding frightened. "What are you kids doing where we are harvesting? Did we hit someone? . . . Oh, little child!"

Willie Bea saw a man in the light. He knelt beside her. "Did the combines scare you, child? We might've run you over!"

Willie Bea was damp and clammy from the gathering cold and mist. Tired and confused, she closed her eyes. Her insides flopped and the inky night of a dizzying universe returned.

It was Monday, the day after. Willie Bea was lying down. There was school, of course, but she didn't go. She had a knot in the center of her forehead as big as a walnut, and it felt bigger than that. They said that one of her stilts hit her as she fell to the ground.

The town doctor, Dr. Taylor, had come to fix her up, at the start of a long, wakeful night — last night. Willie Bea remembered most of it in a kind of dreamy reverie. Her mama and papa telling her things last night sometime. She remembered now, she had the feeling then that they all, even Dr. Taylor, thought she might feel ashamed of herself. Feel foolish, like her mama and papa did. But she didn't. And they were telling her that what they called men from Mars, and what Toughy Clay had called an invasion, *hadn't happened.* That the whole thing, the panic and all, *had been nothing more than a radio play!* On a radio show.

How could that be nothing more than a radio play? she

thought, pulling the covers up over her face. She had the proof of the Kelly farm. What kind of radio play would have the Kelly farm on it!

What I saw wasn't a play or a show, Willie Bea thought, shivering under the covers. The noise I heard. The great white eyes I saw. And *them*, talking to me! Toughy was there, he said it was an invasion. He saw it all. Talked to me right in my ear!

Willie Bea closed her eyes again. A scene flooded the dark redness behind her eyes. She couldn't seem to dam it up and hold it back. There was the white eye of the monster.

No! "Dum-de-dum-de-dum!" Willie Bea hummed, so it would go away. Looking around her room, it was so nice to be safe at home. Warm and safe! With covers and a mama to bring you buttered toast.

Willie Bea's papa came home a little late. She woke up when he came in. "Papa," she said sleepily, "hey."

"Hey, Willie Bea?" said her good papa. "How're you feelin' now?"

"Oh, okay," she said.

He folded her close. She snuggled on his shoulder, wrapped her arms around him. "You had yourself a time last night, didn't you?" he said gently.

"Oh, Papa, don't scold me, please!" she pleaded. Great tears filled her eyes and slid down her cheeks.

"Now, don't cry," her papa said. "I'm not gonna scold — that would be like closin' the barn door after the herd has snuck away. I guess you are just my adventuresome one. You have to go and see."

"Well, I do," she said, leaning back to look at her papa. She wiped her eyes.

"I was just worried you might get yourself hurt out there.

The foreman of the Kelly farm, a Mr. Branner, was here just now," her papa said.

"Goodness!" said Willie Bea.

"You know what a foreman is?" her papa asked.

"The one who runs that Kelly farm," she said.

"Yes, and he was worried about you," her papa said.

"He was?" said Willie Bea, eyes wide, all thought of tears vanished.

"What was all right about him," said her papa, "was that he wasn't peeved that you were out there on private property. He knew I knew you shouldn't have been there. He was just upset at the thought of what might have happened. You see, he and his men were harvesting corn. They, or the Kellys either, didn't know anything was going on. Nobody over there had a radio on."

"Well, it was sure nice he came by."

Her papa paused and took something from the inside pocket of his jacket.

"The foreman showed me that, said I could borrow it to show you," her papa said, as Willie Bea looked at the pamphlet. "Says about those new combine machines they have over there at the Kelly place. Cost a fortune, each one of them. And they are the newest farm machines anywhere, and they are right there over at the Kellys'."

He paused again. "Willie Bea. I brought you all of the papers telling about last night. You weren't the only one seeing monsters. Seems like the whole country was in an uproar."

"But it was just a radio play," her papa went on. "Even *I* got caught up in it." He grinned sheepishly. "Boy, what an imagination can do to you, I'll tell ya! The fellow — Orson Welles is his name — put on a radio show. A radio

587

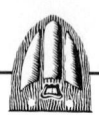

play of this writer's, H. G. Wells's *War of the Worlds*. And folks thought it was real. You look, Willie Bea, it's all there in the newspapers," her papa said, "all that Aunt Leah told us. She heard the radio play, that was all."

"Willie Bea," he said, "I'm not telling you what to believe. I am showing you the facts. And the facts are the truth."

With that, her papa gave her a look of love, of sympathy, and went out, closing her door behind him.

Willie Bea sat still. She had to think. Her papa; all the papers; this pamphlet. She had to look at it, had to see it. You couldn't avoid facts, her papa always did say.

Combine was what it was about, that pamphlet. Right on the front was a drawing of the latest combine design, with a man at its steering wheel, and all of its parts named.

What a combine did was cut a standing crop of grain. Then it separated the grain. (Willie Bea read this inside the pamphlet.) It threshed the grain, and discarded the straw and the husks. The combine that was pictured on the front of the pamphlet was self-propelled. It could cut a crop twenty feet wide at one time. And it could harvest an acre in from five to eight minutes.

Goodness! Willie Bea thought. Even she, who had known nothing about a thing called a combine yesterday, knew today that it was a wondrous machine. A whole acre!

But it was something else about it that really caught her eye. The combine had an auger on one side of it, like a very large stovepipe about twenty feet long. It was used when the machine was ready to unload the corn into the waiting wagons or trucks. Willie Bea stared at it.

The unloading auger went up so high and out away from the combine on a slant. Such a long, long neck it had. At the end of the neck was this peculiar shape, like a triangle.

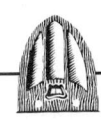

There had been the monster as big as life. Just a silly farm machine. It was almost impossible to believe. But facts were facts.

She felt pretty awful. Not so much from bumps and bruises, but from having to face herself.

"I think I made a fool of myself," she told herself. Sadness came over her and she felt as lonely as she could be. She forced herself to look at a newspaper. The Xenia, Ohio, paper, October 31, 1938.

"That's today," she said out loud.

"MARS INVADES U.S.," she read the lead headline in a whisper, "BUT BY BROADCAST."

The paper went on to say that the radio program caused thousands of people in every part of the country to believe that the eastern United States had been invaded by creatures from the planet Mars.

Willie Bea skipped part of the account. *"Several persons came forward to swear they saw the rocket land and strange creatures climb out of it."*

Well, I'm not the only one, she thought. She didn't feel so bad then. Other folks saw things, too.

"In Newark, N. J., hundreds fled from two city blocks, carrying what possessions they could snatch up." Well, I'll be! she thought.

"Telegraph companies reported that they were delivering telegrams from as distant as California inquiring of the fate of relatives."

Willie Bea read on. The last account of the Mars invasion Willie Bea read came clear from New York, the paper said.

"*The New York Times* reported that it had received a telephone call from a man in Dayton, Ohio . . ." Well, I'll be! Only eighteen miles from here, Dayton. *". . . who wanted to know what time the world was going to end."*

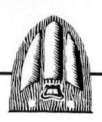

Just like Aunt Leah, Willie Bea thought. Aunt Leah had kept saying the world was coming to an end.

Willie Bea laid the paper aside. Leaned back and closed her eyes.

Somebody came near. She felt the presence sit down gently beside her.

"Willie Beatrime," she dreamed someone called. Mama? Papa?

"Willie Beatrime, wake up!"

Willie Bea came to, but she kept her eyes closed. Huh?

Suddenly, Willie Bea was aware of a scent sweeter than powdered sachet. It was a scent finer than the smell of roses in summer.

No. It couldn't be. "Aunt Leah?" Willie Bea opened her eyes. "Oh, my goodness, it *is* you!"

"Honey, and who else?" Aunt Leah said. There was laughter in her eyes.

Aunt Leah hugged her, kissed her cheek. She leaned back to study her niece's face, that nasty bump.

"Baby girl, you sure suffered, didn't you?"

"Yes," Willie Bea said, holding close.

"Well, don't worry. I've taken all the blame."

"What?" said Willie Bea

"Gettin' everybody all so excited." She watched Willie Bea. "I told your papa it was all my fault, too. Just now."

"They told me over home what happened to you," she went on. "I never knew you were the best of stilting in this whole county, Willie Beatrime."

"Me?" said Willie Bea.

"That's what everybody is sayin', baby. Didn't you know you were the best?"

Willie Bea thought about it. "Not until last night I didn't. I feel awful about what I did," Willie Bea went on. "Everything's just terrible! How will I ever face everybody, especially Papa?"

It was all too much for Willie Beatrime. She lifted Aunt Leah's slender fingers to her eyes and cried bitter tears into the palm of Leah's hand.

"Oh, now, baby, Willie Beatrime, don't do that. I can't stand to see my baby cry!" Aunt Leah said. She really sounded like she cared a lot about Willie Bea.

"Here, baby," Aunt Leah said, taking out a handkerchief. "Don't you cry any more. I can't stay too long. I've been all over the countryside today, seein' folks I upset last night." She grinned, and for the first time seemed slightly ashamed of herself. But quickly that look disappeared.

"Now listen to me, Willie Beatrime." Aunt Leah took Willie Bea by the chin and looked in her face. "You listenin'?"

Willie Bea nodded.

Aunt Leah said, her voice quiet and light as air, "Don't dismiss too soon. Know what I mean by that?"

Willie Bea shook her head. "No, Aunt Leah." She held the hankie tightly.

"I mean, don't think just because it was just a radio play, there was nothing to it. Don't think that because what you saw turned out to be *just* a combine, there wasn't something *behind* it."

"Wha . . . what, Aunt Leah?"

"Honey, when someone don't feel up to scratchin' in the ground with their hand, they will invent a hoe to reach for them that needs scratchin'. When a farmer can't cut the corn fast enough by hand, he'll go make him a *combine* machine to do it faster. Yes," sighed Aunt Leah.

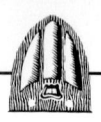

"Baby, do you get my drift?" she went on. "Think of it. Think of it as foretelling. Behind that *machine* of the radio and that *machine* of the combine and all so many folks just seein' monsters, Martians, things that *moved,* maybe was *them. Them* out there tryin' to tell us somethin'."

"Them?" whispered Willie Bea. "Them that talked to me?"

"Whoever talked to you," Aunt Leah said, "it was what was behind the talking. Talking is just a kind of machine for our use, too."

"For someday, sometime, we are going out there," Aunt Leah said. "Up there in the stars."

"Aunt Leah!"

"I mean it, girl," said Aunt Leah. "You just wait! Maybe not in my lifetime, but certainly in yours. Why was there ever a story, *War of the Worlds?* Because somebody realized that we are goin' out there. We will go out to the moon and beyond. We will go to Mars and all so many stars and places."

She smiled brightly at Willie Bea now. "Oooh, pretty Willie Beatrime! And I've got a surprise for you."

Aunt Leah took Willie Bea's face in her hands. Her eyes were deep and dark. She kissed Willie Bea's bump and whispered in her ear: "Don't ever say never!"

Aunt Leah got up. She waved at Willie Bea, although she was right there in front of her.

"Aunt Leah, do you have to go?"

Aunt Leah nodded. "Close your eyes. Don't open them until you count slowly to sixty. Okay?"

"Aunt Leah! What are you up to!"

Willie Bea closed her eyes, grinning from ear to ear. She was facing the bedroom door.

"Bye, Aunt Leah," she said, loud enough for Leah to hear. And then she counted. "One, two, three, four." Out loud. "Fifteen, sixteen, seventeen." All the way to sixty. It felt like a long time.

"Whew!" she said, and opened her eyes.

What she saw made her drop the hankie and cover her mouth with her hands. Hanging there on the back of the door was the most beautiful thing Willie Bea had ever seen in her life.

It was a costume. Of stars. Of sparkles like silver. It was pink and silver. It had a fine pink netting called tulle over the skirt and bodice. The netting was sprinkled with the silver sparkles. And there was a silver rim around the neck and sleeves, a wide silver band around the full silk skirt that stood out. Underneath the see-through tulle was silky pink. A real, silky pink dress of soft folds. It looked like new, and it was, of course.

"Oh, it's beautiful!" sighed Willie Bea. There was a pink mask looped over the hanger by its rubber band. There was a pink wand made out of hard cardboard. The wand was sprinkled with silver stars, she saw, peeking down at it.

"And what's this?" Tenderly, Willie Bea lifted down her dress. She had to stand on tiptoes to do it. Behind her dress were two more sacks covering something.

"A costume for Bay Sister and one for Bay Brother!" She couldn't tell for sure, but she thought Bay's was a pirate and Bay Sister's a gypsy girl.

"Oh, Aunt Leah!" Willie Bea shook her head, she was so thankful.

Then she noticed a note pinned to the paper.

"What in the world!" She put the dress on the bed and took out the pin.

"From Aunt Leah," Willie Bea said. *"Dear WB,"* she read, *"Wave your magic wand and anything can happen. For next year, Halloween."* It was signed, *"Aunt Leah."*

Willie Bea stared at the note. She felt down in the sack. Took out the magic wand. She looked at it long and hard. And waved it. And waved it more.

"Nothin' happened," she said. She shook the wand hard, but nothing occurred that she could see. "Maybe somewhere, something's happening," she told herself. "I know! The note said, *'For next year.'* Wait until next year, when I wave my wand." She laughed. Do you believe that? she thought. "Well, why not? Anything can happen!" She laughed her head off.

Discuss the Selection

1. What did Willie Bea want to do when she thought the Martians had landed?
2. How was Willie's "sighting" of the Martians similar to others' reactions?
3. When you read the story, what did you think Willie Bea was really seeing at the Kelly farm? Did you think she was seeing Martians? Explain your answer.
4. What did Aunt Leah mean when she told Willie Bea that what had happened was "foretelling"?
5. When did Willie Bea find out what had really happened? Find that part of the story and reread it.

Apply the Skills

Knowing the setting—where and when a story takes place—helps you to understand the story better. Setting also helps to set the mood of a story.

Think about the setting in "Willie Bea and the Time the Martians Landed." Then answer the following questions:

1. How did the setting of the story help to make the characters' fear of the Martian landing believable?
2. How did the setting of the story help to explain why Willie Bea had never seen a combine?

Thinking About "Tomorrows"

You have just had a look into the world of tomorrow — by way of science fact and science fiction. The world of tomorrow is rapidly becoming the world of today. Both science and science fiction help us think about the future in exciting new ways. Science gives us the facts upon which to build technological advances. Science fiction provides us with worlds, creatures, and galaxies about which we can dream.

In this unit, you read about the future as imagined by people from the past. Tom Edison's seemingly outlandish visions of electric lights, moving pictures, and the phonograph came true. Many of John E. Watkins's predictions from 1900 have become the reality of the 1980's.

Computers, robots, and space travel once existed only in science fiction. Today they are a part of our everyday lives. But will science ever make it possible to actually "miniaturize" people? Will we ever have a Time Machine in which we can visit ancient peoples? Will there be resort hotels on the moons of the planet Saturn? The answers to these questions still belong to the future. Who knows? As Willie Bea's Aunt Leah would say, "Don't ever say never!"

1. "Fantastic Voyage" described a voyage through the human body. "Let's Take a Trip into Space" described a trip on the space shuttle. How is traveling through the human body like traveling in space? How is it different? What are the dangers in both places?

2. Think about the real and imaginary scientists in this unit: Tom Edison and the characters in "Fantastic Voyage." What character traits did these scientists have in common? What do you think it takes to be a good scientist?

3. Which of the characters in this unit would you most like to meet? Why?

4. How can such inventions as robots, computers, and space shuttles make our lives better? What are some problems associated with these inventions?

5. Willie Bea's world in Ohio was full of love and family customs. It was very much like the world that the Time Children visited. Willie Bea was happy in her world. Two of the Time Children ran away to be a part of that kind of world. List the things that are good and desirable about that world as described in the two stories.

6. If you could travel in a Time Machine, what period of time would you choose to visit? Why?

7. Both "Time in Thy Flight" and "Saturn Rising" described a vision of what the future will be. Briefly summarize each vision of tomorrow. Then tell which one you'd like to see come to pass.

Read On Your Own

Other Worlds, Other Beings by Stanley W. Angrist. Crowell. Is there life on other planets? What might aliens look like? How might one go about talking to aliens? Angrist looks into these questions and others in this far-ranging book.

Fantastic Voyage by Isaac Asimov. Bantam. The exciting story of five people, reduced almost to the size of atoms, who journey into a human body on a lifesaving mission.

Robert Goddard, Space Pioneer by Anne P. Dewey. Little, Brown. A biography of Robert Goddard, the "father of modern rocketry." This is the interesting story of early rockets and someone whose dreams made science fiction come true.

Flying the Space Shuttles by Don Dwiggins. Dodd, Mead. What is it like to fly in a space shuttle? How do space shuttles work? How will shuttles be used in the future? Read more about these cargo ships of tomorrow.

Science Fiction Tales — Invaders, Creatures, and Alien Worlds edited by Roger Elwood. Rand McNally. Journeys through time and space, trips to worlds where dragons are ridden like horses, and visits from aliens who take the form of cats — these adventures all await the readers of this book.

The Trouble With Tribbles by David Gerrold. Ballantine. The account of what happens when you put 1,771,561 small furry animals — tribbles — on board an interstellar star ship. Once they are on board, how do you get them off?

Willie Bea and the Time the Martians Landed by Virginia Hamilton. Greenwillow Books. It is October 30, 1938. Willie Bea's beautiful aunt drives up in her red convertible and announces that Martians will be dropping in too! The complete action-packed story of Willie Bea's adventure.

The Fallen Spaceman by Lee Harding. Harper & Row. A tiny alien, left behind by the ship he was repairing, falls to earth in a computerized spacesuit the size of an office building.

But We Are Not of Earth by Jean E. Karl. Dell. Four teenagers set out across the galaxy in search of new earthlike planets. They find their mission threatened by their own advisor.

Sally Ride and the New Astronauts: Scientists in Space by Karen O'Connor. Franklin Watts. Curious about today's astronauts or how to become one yourself? This book answers all kinds of questions about real space travelers.

The Robots Are Here by Dr. Alvin Silverstein and Virginia Silverstein. Prentice Hall. Robots that arm wrestle, robot seeing-eye dogs, and robots that conduct experiments are all on display in this fascinating book.

The Kids' Whole Future Catalog by Paul Taylor. Random House. Would you like to live in a city that floats or one that's a mile high? Read about eating worm cookies, robots that clean your house, and other ideas of the future . . . and find out where to get more information.

Glossary

The glossary is a special dictionary for this book. The glossary tells you how to spell a word, how to pronounce it, and what the word means.

A blue box ■ at the end of the entry tells you that an illustration is given for that word.

The following abbreviations are used throughout the glossary: *n.*, noun; *v.*, verb; *adj.*, adjective; *adv.*, adverb; *interj.*, interjection; *prep.*, preposition; *conj.*, conjunction; *pl.*, plural; *sing.*, singular.

An accent mark (′) is used to show which syllable receives the most stress. For example, in the word *granite* [gran′ it], the first syllable receives more stress. Sometimes in words of three or more syllables, there is also a lighter mark to show that a syllable receives a lighter stress. For example, in the word *helicopter* [hel′ ə•kop′ tər], the first syllable has the most stress, and the third syllable has lighter stress.

The symbols used to show how each word is pronounced are explained in the "Pronunciation Key" on the next page.

Pronunciation Key*

a	add, map	m	move, seem	u	up, done
ā	ace, rate	n	nice, tin	û(r)	burn, term
â(r)	care, air	ng	ring, song	yo͞o	fuse, few
ä	palm, father	o	odd, hot	v	vain, eve
b	bat, rub	ō	open, so	w	win, away
ch	check, catch	ô	order, jaw	y	yet, yearn
d	dog, rod	oi	oil, boy	z	zest, muse
e	end, pet	ou	pout, now	zh	vision, pleasure
ē	equal, tree	o͝o	took, full	ə	the schwa, an unstressed vowel representing the sound spelled
f	fit, half	o͞o	pool, food		a in *above*
g	go, log	p	pit, stop		e in *sicken*
h	hope, hate	r	run, poor		i in *possible*
i	it, give	s	see, pass		o in *melon*
ī	ice, write	sh	sure, rush		u in *circus*
j	joy, ledge	t	talk, sit		
k	cool, take	th	thin, both		
l	look, rule	*th*	this, bathe		

*The Pronunciation Key and the short form of the key that appears on the following right-hand pages are reprinted from the *HBJ School Dictionary,* copyright © 1985 by Harcourt Brace Jovanovich, Inc.

A a

a·bil·i·ty [ə·bil′ə·tē] *n., pl.* **a·bil·i·ties** Quality of being able; power to perform or do.

ac·ci·den·tal·ly [ak′sə·den′təl·lē] *adv.* In an unexpected or unplanned manner; by chance: I discovered this wonderful book *accidentally*.—**ac·ci·dent·al** *adj.*

A·chil·les [ə·kil′ēz] *n.* In Greek legends, a great Greek hero of the Trojan War. He was killed by an arrow shot into his heel, which was the only place he could be hurt.

A·chil·les ten·don [ə·kil′ēz ten′dən] *n.* A tough band of tissue at the back of the leg; it joins the muscle of the calf to the heel bone.

ac·knowl·edged [ak·nol′ijd] *adj.* Agreed upon by all; generally accepted as true: Don was the *acknowledged* leader of the glee club.

ac·me [ak′mē] *n.* The highest point; peak: Winning an Oscar was the *acme* of her career.

ad·dled [ad′(ə)ld] *adj.* Confused, muddled.

ad·mire [ad·mīr′] *v.* **ad·mired** To look up to; approve of.

ag·i·ta·tion [aj′ə·tā′shən] *n.* Excitement; nervousness; state of being upset or troubled.

ag·o·ny [ag′ə·nē] *n., pl.* **ag·on·ies** Painful, terrible suffering.

air·far·er [âr′fâr′ər] *n.* A traveler by air.

al·ien [āl′yən *or* ā′lē·ən] *n.* A person or being of another country or another place; sometimes an extraterrestrial being.

al·ter·nate [ôl′tər·nit] *adj.* Every other one by turns; first one and then the other.

am·a·teur [am′ə·choor *or* am′ə·t(y)oor] *adj.* Done as a participant in an art, science, sport, or other activity for enjoyment, not for money: an *amateur* scientist.

am·bu·lance [am′byə·ləns] *n.* A vehicle especially equipped to carry sick or injured persons.

an·cient [ān′shənt] *adj.* Of times that are long gone by; a long time ago: *ancient* history.

an·gle [ang′əl] *n.* A surface or line that slopes or slants.

an·guished [ang′gwisht] *adj.* Full of great suffering of mind or body; distressed: He gave an *anguished* cry.

an·nounce·ment [ə·nouns′mənt] *n.* A public statement; something made known, such as details about an event.

an·te·date [an′ti·dāt′] *v.* To come or happen before: Scrolls *antedate* books that have pages sewn at one side.

an·te·room [an′ti·room′] *n.* A small room leading to a larger one.

an·ti·ma·cas·sar [an′tē·mə·kas′ər] *n.* A piece of fabric put high on the back of a seat or chair to prevent soiling.

an·ti·pol·lu·tion [an′tē·pə·loo′shən] *adj.* Designed to reduce or eliminate pollution: The new *antipollution* law will go into effect soon.

an·tique [an·tēk] *adj.* Very old; made a long time ago, used especially about something of value: That *antique* vase is worth thousands of dollars.

an·ti·sep·tic [an′ti·sep′tik] *n.* A substance that prevents infection by stopping the growth of germs: Iodine is an *antiseptic*.

an·ti·so·cial [an′ti·sō′shəl] *adj.* Opposed to ordinary friendliness and social companionship.

anx·i·e·ty [ang·zī′ə·tē] *n.* A feeling of worry or fear about what may happen: Thunder always causes Tom great *anxiety*.

ap·par·ent·ly [ə·par′ənt·lē] *adv.* In a manner that seems plain to see or understand: *Apparently*, we are the first to arrive for the picnic.—**ap·par·ent** *adj.*

ap·peal [ə·pēl′] *v.* To have attraction for; interest: Would that teddy bear *appeal* to a four-year-old child?

ap·pli·ance [ə·plī′əns] *n.* A machine for doing a particular job: Vacuum cleaners, food processors, and steam irons are *appliances*.

ap·ply [ə·plī′] *v.* **ap·plied** To put on: He *applied* the wallpaper in less than a day.

apron   blizzard

a·pron [ā′prən] *n.* In a theater, the part of the stage in front of the curtain.

ar·chi·tect [är′kə·tekt] *n.* A person who designs and makes plans for buildings and sees that the plans are carried out.

ar·range [ə·rānj′] *v.* **ar·ranged** To bring about an agreement or plan: to *arrange* a party.

ar·ri·val [ə·rī′vəl] *n.* The act of arriving at, or coming to, a place.

as·sist [ə·sist′] *v.* To give help to: He *assisted* her with the decorations for the party.

as·ton·ish·ing [ə·ston′ish·ing] *adj.* Amazing; surprising: Her quickness of mind is *astonishing.*—**as·ton·ish·ing·ly** *adv.*

au·thor·i·ty [ə·thôr′ə·tē] *n.* The power to command or make decisions.

a·void [ə·void′] *v.* To stay away from; to stay out of the way of: I try to *avoid* crowds.

a·wait [ə·wāt′] *v.* **a·wait·ing** To wait for; to look forward to or expect.

awe-in·spir·ing [ô′-in·spīr′ing] *adj.* Arousing feelings of great wonder or, sometimes, fear: The colored leaves in the fall are *awe-inspiring.*

B b

baf·fled [baf′əld] *adj.* Confused, puzzled.

ban [ban] *v.* **banned** To forbid or prohibit, particularly by law: Horseback riding is *banned* in the park.

bark [bärk] *v.* **barked, bark·ing** To injure by banging and scraping the skin off: I *barked* my shins on the fence as I ran by it.

ba·sic [bā′sik] *adj.* Forming a basis or foundation for; fundamental: Flour is the *basic* ingredient of bread.

ba·ton [bə·ton′] *n.* A thin stick or wand used by the conductor of a band or orchestra to count the beat and direct the performance.

bea·con [bē′kən] *n.* A light, such as a fire, used as a signal to guide or warn.

bel·fry [bel′frē] *n.* The part of a tower or steeple in which a bell or bells are hung.

bench [bench] *v.* To remove a player from a game.

bi·ol·o·gy [bī·ol′ə·jē] *n.* The science that studies living things, both plants and animals.

bis·cuit [bis′kit] *n.* A kind of bread baked in small cakes; cookie.

bit·ter·ly [bit′ər·lē] *adv.* Very unpleasantly; painfully, stingingly: It was a *bitterly* cold day.

blimp [blimp] *n.* A kind of passenger-carrying balloon that is filled with gas that is lighter than air.

bliz·zard [bliz′ərd] *n.* A heavy, driving snowstorm accompanied by strong winds and extremely cold temperatures.

a add	i it	o͞o took	oi oil
ā ace	ī ice	o͞o pool	ou pout
â care	o odd	u up	ng ring
ä palm	ō open	û burn	th thin
e end	ô order	yo͞o fuse	th this
ē equal			zh vision

ə = { **a** in *above*   **e** in *sicken*   **i** in *possible*
      o in *melon*   **u** in *circus* }

603

boundary — chain mail

bound·a·ry [boun′də·rē *or* boun′drē] *n.* Something, as a line or mark, that forms the outside edges of an area.

boun·ti·ful [boun′tə·fəl] *adj.* Generous; plentiful; abundant.

bow¹ [bou] *v.* To bend the head or body as in greeting.

bow² [bō] *n.* A knot with loops in it.

bril·liant [bril′yənt] *adj.* Splendid; very distinguished: Dr. Chung is a *brilliant* surgeon.

broad·cast [brôd′kast′] *v.* **broad·cast·ing** To make known over a wide area, as though sent over radio or television: to *broadcast* news.

broc·co·li [brok′ə·lē] *n.* A green vegetable of the cabbage family.

browse [brouz] *v.* To eat by nibbling here and there on growing grass, leaves, shoots, or other vegetation.

bun·gle [bung′gəl] *v.* **bun·gled** To do clumsily and badly: to *bungle* a job.

burn out [burn′out′] *v.* **burn·ing out** To use up one's physical or emotional strength.

bus·tle [bus′(ə)l] *v.* **bus·tled** To hurry about busily and excitedly.

butch·er [bŏŏch′ər] *v.* **butch·ered** To kill animals or poultry for food.

C c

ca·boose [kə·bōōs′] *n.* The last car on a freight train, for the use of the train crew.

cal·cu·la·tion [kal·kyə·lā′shən] *n.* Careful planning in advance.

cam·paign [kam·pān′] *n.* A set of activities designed to get something done or to obtain some result: The mayor is starting a clean-up *campaign* for the city.

ca·nal [kə·nal′] *n.* A waterway built to carry ships where they could not otherwise go.

ca·pac·i·ty [kə·pas′ə·tē] *n.* Talent; ability; skill at learning or doing something: He has a great physical *capacity* for gymnastics.

cap·tion [kap′shən] *n.* Written matter placed near or under a picture and describing it.

car·bon di·ox·ide [kär′bən dī·ok′sīd] *n.* An odorless, colorless gas composed of carbon and oxygen. Animals breathe it out; plants take it up from the air and use it to make food.

car·ni·vore [kär′nə·vôr′] *n.* An animal that eats meat.

cat·call [kat′kôl′] *n.* A loud call or whistle to show disapproval of a performer or performance.

cave [kāv] *n.* A hollow space below the surface of the earth, especially one with an opening to the outside.

cen·sus [sen′səs] *n.* An official count of all the people living in a country or some smaller area. Information taken in the census includes the number of people in each household, their ages, the number of each sex, the job each person holds, and so on.

chain mail [chān′ māl′] *n.* A type of armor made of small loops or rings of iron or steel linked together.

604

chairperson   compliments

chair·per·son [châr′pûr′sən] *n.* Someone who heads a committee: The *chairperson* will call the meeting to order.

chan·de·lier [shan′də·lir′] *n.* A lighting fixture that has branches for several lights and that hangs from the ceiling.

chan·dler [chan′dlər] *n.* A dealer who sells supplies and groceries for use on ships.

cir·cuit [sûr′kit] *n.* The arrangement of wires, tubes, and other parts that form an electrical connection or hookup.

cir·cuit break·er [sûr′kit brā′kər] *n.* A switch that cuts off electricity automatically in a circuit when there is an overload of current or a short circuit.

cir·cu·la·to·ry sys·tem [sûr′kyə·lə·tôr′ē sis′təm] *n.* The system of veins, arteries, heart, and lymphatic vessels that pump and transport blood and lymph through the body.

clam·or [klam′ər] *n.* A loud continuing noise.

clap·trap [klap′trap′] *n.* Empty nonsense.

clear·ing [klir′ing] *n.* An area in the woods that has been cleared of trees.

clus·ter [klus′tər] *v.* To grow close together or form into a group: Water lilies were *clustered* at one end of the pond.

coax·ing [kōks′ing] *n.* Persuasion by gentle urging or bribery: The dog would only come after much *coaxing*.

co·in·ci·dence [kō·in′sə·dəns] *n.* An occurrence by chance of two things at the same time or place, in such a way that the occurrence seems remarkable: Both of them being in Rome at the same time was a *coincidence*.

co·lo·ni·al [kə·lō′nē·əl] *adj.* Of or having to do with the original thirteen British colonies that formed the United States of America.

com·mis·sion·aire [kə·mish′ə·nâr′] *n.* A word used mostly by the British for a uniformed attendant who performs a service.

com·mit [kə·mit′] *v.* **com·mit·ted** To do or to perform something, usually something wrong, such as a crime.

com·mu·ni·cate [kə·myōō′nə·kāt′] *v.* To give or exchange information, words, or messages; to send and receive words and ideas.

com·mu·ni·ca·tions [kə·myōō′nə·kā′shənz] *n.* The means of sending messages, such as telephone, telegraph, radio, television, and so on.

com·pan·ion [kəm·pan′yən] *n.* Comrade; friend.

com·pa·ra·ble [kom′pər·ə·bəl] *adj.* Capable of being compared; being similar enough to provide a reason for comparing.

com·par·a·tive [kəm·par′ə·tiv] *adj.* Relative to other things when estimated by comparison: After a noisy morning there was *comparative* quiet in the afternoon.

com·pass [kum′pəs *or* kom′pəs] *n.* An instrument that shows directions, especially one with a magnetic needle that points north to the north magnetic pole.

com·plain [kəm·plān′] *v.* To object or protest; to express dissatisfaction; to find fault.

com·pli·ca·tion [kom′plə·kā′shən] *n.* Something, usually unexpected, that causes a difficulty, a problem, or a change.

com·pli·ments [kom′plə·mintz] *n., pl.* Courtesy. This word is used in the phrase *with the compliments of,* meaning "given with no charge": Take this book with the *compliments* of the author.

a	add	i	it	o͞o	took	oi	oil
ā	ace	ī	ice	o͞o	pool	ou	pout
â	care	o	odd	u	up	ng	ring
ä	palm	ō	open	û	burn	th	thin
e	end	ô	order	yo͞o	fuse	th	this
ē	equal					zh	vision

ə = { **a** in *above*   **e** in *sicken*   **i** in *possible*
     o in *melon*   **u** in *circus* }

605

com·pu·ter [kəm·pyōō′tər] *n.* A machine, usually electronic, that can solve problems and compile, store, and retrieve information.

con·cave [kon·kāv′ *or* kon′kāv′] *adj.* Hollowed or curved inward like the inside of a bowl.

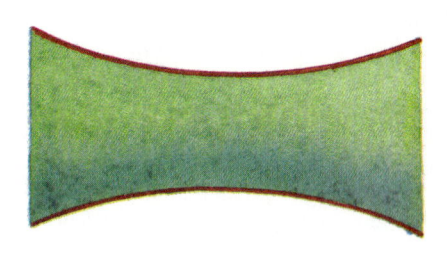

con·cen·tra·tion [kon′sən·trā′shən] *n.* The act of concentrating. Giving full attention to a task or subject.

con·cise [kən·sīs′] *adj.* Expressing a lot while using only a few words.

con·crete [kon′krēt *or* kon·krēt′] *n.* A building and paving material made of cement, gravel, sand, and water.

con·fer·ence [kon′fər·əns *or* kon′frəns] *n.* A meeting for the purpose of discussing a particular subject: a *conference* on world hunger.

con·flict [kon′flikt] *n.* In literature, the struggle in a situation between two or more characters, within one character's personality, or between a character and society or the environment.

con·ser·va·tion [kon′sər·vā′shən] *n.* The protection, as of natural resources, from waste, decay, or overuse.

con·stit·u·ent [kən·stich′ōō·ənt] *n.* A voter; a person who helps elect a government officer.

con·struc·tion [kən·struk′shən] *n.* The act of building a building.

con·ti·nu·i·ty [kon′tə·nōō′ə·tē *or* kon′tə·nyōō′ə·tē] *n.* The quality of being continuous or of going on without interruption.

con·tort [kən·tôrt′] *v.* To twist out of shape: The acrobat *contorted* her body into fantastic shapes.

con·trac·tor [kon′trak·tər] *n.* A person or business that agrees, or contracts, to provide materials and do a job for a stated price.

con·trib·ute [kən·trib′yōōt′] *v.* **con·trib·ut·ing** To take part in; to give money or help a cause.

con·ven·ient [kən·vēn′yənt] *adj.* Suited to easy use; handy.

con·vert [kən·vûrt′] *v.* To cause someone to change to a new belief or religion from another one or from none.

con·vey [kən·vā′] *v.* To communicate; to make known.

con·vinc·ing·ly [kən·vin′sing·lē] *adv.* In a persuasive manner; in a way that makes someone believe what is said.

cor·ne·a [kôr′nē·ə] *n.* The transparent outer coating of the eyeball; it covers the pupil and the iris.

cor·ner·stone [kôr′nər·stōn′] *n.* A stone at the corner of a building, especially one whose placement at the start of construction is accompanied by a ceremony.

cor·o·na·tion [kor′ə·nā′shən] *n.* A ceremony to crown a ruler.

cor·pus·cle [kor′pəs·əl] *n.* Any one of the red or white cells of the blood.

coun·ter·feit [koun′tər·fit] *adj.* Copied to look like something real but meant to deceive; false, but passed off as genuine: *counterfeit* money.

craft [kraft] *n.* A boat, ship, aircraft, or space vehicle.

crane [krān] *n.* A wading bird with a long neck, long legs, and a long pointed beak.

cran·ny [kran′ē] *n., pl.* **cran·nies** A small, narrow opening: We hid the note in a *cranny*.

cred·it [kred′it] *v.* **cred·it·ing** To give credit; to acknowledge something as the work or contribution of a particular person: Kay *credits* me with doing most of the work.

cre·vasse [krə·vas′] *n.* A deep crack or break, as in the ice of a glacier or in the ground during an earthquake.

cru·cial [krōō′shəl] *adj.* Very important; likely to have a significant result or effect.

cum·brous [kum′brəs] *adj.* Cumbersome; unwieldy; clumsy and hard to manage.

curt   displeasure

curt [kurt] *adj.* Short, abrupt, rude.

cus·toms [kus′təmz] *n.* The government agency that collects taxes on goods brought into a country from abroad.

D d

dam·age [dam′ij] *v.* To cause harm or injury to.

debt [det] *n.* A condition of owing something to someone else: Her kindness put me in her *debt*.

de·ceive [di·sēv′] *v.* To fool or mislead; to cause to believe something that is not true: You can easily *deceive* people with that story.

dec·o·rat·ed [dek′ə·rā′tid] *adj.* Made fancier or prettier by the addition of ornaments or trimmings.

de·duc·tion [di·duk′shən] *n.* A conclusion reached by reasoning or inferring; a shrewd guess based on inference.

de·fy [di·fī′] *v.* To stand up against; to resist.

de·ject·ed [di·jek′tid] *adj.* Unhappy; low in spirits; discouraged.

de·par·ture [di·pär′chər] *n.* The act of leaving.

de·scen·dant [di·sen′dənt] *n.* A person born of a particular family; offspring.

de·scent [di·sent′] *n.* The act of coming down from a high place to a lower one: The *descent* of the airplane was much too fast.

de·sign [di·zīn′] *n.* The selecting and arranging of parts (such as size, shape of lines, angles, use of space, and so on) in an art work.

des·per·a·tion [des′pə·rā′shən] *n.* A feeling of despair that leads someone into reckless behavior.

des·ti·na·tion [des′tə·nā′shən] *n.* The place to which one is traveling.

de·tec·tive [di·tek′tiv] *n.* Someone, often a police officer, whose job is to find information about and solve crimes.

de·ter·mi·na·tion [di·tûr′mə·nā′shən] *n.* Strength of character in carrying out a purpose; firmness; courage.

di·ag·o·nal [dī·ag′ə·nəl] *adj.* Extending from one corner or side of a four-sided figure to the opposite corner or side in a slanting direction: a *diagonal* line. ■

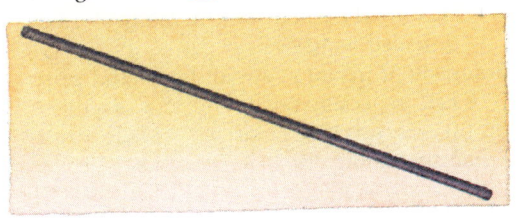

di·rec·tor [di·rek′tər or dī·rek′tər] *n.* A person in charge; someone who manages a group or an organization.

dis·a·bled [dis·ā′bəld] *adj.* Unable to perform normally because of illness or injury.

dis·as·ter [di·zas′tər] *n.* An event that causes great destruction or loss: Earthquakes and floods are *disasters*.

dis·close [dis·klōz′] *v.* **dis·closed** To make known: Reporters will never *disclose* a source of information.

dis·cord·ant [dis·kôr′dənt] *adj.* Harsh, jarring; not in harmony: From the beginner's band class came many *discordant* sounds.

dis·loy·al [dis·loi′əl] *adj.* Not loyal; not faithful; having no feeling of allegiance or devotion to someone or something: When Rae spoke of the school's faults, she felt *disloyal*.

dis·pleas·ure [dis·plezh′ər] *n.* Annoyance; dislike; disapproval; anger.

a	add	i	it	o͞o	took	oi	oil
ā	ace	ī	ice	o͞o	pool	ou	pout
â	care	o	odd	u	up	ng	ring
ä	palm	ō	open	û	burn	th	thin
e	end	ô	order	yo͞o	fuse	th	this
ē	equal					zh	vision

ə = { **a** in *above*   **e** in *sicken*   **i** in *possible*
     o in *melon*   **u** in *circus* }

607

douse · explanation

douse [dous] *v.* To throw water on.

drawl [drôl] *v.* **drawled** To speak in a slow way, making the vowel sounds especially long: Sue was uncertain of her facts, so she *drawled* her words, giving herself time to think.

duct [dukt] *n.* An opening, as a tube or passage, through which air or other things can pass: Air is carried through *ducts* in many buildings with sealed windows.

dun·geon [dun′jən] *n.* An underground prison or cell, especially one found in a castle.

du·pli·cate [d(y)o͞o′plə·kit] *adj.* Made exactly like something else: a *duplicate* key.

E e

ear·nest·ly [ûr′nist·lē] *adv.* In a serious, sincere manner.

e·col·o·gy [i·kol′ə·jē *or* ē·kol′ə·jē] *n.* The relationship between living things and their environment: *Ecology* is a balance between social groupings, natural enemies, light, temperature, food, water, and land.

ec·stat·ic [ek·stat′ik] *adj.* Full of joy or delight; greatly happy.

ed·i·tor [ed′i·tər] *n.* A person who decides on and prepares written material for publication.

ef·fi·cient·ly [i·fish′ənt·lē] *adv.* In a capable manner; in a way that produces results with little effort or waste.

e·lim·i·nate [i·lim′ə·nāt] *v.* To get rid of.

em·broi·der [im·broi′dər] *v.* To decorate with ornamental needlework.

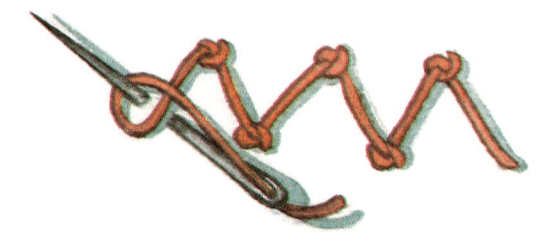

em·pire [em′pīr] *n.* A group of countries or nations held together by a single ruler or a single government.

en·am·eled [in·am′əld] *adj.* Covered with enamel that has been fused to metal by means of heat. It is often applied in many colors and in decorated designs: an *enameled* bracelet.

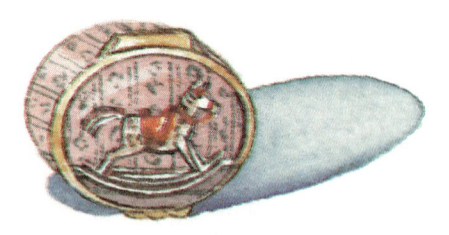

en·coun·ter [in·koun′tər] *n.* A meeting, especially an unexpected one.

en·er·gy [en′ər·jē] *n.* The force or power that makes anything move: The *energy* produced by solar panels warms our water.

en·gi·neer [en′jə·nir′] *n.* Someone who drives a locomotive.

en·ter·tain·ing [en′tər·tā′ning] *adj.* Amusing; giving enjoyment: The performance we saw last night was very *entertaining*.

en·vi·ron·men·tal [in·vī′rən·men′təl] *adj.* Having to do with the conditions and surroundings that affect the development of people, animals, and plants: Pollution may have long-term *enviromental* effects.

e·ra [ir′ə *or* ē′rə] *n.* A specific period of time in history: the colonial *era*.

es·sen·tial [ə·sen′shəl] *adj.* Extremely important; basic; necessary: Great care is *essential* in precision jobs such as watchmaking.

ex·ca·va·tor [eks′kə·vā′tər] *n.* A person or a machine that digs holes or scoops out dirt.

ex·haust [ig·zôst′] *v.* To become extremely tired; to use up completely: We *exhausted* our supply of water.

ex·pand·ing [ik·spand′ing] *adj.* Becoming larger; growing: Eating too many creampuffs is giving him an *expanding* waistline.

ex·pla·na·tion [eks′plə·nā′shən] *n.* The act or process of making understandable: I didn't

608

exuberant · friction

understand how the machine worked, so I asked for an *explanation*.

ex·u·ber·ant [ig·zōō'bər·ənt] *adj.* Overflowing with energy and high spirits: Winning the prize made Tomiko *exuberant*. —**ex·u·ber·ant·ly** *adv.*

F f

fa·cil·i·ty [fə·sil'ə·tē] *n.* Something, as a library or a school, that is designed, built, or established to serve a special purpose or to perform a service: This town needs a new garbage-disposal *facility*.

fac·tu·al [fak'chōō·əl] *adj.* Based on facts; made up of facts.

fan·ci·ful [fan'si·fəl] *adj.* Existing only in the imagination; unreal: The creature in the fun house was a *fanciful* animal with string for a mane and polka-dotted velvet for its hide.

fan·ta·sy [fan'tə·sē] *n.* A work or creation of the imagination.

fil·a·ment [fil'ə·mənt] *n.* A very thin thread or wire.

fin·ish line [fin'ish līn] *n.* The line or tape that marks the end of a race course: Hector was the first to cross the *finish line*.

flail [flāl] *v.* **flailed** To move about wildly, flapping one's arms.

flats [flatz] *n.* Lands such as marshes that are flat and level.

fleck [flek] *n.* A small spot or speck.

flick [flik] *v.* To move or strike at with a light, quick snap.

flim·flam [flim'flam] *v.* **flim·flammed** To cheat by making something appear real: The carnival barkers *flimflammed* the audience into believing there was a two-headed man inside the tent.

flip·pan·cy [flip'ən·sē] *n.* Speech or behavior that is pert and not respectful.

flue [flōō] *n.* A tube or pipe within a chimney through which smoke or hot air flows: One chimney may have several *flues*.

folktale [fōk'tāl'] *n.* A kind of folklore story with a simple plot and with ordinary people or animals as heroes.

fore·warn [fôr·wôrn'] *v.* **fore·warned** Warned beforehand or in advance.

for·mal [fôr'məl] *adj.* Following set rules and customs.

for·tu·nate [fôr'chə·nit] *adj.* Having or bringing good luck; lucky.

foun·da·tion [foun·dā'shən] *n.* A base that supports other things above it: The statue won't topple because the *foundation* it sits on is very firm.

foun·dry [foun'drē] *n.* A place where metals are melted and poured into molds.

fran·ti·cal·ly [fran'tik·lē] *adv.* **In a wildly nervous, excitable manner:** He searched *frantically* for the lost papers.

freight [frāt] *n.* Goods shipped by trains, ships, trucks, or airplanes.

fric·tion [frik'shən] *n.* A force of resistance produced when one object rubs against another object: A fire can be started by *friction*.

a	add	i	it	oo	took	oi	oil
ā	ace	ī	ice	ōō	pool	ou	pout
â	care	o	odd	u	up	ng	ring
ä	palm	ō	open	û	burn	th	thin
e	end	ô	order	yōō	fuse	th	this
ē	equal					zh	vision

ə = { **a** in *above* **e** in *sicken* **i** in *possible*
      o in *melon* **u** in *circus* }

609

fuse [fyo͞oz] *n.* A thin enclosed strip of metal that completes an electrical circuit. When an overload of current occurs, the metal strip melts and breaks the circuit.

G g

ga·lac·tic [gə·lak′tik] *adj.* Having to do with a galaxy, a group of millions of stars formed into a single system: Our solar system is part of a *galactic* group called the Milky Way.

ge·ol·o·gist [jē·ol′ə·jist] *n.* Someone who studies the origin, history, and structure of the earth, paying particular attention to rock formations.

ghet·to [get′ō] *n.* A part of a city into which people of a minority group or the very poor are crowded.

glid·er [glī′dər] *n.* A light aircraft that has no engine. It soars on air currents.

glow·er [glou′ər] *v.* To stare at someone angrily.

god [god] *n.* In myths, a male being whose supposed supernatural and superhuman powers were considered to be worthy of worship by people.

god·dess [god′is] *n.* In myths, a female being whose supposed supernatural and superhuman powers were considered to be worthy of worship by people.

grant [grant] *n.* A sum of money awarded for a particular purpose, such as study or research.

grav·i·ty [grav′ə·tē] *n.* A natural force that pulls objects toward the center of the earth and that causes objects to have weight: Things fall to the ground because of the pull of *gravity*.

gri·mace [gri·mās′ *or* grim′əs] *v.* To twist the face to express disgust, disapproval, or pain.

grouse [grous] *n.* Any of several small, plump game birds often hunted for sport.

grudg·ing [gruj′ing] *adj.* Unwilling; resentful.

guilt·i·ly [gil′tə·lē] *adv.* With a feeling of guilt, or of having committed a wrongdoing.

gul·li·ble [gul′ə·bəl] *adj.* Easily cheated; ready to be deceived.

gym·nas·tics [jim·nas′tiks] *n. pl.* Exercises for developing muscular strength and control. ■

H h

hand·i·capped [han′dē·kapt′] *adj.* Having a handicap; disabled.

haugh·ti·ly [hô′tə·lē] *adv.* In a scornful, self-satisfied, proud manner.

haz·ard·ous [haz′ər·dəs] *adj.* Full of danger; risky.

heart·beat [härt′bēt′] *n.* The pulsating sound that the heart makes.

her·bi·vore [(h)ûr′bə·vôr′] *n.* An animal that eats only plants.

herd [hûrd] *n.* A large group of animals, all of one kind, kept, fed, or moved together.

he·ro [hir′ō *or* hē′rō] *n., pl.* **he·roes** Someone admired for great deeds and for personal characteristics such as courage and nobility of spirit.

hon·or·ar·y [on′ə·rer′ē] *adj.* Given or done as a matter of respect.

hinge [hinj] *n.* A joint, usually of metal, with movable parts that allow a door, gate, cover, or lid to open and shut.

hur·ri·cane [hûr′ə·kān′] *n.* A storm that begins over a tropical ocean and has very heavy rains and violent whirling winds.

hyacinth   interference

hy·a·cinth [hī'ə·sinth] *n.* A fragrant spring flower related to the lily family with a cluster of bell-shaped flowers growing in a spike.

hys·ter·i·cal [his·ter'ə·kəl] *adj.* Showing unusual excitement or emotion.

I i

i·den·ti·ty [ī·den'tə·tē] *n.* The fact of being oneself and not another: Be proud of your *identity*.

ill·ness [il'nis] *n.* Sickness; bad health; disease.

im·ag·i·nar·y [i·maj'ə·ner'ē] *adj.* Occurring only in the imagination; not real.

im·mense [i·mens'] *adj.* Very large or huge.

im·pa·tient [im·pā'shənt] *adj.* Unwilling to put up with having to wait, things that annoy, opposition, or pain.

im·press [im·pres'] *v.* To have an effect on the thoughts or feelings: The speaker *impressed* me very favorably.

im·pres·sion [im·presh'ən] *n.* A feeling, notion, or idea: I got the *impression* that the math test would be easy.

im·prove [im·proōv'] *v.* To make better or to become better.

im·pu·ri·ty [im·pyoor'ə·tē] *n.* Something that prevents another thing from being pure: Be sure there is no *impurity* in your drinking water.

in·ad·ver·tent·ly [in'ad·vûr'tənt·lē] *adv.* Not on purpose; unintentionally.

in·cog·ni·to [in·kog'nə·tō *or* in'kog·nē'tō] *adj.* Having a concealed, or hidden, identity; in disguise.

in·cur [in·kûr'] *v.* **in·curred, in·cur·ring** To be the receiver of something unpleasant: We hoped to be able to perform without *incurring* the boos of the audience.

in·de·pen·dent [in'di·pen'dənt] *adj.* Acting and thinking for oneself; free.

in·dus·tri·al [in·dus'trē·əl] *adj.* Having to do with industry, or manufacturing.

in·fec·tion [in·fek'shən] *n.* The condition of sickness caused by a germ or virus: Colds and other *infections* are contagious.

in·fer [in·fûr'] *v.* To come to a conclusion by reasoning.

in·fer·ence [in'fər·əns] *n.* A conclusion arrived at through reasoning.

in·got [ing'gət] *n.* A mass of metal shaped into a bar or block so that it can be reworked later by melting, rolling, or hammering.

in·grat·i·tude [in·grat'ə·t(y)oōd'] *n.* The state of not being grateful or appreciative.

in·ject [in·jekt'] *v.* To force a substance into the body through a needle: The doctor *injected* the patient with an antibiotic.

ink·ling [ingk'ling] *n.* A hint; a slight notion or suggestion: I had an *inkling* of what the gift would be.

in·stall [in·stôl'] *v.* **in·stalled** To put something into place and make it ready for service or use: Don *installed* the air conditioner.

in·stance [in'stəns] *n.* A particular case or example.

in·su·la·tion [in'sə·lā·shən] *n.* Material used to cover, pack, or surround something to keep heat, electricity, or sound from leaking out.

in·sult [in·sult'] *v.* To speak scornfully or rudely to.

in·ter·fer·ence [in'tər·fir'əns] *n.* The act of meddling in someone else's business or of getting in the way.

a	add	i	it	o͞o	took	oi	oil
ā	ace	ī	ice	o͞o	pool	ou	pout
â	care	o	odd	u	up	ng	ring
ä	palm	ō	open	û	burn	th	thin
e	end	ô	order	yo͞o	fuse	<u>th</u>	this
ē	equal					zh	vision

ə = { **a** in *above*   **e** in *sicken*   **i** in *possible*
      o in *melon*   **u** in *circus* }

611

in·ter·rup·tion [in′tə·rup′shən] *n.* A break or stop for a time before continuing: There was an *interruption* in the TV drama so that the news could be broadcast immediately.

in·ter·view [in′tər·vyoō′] *n.* A meeting of two people for a special purpose, or a reporter asking questions of someone to get information for publication.

in·tro·duc·tion [in′trə·duk′shən] *n.* The act of making people acquainted with each other: A new visitor needs an *introduction*.

in·var·i·a·bly [in·vâr′ē·ə·blē] *adv.* Without varying or changing; with no exceptions: He *invariably* stopped at construction sites to watch the huge buildings being built.

in·va·sion [in·vā′zhən] *n.* Entry into a country or region by force with the purpose of conquering it: The armed forces defend us against foreign *invasion*.

in·ven·tion [in·ven′shən] *n.* Something thought about and brought into being for the first time: The *invention* of the airplane was a step in conquering space.

in·ves·ti·ga·tion [in·ves′tə·gā′shən] *n.* A careful search or inquiry to find out details or facts: The detective made a thorough *investigation* at the scene of the crime.

in·vis·i·ble [in·viz′ə·bəl] *adj.* Incapable of being seen; not visible: You can see otherwise *invisible* life forms through a microscope.

ir·ri·ta·bly [ir′ə·tə·blē] *adv.* In an annoyed, snappish, or angered manner: When ill, he always behaved *irritably*.

J j

jail·bird [jāl′bûrd′] *n.* An informal word for someone who is serving a term in a jail or a prison.

jeal·ous [jel′əs] *adj.* Fearful of losing someone's affection or love to another person: The child was *jealous* because she was afraid her parents would love her baby brother more.

jour·nal·ist [jûr′nəl·ist] *n.* Someone whose job is writing for, editing, or managing a newspaper or a magazine: Reporters and columnists are *journalists*.

ju·bi·lant [joō′bə·lənt] *adj.* Showing or expressing great joy or triumph: Jan and Bill were *jubilant* when they heard the good news.

jug·u·lar [jug′yə·lər] *n.* The jugular vein, one of the two major veins in the neck that return blood from the brain to the heart.

K k

khak·i [kak′ē *or* kä′kē] *n.* A strong cotton cloth of a greenish-brown color: *Khaki* is often used to make uniforms.

knowl·edge [nol′ij] *n.* That which is known or can be learned.

L l

lan·tern [lan′tərn] *n.* A case with transparent sides that holds a light: A *lantern* is a help on a dark and snowy night. ■

612

ledge   natural

ledge [lej] *n.* A narrow, shelflike piece of rock.

leg·en·dar·y [lej′ən·der·ē] *adj.* Connected with a story that has come down from earlier times and is sometimes thought to be partly true.

leg·is·la·ture [lej′is·lā·chər] *n.* A group of people that makes laws for a nation or state.

life·blood [līf′blud′] *n.* The vital force necessary to life: Voters are the *lifeblood* of a democracy.

log·ic [loj′ik] *n.* Sound reasoning: You can use *logic* to solve most problems.

lone·li·ness [lōn′lē·nəs] *n.* The quality or state of being alone.

lunge [lunj] *v.* **lunged** Make a quick movement forward.

M m

mag·got [mag′ət] *n.* An early wormlike stage in the development of an insect.

mag·ni·fy·ing glass [mag′nə·fī·ing glas] *n.* A lens that makes objects look larger.

man·u·script [man′yə·skript′] *n.* An original book or article written by hand or on a typewriter word processor.

mar·vel [mär′vəl] *v.* **mar·veled** To be astonished; to wonder: They *marveled* at the exhibit.

mas·sive [mas′iv] *adj.* Large or bulky.

maze [māz] *n.* A network of paths or passages designed to be very hard to follow: Once you enter a *maze*, it is almost impossible to find the center or the exit.

med·ley [med′lē] *n.* A jumble of unrelated sounds or things.

mem·brane [mem′brān′] *n.* A thin layer of tissue, covering certain parts of animals or plants.

mem·o·ra·bil·i·a [mem′ə·rə·bil′ē·ə] *n. pl.* Things worth remembering or records of them: She collected *memorabilia* of the Beatles.

mer·ry [mer′ē] *adj.* Joyous; gay.

mill [mil] *v.* **mil·ling** To move around without order or method.

mi·nor·i·ty [mə·nôr′ə·tē] *n.* A group of people in the population different from the larger group of which it is a part.

mis·sion·ar·y [mish′ən·er′ē] *n, pl.* **mis·sion·ar·ies** A person sent out to convert people to a religion.

mo·lec·u·lar [mə·lek′yə·lər] *adj.* Having to do with molecules, the smallest parts of an element or compound that can exist separately while still keeping their chemical properties.

mo·tion sick·ness [mō′shən sik′nes] *n.* Sickness, such as dizziness, resulting from motion during travel.

mus·cle [mus′əl] *n.* A bundle of fibrous tissue in the body that, by contraction and stretching, produces body movement.

myth [mith] *n.* A traditional story that explains something in nature or a past event: The story of how Pandora opened the box of troubles is a *myth*.

N n

nar·ra·tive [nar′ə·tiv] *n.* An account, story, or tale.

nat·u·ral [nach′ər·əl] *adj.* Produced by or existing in nature: Poison ivy contains a *natural* irritant.

a	add	i	it	o͞o	took	oi	oil
ā	ace	ī	ice	o͞o	pool	ou	pout
â	care	o	odd	u	up	ng	ring
ä	palm	ō	open	û	burn	th	thin
e	end	ô	order	yo͞o	fuse	th	this
ē	equal					zh	vision

ə = { a in *above*   e in *sicken*   i in *possible*
      o in *melon*   u in *circus* }

613

nausea — permit

nau·se·a [nô′zē·ə *or* nô′zhə] *n.* A sick feeling, accompanied by an urge to vomit.

nav·i·ga·tion [nav′ə·gā′shən] *n.* Charting the position or course of an aircraft or ship: Expert *navigation* is needed for today's aircraft.

nudge [nuj] *v.* **nudged** To push gently: He *nudged* the sleeping dog.

O o

o·blige [ə·blīj′] *v.* **o·bliged, o·blig·ing** To owe gratitude: We are much *obliged* to you for your help.

o·blig·ing·ly [ə·blī′jing·lē] *adv.* Kindly; politely: He *obligingly* got up so his grandmother could sit.

oc·cu·pant [ok′yə·pənt] *n.* Inhabitant; person who occupies a house or lands.

om·i·nous [om′ə·nəs] *adj.* Threatening or forbidding: an *ominous* cloud.

om·ni·vore [om′ni·vôr′] *n.* An animal that eats both meat and plants.

o·pin·ion [ə·pin′yən *or* ō·pin′yən] *n.* Something a person believes to be true; judgment: Do you have an *opinion* about the latest movies?

op·po·nent [ə·pō′nənt] *n.* A competitor; a person who resists or fights another.

op·pose [ə·pōz′] *v.* To be against a person or thing; resist; fight against.

op·ti·cal [op′ti·kəl] *adj.* Having to do with optics, the science that deals with light and its properties.

op·tic nerve [op′tik nûrv] *n.* The nerve that carries impulses between the brain and the eye, enabling one to see.

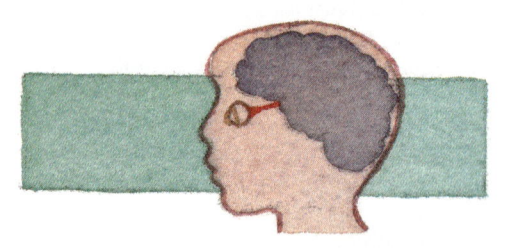

o·ral [ôr′əl] *adj.* Uttered through the mouth; spoken: an *oral* exam.

o·ral his·tor·y [ôr′əl *or* ō′rəl his′tə·rē] *n.* History

or·bit·ing [ôr′bit·ing] *adj.* Revolving around a center, as the moon.

or·di·nar·y [ôr′də·ner·ē] *adj.* Average; common; everyday.

or·gan·ic [ôr·gan′ik] *adj.* Fundamental; basically integrated with a system.

o·ver·load [ō′vər·lōd′] *v.* To put too large or too heavy a load on.

ox·y·gen [ok′sə·jin] *n.* A gas in the air necessary for breathing.

P p

pan·ic [pan′ik] *n.* Sudden, overwhelming fear.

pas·sive [pas′iv] *adj.* Quiet; not fighting openly against: *passive* resistance.

pat·tern [pat′ərn] *n.* Design.

peer [pir] *v.* **peered** To look closely; strain to see: We *peered* into the doghouse, looking for the puppies.

per·form [pər·fôrm′] *v.* **per·form·ing** To carry out; accomplish.

per·il·ous [per′əl·əs] *adj.* Risky; dangerous.

per·mit [pûr′mit] *n.* A license; an official document giving permission.

persistent   quiver

per·sis·tent [pər·sis′tənt] *adj.* Continuing firmly; lasting: a *persistent* illness.
pes·ter [pes′tər] *v.* **pes·tered** To annoy; bother.
phan·tom [fan′təm] *n.* A ghost.
phar·ma·cist [fär′mə·sist] *n.* A person licensed to prepare and sell drugs to fill doctors' prescriptions.

pip [pip] *n.* A small fruit seed.
plain·tive [plān′tiv] *adj.* Sad; mournful: a *plaintive* tune.
plug [plug] *n.* A flat cake of tobacco for chewing.
poi·son·ous [poi′zən·əs] *adj.* Containing poison; harmful.
pol·i·tics [pol′ə·tiks] *n. pl.* Affairs and activities of those already in or those trying to get into a government.
pop·py·cock [pop′ē·kok′] *n.* Meaningless talk; nonsense.
pop·u·lar [pop′yə·lər] *adj.* Liked by or suited to many people; well-liked.
pop·u·la·tion [pop′yə·lā′shən] *n.* The people living in a place.
prank [prangk] *n.* A playful trick.
pre·serve [pri·zûrv′] *v.* **pre·serv·ing** To keep unchanged; to maintain; to keep safe: to *preserve* old buildings.
prin·ci·pal [prin′sə·pəl] *adj.* Chief; main.
pri·vate [prī′vit] *adj.* Away from public view; secluded.
pro·ceed·ings [prə·sē′dingz] *n. pl.* Legal actions started in court.
pro·duc·tion line [prə·duk′shən līn] *n.* A system for assembling the parts of a product: Automobiles are produced on a *production* line.
pro·nounce [prə·nouns′] *v.* **pro·nounced** To make the sound or sounds of a word.

pro·posed [prə·pōzd′] *adj.* Put forward for acceptance or consideration.
pro·voke [prə·vōk′] *v.* **pro·voked** To stir up; annoy: A tiger will attack if *provoked*.
prow [prou] *n.* The pointed, forward end of a ship or boat.

prowl [proul] *v.* **prowl·ing** To roam about slyly, in search of food or something to steal.
pur·pose·ful [pûr′pəs·fəl] *adj.* For a purpose; intentional.

Q q

quiv·er [kwiv′ər] *v.* **quiv·er·ing** Trembling or shaking slightly.

a	add	i	it	o͞o	took	oi	oil
ā	ace	ī	ice	o͞o	pool	ou	pout
â	care	o	odd	u	up	ng	ring
ä	palm	ō	open	û	burn	th	thin
e	end	ô	order	yo͞o	fuse	th	this
ē	equal					zh	vision

ə = { a in *above*, e in *sicken*, i in *possible*, o in *melon*, u in *circus* }

615

R r

rage [rāj] *n.* Violent anger.
ram·shack·le [ram′shak′əl] *adj.* Rickety; about to fall apart: a *ramshackle* beach house.
ran·som [ran′səm] *adj.* Having to do with the price demanded for the release of a captive: a *ransom* note.
rate [rāt] *v.* **rat·ed** To give a value, ranking, or category to.
rat·tle [rat′(ə)l] *v.* **rat·tled** To speak rapidly; chatter.
re·ac·tion [rē·ak′shən] *n.* An action in response to something.
re·al·is·ti·cal·ly [rē′əl·is′tik·(ə·)lē] *adv.* In a lifelike, vivid way.
re·al·i·ty [rē·al′ə·tē] *n.* The real world of facts; true existence: What you see on television does not necessarily represent *reality*.
re·al·i·za·tion [rē′əl·i·zā′shən] *n.* A sudden understanding; the act of realizing.
re·bel [ri·bel′] *v.* To rise up in resistance; to oppose authority.
re·call [ri·kôl′] *v.* **re·called** To remember; bring to mind.
re·cep·tion desk [ri·sep′shən desk] *n.* A desk in an office or hotel where callers or guests are greeted. ■

reck·on [rek′ən] *v. informal* To guess; suppose: I *reckon* the train will be late.
rec·og·nize [rek′əg·nīz′] *v.* To be aware of; to understand as true: The world *recognized* Einstein's genius.

re·cord [rek′ərd] *n.* The best achievement recorded, as in a sport: That dive set a *record*.
re·frig·er·ate [ri·frij′ə·rāt′] *v.* To keep or make cold. **re·frig·er·a·tion** *n.*
re·ject [ri·jekt′] *v.* **re·ject·ed** To refuse to take.
rel·a·tive·ly [rel′ə·tiv·lē] *adv.* Comparatively; as compared with something else: *relatively* cold.
re·lent [ri·lent′] *v.* **re·lent·ing** To become gentler; to soften: Please *relent* and let us have a party.
re·luc·tant [ri·luk′tənt] *adj.* Unwilling; not eager.
REM Rapid eye movement. A type of sleep.
re·mark·a·ble [ri·mär′kə·bəl] *adj.* Extraordinary; unusual.
re·peat·ed [ri·pē′tid] *adj.* Done again and again; frequent.
rep·e·ti·tion [rep′ə·tish′ən] *n.* An act or operation performed again and again.
re·port·er [ri·pôr′tər] *n.* A person who reports the news. ■

rep·re·sen·ta·tive [rep′ri·zen′tə·tiv] *n.* An elected member of the House of Representatives in Washington, D. C., or of a state legislature.
re·quire·ment [ri·kwīr′mənt] *n.* Something needed or demanded.
re·search [ri·sûrch′ *or* rē′sûrch′] *n.* Careful study and investigation.
re·sent·ful [ri·zent′fəl] *adj.* Full of ill will and anger.
re·sign·ed·ly [ri·zī′nid·lē] *adv.* Patiently; submissively.
re·solve [ri·zolv′] *v.* **re·solved** To solve or make clear; to work out a solution.
re·source [ri·sôrs′ *or* rē′sôrs′] *n.* Something vital that can be used or drawn upon: Water is a natural *resource*.

616

respect / short circuit

re·spect [ri·spekt'] *v.* To treat with politeness; to honor.
re·treat [ri·trēt'] *v.* To withdraw.
re·un·ion [rē·yoon'yən] *n.* A meeting of a group of people after time has passed: a class *re-union*.
riv·er·bed [riv'ər·bed'] *n.* The ground over which a river flows.
rock [rok] *n.* A stone that can be picked up.
rou·tine [roo·tēn'] *n.* A fixed or usual way of doing something.
ruf·fi·an [ruf'ē·ən *or* ruf'yən] *n.* A person who behaves badly and possibly criminally.

S s

sa·ga [sä'gə] *n.* A long story, often telling the history of a family or a country.
sam·pan [sam'pan] *n.* A small boat wth oars and a sail, used in China and Japan.
sap·phire [saf'īr] *n.* A precious gem with a deep blue color.
sat·el·lite [sat'ə·līt] *n.* An object made to be put into a space orbit around the earth.

saun·ter [sôn'tər] *v.* **saun·tered** To walk slowly and casually; to stroll.
schol·ar·ship [skol'ər·ship'] *n.* A grant of money awarded to pay for a student's education.
scoun·drel [skoun'drəl] *n.* Evil-doing person; criminal.
scout [skout] *v.* To guide: They *scouted* the hunter though the woods.
scruff [skruf] *n.* The back part of the neck.

scrunch [skrunch] *v.* To squeeze so as to make smaller; fold up: We'll have to *scrunch* to get into that space.
scud·ding [skud'ing] *adj.* Flying swiftly: Watch the *scudding* clouds.
sea·far·er [sē'fâr'ər] *n.* A sailor.
se·cure [si·kyoor'] *adj.* Safe; protected.
se·cur·i·ty [si·kyoor'ə·tē] *adj.* Having to do with protection or safety.
sem·i·cir·cle [sem'ē·sûr'kəl] *n.* A half circle.
sen·si·ble [sen'sə·bəl] *adj.* Having wisdom or good judgment.
se·rene [si·rēn'] *adj.* Calm; peaceful.
ser·ies [sir'ēz] *n.* A group of things coming one after another; a connected group: a *series* of programs on space.
sev·er [sev'ər] *v.* **sev·ered** To cut; separate.
shade [shād] *v.* **shad·ed** To color darkly.
shin·gle [shing'gəl] *v.* **shin·gled** To cover a roof or a building with pieces of wood or other material usually placed in an overlapping manner.

short cir·cuit [shôrt sûr'kit] *n.* An electrical problem that can cause a fire.

a	add	i	it	oo	took	oi	oil
ā	ace	ī	ice	oō	pool	ou	pout
â	care	o	odd	u	up	ng	ring
ä	palm	ō	open	û	burn	th	thin
e	end	ô	order	yoo	fuse	th	this
ē	equal					zh	vision

ə = { **a** in *above*   **e** in *sicken*   **i** in *possible*
      o in *melon*   **u** in *circus* }

617

silhouette   tension

sil·hou·ette [sil'ōō·et'] *n.* Outline of an object seen against a light background.
sin·ew [sin'yōō] *n.* A band of strong tissue, attaching a muscle to a bone; a binding.
sin·is·ter [sin'is·tər] *adj.* Threatening evil or bad luck: a *sinister* look.
sit·u·a·tion [sich'ōō·wā'shən] *n.* A state of affairs or circumstances.
slope [slōp] *n.* A slanting surface or piece of ground.
snarl [snärl] *v.* **snarl·ing** To growl harshly or angrily.
sniv·el [sniv'əl] *v.* **sniv·el·ing** To cry; to whine tearfully.
so·ci·o·log·i·cal·ly [sō'sē·ə·loj'ə·kəl·lē] *adv.* In a manner having to do with *sociology*, the study of people living in groups or communities.
som·er·sault [sum'ər·sôlt] *n.* An acrobatic stunt in which a person jumps or rolls completely over.
space shut·tle [spās shut'əl] *n.* A vehicle for travel in space.
spear [spir] *n.* A long pole with a pointed head at one end, used in war or in hunting.

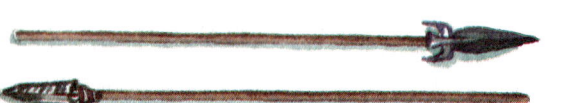

spe·cif·ic [spi·cif'ik] *adj.* Particular; definite.
sprint [sprint] *v.* **sprint·ed** Ran very fast: The runner *sprinted* to the finish line.
stag·nant [stag'nənt] *adj.* Motionless, stale, and dirty: Fish can die in a *stagnant* lake.
sta·tion·a·ry [stā'shən·er'ē] *adj.* Fixed; remaining in one place.
steep [stēp] *adj.* Having a sharp incline or slope.
steer[1] [stir] *v.* To direct, guide, or control the course of a vehicle.
steer[2] [stir] *n.* A male of beef cattle, usually between two and four years old.
stray [strā] *v.* To wander.

stream [strēm] *n.* A small body of flowing water. 
style [stīl] *n.* A distinctive or individual manner of expression.
sub·stance [sub'stəns] *n.* Solid material.
sub·stan·tial [səb·stan'shəl] *adj.* Large; considerable.
sub·sti·tute [sub'stə·t(y)ōōt'] *n.* A thing or person that takes the place of something or someone else.
sur·ger·y [sûr'jər·ē] *n.* An operation to repair or remove injured or diseased parts of the body.
sur·viv·al [sər·vī'vəl] *n.* Outlasting; outliving.
sus·pect [sus'pekt'] *n.* A person thought to have committed a crime.
swal·low [swol'ō] *n.* A small bird with a short bill, long pointed wings, noted for being fast in flight.
swiv·el [swiv'əl] *v.* To turn or rotate.
swoon [swōōn] *v.* **swoon·ing** To faint.
symp·tom [sim(p)'təm] *n.* A sign of a bodily disease or disorder: Sneezing can be a *symptom* of a cold.
syn·chro·nized swim·ming [sing'krə·nīzd' swim'ing] *n.* An event arranged so that swimmers keep to the same time or speed.

T t

tall tale [tôl tāl] *n.* A funny story that is usually exaggerated beyond belief.
ten·sion [ten'shən] *n.* Nervous anxiety; suspense.

618

testily   undiluted

tes·ti·ly [tes′tə·lē] *adv.* In a touchy manner; angrily: He refused *testily* when asked for a loan.

tes·ti·mo·ni·al [tes′tə·mō′nē·əl] *n.* A persuasive speech or piece of writing that gives the opinion or endorsement of a celebrity or a well-known person.

ther·mo·stat [thûr′mə·stat′] *n.* A device that automatically regulates temperature. ■

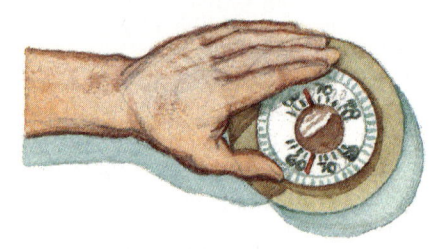

the·sis [thē′sis] *n.* A formal essay.

threat [thret] *n.* A warning; a statement that one intends to harm another person.

threat·en·ing [thret′ən·ing] *adj.* Promising harm; menacing.

thy [t͟hī] *adj.* An old-fashioned form of *your.*

tier [tir] *n.* One or more rows that are placed on top of each other. ■

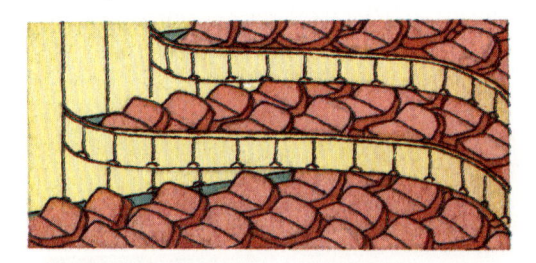

till [til] *v.* **til·ling** To work the soil.

tilt [tilt] *n.* A slant or slope.

toll [tōl] *v.* **tol·ling** To sound slowly and regularly, as a bell.

trai·tor [trā′tər] *n.* A person who betrays, especially one who betrays his or her country.

trans·plant [trans′plant] *n.* A transfer of tissue or of a bodily organ from one person to another.

trem·bling [trem′b(ə)ling] *n.* The act of shaking.

tri·al [trī′əl] *adj.* Having to do with a test; preliminary.

tri·um·phant [trī·um′fənt] *adj.* **tri·um·phant·ly** Joyful; victorious.

trudge [truj] *v.* To walk slowly and wearily.

tur·moil [tûr′moil] *n.* Great confusion; disturbance.

ty·phoon [tī·foon′] *n.* A violent hurricane.

type [tīp] *v.* **typ·ing** To use a typewriter for writing. ■

U u

un·beat·a·ble [un·bē′tə·bəl] *adj.* Not capable of being beaten.

un·de·vel·oped [un′di·vel′əpt] *adj.* Not yet developed or cultivated, as with land.

un·di·lut·ed [un′di·loot′id *or* un′dī·loot′id] *adj.* Pure; not mixed with anything.

a	add	i	it	o͝o	took	oi	oil
ā	ace	ī	ice	o͞o	pool	ou	pout
â	care	o	odd	u	up	ng	ring
ä	palm	ō	open	û	burn	th	thin
e	end	ô	order	yo͞o	fuse	t͟h	this
ē	equal					zh	vision

ə = { **a** in *above*, **e** in *sicken*, **i** in *possible*, **o** in *melon*, **u** in *circus* }

619

unerringly　　　　　　　　　　　　　　　　　　wound

un·err·ing·ly [un·er′ing·lē] *adv.* Without mistakes; faultlessly: Even in the dark, he went *unerringly* to the right door.
un·ex·pect·ed·ly [un′ik·spek′tid·lē] *adv.* Without warning: My grandmother visited *unexpectedly.*
un·fore·seen [un′fôr·sēn′] *adj.* Not expected beforehand.
ut·ter·ly [ut′ər·lē] *adj.* Completely; totally.

V v

vac·cine [vak·sēn′ *or* vak′sēn′] *n.* A substance made from weak or dead viruses and used to protect people and animals from serious diseases, such as polio and smallpox.
val·u·a·ble [val′y(o͞o·)ə·bəl] *adj.* Useful; worthy of respect.
van·tage point [van′tij point] *n.* A position from which one has a broad or commanding view.
veiled [vāld] *adj.* Covered; hidden. ■

Ven·u·sian [və·no͞o′zhən] *n.* An inhabitant of the planet Venus.
ver·sion [vûr′zhən] *n.* A specific form or account of something: What is your *version* of the story?
vet·er·i·nar·i·an [vet′ər·ə·nâr′ē·ən *or* vet′rə·nâr′ē·ən] *n.* A doctor who treats animals.
vi·brate [vī′brāt] *v.* To move rapidly back and forth.

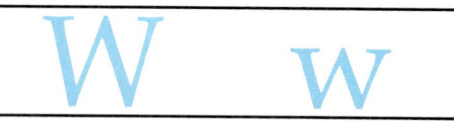

W w

wan·gle [wang′gəl] *v.* To get or accomplish something by sly means: to *wangle* a privilege.
wa·ver [wā′vər] *v.* To move from side to side.
weap·on [wep′ən] *n.* A tool or device used for fighting or hunting.
weld [weld] *v.* **weld·ing** To join pieces of metal by softening them with heat and pressing them together.
well-or·gan·ized [wel·ôr′gən·īzd′] *adj.* Arranged in good order.
whirl·wind [(h)wûrl′wind] *adj. use* Rushing and spinning like a whirlwind: a *whirlwind* tour.
wick [wik] *n.* A string in a lamp or candle that burns when lighted. ■

wig·wam [wig′wom′] *n.* A cone-shaped hut built by North American Indians. ■

wis·dom [wiz′dəm] *n.* The quality of knowledge and good judgment.
wisp [wisp] *n.* A small amount; shred: a *wisp* of cloth.
won·drous [wun′drəs] *adj.* Inspiring wonder or admiration.
wound [wo͞ond] *v.* **wound·ed** To injure by penetrating the skin.

620

Pronunciation Guide to Names, Words, and Phrases

Acraud [ak′rōd]
Aleut [ə·lo͞ot]
Alioto, Michela [a·lē·ō′tō, mi·kä′lä]
Alpha [al′fə]
amah [ä′mə]
Andes [an′dēz]
aremus piz wat [ə rē′məs piz wat]
Asimov, Isaac [a′zi·môf, ī′zək]
Atlas [at′ləs]
Attean [a·tē′ən]

Babylon [bab′ə·län]
Beijing [bā′jing′]
Benes, Jan [be′nəs, yän]
Berne [bûrn]
Burma [bûr′mə]

Capek, Karel [chä′pek, kä′rel]
Caribbean [kar·ə·bē′ən]
Cathay [ka·thā′]
Chaudron, Yves [shō·droh(n)′, ēv]
Confucius [kən·fyo͞o′shəs]
Copreus [kop′ryo͞os]
Covent Garden [kuv′ənt gär·dən]
Creole [krē′ōl]
Czech [chek]

Damascus [də·mas′kəs]
da Vinci, Leonardo [də vin′chē, lē·ō·när′dō]
Dione [dē′ō′nē]

Edinburgh [ed′(ə)n·bûr·ō]
Emer [ā′mer]
Enceladus [en·sel′ə·dəs]

Gau Qing [gou king]

Geri, Alfredo [je′·rē, al·frä′dō]
Gonfil [gon′fil]

Hangku [hāng·ko͞o′]
Hankou (also **Hankow**) [hän·kou′]
Haranati [hä·rä·nä′tē]
Hera [hir′ə]
Hercules [hûr′kyə·lēz]
Hesperides [hes·per′ə·dēz]
Higa [hē′gə]
Hyperion [hī·per′ē·ən]

Iapetus [yap′ə·təs]
Inca [ing′kə]
Incognito [in·kog·nē′tō]
Indonesia [in·də·nē′zhə]

Jupiter [jo͞o′pə·tər]

kai bitzi [kī bit′sē]
Kampuchea [kam·po͞o·chē′ə]
Karana [kä·rä′nä]
kweh [kwe]

Ladon [lā′dōn]
Lebanon [leb′ə·non]
Leiden [lī′dən]
Le Matin [lə ma·tənh]
Lin Nai-Nai [lin nī′nī]
lire [lir′ā]
llama [lä′mə]
Louvre [lo͞o′vr(ə)]

Malay Peninsula [mə·lā′ pə·nin′sye·lə]
Malaysia [mə·lā′zhə]
matinee [mat′ə·nā′]
memorabilia [mem′ə·rə·bil′ē·ə]
Michaelmas [mik′əl·məs]

621

Miguel [mē·gel′]
Miko [mē′kō]
Mimas [mē′mäs]
Mona Lisa [mō′nə lē′zə]
Morcar [môr′kär]
Mount Palomar [mount pa′lō·mär]
Muckluk [muk′luk]

naip [nīp]
Napoleon [nə·pō′lē·ən]
Ner [när]
Nereus [nir′ē·əs]
Nicaragua [nik·ə·rä′gwa]
Nicolletti [nē·kō·let′tē]
Notre Dame [nō′tr(ə) däm]

Olympus [ō·lim′pəs]

Pecos Pete [pā′kəs pēt]
Peruggia, Vincenzo [pe·roo′jə, vin·chen′zō]
Philippines [fil′ə·pēnz]
Phoebe [fē′bē]
Poggi, Giovanni [pô′jē, jō·vän′nē]
Polo, Marco [pō′lō, mär′kō]
Portuguese [pôr·chə·gēz′]
Proteus [prō′tyoos]
Prussia [prush′ə]

Renaissance [ren′ə·säns]
Rhea [rē′ə]
robota [rō·bô′tə]
Rontu [ron′too]
Rue de Paris [roo də pär·ē′]

St. Drimma [drim′mə]
St. Felin [fel′ən]
St. Froida [froi′də]
St. Melin [mel′ən]
St. Misham [mē′shəm]
St. Petrag [pet′rəg]
Saknis [sak′nis]

Salon Carrée [sə·lohn′ kä·rā′]
Sammle [sam·le]
sampans [sam′panz]
Sandoz, Fritz [san′doz, frits]
Sandri [san′drē]
Saturnian [sat·ərn′ē·ən]
Shanghai [shang′hī]
Shengli [sheng′lē]
Singapore [sing′(g)ə·pôr]
Soviet Union [sō′vē·et]
Stampfl, Franz [stamp′fəl, frants]

ta ho [tä hō]
Tethys [teth′is]
Thailand [tī′land]
Titans [tīt′ənz]
Tsai loushang [sī lou′shäng]

Uchida, Yoshiko [yoo·chē′də, yō·shē′kō]
Uffizi [yoo·fēts′ē]

Valfierno, Eduardo [val·fyär′nō, ed·wär′dō]
Valfierno, Marques de [val·fyär′nō, mär·kes′ də]
Vietnam [vyet′nam]
Vincenzo, Leonardo [vin·chen′zō, lē·ō·när′dō]

Waco [wā′kō]
waigwo ren [wī′gwō ren]
wigwam [wig′wom]
Woo [woo]
Wuchang [woo′ chang]
Wuhan [woo′hän]

xiaosyin [shou·syin′]

Yangtse [yang′sē]
ye hye hye [ye hye hye]

zalwit [zäl′ wit]
Zeus [zoos]

622

Index of Titles and Authors

Adventure of the Blue Carbuncle, The, 274
Aiken, Joan, 188
Alfred Hitchcock's The Mystery of the Seven Wrong Clocks, 158
Asimov, Isaac, 436

Bannister, Roger, 108
Billings, Charlene, 214
Borland, Hal, 553
Bradbury, Ray, 458

Chang, Diana, 324
Charles, Donald, 105
China Homecoming, 328
Clarke, Arthur C., 470
Computer Screen Imagery, 234
Cullinan, Bernice E., 366

de Alarcón, Pedro Antonio, 258
Doyle, Sir Arthur Conan, 272, 274
Dwiggins, Don, 496

Electronic Revolution: Robots, The, 534
Evslin, Bernard, 20

Fallow Deer at the Lonely House, The, 344
Fantastic Voyage, 436
Fleischman, Sid, 378
Four-Minute Mile, The, 108
Fritz, Jean, 306

Golden Apples, The, 20
Ghost on Saturday Night, The, 378
Gift-Giving, The, 188

Hass, E. A., 174
Hamilton, Virginia, 564, 566
Hardy, Thomas, 344
Hawkes, Nigel, 534
Henniker-Heaton, Peter J., 488
Hitchcock, Alfred, 158
Homesick, 306

Incognito Mosquito and the Miscast Dancer Mystery, 174
Island of the Blue Dolphin, 78

Joan Benoit, 98

Kort, Michele, 98

Let's Take a Trip into Space, 496
Letters to a Black Boy, 352

Meet Don Madden, 554
Merriam, Eve, 224
Michela Alioto: Computer Teen, 230
Microchip: Small Wonder, 214
Morning the Sun Refused to Rise, The, 4
Mrs. Frisby and the Rats of NIMH, 404

Naman, Mard, 230

O'Brien, Robert C., 402, 404
O'Dell, Scott, 78

Parker, Faye, 506
Post Early for Space, 488

623

Predictions from 1900, 544

Reeves, Barbara, 554
Roads Go Ever On and On, 207
Rounds, Glen, 4
Runner, The, 105

Sadler, Catherine Edwards, 274
Sandburg, Carl, 18
Saturn Rising, 470
Saying Yes, 324
Sign of the Beaver, The, 122
Speare, Elizabeth George, 122
Stover, Marjorie Filley, 52
Stub-Book, The, 258

Teague, Bob, 352

They Have Yarns, 18
Think Tank, 224
Time in Thy Flight, 458
Tolkien, J. R. R., 207
Tom Edison and the Wonderful "Why", 506
Trail Boss in Pigtails, 52
True or False? Amazing Art Forgeries, 246

Uchida, Yoshiko, 36, 366

Waldron, Ann, 246
Watkins, John Elfreth, 544
Westward Bound, 66
Willie Bea and the Time the Martians Landed, 566
Wise Old Woman, The, 36